AN ANCIENT LINEAGE

AN ANCIENT LINEAGE

European Roots of a Jewish Family

Gelles–Griffel–Wahl–Chajes–Safier–Loew–Taube

EDWARD GELLES

VALLENTINE MITCHELL
LONDON • PORTLAND, OR

First published in 2006 in Great Britain by
VALLENTINE MITCHELL
Suite 314, Premier House, 112–114 Station Road,
Edgware, Middlesex, HA8 7BJ

and in the United States of America by
VALLENTINE MITCHELL
c/o ISBS, 920 NE 58th Avenue, Suite 300
Portland, Oregon, 97213-3786

Website: www.vmbooks.com

British Library Cataloguing in Publication Data
A catalogue record for this book has been applied for

ISBN 0-85303-680-2 (cloth)
ISBN 978-0-85303-680-7 (cloth)

Library of Congress Cataloging-in-Publication Data
A catalog record for this book has been applied for

Typeset by FiSH Books, Enfield, Middx.
Printed in Great Britain by MPG Books Ltd, Bodmin, Cornwall

To the Memory of my Ancestors

Pride and humiliation hand in hand
Walked with them through the world whe'er they went;
Trampled and beaten were they as the sand,
And yet unshaken as the continent.

For in the background figures vague and vast
Of patriarchs and of prophets rose sublime,
And all the great traditions of the Past
They saw reflected in the coming time.

And thus for ever with reverted look
The mystic volume of the world they read,
Spelling it backward like a Hebrew book,
Till Life became a Legend of the Dead.

Henry Wadsworth Longfellow

Contents

List of Documents and Photographs

List of Maps

List of Tables and Charts

Letter of Approbation

Genealogical research has become a prevalent occupation to which people devote much time and effort. It satisfies their curiosity about their ancestors, who they were, where they settled, and what can be learnt about their way of life. Genealogists face great challenges in utilizing the often-limited resources available to assemble the great puzzle of the past, records which were scarce and irregular to start with having been lost over the passage of time.

Jews always placed great emphasis on lineage, for both hierarchical and practical reasons. This tradition goes back to the Bible itself, which contains a book specifically devoted to genealogy (Chronicles). Our people have suffered pogroms and libels, expulsions and wandering, culminating in the Holocaust of our era and the murder of six million Jews. With this loss of life, precious records and valuable sources of historical and genealogical information have also been destroyed. From the halachic perspective, particular importance is attached to the preservation of the lineage of the priestly Cohen and Levy families and the descent from the House of David from whose seed the Messiah will come. Maimonides (Mishneh Torah, Laws of Kings 12:3) emphasizes the task of the Messiah in identifying which of the twelve tribes of Israel each Jew is descended from, as an integral part of his role in the future redemption.

Dr Edward Gelles has succeeded in overcoming the inherent difficulties with great success and the fruits of his labours are gathered in this book. He has spent many years researching his own family and its connections, laboriously gathering material from books and newspapers, libraries and archives, websites and the testimony of family members. The resulting creation is not a dry collection of names, dates and figures, but is a fascinating story of Jewish life expressed in an interesting and flowing language. The reader travels with the author through many historic European towns and cities, and is exposed to accounts of the life of their Jewish communities over a period of hundreds of years. This is an important document not only for members of the author's extended family, but for all seekers of knowledge, who will find themselves enriched socially and historically as well as by the deepening of their Jewish roots.

Rabbi Meir Wunder
Jerusalem
March 2006

Foreword

I am pleased to present Edward Gelles's An Ancient Lineage to potential readers. It is the magnum opus of a determined, resourceful and imaginative genealogist based on many hundreds of records in libraries and archives on three continents. Dr Gelles's efforts have produced a book that is inspiring and even moving at times as the documents reflect the vicissitudes of European Jews over a thousand years and many countries. The book lets us see the world of Jewish experience through the grains of sand of the particular lives of individual Jews. Forty stimulating chapters are accompanied by illustrations, maps and genealogical tables. There are innumerable surprising and stimulating linkages here for the historian too. There is both the history and the legend of Saul Wahl of Padua who came to Brest-Litovsk and, according to a widespread tale, became king of Poland for a day. One learns also of Hayyim (Joachim), the nephew of David Gans, the Prague Jewish historian and scientist, who was apparently the first Jew to set foot in English America in the sixteenth century under the patronage of Sir Walter Raleigh. Who would have expected to find, on the same genealogical chart, the names of Moses Isserles, the great legalist and codifier of the sixteenth century; Moses Mendelssohn, the outstanding Jewish philosopher of the Enlightenment; and Israel Friedman, the founder of the Ruzhin-Sadagora line of Hasidic leaders in the nineteenth century? In addition to the seven families whose lineages the author highlights, there is much here on many other distinguished lines such as Landau, Yaffe, Popper, and Fraenkel. This book has much to teach aspiring genealogists who will profit not only from the practical advice Dr Gelles provides but cannot fail to be inspired as well by the dogged determination of the author to follow up any hint and pursue any clue in the quest for his ancestors.

Profesor Gershon David Hundert
McGill University
March 2006

Acknowledgements

I have been fortunate in the help I received from scholars, archivists, curators and librarians, relatives and friends. They are too numerous to list here but many of them are referred to in the following pages. I am particularly indebted to my cousin Tad Taube and the Taube Family Foundation for a grant towards my research expenses, to Yissochor Marmorstein for finding some important sources and for translating Hebrew texts, and to Frank Cass and his staff at Vallentine Mitchell for publishing my book.

When I began these studies seven years ago I sought advice in various quarters. Saul Issroff gave me a few practical hints while Michael Honey, Harold Rhode and Dr Neil Rosenstein introduced me to some genealogical reference works. I had early guidance from Rabbi Meir Wunder of Jerusalem and Rabbi Dov Weber of New York. Alexander Dunai carried out extensive archive searches for me in Lviv. Ilana Tahan of the British Library and Huw Williams are among several librarians who have been helpful. The directors of the Jewish Theological Seminary in New York and of the Central Archives of the History of the Jewish people in Jerusalem kindly supplied microfilms of relevant source material in their collections. Dr Bernardo Vasconselos e Sousa of the Portuguese National Archives, Dr Paolo Castignoli, of the Livorno Archives, Dr Tadeusz Zych, the deputy mayor of Tarnobrzeg, Mrs Heidrun Weiss of the Jewish Community Offices in Vienna and Walter Pagler of Verein 'Shalom' also provided valuable information. Thanks are due to the coordinators of Jewish genealogical websites for Tarnobrzeg and Kolomea, Gayle Schlissel Riley and Alan Weiser. My cousins who contributed genealogical data include Andrew, Boruch and Eric Griffel, Lucy Lamm, Marilyn Low, Judith Ritter, Viola Sachs, Marcel Safier, Elsa Schmaus, Elaine Weinstein and Barbara Safier Welner. Nita Hirsch, Bracha Weiser and Raffaele de Banfield-Tripcovich were among correspondents close to my family circle. Among many others who evinced an interest in my work were Yehudah Klausner, Peter Trawnicek, and Yisrael Asper. Elly Miller, Pauline James, and other friends encouraged me in various ways. Alan Horan and Miles Saltiel allowed me to call on their computer skills. My special thanks are due to the editors of the genealogical journals who published my articles including Yocheved Klausner, Sallyann Amdur Sack, Edward Goldstein, David Fielker and Judith Samson.

PERMISSIONS TO REPRODUCE ILLUSTRATIONS

The Seal of Kalonymos ben Todros of Narbonne is reproduced by permission of the Archives Municipales de Narbonne (courtesy of M. Paul-Henri Viala).

The dust jacket of *My Dear Ones* by Neil and Margaret Rau is reproduced by permission of the copyright holders, Recovery, Inc.

The dust jacket of *Dateline Istanbul* by Joseph Friedenson is reproduced by permission of the copyright holders, Artscroll/Mesorah Publications, Ltd

Names of People and Places

Commonly used Hebrew and Yiddish first names such as Arieh (Leib, Leo), Zvi (Hirsch) or Naftali Zvi (Naftali Hirsch), Dov (Ber, Baer) and Zeev (Wolf) were used separately or in combination, as in Arieh Leib, Zvi Hirsch, Dov Ber and Zeev Wolf. In the book we will meet a Wahl and a Weinstein who are referred to alternately as Zvi Arieh or Hirsh Leib. I cannot go here into the complexities of abbreviations, diminutives and nicknames.

The spelling of family and town names changed with time and social context. Even at the same time and place members of a given family might come to write their names in different ways. Transliteration from the Hebrew often led to ambiguities. Continual political upheavals and migrations were the primary causes of change. Different ethnic groups, living side by side in central and eastern Europe, rendered names in Yiddish, German, Polish, Ukrainian, Russian and so forth.

Spellings to be found in this book include, for example: first names – Yitzchak / Isaac and Yechezkiel / Ezekiel; second names – Chayes / Chajes (the Hebrew alphabet does not have a 'j'), Gelles, Gellis and occasionally Gellies or Gelis, Halpern, Heilprin, etc, Shapiro, Spiro etc, Wahl / Wohl (German / Polish), Horowitz / Horovitz (German / Slav); town names – Solotwina / Solotvina, Stanislau / Stanislawow (now renamed Ivano-Frankivsk), Lemberg / Lwow / Lvov / Lviv (German / Polish / Ukrainian), Grodno / Horodna (Polish-Lithuanian / Russian). The appended Index of Place Names lists just a few of many alternative spellings.

Examples of Jewish usage included Mikulov for Nikolsburg, Apt for Opatow, Tiktin for Tykocin, Krotchin for Krotoschin / Krotoczyn, Tzoismer or Zausmer for the Polish town of Sandomierz (whose Zausmer Rabbis thus came by their family name).

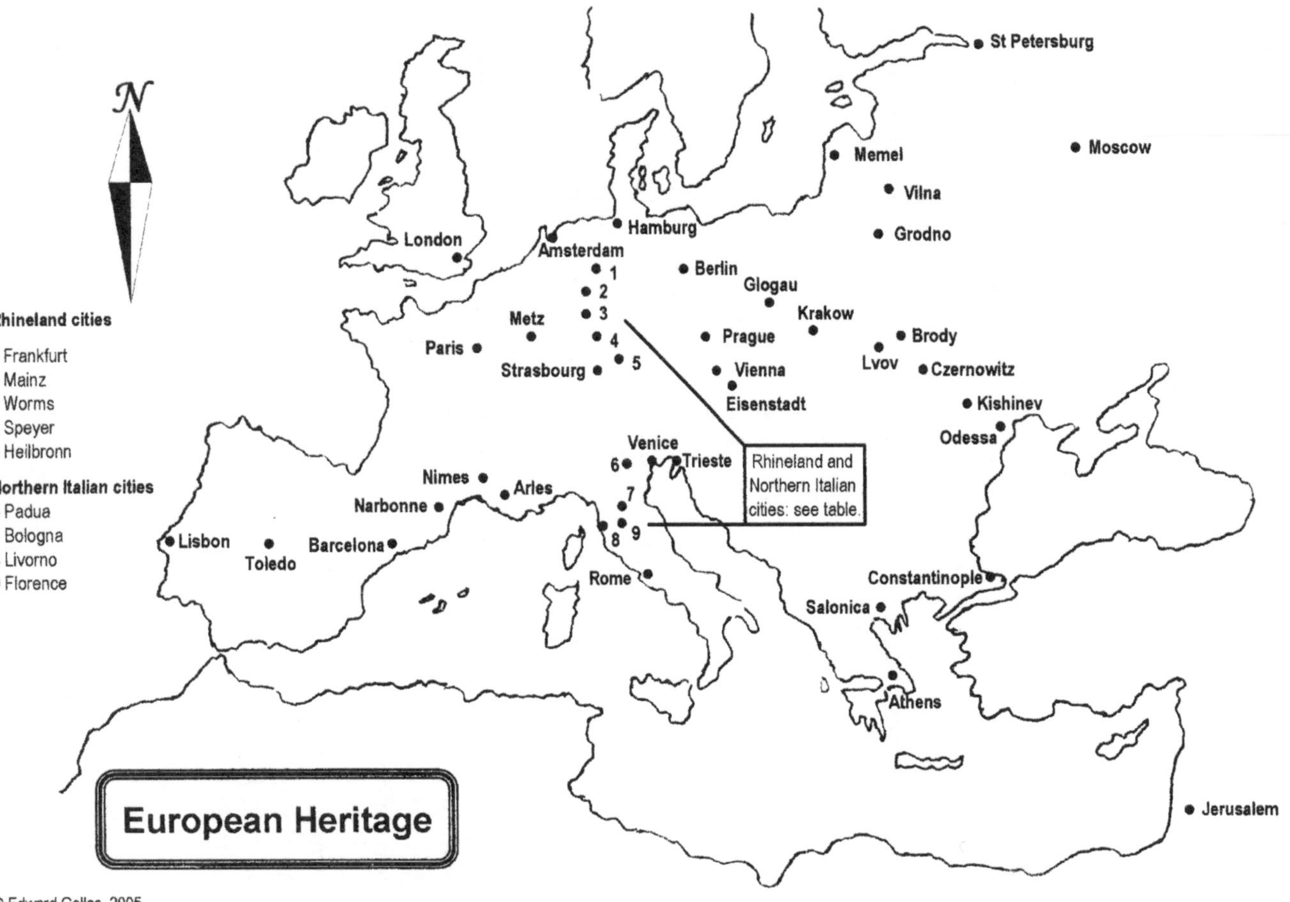
European Heritage
N
Rhineland cities
1 Frankfurt
2 Mainz
3 Worms
4 Speyer
5 Heilbronn
Northern Italian cities
6 Padua
7 Bologna
8 Livorno
9 Florence
Rhineland and Northern Italian cities: see table.
St Petersburg
Moscow
Memel
Vilna
Grodno
London
Hamburg
Amsterdam
Berlin
Glogau
Krakow
Brody
Lvov
Czernowitz
Paris
Metz
Strasbourg
Prague
Vienna
Eisenstadt
Kishinev
Odessa
Venice
Trieste
Nimes
Arles
Narbonne
Barcelona
Lisbon
Toledo
Rome
Constantinople
Salonica
Athens
Jerusalem

European Heritage

When Jerusalem fell to the Babylonians two and a half thousand years ago there was already a scattering of Jews all over the Mediterranean littoral. A few refugees from Judea reached Europe at that time. The Rhine was one of the main routes that led them to the heart of the continent. A large Jewish community remained in exile in Mesopotamia, and from this reservoir immigrants came to Greece, Constantinople and the Black Sea coast. They pressed on to Moldavia, Galicia, Lithuania and Hungary, following rivers such as the Pruth, Bug, Vistula and Danube. The Jewish colony in Rome predated the influx of prisoners after the fall of the second temple. Sephardic Jews, who were uprooted from the Iberian peninsula and Provence at the end of the middle ages, came to Italy, to the Ottoman Empire, and later also to Holland, England and the New World. In the east, such Sephardim absorbed earlier Romaniot settlers. In the west, Ashkenazi Jews left medieval northern France and the Rhineland. From these areas of ancient settlement and persecution, and also from Italy, they made their way to Bohemia and then to Poland, Lithuania and beyond. There they mingled with earlier arrivals from Germany and the Austrian lands and absorbed the smaller number of immigrants who had followed an eastern route and any Khazar converts to Judaism who had come to Poland after the fall of their tribal kingdoms by the Black Sea. The flow to eastern Europe was reversed in the ages of enlightenment and emancipation. Many Jews then returned to the western lands from which their ancestors had fled centuries before.

For consistency with the European Heritage map the Polish names of Krakow and Lvov are used instead of the Austrian Krakau and Lemberg.

Galicia

Thc three partitions of Poland in 1772, 1793 and 1795 carved up the country between Prussia. Austria and Russia. The ancient land of Galicia and Ladomeria became part of thc Austro-Hungarian Empire in 1772 and remained so until the end of the First World War, when a new Republic of Poland was reconstituted. After the Second World War Galicia was divided between Poland and the Ukraine.

In 1795 land around Lublin was added to the province but this accretion was transferred to Russian Poland at the Congress of Vienna in 1815. The city of Krakow and a small surrounding area was then quasi-independent. It was incorporated into Austrian Galicia in 1846. Thc Duchy of Bukowina, with its capital at Czernowitz, was annexed by Austria in 1775 and united with Galicia until 1849. From 1849 until 1918 the Bukowina was a separate Crown land of the Austrian Monarchy.

During this period, the western half of Galicia had a Polish-speaking Catholic majority while an orthodox Ukrainian-speaking population predominated in eastern Galicia. Jews formed a sizeable minority, particularly in the eastern part of the province. The population of the Bukowina had a different ethnic mix with a Moldavian or Romanian stock and the Jews formed a smaller part of the population than in Galicia. During thc nineteenth century the movement between Galicia and Bukowina continued to increase. The relatively favourable political and economic conditions in the Bukowina led to a substantial Jewish inflow from Galicia and the Russian Empire.

I.

THE BOOK'S SCOPE AND ORIGINS

There's a divinity that shapes our ends
Rough-hew them how we will

Hamlet, Act 5 Scene 2

CHAPTER ONE

Genealogical Key for a Millennial History

Synopsis

My ancestors moved across Europe from Portugal, Spain and Italy to France and Germany, Austria, Bohemia, Poland, Lithuania, Russia, Galicia and Hungary. Some of these migrations were often a two-way process over time, but the general direction persisted for centuries until it was reversed in the more recent period. I did not find the details of their millennial journey in history books, nor was it revealed in geographical texts and atlases. The story slowly emerged from the genealogical connections of individual people and families. The tapestry of interwoven family relations, particularly of century-old rabbinical clans, provides a fascinating database for the study of inheritance. It is genealogy rather than history or genetic science that has primacy in my study, and I believe that the results illustrate the contribution genealogical methodology can make to historical enquiry.

Major difficulties abound in the study of Jewish genealogy. Firstly, so many records were destroyed over the centuries in the long catalogue of disasters that overtook the Jewish people, including the expulsions from the Iberian peninsula at the end of the fifteenth century, the persecutions in France and Germany, the periodical expulsions from major centres such as Vienna and Prague, the Thirty Years War and the Chmielnicki massacres in central and eastern Europe in the mid-seventeenth century, the nineteenth-century Russian pogroms, and the climax of millennial persecution in the twentieth century holocaust. Only a fraction of civil authority and Jewish community records and of tombstone inscriptions has survived. Secondly, family names were not universally adopted in Europe until the late-eighteenth or early-nineteenth centuries. In earlier periods, a variety of patronymics, names derived from places of origin, occupational soubriquets, and nicknames could give rise to much confusion. Not only could siblings have completely different second names, but also one and the same person might be called by different names, according to circumstance. Thirdly, the details of wives are often inadequately recorded. Girls were once married at a very young age and many died giving birth to their first child. The issue of subsequent marriages is often difficult to identify. Name changes can be a problem or sometimes be turned to advantage.

Matronymics were revealing of family connections, and so was the adoption of the father-in-law's family name, which was quite common for a considerable time in Eastern Europe. Fourthly, there is the question of mobility. Wars, political persecutions and economic pressures were the root causes of the major migrations over the centuries, from west to east and back again. The Jews were forced to be mobile and none were more so than the rabbis, who went where new communities required their ministrations. Demographic and economic pressures fluctuated. The birth rate was high but infant mortality was at times quite appalling. Family and trade connections led to arranged marriages involving distant towns, so that some dominant lines spread over a whole province, and from country to country.

It should be clear from these few generalizations that genealogical search is not simply a matter of following some names in a particular locality backward in time. Changing names and locations call for a wide-ranging and flexible genealogical methodology.

Against the established background of European history there is the framework of a limited number of great families whose lines of descent were studied and preserved over the centuries. These families include some that rose to eminence through the great distinction of one or two individual figures and others that produced scholars or community leaders over many centuries. They tended to intermarry to produce an intellectual elite that contributed considerably to European culture while holding the Jews together through millennia of hardship and periods of persecution. Particularly relevant to my story are the Treves, Spiro and Luria families, whose nexus leads back to the medieval rabbis of France, to the great scholar and biblical commentator Salomon ben Isaac, known as Rashi of Troyes (1040–1105), and forward to the Katzenellenbogen Rabbis of Padua and Venice who hailed from the eponymous town in Hesse-Nassau. A scion of this family was Saul Wahl (1545–1617), who became an important figure in the Polish-Lithuanian state and left a large and enduring progeny. The Spiro (Shapiro) took their name from Speyer and the ancient Halpern or Heilprin were from Heilbronn. The names of Horowitz and Landau reveal their ancient connections with a Bohemian and a German town. Yaffe, from Italy and Bohemia, and Rapaport, with German and Italian roots, are also among the important rabbinical clans who trod the familiar paths leading to Eastern Europe. The *Kohanim* or priestly caste was represented by various families from Germany and Austria who were translated to Poland, Lithuania, and elsewhere. One such sacerdotal family from Frankfurt, who moved to Lithuania at the beginning of the seventeenth century, produced Rabbi Shabatai Katz, a leading *halachic* authority of his day who married a descendant of the great sixteenth-century Rabbi Moses Isserles of Cracow. The latter's near contemporary, Rabbi Judah Loew of Prague, had distinguished forebears in Worms. *Der Hohe Rabbi* Loew became a legendary figure in Prague. His pupils included the renaissance historian and astronomer Rabbi David Gans, whose family can also be traced from West Germany to Prague and then to Poland. The latter's nephew Chaim, aka

Joachim Gaunse, a distinguished mining engineer who worked in England in the 1580s, was perhaps the first professing Jew to reach the shores of North America.

Some of the Chayot from Portugal settled in Provence long before the general expulsions from the Iberian peninsula, as did the Chalfan who were also of Sephardic origin. From Provence they found their way to Italy and Bohemia. Isaac Chayot or Chayes became Chief Rabbi of Prague and was a brother-in-law of Judah Loew. He was closely related to the Eberles, who acquired the name of Altschuler (from the Prague synagogue they helped to build). Chayes and Altschulers later spread to Galicia and elsewhere. Chalfans distinguished themselves in Venice, Prague and Vienna for two centuries, until the general expulsion of the Jews from the last-named city in 1670. Later they connected with the Yollis family of Cracow, who were allied to the Heschel branch of Katzenellenbogen. The Chalfan forebears go back to Kalonymos, who were in northern Italy in the tenth century or earlier, flourished in Speyer and Mainz in Germany, and were community leaders in Narbonne and Arles.

Amongst these ancient families some are of particular genealogical interest in that their claims of descent from biblical times and even from King David are taken seriously by some genealogists. These include a number who are generally believed to be descended from Rashi of Troyes. The forebears of Judah Loew of Prague are also sometimes claimed to be of Davidic descent.

The modest ambition of a family genealogist might be to find evidence for links with some of these well-established ancient lineages. Many branches of my family remain unexplored and there are many gaps in my knowledge of even nineteenth-century kinsfolk, but at the same time there are connections to famous lines going back to the sixteenth century and earlier, so that a picture of our forebears and how they moved about Europe is beginning to emerge.

My sources are national, municipal and Jewish community archives, museums and libraries, the internet, and many private correspondents, and the material comprises tombstone inscriptions, birth, marriage, death and property records, a variety of other documents such as taxation records, business directories, patents of nobility, newspaper clippings, book subscription lists, school reports, army lists, ships' manifests, immigration records, and all manner of references in the secular and rabbinical literature. This material comes from all over Europe.

Moses Gelles was a scholar of the Brody *Klaus* in the early eighteenth century. He and some of his progeny carried the epithet *Levush,* perhaps in recognition of their descent from Rabbi Mordecai Yaffe of Prague. My paternal line can be traced back to this Gelles family in Brody. This involved *inter alia* an analysis of house numbers and residents' names over several generations. The descendants of Moses Gelles married into various rabbinical families, including those of Rabbi Pinchas Shapiro of Koretz, and of the Brody families Hakohen, Fraenkel, Margoshes and Zundel. We had close connections with the Shapiro rabbinical line and with the Friedmans of Czortkow. Rabbi Yehuda Leib Zundel of Brody was a scholar of the Brody *Klaus* like Moses Gelles. He was the grandfather of Shalom Rokeach, the first Rabbi of the chasidic Belz dynasty. Rabbi Zundel carried the suffix *Ramraz* being the acronym for his father, Rabbi Moses Reb Zelig's of Brody, who was the son of Rabbi Todros, a descendant of the Abulafia family who flourished in thirteenth- and fourteenth-century Spain.

My forebear Rabbi Shmuel Helman was born and married in the Silesian towns of Krotoschin and Glogau. He studied in Prague, and held rabbinical posts in Moravia and Germany before becoming the prominent Chief Rabbi of Metz, where he died in 1764. His daughters were allied to Katzenellenbogen, Fraenkel and Rapaport, and he was also related to Ezekiel Landau, the Chief Rabbi of Prague. Helman's progeny occupied rabbinical positions in France, Germany, Poland and beyond.

Lithuanian rabbis by the name of Gelles go back to Uri Feivush, who was Chief Rabbi of Vilna and became head of the Ashkenazi community in Jerusalem around 1650. He was given the title of *Nasi* in the Holy Land, following a similar conferment on Isaiah Halevi Horovitz in the preceding generation. Possible connections of the later Gelles rabbis with Uri Feivush and also with Moses Isserles are suggested by the recurring names of Uri, Isaac and David in their respective lines of descent and their coincidence in the towns of Brody and Glina.

My mother's family were the Griffels of Nadworna and Stanislau. According to family tradition they were descended from Rabbi David Halevi Segal, the seventeenth-century Chief Rabbi of Lvov. Eliezer Griffel was the patriarch of a clan centred on Nadworna that extended over stretches of Galicia and beyond. He owned oil wells and refineries, sawmills and other enterprises, and they had a large-scale timber export business. His wife Sarah Chayes came from the Kolomea branch of a family that produced distinguished rabbis over a period of several centuries, and spread from their base in Brody to establish branches as far afield as Livorno and Florence. A scion of the latter branch was ennobled by the King of Portugal.

Zvi Hirsch Perez Chajes, the Chief Rabbi of Vienna in the inter-war years, was a distant cousin. The family, still flourishing in worldwide dispersal, once produced scholars, lawyers, doctors, a world-class chess player, and a distinguished pianist and composer.

Eliezer and Sarah's eldest son was my grandfather David Mendel Griffel who married Chawa Wahl of Tarnobrzeg. She came from a family who were held to be descendants of Saul Wahl, son of the Rabbi of Venice. Chawa's father Shulem Wahl, described in contemporary records as a capitalist, married Sarah Safier of another prominent family. A number of Safier descendants established new roots in America and Australia. Our cousins descended from Chawa Wahl's sisters included the Loews of Sedziszow, the Ohrensteins, and the Taube family. Abraham Low was a distinguished psychiatrist in Chicago, Lucia Ohrenstein became Countess Tripcovich and a leading figure in Rome café society during the 1950s, and Thaddeus Taube is an outstanding businessman and philanthropist in California, whose notable benefactions extend beyond that State. Another Taube cousin is Viola Sachs, sometime Professor of American literature in Paris. The Taube family can be traced from eighteenth-century Belz and Krystynopol, to Lemberg (Lvov) and Cracow. The Griffels, who were once in Stanislau, Lemberg, Cracow and Vienna, have numerous descendants in America and Israel. My mother's first cousin, Dr Jacob Griffel is credited with saving thousands of Jewish lives during and after the Second World War through his work with the rescue committee based in Istanbul and in other ways. Relatives of the Griffels, such as the Wohls of Cracow, appear among the crowd of in-laws in the family history.

It would have been impossible to unravel even a small part of our heritage if so many forebears had not been rabbis or connected with rabbinical families. The most prominent and best-documented branches are those of the Wahl and Chayes families. The trail from my grandfather Rabbi Nahum Uri Gelles is necessarily more tentative, but it is revealing an ancient and illustrious ancestry.

The material I have gathered on Gelles, Griffel, Weinstein, Wahl, Chayes, Safier, Loew and Taube forms the basis for this book, which features their links with many other families. These genealogical studies have revealed a family that through its multiplicity of connections to famous ancient lines can be seen as a microcosm of the millennial Jewish presence in Europe.

Table 1
CHRONOLOGICAL TABLE

A.D.
800 Jewish emissaries between courts of Charlemagne and Caliph
Haroun al Rashid of Baghdad
Legendary ancestry of Kalonymos family
900 from Italy to the Rhineland and Provence.
Kalonymos saves life of Otto II at battle of Cotrone, 982.
1000 Kalonymos family flourish at Mainz, Speyer and Worms.
Great Schism, 1054. Byzantine Emperor Constantine X sends Jewish
doctor to treat Pope Urban II.
First crusade, 1096. The biblical scholar and translator Rashi of
Troyes meets Geoffrey of Bouillon.
1100 Flourishing communities on the Iberian peninsula. Jewish
Renaissance in Spain.
1200 Kalonymos lead communities at Narbonne and Arles.
Abulafia, distinguished family in thirteenth- and fourteenth-century
Spain.
1300 From the time of Casimir the Great, Poland gives refuge to Jews
fleeing from persecution in the West.
Spiro (Shapiro), Treivish (Treves) and Heilprin (Halpern) clans take
names from Speyer, Trier and Heilbronn. Joseph Treves, the Great, of
Marseilles. Mattityahu Treves of Provence, Ch. Rabbi of Paris.
General expulsion of Jews from France, 1394
1400 Yaffe in Bologna (some later move to Bohemia and later still to Poland).
Nexus of the Treves, Spiro and Luria families. Yechiel Luria of
Alsace, father-in-law of Isaac Katzenellenbogen. Elijah Delmedigo,
professor at Padua, translates the works of Averroes.
Joseph Colon, the Maharik of Mantua, descendant of the French
Trabots. His son-in-law, the astronomer Abba Mari Delmedigo
Chalfan settles in Italy.
General expulsions from Spain and Portugal, 1492–97 to Holland,
Italy and Ottoman Empire.
Chayot (Chayes) of Provence later in Prague and Poland.
1500 Abba Mari Chalfan's son, Elias Menachem Chalfan of Venice, rabbi,
doctor, friend of Pietro Aretino, sits on Venice rabbinical court to
consider Henry VIII's divorce case. He marries daughter of
Kalonymos ben David. His descendants flourish in Venice, Prague
and Vienna in spite of periodical expulsions.
Katzenellenbogens from Hesse-Nassau establish rabbinical dynasty
in Padua and Venice.
Rabbis Moses Isserles of Cracow and Shlomo Luria of Lublin.
Union of Lublin, 1569, creates greater Poland-Lithuania, where the
Jewish community continues to flourish and Saul Wahl, scion of the
Katzenellenbogens, plays important role.

Renaissance Rabbis of Prague include Judah Loew, Mordecai Yaffe, Isaac Chayot and David Gans.
Series of temporary expulsions from Prague.

1600 Persecution in Frankfurt, 1612. Isaiah Halevi Horovitz moves to Holy Land.
Chmielnicki massacres in Poland, 1648 mark Poland's decline.
Sephardic Jews formally readmitted to England by Oliver Cromwell, 1656.
Uri Feivush, Ch. Rabbi of Vilna and Nasi in Jerusalem. Nathan Nata Spiro, Abraham Joshua Heschel and Aryeh Leib Fischls, Ch. Rabbis of Cracow. Chaim Menachem Man (Chalfan) Ch. Rabbi of Vienna.
General expulsion from Vienna 1670.

1700 Era of the Court Jews. Samson Wertheimer in Vienna.
Jewish communities flourish in Amsterdam, Brody, and Livorno.
Samuel Helman, Ch. Rabbi of Metz. Ezekiel Landau, Ch.R. of Prague.
Chasidic movement. Rabbi Pinchas Shapiro of Koretz.
The enlightenment. Moses Mendelssohn.
The three partitions of Poland (1772–95).
Emperor Joseph II and the beginnings of emancipation.

1800 Napoleon summons Grand Sanhedrin, 1806 attended by Naftali Hirsch Katzenellenbogen.
His grandson, Isidor Lazare becomes Ch. Rabbi of France.
Reversal of centuries-old migrations to the east. Rise of nationalism.
Russian pogroms and increasing emigration to the west and to America.
Beginnings of modern Zionism.

1900 First World War.
Zvi Hirsch Perez Chayes, Ch. Rabbi of Vienna and David Tebele Katzenellenbogen, Ch. Rabbi of St Petersburg.
Second World War and Holocaust. Establishment of the State of Israel, 1948.

Chapter Two

Introduction

Background to the book

A study of lineage has been of importance to the Jewish people since biblical days, and at different times it appears to have assumed greater or lesser religious and mystical significance.[1] The eighteenth-century enlightenment and gradual emancipation led many in succeeding generations to look towards assimilation as a way of escaping from their historical sufferings. They continued to remember their past, but they did not see family lineage as the moral support it could become in evil times. The aftermath of the Chmielnicki massacres in the mid-seventeenth century stimulated the need to study and cherish one's roots. So it is today after the catastrophes of the century which has just ended.

I grew up with only a dim awareness of my ancestry, but it was inevitable that I should turn sooner or later to a serious study of my family origins. The present enquiry has confirmed my belief that I have been shaped to a large degree by what my ancestors have passed down to me. I accept that it is the duty of succeeding generations to cherish their inheritance and to seek inspiration from it for their own lives.

Genealogy now has a potent ally in the modern science of genetics. Thus, recent DNA studies indicate that the 'seed of Aaron', the descendants of the ancient Jewish high priests, has managed to maintain a genetic particularity for over three thousand years.[2] Studies of the genetic particularity of other groups are in progress.[3]

As for the rabbinical clans that emerged in the middle ages, they intermarried for centuries to produce a genetically inbred elite. There is no doubt that it was this caste which held the Jewish people together for so long. They provided guidance and leadership, and while there was a measure of communal self-government, they were the interpreters of Jewish law and the guardians of Jewish ethics. The migrations of my ancestors, following on persecution, economic pressures and periodical expulsions, are in themselves an integral part of European history.[4] Rabbis were particularly peripatetic in good and bad times. For centuries, their movements back and forth across the continent followed to some extent the rise and decline of their flocks and changing needs for spiritual care.

It has been claimed that in a cultural sense the Jews were the first Europeans.[5] From the days of the biblical scholar Rashi of Troyes, who flourished in the eleventh century, the network of descent has been so close knit that a connection to any rabbinical family possessing an established pedigree opens up the possibility of tracing one's ancestry back to the distant past.[6]

While I come from such a background, many of my forebears were inevitably involved in a variety of secular pursuits. This family history is in a way a microcosm of the Jewish contribution to the story of Europe. Some positive aspects of this contribution may not have been adequately recognized. We have all been shaped by more than a thousand years of a common European culture, and if a future is to be built on this foundation, it must be secured through a better understanding of our roots. My old family tree had innumerable worthies who were unremarkable rabbis in distant provincial towns, but every so often the tree bore remarkable fruit. From so many generations there remains much to cherish and much can still be learnt.

When I determined to find out more about my family, I just had a couple of documents and a few fading childhood memories. I decided to record my progress in the form of a series of short articles. It was my intention to demonstrate how I went about finding my forebears, including early mistakes and going up a blind alley or two, an almost inevitable consequence of the dearth of primary source material.

The collection of essays, some of which have already been published elsewhere, together with some added tables and notes, build up into a picture of my ancestry. I have been concerned not only with the discovery of ancestors and the methodology of genealogical research, but with understanding the connection between the fortunes of individuals and of families and the great movements of European history over the past thousand years. These include the crusades, the discovery of the new world and expulsions from the Iberian peninsula, religious wars, the Italian Renaissance, the Reformation and Counter-Reformation, the rise of modern states and money economies, the Thirty Years War, contemporary upheavals concomitant on the decline of Poland and the rise of Russia, the rise and fall of the Ottoman Empire, developments in Prussia, Russia and Austria including the consequences of the eighteenth-century partitions of Poland, emancipation, assimilation, nationalism, modern anti-Semitism and Zionism, two world wars and the holocaust, a world-wide dispersion of the survivors and the creation of the State of Israel.

NOTES

1. Rabbi Meir Wunder, 'The Reliability of Genealogical Research in Modern Rabbinic Literature', *Avotaynu*, XI, 4 (winter 1995).
2. K. Skorecki *et al.*, 'Y Chromosomes of Jewish Priests', *Nature*, 385 (2 Jan. 1997), p.32; idem, 'Origins of Old Testament Priests', *Nature*, 394 (9 July 1998), p.138.
3. Rabbi Yaakov HaKohen Kleiman, 'Jewish Genes: DNA Evidence for Common Jewish

Origin and Maintenance of Ancestral Genetic Profile', *Sharsheret Hadorot*, xvi, 1 (Oct. 2001).

4. Rabbi Yaakov HaKohen Kleiman, *DNA and Tradition – the Genetic Link to the Ancient Hebrews* (Devora Publishers, 2004).
5. The 24th *IAGS* International Conference on Jewish Genealogy (Jerusalem 2004) devoted a session to developments in this rapidly moving field. For a summary, see Saul Issroff, 'Genetics and Genealogical Discoveries', *Shemot*,12, 4 (Dec. 2004).
6. Martin Gilbert, *Atlas of Jewish History* (London: Routledge, 1993). Edwyn R. Bevan and Dr Charles Singer (eds.), *The Legacy of Israel* (Oxford: Clarendon Press, 1927), p.180. Yehuda Klausner, 'Torah and Jewish Genealogy', *Sharsheret Hadorot*, XV, 1 (Autumn/ Winter 2000).

Chapter Three

In Search of My Pedigree

My parents' marriage certificate and a few childhood memories

My father came from an old rabbinical family and my mother's people, the Griffels, were entrepreneurs with a variety of business interests. Both families had been in the Galician province of the Austro-Hungarian Empire for many generations.

My father, David, grew up in a small provincial town, but he was determined to seek a secular education. From a yeshivah in Munkacz he ran away to Czernowitz, worked his way through college and began his legal studies, which he completed in Vienna, where he obtained his doctorate in 1915. He set up as an advocate there shortly afterwards.

My mother, Regina, came to Vienna with her parents after the outbreak of the First World War, to escape from the conflict that engulfed their home town on the eastern front. My parents married in 1921 and had two sons. My elder brother Ludwig was born in 1922 and perished in 1942. My father brought his brother Max and sister Lotte to Vienna and supported them through university, where they both gained doctorates in law. Max also practised as an advocate in that city and wrote a standard work on company law which is now in its 5th revised edition. Lotte emigrated to Palestine and married Dr Curt Kallmann, a physician from Berlin. My mother had two brothers, Zygmunt and Edward, who were successful businessmen in Lvov and Warsaw. They visited us in Vienna quite frequently. I went to Poland once to spend a summer holiday with my grandmother at Zopot, a resort on the Baltic coast. My family enjoyed a comfortable middle-class life in Vienna between the two world wars. We were largely assimilated. We went to the synagogue twice a year and I had Hebrew lessons for a while. My father was actively involved in Zionist circles. We felt we had little in common with our orthodox relations and we were completely severed from them culturally.

My paternal grandfather came to Vienna shortly before his death in 1934, so I have a memory of him and of my maternal grandmother. After the Anschluss we fled to England, and my uncles managed to leave Poland in time, but their parents vanished in the holocaust. My mother died in London in 1954 and my father died in Vienna in 1964.

Half a century later I feel that I have to pay my respects to my ancestors. In a way it is like placing flowers on their graves, but I hope that this record will be longer lasting. I consider that I am fulfilling a religious duty.

When I embarked on my genealogical odyssey in 1998 I had a few fading childhood memories, my birth certificate, and my parents' marriage certificate, supplied by the Israelitische Kultusgemeinde in Vienna.[1] It states that David Gelles, advocate of Vienna, son of Nahum Uri Gelles and Esther Weinstein, born at Kudrynce on 24 December 1883, married Regina Griffel, daughter of David Mendel Griffel and Chawa Wahl, of Vienna, born at Nadworna on 18 March.1900. The marriage took place at the main synagogue in Vienna on 18 August 1921.

According to family legend my grandmother was descended from Saul Wahl, a scion of the Katzenellenbogen rabbis of Padua and Venice, who became an important figure in sixteenth-century Poland. I knew his name from such books as Simon Dubnow's *Weitgeschichte des Jüdischen Volkes*. In due course I found Neil Rosenstein's *The Unbroken Chain*, the genealogical source book on the Katzenellenbogen descendancy. I could not derive any immediate assistance from this magnum opus on the connection between Saul Wahl and my family. However, I had speedier success in searching for the Gelles ancestry. Rosenstein's invaluable book first drew my attention to the connection by marriage between my father's family and the famous Chasidic Rabbi Pinchas of Koretz. The well-known reference works on the Galician Rabbinate, *Otzar Harabbanim, Ohalei Shem* and *Meorei Galizia*, had entries for my grandfather, refer to my great-grandfather, and confirm that the family came from Brody and was descended from Samuel Hillmann, an eighteenth-century Chief Rabbi of Metz.

By this time I had found my way to the *Jewish Genealogical Society of Great Britain*, some of whose members, notably Michael Honey, helped me at the start and pointed me towards some of these standard reference works. That is not to say that they did not sometimes lead me up blind alleys! I found out in due course that Jewish genealogy is not so simple, and that there is still a great deal of uncertainty and argument about some links which were generally accepted for a long time – but more of that later.

There are clearly several approaches to the study of pedigree, and the most obvious is to work backwards in time, as I did with the Gelles and Griffel families. I knew my mother's place and date of birth and that the Griffels came from Nadworna and later also lived at Stanislau, but I had no idea where my grandmother's family came from. I did not have Chawa Wahl's birth date or the names of her parents. For a long time I was unable to trace any surviving Wahl relations. However, my desire to get behind the family legend made me press on with the study of Saul Wahl and of his multitudinous descendants, in a firm belief that going forward and back in time my ancestral lines would meet at some point.

Soon after I began my researches some obscure Hebrew books came to light through my translator Yissochor Marmorstein and information supplied by Rabbis Meir Wunder of Jerusalem and Dov Weber of New

York. From the correspondence recorded in these books I was able to construct a partial family tree for the Wahls of Nadworna. It was like solving a jigsaw puzzle in which the details from apparently unrelated families slowly came together. Librarians at the London School of Jewish Studies, at the British Library, and elsewhere facilitated these efforts.[2]

During this time I wrote to Jewish community offices in Vienna and Zurich,[3] and ultimately made contact with a Wohl family of Zurich and New Jersey. They were in touch with some Griffels from Nadworna. These Wohls told me that they were descended from Zvi Arieh Wahl, the nineteenth-century Chief Rabbi of that town. Unfortunately they did not have any documents or detailed information, but the reference books had already indicated that Zvi Arieh Wahl was a likely connection to the Wahl family tree. With the Griffels, too, this approach bore fruit in the end. I established contact with long lost cousins in America, and they had something to tell me about Jacob Griffel who rescued thousands of Jews from Eastern Europe during and immediately after the war. These contacts jogged my memory and led me to the Wohls of Krakow with whom we are connected. My aunt, Maryla Suesser, was the grand-daughter of Salomon Meier Wohl, who was a merchant banker, and whose family at one time had a business in Vienna and a bank in Zurich. I had forgotten the connection when I came across a reference to their descent from Saul Wahl in J. Burnford Samuel's book, *The History of the Samuels* (Philadelphia: Lippincott, 1912). Another aunt, Susan Manson, turned out to be descended from the famous Chasidic dynasties of Ruzhin and Sadegura.

In my archive searches those at Vienna were the most easily accessible, and the Jewish community offices supplied me with birth, death and burial records for my father, uncle and grandfather. Polish and Ukrainian archives are more of a challenge. The starting point was the Mormons' Family History Library in South Kensington, but their material on Galician Jewry is patchy with respect to both time and place. The number of Jews who survived the war in Brody, Stanislau and Nadworna was pitifully small, yet there is a Rabbi Kolesnik in Stanislau today who unearthed several birth records for Griffels and Wahls from Nadworna at the relevant period. Government archives in Warsaw[4] and L'viv[5] are slowly yielding vital data. I have thus obtained the birth records for my maternal grandfather and great-grandfather. Recently some fascinating early-nineteenth-century records from the *Beth Din* at Brody have come my way. They contain entries for numerous transactions involving my paternal ancestors.

Information from tombstones such as place of residence, father's name and date of death is being gathered wherever possible. I had the data from my father's and grandfather's graves in Vienna, but thanks to a major project on the Jewish tombstones in Brody, conducted by Neil Rosenstein and Dov Weber, much more on the Gellis family is emerging.

My grandfather, Nahum Uri Gelles, died in Vienna in 1934 and is buried in that city's central cemetery. He was born at Narajow in 1852 and was the Rabbi of Solotwina near Stanislau for half a century. His tombstone states that he was the son of Rabbi David Isaac Gellis and that the family came from Brody.

The photo of the tombstone of my great-grandfather was supplied by Dov Weber of New York (see Figure 5). He is described in the rabbinical reference books as Rabbi Gaon David Isaac, blessed *Zaddik*, Gellis. He was born around 1790 and died about 1870. He is buried with his forefathers in Brody and his tombstone confirms the name of his father as Rabbi Moshe Gellis. This photo is one of numerous tombstones in the new Jewish cemetery at Brody that have recently been taken and the details of some are being put on computer. It took me quite some time to become familiar with the computer aids to genealogical research, but in due course information began to reach me from various web sites (see Postscript).

At this stage I had established a direct descent from Moses Gelles, who was a member of the prestigious *Klaus* of Brody in the eighteenth century. A line of cousins also descending from him were rabbis in Podolia: Shmuel Dov (Gelles), was the son-in-law of Pinchas Shapiro of Koretz (1726–90). The latter was a direct descendant of Nathan Nata Spiro of Krakow (1585–1633), whose ancestry goes back to Rashi.

I now knew a little about my maternal great-grandfather Eliezer Griffel and his wife Sarah Chayes of Kolomea, but the Chayes and Wahl connections of my great-grandmother and my grandmother still remained a major challenge.

POSTSCRIPT

The above account is a slightly revised version of the article I published in the magazine *Shemot* in June 2000. By that time I had a rough outline of my father's rabbinical pedigree going back to Brody in the eighteenth century. As for my mother's background, the most distinguished names were clearly those of my grandmother, Chawa Wahl, and of my great-grandmother Sarah Chayes. I had not yet confirmed their places of birth and vital details. While pursuing these questions I looked into the history of the Wahl and Chayes clans and the two following articles are based on these studies.

NOTES

1. Israelitische Kultusgemeinde, 1010 Vienna, Seitenstettengasse 4, tel: 531 04 172, fax: 531 04 179, e-mail: h.weiss@ikg.wien.at.
2. Libraries: London Library in St James's Square, SW1; Jewish Studies Library at University College London; Oxford Centre for Hebrew & Jewish Studies, Yarnton Manor, near Oxford; London School of Jewish Studies, 44a Albert Road, Hendon, NW4; The British Library, 96 Euston Road, NW1; The Wiener Library, 4 Devonshire Street, W1; Yad Vashem, Jerusalem; Diaspora Museum, Tel Aviv; The Leo Baeck Institute, 15 West 16th St., New York.
3. For Vienna, see Note 1. Israelitische Kultusgemeinde Zurich, PO Box 8027, Zurich, Switzerland.

4. Warsaw State Archives, Archiwum Glowne Akt Dawnych, ul. Dluga 7, 00-263 Warszawa.
5. Tsentralnyi Derzhavnyi Istorychnyi Archiv u.m. L'vivi; Ploshna Soborna 3a, Lviv 290008, Ukraine. Archive searches in Lviv were carried out by Alexander Dunai, a resident of that city (Stepanivny Street 17/2, Lviv)

Figure 1
Edward Gelles and his father, Dr David Gelles

F 1

Heiratsurkunde

(Standesamt) Israelitische Kultusgemeinde Wien Nr. 83/1921/I)

Der Dawid Itzig G e l l e s , Rechtsanwalt, - - - - - - - - - -

- -,

- - - - - - - - - - -, wohnhaft Wien IX, Währingerstraße 5 - 7 - -,

geboren am 24. Dezember 1883 in Kudrnyce - - - - - - - - - - - -,

(Standes-/Pfarr-)amt - - - - - - - - - - - - - - - - - Nr. - - -), und

die Regina G r i f f e l -

- -,

- - - - - - - - - - -, wohnhaft Wien IX, Währingerstraße 2 - - - -,

geboren am 18. März 1900 in Nadworna - - - - - - - - - - - -

(Standes-/Pfarr-)amt - - - - - - - - - - - - - - - - - Nr. - - - -),

haben am 18. August 1921 - - - - - - - - - - vor dem Standesamt

der Israelitischen Kultusgemeinde Wien, Tempel die Ehe geschlossen.

Vater des Mannes: Nuchem Ira Gelles - - - - - - - - - - - - - - - -

Mutter des Mannes: Ester geb. Weinstein - - - - - - - - - - - - - -

Vater der Frau: Dawid Mendel Griffel - - - - - - - - - - - - - -

Mutter der Frau: Chawy geb. Wahl - - - - - - - - - - - - - - - - -

Vermerke: -

(Siegel)

Wien, den 21. August 1964.

Der beeidete Matrikelführer:

(Der Standesbeamte)

f. Margarethe Mezei

Eheschließung der Eltern:

des Mannes am .... (Standes/Pfarr)amt .... Nr. ....)

der Frau am .... (Standes/Pfarr)amt .... Nr. ....)

A 151 Heiratsurkunde (mit Elternangabe)
Verlag für sämtlichen Standesamtsbedarf Oskar Höfels, Wien I, Seilerstätte 28.

Figure 2
Marriage certificate of my parents

Figure 3
Tombstone of Dr David Gelles, Vienna 1964

Figure 4
Tombstone of Rabbi Nahum Uri Gelles, who died in 1934 and is buried in Vienna

Rabbi Nahum Uri Gelles

Here lies Rabbi Nahum Uri who served for fifty years as Av Beth Din of Solotwina
son of the pious Rabbi David Isaac of blessed memory from Brody
both of them spent time in the shadow of tzadikim
Born 20th Shevat 5612
Passed away 11th Kislev 5698
May his soul be bound in the bond of everlasting life

Figure 5
Brody Tombstone of
Rabbi David Isaac Gellis
(ca. 1790–1870)

Rabbi David Yitzchak Gellis[1]

The tombstone marking the burial place of a man who was truly honest and God fearing from an early age
He sat in "the dust of the feet of tzadikim"[2] despite all the travails of his days
He is the learned and outstanding Rabbi David Yitzak zt"l[3]
Son of the late Rabbi Moshe Gellis zt"l[3]
May his soul be bound in the bond of everlasting life

1 *Dates are not visible on the photograph of this tombstone*
2 *Quotation from Mishna: Ethics of the Fathers, Ch.1:4*
3 *abbreviation of the phrase (Proverbs 10:7)*
"the memory of the righteous should be blessed"

Table 2
EDWARD GELLES

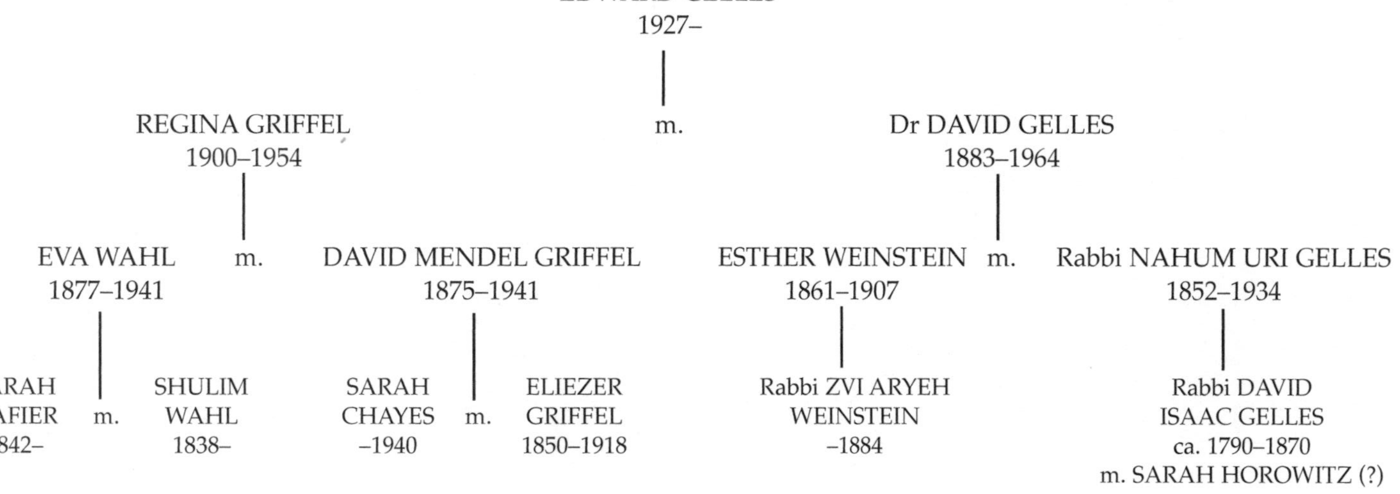

II.

CONCERNING THE WAHL AND CHAYES FAMILIES

Let us now praise famous men
and our fathers that begat us

Ecclesiasticus, 44: 1

Chapter Four

Saul Wahl

Where legend meets history

How could the Italian grandson of a German Jew become king of Poland? According to Jewish tradition, it happened in 1587. Poland at that time had an elective kingship. The throne was vacant. The electors were divided. Saul Wahl, a leading financier, was well connected with the biggest magnates in the land and in a position to play an important role during the interregnum. An extraordinary man was in the right place at the right time.

What was so special about the sixteenth century and the condition of the Jews in Europe and in Poland in particular? Who was Saul and where did he come from?

The discovery of the New World in 1492 heralded a period of rapid expansion across Europe. Spanish bullion fuelled financial liquidity, trade and mobility. Rising populations required more food. This trend favoured the land-owning nobility, and nowhere more so than in Poland, which became the granary of Europe. At the same time, the Renaissance and the Protestant Reformation brought about a revolution in culture, religious diversity and political ideas.

THE STATE OF POLAND

Poland flourished under the Jagiellonian kings who were also grand dukes of Lithuania. With Sigismund I (1506–48) the Renaissance came in the person of his queen, Bona Sforza, daughter of the Duke of Milan. Her retinue included Jewish doctors who had studied at the great Italian universities, particularly Padua, which was also the Alma Mater of many notable Poles. Thus, Poland's greatest scientist of the age, Nicolas Copernicus, and one of her leading statesmen, Jan Zamoyski, were graduates of both Cracow and Padua.

Jews had been fleeing to Poland from persecution in Germany since before the time of Casimir the Great (1333–70), who ratified and extended an earlier charter of toleration. As elsewhere in Europe, the Jews met religious intolerance from the clergy, and marked hostility from townspeople, who felt themselves economically threatened, in contrast to the king and the magnates who benefited from their activities.

The direct Jagiellonian line came to an end shortly after the formal union of the Kingdom of Poland with the Grand Duchy of Lithuania (Lublin 1569). The death of Sigismund II August marked the beginning of the era of elective kingship. In the new 'Republic', political power was vested in the nobility. The election depended on the balance between the great magnates of the land and of the neighbouring states such as Austria and Sweden. It was an oligarchy with a titular royal head and with a constitution that bore some resemblance to those of the Serene Republic of Venice and the Holy Roman Empire. The Jews benefited from the new system in so far as newly elected kings needed ready funds, which they could supply.

The brief reign of Henri Valois (1573–75) was followed by that of the Transylvanian Prince Stefan Bathory (1576–86). Then the Swedish Prince Sigismund III Vasa and his two sons successively held the Polish crown through a century of expansion, which saw Poland-Lithuania briefly become the most powerful state in Eastern Europe. At its widest boundaries, it included White Russia and Ukraine, and extended beyond Smolensk and Kiev to the land of the Zaporozhe Cossacks. In this age Catholic kings maintained the rights of religious minorities and the privileges accorded to the Jews. An extensive system of Jewish autonomy developed with substantial juridical and fiscal powers, such as the assessment of taxes by the rabbinate and local councils.

Their numbers grew rapidly to over 5 per cent of the population, and they extended their activities from the traditional money-lending to all branches of the economy. They became the favoured agents of the crown and magnates as rent, tax, toll and tithe collectors, and estate managers, which involved running the mills, distilleries, taverns and other enterprises. Inevitably the resentment of the peasantry was directed against the Jewish agents rather than the absentee landlords.

For a long time Poland more than held its own against the rising powers of Sweden and Muscovy, the more distant threats of the Tartars and Ottoman Turks, and the ambitions of their Hohenzollern vassals. The deluge came in 1648 with the rebellion of Bogdan Chmielnicki, Ataman of the Dnieper Cossacks, which ultimately led to the transfer of their allegiance to Muscovy and to the loss of Ukraine and much else for Poland. This blow to the Polish state was also a catastrophe for the Jewish communities, which suffered enormous losses in lives and property.

ACROSS EUROPE

Conditions were changing elsewhere in Europe. While large numbers of German Jews migrated directly to Poland over a long period, others went to join existing communities in Italy. There the Jews suffered under the religiously inspired intolerance that waxed and waned during the Renaissance,

Reformation and Counter-Reformation periods. They were confined to ghettos and severely restricted in the occupations and professions that were open to them. The Church had long forbidden Christians to receive interest, but tolerated or even encouraged Jewish moneylenders, who enjoyed a near monopoly in some countries, though at times they met strong competition from the Lombards. Jews did not have full civil rights, but their lives and property were generally protected by the secular authorities. The universities gave them access in very limited numbers. Padua was for a long time one of the few schools where they could study medicine.

The mass expulsions from the Iberian peninsula at the end of the fifteenth century were the greatest disaster for Sephardic Jewry, which had flourished in Spain and Portugal for centuries. Many fled to Holland, Italy and Turkey. The Ottomans maintained a hospitable and tolerant attitude for a considerable period. Jews prospered in Constantinople but, after the battle of Lepanto in 1571, the Sultan's power and protection declined. Prominent at that time was Joseph Nasi, who had fled from Portugal to Holland, and later not being made welcome in Venice, accepted an invitation to move to Constantinople. He became the powerful favourite of Sultan Selim and was created Duke of Naxos and Prince of the Cyclades. Salomon Ashkenasi, whose family had come to Italy from Germany, was physician to Sigismund August in Cracow and later to the Grand Vizier in Constantinople. He is reputed to have been influential in the negotiations leading to the election of Henri Valois and later of Stefan Bathory to the Polish throne, and he was sent as ambassador of the Sublime Porte to the Serene Republic of Venice in 1574. His son, Nathan, who also studied medicine at Padua, was Ottoman ambassador to Venice in 1605. These men were favourably placed to conduct discreet diplomatic and financial negotiations by nature of the dispersion and their wide international contacts.

In contrast to the fifteenth-century persecutions in Germany and the Empire, the Reformation ushered in a better time for the Jews there, perhaps because it divided their potential oppressors. The ensuing turbulence, changing alliances, fluctuating fortunes of war, and the expanding need for credit and finance led the Habsburg emperors to adopt a friendlier policy. Maximilian II allowed the Jews to return to Bohemia, and in 1577 Rudolph II gave them a charter of privileges. One of his agents, Marcus Meisel, was a prototype of the 'Court Jew'. He helped to finance the war against the Ottoman Turks.

THE FAMILY BACKGROUND

Returning to the importance of Padua in this period, noble Poles travelled in Italy and learned Jews went to Poland. That is the background to the career of Saul Wahl, scion of the Katzenellenbogen family, hailing from the town of that name in the German state of Hesse-Nassau.

The name Katzenellenbogen is believed to derive from the Catti, an ancient Frankish tribe. It may refer to their settlement near the bend (elbow) of the Rhine or to another geographical feature in that area known by the Latin name of Cattimelibocus. Descendants of Hugh Capet became counts of Katzenellenbogen in the twelfth century and gradually permitted small numbers of Jews to settle there. A Jewish community was firmly established early in the fourteenth century. Rabbi Isaac of Katzenellenbogen married the daughter of Rabbi Jehiel Luria of Alsace and later moved to Prague, where his son Meir (1482–1565) studied before going on to Padua. There he married Hannah, the granddaughter of his teacher Judah Minz. The latter had come to Padua when the Jews were expelled from Mainz in 1461. He established a talmudic academy which achieved worldwide fame, attracting students from north of the Alps and as far as the Levant. Meir took over the leadership from Judah's son, Abraham in 1541. He is considered the patriarch of the Katzenellenbogen family.

According to the historian Cecil Roth, Rabbi Meir was among the most eminent talmudic authorities of his day and his opinion was consulted from every quarter of Europe in connection with knotty problems of Jewish law. His son, Samuel Judah (1521–97), succeeded him in Padua which was conjoined with Venice in his rabbinate. His reputation extended to non-Jewish scholars. Paul Weidner dedicated his works to him (Vienna 1562). Like his father, he wrote numerous *responsa* and some of his sermons were published in Venice in 1594. His friend Leone da Modena delivered his funeral oration in 1597. He and his wife Abigail had two daughters and a son Saul, born in Padua about 1541–5. The family background was thus distinguished for learning, wealth and social position in one of the most flourishing Jewish communities.

FROM ITALY TO POLAND

Saul attended the university of Padua, and around 1560 he set out for Poland to study at the *yeshiva* of the Maharshal (R. Shlomo Luria) in Brest. There he settled after marrying the daughter of a local rabbi. Brest was fast becoming an important centre for Lithuanian Jewry and he might well have ended his days as the respected rabbi of this distant town. But now there occurred one of those chance events that shape the lives of individuals and nations. The path of the Katzenellenbogens crossed that of the Radziwills, the richest and most powerful nobles in Lithuania, who remained prominent in the councils of Poland for several centuries.

Nicholas Radziwill, who died in 1477, was Marshal of the Court of Lithuania and Palatine of Wilno, the most important person in the country after the Grand Duke. His two great-grandsons, Nicholas 'Rufus' and Nicholas 'the Black', were given the title of Prince of the Holy Roman Empire by Charles V as part of the latter's machinations to prevent the union of Lithuania with Poland. But this was trumped by Sigismund August, who not only confirmed their princely status but granted them the freeholds of their enormous estates of Olyka and Nieswiez, from which they henceforth took their ducal titles. All this was reaffirmed by both king and parliament in Lublin in 1569. The position of the Radziwills in Poland was further strengthened by the king's marriage to Barbara, Prince Rufus's sister. Nicholas the Black's son, Prince Nicholas Christoph 'the Orphan' (1549–1616), returned to the Catholic faith and undertook a pilgrimage to Jerusalem which he recorded in his *Peregrinatio Hierosolymitana.* He also offered to buy up the extant copies of the Protestant 'Radziwill Bible' published by his father, intending to have them destroyed. According to legend, this is the Prince Radziwill who, returning from the Holy Land, found himself short of funds in Italy and appealed to Rabbi Samuel Judah for assistance, which was amply provided. Regaining his domain, he repaid the Rabbi's kindness by seeking out his son Saul and taking him under his wing. Not so strange when one considers that they had been contemporaries at Padua! Radziwill and his friends favoured Saul with appointments and eased his advancement to wealth and influence.

There are records that Saul leased breweries at Kandawa (west of Riga) in 1578 and owned ships for this business, and that he acquired similar interests at Wieliczka near Cracow in 1580. In these years King Stefan Bathory leased him the salt pans in the Grand Duchy, giving him the sole rights to sell their products, and also the salt mine at Wieliczka. Since at one time salt furnished nearly a fifth of the crown revenues, these were major commercial concessions. There are also documents relating to Saul's paying a large sum for the right to farm the Lithuanian taxes for three years and, again, the sum of 150,000 gold florins for the right to collect tolls on bridges and duties on flour and brandy for ten years. In 1589 King Sigismund gave him titles and privileges in a decree granting him 'a place among our royal officials and that he may be assured of our favour we exempt him and his lands for the rest of his life from subordination to the jurisdiction of any court in our lands'. Saul, referred to as 'Servus Regis', the King's Servant, became the king's principal agent in the opening up of commerce in Lithuania and Courland in particular.

From the 1580s onwards Saul was among the leaders of the Brest community, taking an important part in the Council of the Lands. He interceded in a number of lawsuits on behalf of Jewish communities, as for example in 1592 when the Jews of Brest appealed to the king against the local municipality. In the same year, he persuaded the king to order the courts in Courland to judge disputes with Jews according to Polish, rather than the less favourable Prussian, law. This ruling was extended and confirmed by later kings. Saul was also given credit for the confirmation that disputes between Jews should be subject only to Jewish courts, thus strengthening the autonomy rights of Lithuanian Jewry. During this time, he brought up a family and united himself with the most prominent Jewish rabbis through the marriages of his children. His son Meir, who later became Rabbi and Head of the Rabbinical Court at Brest, married Heinde, the daughter of

Rabbi Pinchas Horowitz, the brother-in-law of the great Rabbi Moses Isserles. He built a synagogue, a house of learning and public baths, and made many other benefactions. When the Brest synagogue was demolished in 1842, a plaque was discovered with the following inscription: 'Saul, son of the Chief Rabbi of Padua, built this synagogue in honour of his pious wife Deborah, daughter of (David) Drucker'. Other information that has come down to us includes references to the gold chain which Saul wore with other decorations and which he bequeathed to the poor, as well as a trust fund of 20,000 Polish gulden, to a seal displaying a lion (rampant) holding in its paw two tablets with a Latin inscription (representing the ten commandments), and to title deeds for property still recorded as extant in the mid-nineteenth century.

HISTORICAL RECORDS AND ORAL TRADITION

Saul became an intimate of the Radziwills and other magnates and of King Sigismund, who is supposed to have addressed him as Wahl. As for the adoption of that name, it could be a reference to his Italian origin. Another possible derivation is from a trade or tavern sign. A closely related family had the name of Shor. This is Hebrew for ox, and the Polish for ox is wo(h)l. A similar type of name derivation applies to the Rothschilds. A third possibility is that mentioned by early writers such as his direct eighteenth-century descendant Rabbi Phineas ben Moses Katzenellenbogen. He set down the oral tradition passed from Saul's contemporaries to his father. This describes Saul's election as king for a day during the interregnum of 1587 and asserts that the name Wahl (German for election) was given to him at that time:

> Rabbi Samuel Judah's son was the great Saul Wahl of blessed memory. All learned in such matters well know that his surname Wahl was given him because he was chosen king of Poland by the unanimous vote of the noble electors of the land. I was told by my father and teacher of blessed memory that the choice fell on him in this wise. Saul Wahl was a favourite with the Polish noblemen and highly esteemed for his shrewdness and ability. The king of Poland had died. Now it was customary for the great nobles of Poland to assemble for the election of a new king on a given day on which it was imperative that a valid decision be reached. When the day came many opinions were found to prevail among the electors, which could not be reconciled. Evening fell and they realised the impossibility of electing a king on the legally appointed day. Loath to transgress their own rules the nobles agreed to make Saul Wahl king for the rest of the day and the following night and thus conform with the letter of the law. And so it was.

In earlier Polish and Lithuanian state documents Saul had been variously referred to as Saul Judicz, that is, Saul the Jew. These records are scanty. Much was lost or deliberately destroyed in the late seventeenth century and during the eighteenth-century partitions. However, the oral tradition and the weight of anecdotal evidence that Saul carried out royal functions prior to the election of Sigismund III is impressive. For example, Edelmann sent out a circular to the rabbis in 'Ashkenaz' in the mid-nineteenth century and received several hundred letters and manuscripts from all over Central and Eastern Europe. These dealt with aspects of Saul's career in finance and commerce, as a civic leader in Lithuania, with his royal election, and with the laws he is supposed to have rushed through to improve the legal status of the Jews. When Prince Radziwill proposed Saul to the deadlocked electors to be king for a day in order to gain time for a resolution of the impasse, Saul is supposed to have insisted as a condition of accepting the honour that certain laws should be enacted forthwith, that in future the spilling of Jewish blood was to be treated in the same way by the courts as the murder of a Christian, and that no further blood libel allegations (to which there was no basis) were to be considered.

Other legends grew up around Saul's name. The story that Sigismund had an affair with his daughter Hanele has a degree of plausibility. Saul married her off in a hurry to a septuagenarian rabbi, Ephraim Zalman Shor, and she promptly produced a son, Jacob. The subject has continued to fascinate for centuries.

CONCLUSION

In this essay I have attempted to sketch in the state of Poland-Lithuania in the later sixteenth century against the general European background. The salient points were the political balance between the king, the magnates, the lesser nobility, and the other estates of the land, the economic importance of the Jewish community, the great wealth of Saul, his influence at court and with the higher nobility, and particularly the patronage of the Radziwills.

Against this historical background and with the documented facts of his life, it is plausible that Saul should have played an important role after the death of Stefan Bathory. Many of the principal players would have been beholden to him. The long interregnum of 1586–87 saw an intense struggle between the parties of the leading candidates. The crown was the prize to be won by a Catholic prince who could take the required coronation oath after gaining the support of the magnates and the acclaim of the nobility.

Sigismund Vasa was backed by his aunt, Queen Anna Jagiellonka (the widow of Stefan Bathory), by the Primate, and by the Zamoyski faction. They were ultimately successful against the Habsburg candidate, the Archduke Maximilian, brother of the Emperor Rudolph II, who was supported by the Empire, Spanish silver, the Zborowskis and others. Sweden and the Papacy were in the front rank of players; Muscovy and the Duke of Ferrara were also involved in the struggle. Lithuania pursued its own line within the Union with a delaying policy. The Swedish prince was chosen in August 1587 and crowned in December of that year. When it came to a crucial vote on 18 August, the delaying tactics in which Saul was involved redounded to Sigismund's advantage. His services were certainly appreciated, not least by Sigismund, who showed him marked favour soon after his accession to the throne.

Saul Wahl combined talmudic learning and a classical education with outstanding business ability and leadership of the Jewish community with an important role in the councils of state. He died around the year 1617. One of his sons, Rabbi Meir Katzenellenbogen Wahl, was among the founders of the Council of Lithuania in 1623. Saul's children left a numerous progeny and later descendants included many leading personalities in Jewish communities throughout Europe.

NOTES

The original account of Wahl's 'Election' was set down by his direct descendant Phineas ben Moses Katzenellenbogen in the early eighteenth century. An edited version of the original manuscript Yesh Manhilin was published in Jerusalem in 1984.

Hirsch Edelmann, *Gedullath Shaul* (The Glory of Saul) (London: 1854) has a large body of material on the life of Saul Wahl from many sources.

Other references include Ahron Walden, *Shem Hagedolim Hachadash* (Warsaw: 1864); Ephraim Zalman Margolis, *Ma'aloth Hayochasin* (Lemberg: 1900); and Rabbi Meir Padua of Brest, who recalls having seen the ethical will left by Saul Wahl to his descendants. S.A. Bershadski, 'Yevrei Korol Polski', *Voskhod* 1889 *et seq.* (a number of articles in Russian). Majer Balaban, 'Shaul Wahl: Der Yidischer melekh in Poyln: Emes un legende' (The Jewish King in Poland: Truth and Legend) in *Yidn in Poyln* (The Jews in Poland) (Wilno: B. Kietzkin, 1930); also cited in Yakov Leib Shpiro, *Mishpachot Atikot BeIsrael* (Ancient Families of Israel) (Jerusalem: Chulyot, 1981).

There are also numerous magazine articles such as: Gustave Karpeles, 'A Jewish King in Poland' (Jewish Publication Society of America 1895); D. Wasserzug, 'A King for a Night. The Polish Jew who Reigned', *Jewish World* (24 July 1903). J. Burnford Samuel, *History of the Samuels* (Philadelphia: Lippincott, 1912) cites an unpublished manuscript by B. Marcus and Sons, Vienna 1911, said to give details of the descent of Salo Meir Wohl of Cracow from Saul Wahl.

The appended chart shows some lines of descent from Saul Wahl which are relevant to the discussion of the Gelles rabbinical ancestry (see Chapter 36). Chapter 5 traces the ancestry of a Wahl family from my mother's home town, Nadworna.

Table 3
ASHKENAZI RABBINICAL ORIGINS

Katzenellenbogen	**Mainz**	**Heilbronn**	**Speyer**	**Treves**
			Samuel Spira m.	Vergentlin, d. of Mattityahu Treves *Ch. R. of Paris 1364*
			Shlomo	
Isaac K. m. d. of Jehiel Luria *moved to Prague then to Padua*	Judah Halevi Minz 1411–1508 *Chief Rabbi of Padua*		Perez of Constance	
		Zebulon Eliezer Ashkenazi Halpern	Nathan Nata of Posen	
Meir Judah K. m. 1483–1565 *Chief Rabbi of Padua*	Hannah Minz [grand-daughter of the above]		Simson of Posen	
Samuel Judah K. m. Abigail Yaffe 1521–97 *Chief Rabbi of Padua and Venice*		Moses Ashkenazi Halpern d. 1603, *R'M of Lvov* m. Aidel Lipshitz	Natan Nata Spira of Grodno, d. 1577	
			Solomon	
Saul Wahl m. Deborah Drucker 1545–1617 *Rex Pro Tempore, Poland 1587*		Abraham Halpern 1578–1649, *ABD of Lvov* m. d. of Shmuel Judah Wahl	Natan Nata Spiro 1585–1633 *ABD of Cracow* m. Roza Avarles d. 1642	
Meir K. m. Heinde, d. of Pinchas Horovitz d. 1631 1535–1617		Eliezer Lipman Halpern		
Moses K. of Chelm m. d. of Benjamin Benas d.ca. 1650 of Posen		Israel Halpern of Krotoschin m. Lifsha, d. of Natan Nata Spiro		
Saul K. of Pinczow m. Yente, d. of Jacob Shor 1617–91 d. 1655		?		
Moses K. of Anspach m. d. of Eliezer Heilprin of Fuerth 1670–1733 1649–1700		Shmuel Hillman, *ABD* of Metz ca. 1670–1764		
Eliezer Katzenellenbogen of Hagenau & Bamberg m. 1700–71		Yached		
	Naftali Hirsch Katzenellenbogen ca. 1745–1823			

CHAPTER FIVE

The Wahls of Nadworna

Genealogy of a family descended from Saul Wahl

The basis of this chapter is an article published in the magazine *Shemot* in the centenary year of my mother's birth. My mother was born in Nadworna, a little town in south-eastern Galicia, which was part of the Austro-Hungarian Empire. Her father David Mendel Griffel came from an old Galician family. Her mother Chawa Wahl claimed descent from Saul Wahl, the legendary one-day King of Poland. Belief in this tradition was not confined to my mother's family, but was widespread among friends and acquaintances at that time. When I embarked on a serious study of the subject fairly recently, I discovered that much had been written about the man and the legend.

Saul ben Judah Katzenellenbogen, known as Saul Wahl, was born into a family from the eponymous town of Katzenellenbogen in Hesse-Nassau. His grandfather, Chief Rabbi Meir of Padua, was a most eminent authority on Jewish law in his time. His father, Samuel Judah, followed on as a distinguished Chief Rabbi of Padua and Venice. Saul travelled to Poland as a young man, and ultimately became Parnas of Brest, a leader of Lithuanian Jewry, a great financier and entrepreneur, and an influential figure behind the vacant throne during the interregnum of 1587.[1] Saul Wahl had at least eleven children and they married into the leading Jewish families of their time, so there are a number of distinct lines of descent, and many old families claim him as an ancestor. He was possibly called Wahl by the Poles because he came from Italy: in medieval German, the Italians were called *Walen*, and the important law compendium, the *Sachsenspiegel*, refers to the King of Italy as *Here der Walen*.[2] Later generations used the form Wohl or Wahl, as was discussed in my earlier chapter.

Dr Neil Rosenstein has amassed a vast corpus of genealogical data on the descendants of Saul Wahl, but the 1990 edition of his work did not have any references to the Wahls of Nadworna or to the nineteenth-century Rabbi Zvi Arieh Wahl.[3] It is not entirely surprising that few people had heard of him. He was a worthy and not particularly distinguished rabbi in a small provincial town, but he did have an interesting pedigree which could turn out to be of some relevance to my immediate family.

From the well-known genealogical works dealing with the Galician rabbinate and a few hints from other experts, the search finally led to two rather obscure books in a private collection.[4] They would be in a few of the principal libraries such as the Jewish National and University Library in Jerusalem. These books contain texts of letters written by Zvi Arieh Wahl to various relatives.

In *Chidushei Hagershuni* (Note 4), Zvi Arieh sets out his family tree, signing himself Hirsch Leib Wahl of Nadworna. He says that most of his information was derived from his grandfather, Samson, and traces his line back through his father, Israel Wahl of Brodshin, Samson Wahl and David Wahl. David was the son of a magnate called Israel Stariner, who was connected directly and by marriage with many famous rabbis, and was himself descended from Saul Wahl and Yomtov Lipmann Heller. Zvi Arieh Wahl noted that Saul Wahl had a son who died during his father's lifetime and that the latter's son married Heller's granddaughter. Stariner was the grandson or great-grandson of that union. Zvi Arieh's letter also mentions many related rabbis, including Chaim of Czernowitz and Moshe Teitelbaum, two Chasidic leaders, descendants of Stariner and hence cousins of Zvi Arieh's grandfather. Another cousin of the latter, and apparently a grandson of Stariner, was Rabbi Avraham Reb Shachna's, who was connected with a number of prominent rabbinic lines.[5] David Wahl was the father of several rabbis.[6]

The Wahl-Heller line is linked with the Katzenellenpogen line originating with the marriage of a daughter of Rabbi Samuel Judah Katzenellenbogen of Venice to Rabbi Yoel Ashkenazi. Yomtov Lipmann Heller, the famous author of *Tosafot Yomtov* and Chief Rabbi of Vienna, Prague and Cracow, was the grandson of Moses Halevi Heller of Wallerstein, Chief Rabbi of the German communities, and reputedly descended from Jewish prisoners brought to Rome by Titus Vespasianus. Yomtov had nine children and several of them married into the Wahl family. There were also numerous alliances between grandchildren. To quote from the recent edited translation of Heller's autobiography, *Megilas Eivah:*[7]

> I travelled to Nemirov with my son Shmuel, his wife Devorah, the daughter of Gaon Avrashak and granddaughter of the benevolent Saul Wohl.

and again,

> I travelled with my grandson Nathan to Chelm in preparation for his marriage to the daughter of Gaon Moshe ABD [Av Beth Din], who was the son of Gaon Rav Meir, ABD of Brest and grandson of the communal leader Saul Wohl.

The millennial priestly family to which the eminent Rabbi Shabatai Katz belonged is interwoven with the Wahl pedigree as shown in Table 6. These connections are discussed by Zvi Arieh in a letter addressed to a relative, a member of the HaKohen (Katz) family. It is reproduced in *Chasdei Avoth*:

> The wife of your ancestor Rabbi Michel Katz, whose name was Taube, was the daughter of my ancestor Rabbi Abraham. The mother of Rabbi Michel was a daughter of the saintly Gaon, the holy Rabbi Moshe Heilprin, who was ABD of Berdichev ... When I visited the holy Rabbi of Sadegura, whose son-in-law is also a descendant of Rabbi Moshe Heilprin, he told me that this saintly Rabbi was the eighteenth generation in direct line from the Tosafist Rabbenu Elchanan, whose mother was a daughter of Rabbenu Yitzhak, whose mother was a granddaughter of Rashi. I told him that my grandfather had said that we are descendants of Rashi ... The wife of your ancestor Rabbi Shmuel Katz (the grandfather of Rabbi Michel), Temah, was the daughter of Beila, the daughter of Rabbi Moshe Gad, a grandson of the great Rabbi David Halevi Segal (whose work the *Turei Zahav* he published) by his first wife, the daughter of the famous Rabbi Yoel Sirkis, author of the *Bayis Chadash*.

Zvi Arieh also wrote about Rabbi Abraham:

> He knew the whole Torah by heart, back-to-front, and used to study the Talmud tractate Sabbath every Sabbath. He was the grandson of the Gaon, the author of *Knesset Yehezkel* (Rabbi Ezekiel of Altona-Hamburg).

Zvi Arieh Wahl's letters provide a starting point for the construction of the Wahl family tree. This involved the reconciliation of Zvi Arieh's data with information from authoritative reference works[8] and with genealogical data on families linked to the Wahls and Katzenellenbogens. Rabbi Fischler[9] states that another relative, the son of his great-uncle, the learned and saintly Rabbi Saul Hakohen Adlersberg, the ABD of Brodshin, gave him information similar to that provided by Zvi Arieh Wahl. Adlersberg's ancestry is also discussed elsewhere.[10]

The connections of the Hakohen line from Shabatai Katz are supported by the pedigrees provided by a member of the Hirsch family, Yehudah Arieh Zvi[11] and they tie in with the details given by Fischler and Pickholz (Note 4).

Generally speaking, full details such as precise dates and the names of wives and children have come down to us only in exceptional cases. The family is fortunate in having a number of eminent rabbis for whom such records survive. Inevitably, many gaps remain. Some ambiguous connections have been resolved using data directly provided by descendants of Zvi Arieh Wahl, found through enquiries in Europe and America. Zvi Arieh's son, Isaac David Wohl, was Rosh Yeshiva at Nadworna. His son Isidore Azrael Wohl (1887–1963) had two sons, Isaac David (born 1921) and Zvi Arieh (born 1914). The former has a daughter and a son, Ronnie Wohl of San Francisco, while the latter's son, Ilan Wohl, lives in Switzerland.[12]

Another line to be dovetailed into the family tree is that of the Halperns. Moshe Heilprin or Heilpern, scion of the Halpern clan, who can be seen from Tables 5 and 6 to be a linchpin of the Nadworna Wahl's family tree, and descended from Mordechai Yaffe of Prague. He was ABD of Berdichev before moving to Solotwina near Brodshin. His wife Mindel was a descendant of Rabbi Shabatai Katz.

Zvi Arieh Wahl and Alexander Hakohen Adlersberg, among others, have outlined Heilprin's illustrious pedigree. To describe him as holy and saintly does not adequately convey the veneration he inspired in his followers. This can be gauged from the legends which have come down to us:[13]

> A local priest tried to revive the infamous blood libel against the Jews of Brodshin, having killed his maidservant and deposited the corpse in the woodshed of a Jew. The latter was sentenced to death and all the local Jews were to be expelled from the town. Rabbi Moshe instructed them to lodge an appeal saying that he wished to give evidence as to the identity of the murderer. He had the corpse exhumed and brought into the courtroom. He then spoke to the dead girl asking her to reveal who had killed her. Miraculously, she began to speak and declared that the priest was in fact the murderer. The priest fainted and later admitted his guilt, and the Jews were saved. Rabbi Moshe said that he would not return home to Solotvina, and that he was going to die as he had invoked the Divine Holy Name. He died the next day and was buried in Brodshin. Before his death he gave instructions that his descendants up to ten generations should come to pray at his grave in times of trouble. He did however request that they should only disturb him in matters of life and death.

Other stories tell how he persuaded a brigand who was feared all over the Carpathian mountains to promise not to harm any Jews, and how the Baal Shem Tov (the founder of the Chasidic movement) came to spend a Sabbath with him at Solotvina.

This study was initiated to define the connection between Saul Wahl and the Wahls of Nadworna. It has achieved this, and furthermore it has amply demonstrated the richness of the links between the ancient rabbinical families. There are many holy and saintly men in the Wahl ancestry, and many of the most famous rabbinical scholars are associated with the family in one way or another. The tree can only show a bare outline of this inheritance.

NOTES

1. Edward Gelles, 'Saul Wahl. A Jewish Legend', *Judaism Today* (Dec. 1999).
2. Lord Bryce, *The Holy Roman Empire* (London: Macmillan, 1961), p.190.
3. Neil Rosenstein, *The Unbroken Chain*, revised edition (New York, London, Jerusalem: CIS Publishers, 1990).
4. Judah Gershon Pickholz, *Chidushei Hagershuni* (Kolomea: 1890). Yehiel Michel Fischler, *Chasdei Avoth* (Lemberg: 1880).
5. David Steinberg, *Machazeh Avraham* (Brody, 1927). Ephraim Zalman Margolis, *Ma'alot Hayochasin,* ed. Abraham Segal Ettinge (Lemberg: 1900).
6. Zvi Horowitz, *Letoldoth Hakelot BePolin* (Jerusalem: Mosad Horav Kook, 1978).
7. C.U. Lipschitz and Neil Rosenstein, *The Feast and the Fast* – edited translation of *Megilas Eivah* with additional material (New York and Jerusalem: Maznaim Publishing Corp., 1984), pp.36–7 and 41.
8. Meir Wunder, *Meorei Galicia* (Jerusalem: Institute for the Commemoration of Galician Jewry, 1978).

9. Fischler, *Chasdei Avoth.*
10. Alexander Yoel Hakohen Adlersberg, *Magen Avoth* (Stanislau: ed. and published by Benjamin Schmerler, 1936).
11. Yehudah Arieh Zvi, *Nachalot Zvi* (Bnei Brak, Israel: 1994). Moses Yaakov Schwerdscharf, *Hadras Zvi* (History of the Hirsch family of Kolomea) (Sziget: 1909).
12. Information from the Wohl family.
13. Adlersberg, *Magen Avoth.* C.Y.D Azulai, *Shem Hagedolim* (Cracow, 1930).

Additional Notes to Tables 4, 5 and 6
[see the Glossary for some of the rabbinical works mentioned below]

Israel Stariner's great-uncle was Samson of Ostropol, a cabbalist who was martyred in 1648 and who was also a kinsman of the eminent Rabbi Yehoshua Heshel Charif of Cracow, author of *Meginei Shlomo* and *Pnei Yehoshua.*

David Wahl's wife was Deborah, daughter of Zvi Hersch, ABD of Drohobycz, son-in-law of Yaakov Ashkenazi, ABD of Jaroslaw, who was descended from a German rabbinical line, his father Israel Ashkenazi being the son of Rabbi Ze'ev Wolf, ABD of Hildesheim.

Shabatai Katz was the author of *Siftei Kohen* and *Nekudot Hakesef,* and the most famous member of a millennial priestly family. He was the son of Meir and grandson of Moshe Katz, who moved to Lithuania from Frankfurt-on-Main, when the Jews were imperilled there in the early seventeenth century. The chart shows later links between the descendants of Shabatai Katz and Moshe Heilprin of Berdichev. The descendants of Shabatai's brother, Yonah Nachum, are linked to the progeny of David Halevi Segal, the lines from these two brothers coming together with the marriage of Gershon Mendel Katz and Rodel Heilprin. The offspring of that union link the Katzenellenbogen and Wahl-Heller lines.

Moshe Heilprin's son Yosef Heilpern succeeded him at Berdichev. There is a connection between this Halpern line and that of Jechiel Heilprin of Minsk (1660–1747) the author of *Seder Hadoroth,* and there may be a link to Samson Wertheimer of Vienna, Court Jew and Chief Rabbi of Hungary (1659–1724).

Mordechai Yaffe was the author of *Aseret Levushim.* He was related to Sirka Yaffe, the mother of Joel Sirkes, the Chief Rabbi of Cracow who wrote *Bayis Chadash,* and to Abigail Yaffe. Mordecai Yaffe was known as the Levush after the title of his magnum opus. He was an outstanding Rabbi in Prague, Lithuania and Poland, and took the lead in the establishment of the Council of the Four Lands which remained the semi-autonomous governing body of Polish Jewry for two centuries (see Chapters 29, 30, 32 and 36)

David Halevi Segal, the son-in-law of Rabbi Joel Sirkes, became a distinguished Chief Rabbi of Lvov and wrote the important commentary *Turei Zahav* (for family connections, see further, Chapters 15 and 34).

Table 4
KATZENELLENBOGEN

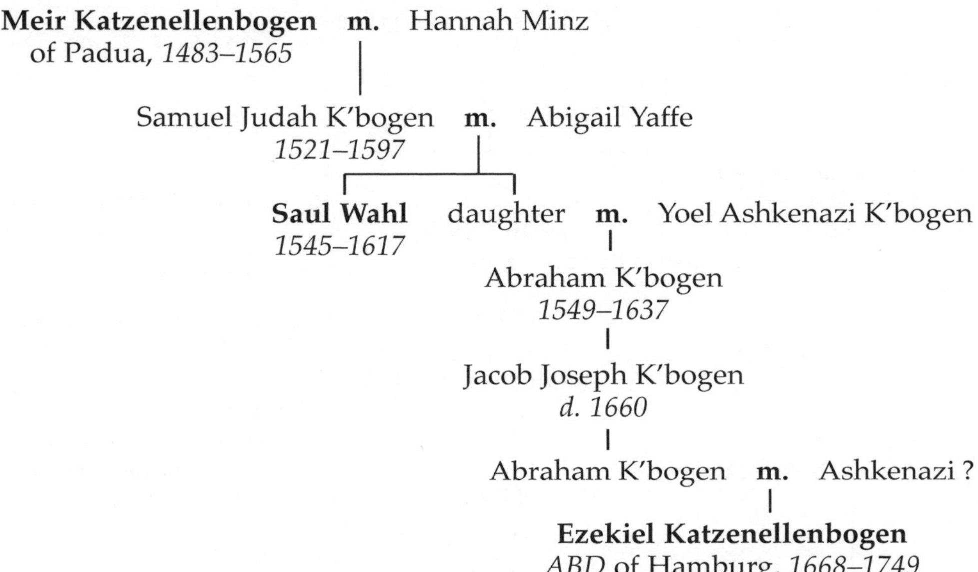

Table 5
A YAFFE DESCENT

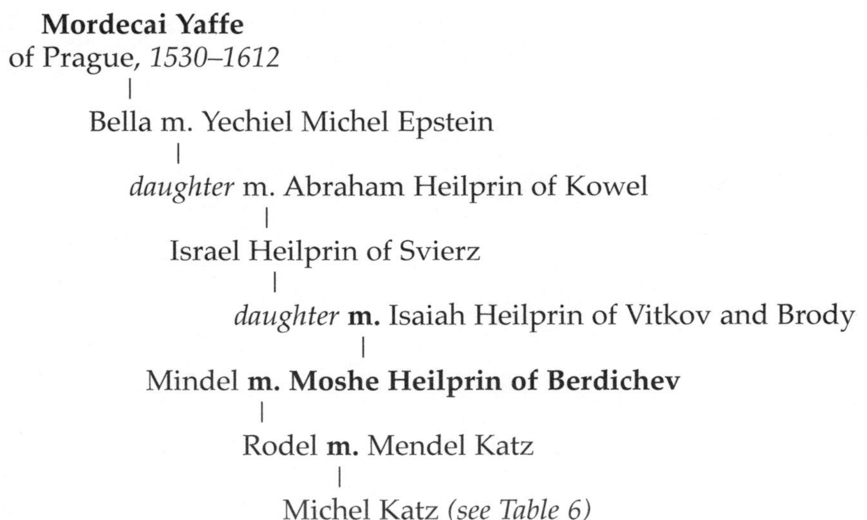

Table 6
ZVI ARIEH WAHL

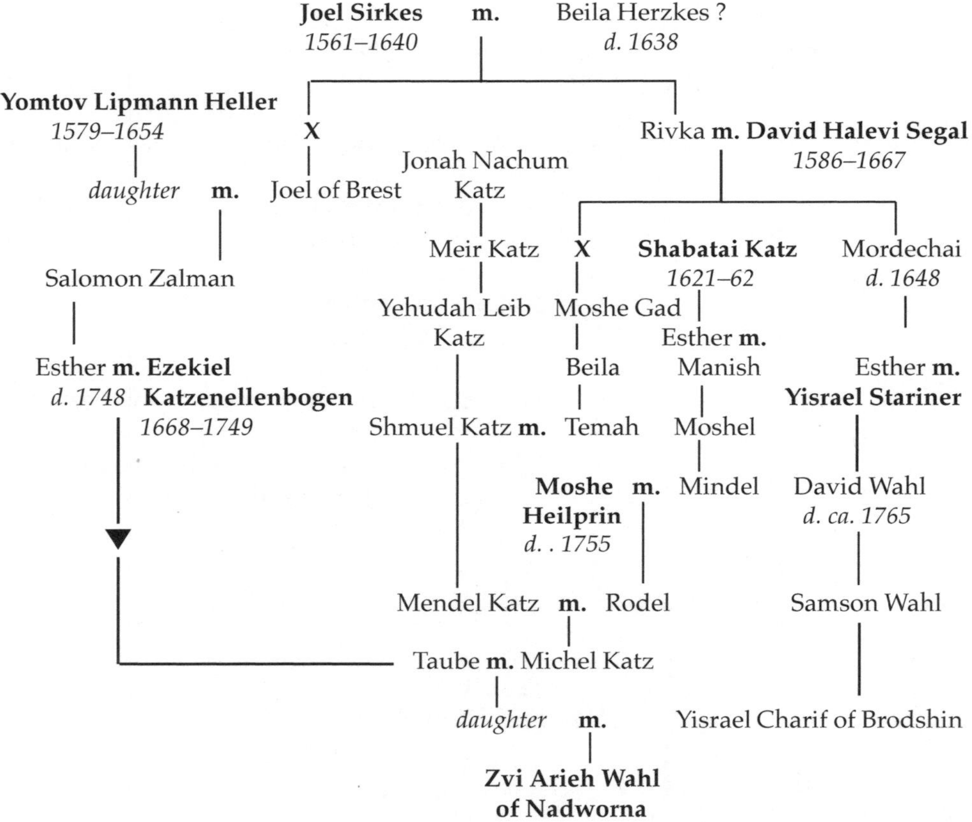

Figure 6
Zvi Perez Chajes (1910)

Chapter Six

History of the Chayes Family

From Prague to Brody and Vienna

FAMILY ORIGINS

The pan-European background of many rabbinical families reflects historical movements such as the great persecutions and expulsions, innumerable wars, and changing economic and social conditions. None exemplify this better than the Chajes family, which has produced many rabbis and other men of note over the past five hundred years.

At the end of the fifteenth century catastrophe overtook the Jews of Portugal and Spain. A graphic account of the dreadful sufferings in this period was given by the scholar Judah ben Jacob Chayot, who set sail from Lisbon with his family in 1493.[1]

Isaac ben Abraham Chayot came from kinsfolk who had long been settled in Provence. He migrated to Bohemia and was chosen to be Chief Rabbi of Prague in 1584. He was a brother-in-law of the great Rabbi Jehuda Loew ben Bezalel,[2] and was related to the Altschulers, who were descended from Rashi.[3] Isaac's son, Menachem Manish Chajes became Rabbi of Vilna in 1617 and participated in the Council of the Four Lands which met at Lublin in the same year.

The family, which was known as Chajes in Poland, established itself in the Galician town of Brody. Poland underwent a series of partitions in the eighteenth century, as a result of which the province of Galicia became Austrian, and Brody attained a measure of importance as a border town between the Austrian and Russian Empires. Given the status of a 'free' city, it flourished commercially for more than a century. The Jews were at times numerically preponderant and there was a vibrant Jewish cultural life. A writer on its history described it as 'The Jerusalem of Austria'. The Chajes became one of the town's leading families.

At this time, a namesake of the old Chief Rabbi of Vilna, Menachem Manish Chajes, a prosperous wood merchant of Brody, married the daughter of Wolf Berenstein, son of the first Chief Rabbi of Galicia (Aryeh Leib Berenstein 1708–88). Chajes was a cultured and well-travelled man who came to see opportunities for trade in the Tuscany that had given refuge to some of his forebears. Just as Brody under Austrian rule provided a beneficent climate for Jewish cultural life and business enterprise, so Florence and the busy harbour town of Leghorn were havens of tolerance in eighteenth-century Italy. The Jews of Leghorn enjoyed the distinction among Italian communities of never having suffered any significant persecution. There were no ghettos or dress ordinances but an enlightened economic regime and a liberal approach to Jewish communal autonomy.

The charters and privileges granted by the Medici in the sixteenth century were upheld by the House of Lorraine, which succeeded to the Grand Ducal titles in 1737. Leghorn had risen to importance before that time. It maintained its status as a 'free' city from 1691 to 1867. The old synagogue dating from 1583 was embellished for centuries and became a famous showpiece. A majority of the early Jewish settlers were from the Iberian peninsula, and much of the community's business was for long transacted in Portuguese. Among the many products traded here was coral, which became very fashionable for use in jewellery and other artefacts. The story of the rise and fall of the Leghorn community is measurable in part in terms of the popularity of this substance.[4] Coral artefacts were exported particularly to Russia, India and China, and often traded for diamonds.

Chajes and his kinsfolk prospered in the coral trade, which laid the basis for the commercial bank, Berenstein, Chajes & Co. of Florence, in which his son Meir became a partner. He later returned to his family's base in Brody, where he founded Meir Chajes & Son. Leghorn was the entrepot for the Levant, Brody for the Russian markets. With their Portuguese origins, Italian ancestors and multi-lingual skills, the Chajes would have felt very much at ease in both communities, which were also both distinguished for Jewish learning. Meir continued to spend part of each year in Italy. Some of his relations stayed there. One of their descendants, Guido Chajes, a banker in Leghorn, was made a Count for services to the Portuguese crown, thus providing a measure of symbolic redress for the great injustice suffered by his ancestors hundreds of years earlier. The line survived well into the twentieth century.[5]

ZVI HIRSCH CHAJES

One of the sons of Meir Chajes was the scholar Zvi Hirsch Chajes, who was born at Brody in 1805. A polymath by all accounts, Zvi Hirsch combined an encyclopaedic knowledge of the Talmud and Jewish literature with fluency in numerous modern languages, and a special interest in history and philosophy. His favoured reading included the French and German classics. According to an anecdote, he referred to the greatest of German writers as 'Reb Goethe'. Most unusually for his time, he qualified as *Magister* in the philosophical faculty of Lemberg University. In his numerous religious works he took an orthodox position, while encouraging an approach to secular education and other matters which followed the spirit of the age. He was close to the Enlightenment thinker Nachman Krochmal and corresponded with philosophers and literati including the Italian scholars Samuel David Luzzatto and Isaac Samuel Reggio. As Chief Rabbi of Zolkiew and Kalicz he made an important contribution to the social and political discussions of the day. His sons included Isaac, who was Rabbi of Brody in the closing years of the nineteenth century and Salomon, who was the father of the Chief Rabbi of Vienna and Zionist leader, Hirsch Perez Chajes.[6]

HIRSCH PEREZ CHAJES

The grandson and namesake of the Rabbi of Zolkiew was born in Brody in 1876. He was an acknowledged infant prodigy, and he had every advantage of an affluent and cultured background, including the best available teachers. He went to the Jewish Theological Seminary and graduated from the University of Vienna in 1901. From 1904 he was professor at the University of Florence. Incidentally, one of his pupils there was Umberto Cassuto, who wrote a thesis on Bialik's poetry. Chajes was an ardent Zionist from his earliest days and he put forward his views in such media as the weekly *Settimana Israelitica*. When he became Chief Rabbi of Trieste in 1912 he founded *Il Messaggero Israelitico*. His sojourn in Italy was the most productive for scholarly output.

In 1918 he went back to Vienna and shortly afterwards became its Chief Rabbi, remaining at this post until his death in 1927. During these nine years he was the spiritual leader of the second largest Jewish community in Europe. He was a great orator and a very popular preacher. He threw himself behind many charitable causes, and in particular did much for secular Jewish education, founding several schools including a high school which was later named after him, and he also involved himself with all aspects of religious teaching. His work in the Zionist cause led him to attend the San Remo Peace Conference in 1920, and he was chairman of the Zionist Action Committee from 1921–25. His contributions to modern Jewish scholarship were embodied in numerous works including hundreds of articles and reviews. Published tributes to his achievements are listed in an article on his life in the *Encyclopaedia Judaica*. His funeral in Vienna drew tens of thousands of mourners. Such crowds had not been seen since the funeral of Dr Theodor Herzl.[7] The service in the Seitenstetten Tempel, Vienna's main synagogue, was attended personally by the Austrian State President, Dr Michael Hainisch, and by the former Chancellor, Hans Schober.[8]

The three rabbis, Isaac ben Abraham of Prague, Zvi Hirsch of Zolkiew and Hirsch Perez of Vienna were all men of great culture and wide horizons. They were steeped in Jewish traditional learning, but they were also multi-lingual and exceptionally receptive to the intellectual currents of their day. As teachers and communal leaders their standpoint on religious, social and political issues became paradigmatic of their time. The sixteenth-century

Rabbi of Prague was a scholar acquainted with the literature and science of the Renaissance, but he lived in a period when Cabbalistic lore and Jewish mysticism were most influential. The nineteenth-century Rabbi of Zolkiew was very much a man of the Enlightenment, while still remaining within the orthodox fold. The great twentieth-century Rabbi of Vienna was equally a man of the widest European culture. He grew up in an age of burgeoning nationalism and the beginnings of racist anti-Semitism. These led to the founding of the Zionist movement with which he had a life-long involvement. The trauma of the First World War and its aftermath affected his views on social policy, and his became the model for a modern liberal worldview in which the rabbinical tradition could be subsumed.

Brody and Leghorn were already in economic decline in the later nineteenth century. The upheavals of the twentieth century dispersed the family, and of those who survived some made their way to the United States and Israel. They have distinguished themselves in various walks of life, including literature, music, law, medicine and commerce. They include the gynaecologist Josef Chajes (1875–1944), the bibliographer Saul Chajes (1884–1935), and the composer, pianist, and teacher Julius Chajes, who was born in Poland in 1910 and went to America in the 1930s. Sophie, a cousin of the Chief Rabbi, married the Austrian philologist Professor Solomon Frankfurter (1854–1941), who was the uncle of US Supreme Court Justice Felix Frankfurter. A chess master and numerous scientists prove the continued intellectual vigour of the Chajes clan.

FAMILY CONNECTIONS

Chajes connections with the Wahl–Katzenellenbogen family tree include Rabbi Jacob Isaac Chajes, the son of Rabbi Eliezer of Cracow (d. 1623), and grandson of Rabbi Isaac ben Abraham Chayot. Rabbi Jacob Isaac was a judge and *Moreh Zedek* in Prague, where he died in 1687. He married Eidel, the daughter of Abraham ben Yoel Ashkenazi Katzenellenbogen, Chief Rabbi of Lvov (1549–1637), who was the grandson of Chief Rabbi Samuel Judah of Padua and Venice.[9]

My great-grandmother Sarah Matel Chayes, who married Eliezer Griffel of Nadworna, was the daughter of Isaac Chaim Chajes of Kolomea.[10] The Kolomea family connection is mentioned in the Brody Yizkor book.[11]

Rabbi David Tebele, son of Chief Rabbi Nathan Nata of Brody, became ABD of Lissa where he died in 1792. His sister married Rabbi Isaac Chayes of Brody. This couple were the great-grandparents of Rabbi Zvi Hirsch Chayes of Zolkiew.[12]

The five-hundred-year story of this family is truly a microcosm of the Jewish presence in Europe, their sufferings and achievements. Combining a Sephardic and Ashkenazic heritage, and deeply involved in successive cultural movements, their history is inextricably bound up with that of the continent in which they made their home.

NOTES

1. H. Graetz, Volkstümliche Geschichte der Juden (Berlin and Wien: B. Harz, 1923), Vol.3, p.131.
2. *Encyclopedia Judaica* (Jerusalem: Keter Publ., 1972) for articles on Chajes and Judah Loew of Prague.
3. R. Meir Perels, *Megillath Yuchasin Mehral miPrag* (Warsaw: 1864). See also David Nachman Rutner, *Beth Ahron Veyisrael* (18:2), Jerusalem, pp.170–5 quoting a work by Rabbi Yair Chayim Bacharach, grandson of the Maharal, in a periodical 'Bikurim' published in Vienna in 1865, clearly identifying Judah Loew's first wife as the sister of Rabbi Isaac Chayes, son of Rabbi Abraham Chayes of Prague (known as Reb Eberel Altschuler).
4. Cecil Roth, *The History of the Jews in* Italy (Philadelphia: Jewish Publication Society of America, 1946), p.349.
5. N.M. Gelber, 'Aus Oberrabbiner Prof. Chajes' Ahnensaal', *Die Stimme*, No.2 (Vienna, 1928), pp.2–4.
6. See notes 3, 4 and 5. Neil Rosenstein, *The Unbroken Chain* (New York, London and Jerusalem: CIS Publishers, 1990), pp.803–6 and 583–4.
7. Ibid.
8. Hugo Gold, *Zvi Perez Chajes* (Tel-Aviv: Olamenu, 1971).
9. See notes 2 and 6.
10. See chapter 8.
11. *An Eternal Light. Brody in Memoriam* (Israel: Organisation of former Brody Residents, 1994), p.324.
12. R. David Tebele Efrati, *Toldot Anshei Shem* (Warsaw: 1875), pp.34–5. Louis Lewin, *Die Geschichte der Juden in Lissa* (Pinne: N. Gundermann, 1904), p.204.

CHAPTER SEVEN

An Italian Branch

From Brody to Florence and Livorno

Brody in Galicia and Livorno in Tuscany had ancient Jewish communities, which in their day enjoyed a rich communal life. It is an astonishing fact that in the mid-eighteenth century Brody had the second largest Jewish population in Europe and Livorno came in third place. The leading community at that time was Amsterdam. Brody had more Jews than say Cracow or Lvov, and Livorno many more than say Rome or Venice. The number of Jews greatly multiplied in the course of the next 150 years. This was accompanied by remarkable demographic shifts. After the First World War the largest Jewish centres included Warsaw, Vienna, Budapest and Berlin, while Livorno and particularly Brody had faded away.

What explained their rise and fall, and what did a famous old seaport in Italy have in common with a border town lying at the furthest corner of the Austro-Hungarian Empire? The fortunes of an ancient Jewish family with links to both of them provide the answer and an interesting sidelight on their distant past.

Livorno, or Leghorn as the English called it, was the third largest port in Italy. It was the busy harbour of Florence and an entrepot for the Levant. Its varied commerce included a flourishing coral trade. Artefacts of this material became very fashionable in the eighteenth century when they were exported particularly to Russia, India and China. Florence and Livorno were havens of tolerance under the Medici, whose beneficent rule was continued by their successors, the House of Lorraine. The Jews of Livorno had the distinction among Italian communities of never having suffered any significant persecution. An enlightened economic regime went hand in hand with a liberal approach to Jewish communal autonomy. Livorno maintained its status as a 'free' city from 1691 to 1867. With the gradual loss of its ancient trading pre-eminence, the prosperity of the town and of its Jewish community inevitably declined.

Brody was once a small town with Polish overlords. When Poland underwent the first of three partitions in the late eighteenth century, the town came under Austrian rule. It was situated near the frontier of the Tsarist Empire, and acquired a modest importance as an entrepot for the Russian trade. In cultural as well as economic terms, it lay at the crossroads between central and eastern Europe. The Jews of Brody continued to enjoy a large degree of self-government, which had attracted so many of them to different parts of Poland in past centuries. The liberal Austrian regime, including just over a hundred years of 'free' city status, gave the town a measure of prosperity until the middle of the nineteenth century. The first railway line by-passed Brody, intensifying the diminution in its trading position. A natural population increase was later exacerbated by the inflow of refugees from Russian pogroms. Changing economic circumstances and overcrowding led to an ongoing impoverishment and decline. The remains of some tombstones are among the reminders of a community that was finally destroyed in the holocaust.

In their heyday, both the Italian port and the Austrian border town were strategically situated and apparently had many similar features. Its Jews had certain economic privileges and a vibrant cultural life. These factors have a direct bearing on the demographic changes that ensued.

The above historical outline may give an indication why some Jews might have felt equally at home in either Livorno or Brody during the later eighteenth century. They were then in the bosom of substantial orthodox communities and could participate in the thriving entrepot trade which both towns enjoyed. The produce and manufactures of the Mediterranean littoral could find their way to eastern Europe and vice versa. A pre-eminent example was provided by the export of coral products from Livorno to the east via Brody, with diamonds and other precious stones, furs, and so on coming the other way. All this is exemplified by the history of one ancient family, which contributed much to both towns.

From their ancestral homes on the Iberian peninsula some of the Chayots took refuge in Southern France and in Italy. Isaac ben Abraham Chayot of Provence became chief rabbi of Prague in 1584 and later moved to Poland. His family ultimately settled in Brody where their name was *polonised* to Chajes. For three centuries they produced a succession of rabbis and distinguished scholars culminating in Zvi Perez Chajes (1876–1927), who was born in Brody, became professor at the University of Florence, Chief Rabbi of Trieste, and finally Chief Rabbi of Vienna between the two world wars. He was a great-grandson of Meir Chajes of Brody, whose father had grown rich in the coral trade in Livorno. The latter married the granddaughter of the first Chief Rabbi of Galicia and founded the banking house, Berenstein, Chajes & Co. in Florence. Many Jews of Livorno were of Portuguese extraction and in earlier times much business was indeed conducted in Portuguese. Their Sephardic origin, Italian ancestors and multi-lingual skills put the Chajes particularly at ease in Livorno, while they had made their mark in Galicia in scholarship as well as in business. Meir Chajes was a partner in the Italian family bank but eventually returned to his base in Brody, where his firm continued to maintain trading connections with the Tuscan branch.

A Leone Chajes is listed in the 1841 Livorno census as born in Brody, aged 47, and engaged in the coral trade. He would have been closely related to

Meir Chayes, who had numerous sons and nephews. The director of the Archivio di Stato di Livorno, Dr Paolo Castignoli, has sent me details of family members entered in the register from 1869 to 1928, and the director of the Portuguese National Archives, Dr Bernardo Vasconselos e Sousa, has kindly provided me with references to family documents. These records chart the rise and decline of the family in Tuscany. Guido Chajes was given the title of Count by King Carlos I of Portugal in 1904 for his services as Vice-Consul in Livorno. A letter issued by King Manuel II in 1909 confirms the title to Giorgio de Chajes, son of the 1st Count. It is gratifying that some amends were made after four centuries for the great wrong suffered by this family in Portugal.

The Villa Chajes is a fine mansion and still a landmark in Livorno. It was acquired by the Count and his brother in 1906 and passed to several of their descendants. When I enquired of a local scholar whether the name of Chajes is still remembered in Livorno, I was amused to learn that everyone is familiar with the name, as the Villa Chajes is located near the football club. Paolo Galmarini of Livorno kindly sent me a book entitled *The Villa Chajes and its Surroundings*. The mansion is now converted into a hotel.

Livorno, 10 Ottobre 2000

Oggetto: Ricerca sulla famiglia Chayes a Livorno

In riferimento alla ricerca promossa dal dr. Edward Gelles, questo istituto ha svolto una ricvognizione nei fondi Catasto e Satto Civile di Livorno. Dalla consulatzione dei registri e emerso:

Anno 1869	Chayes Giacomo di Leone Catasto Terreni partita 425
Anno 1889	Chayes Adolfo, Guido e Giulio e Vittorio fu Giovacchino Israel Catasto Fabbricati partita 839
Anno 1906	Chayes Guido e Adolfo fu Giovacchino Catasto Terreni partita 9106
Anno 1913	De Chayes Giorgio fu Guido, Chayes Maria e Nella Fu Vittorio Catasto Fabbricati partita 12393
Anno 1919	Chayes Vittorio e Adolfo fu Giovacchino Catasto Fabbricati partita 12387
Anno 1923	Nasce De Chayes Giorgio Stato Civile 2m
Anno 1923	Nasce Chayes Maria Luisa di Vittorio Stato Civile 2/II
Anno 1924	Nasce De Chayes Costanza di Giorgio Stato Civile
Anno 1928	Si sposa De Chayes Giorgio di Guido Stato Civile

R.C./

DEGMA 205

DEGMA 233

Figure 7
Chayes records in Livorno
including extracts from the 1841 census

Cavalieri Ester v. va di Giuseppe	51	Alla Villa	Livorno	Benestante				vedova
Cave Giuseppe	30	Via Leopolda – 3° p.	Roma	Possidente Negoziante			moglie domestico	
Cettone Fortunata	65	Via Reale 1071 – p. terreno	Roma				2 nipoti	vedova indigente casuale
Cesana Elia	46	Via Leopolda – 4° p.	Tunisi	Negoziante	1	1	moglic cuoca	
Cettone Grazia	30	Via Reale 1032 – 3° p.	Livorno	Attende a casa	2	3		vedova
Cettone Moise Sabato	32	Via Reale 1047 – 6° p. .	Livorno	Commerciante di manifatture	2	1	moglic	
Cettone Sabato	60	Via Reale 1049 – 6° p. .	Roma	Commerciante di manifatture	2	1	moglic	
Chajes Leone	47	Via Leopolda – 1° p.	Brody	Negoziante di pellicceria/corallo			moglic fratello	
Chimichi Ester	50	Via S. Martino 1091 – 1° p.	Livorno	Cuoca				nubile
Chimici Giuseppe di Sansone	58	Via Reale – 1° p.	Roma	Scritturale		3	moglic	indigente casualr
Ciaves Aron	40	Via Reale 1039 – 2° p.	Livorno	Merciaio		2	moglic sorella	
Ciaves Isach	23	Via G. del Governatore 950 – 2°p.	Livorno	Venditore di manifatture				celibe
Coen Abram di Sam	42	Alla Villa	Livorno	Negoziante			moglic domestica	
Coen Alessandro	68	Via Malenchini – 2° p.	Livorno	Possidente	1		nuora	vedovo

ASSUNTO: **Documental research – Count Guido Chajes**

INFORMAÇÃO Nº 92/2000

Following the letter sent by Dr. Edward Gelles, from London – United Kingdom, who wants to know if this Archives preserves any record related Count Guido Chajes, we have done the research required.

We have found the following documents:

1904, March 17
Decree signed by the King D. Carlos I agreeing the title of Count of Chayes to Mr. Guido Chayes, Austrian, according the excellent services helped to Portugal as Vice-Consul in Livorno (Italy).
IAN/TT, *Ministério do Reino.ASE. Decretos*, 1904 Março

1904, March 24
Record of the letter agreeing the title of Count of Chayes to Mr. Guido Chayes.
IAN/TT, *Registo Geral de Mercês. Mercês de D. Carlos I*, liv. 18, fl. 294v-296

1909, April 22
Record of the letter agreeing the title of 2nd Count of Chayes to Mr. George de Chayes, son of the first Count.
IAN/TT, *Registo Geral de Mercês. Mercês de D. Manuel II*, liv. 4, fl. 97v

We inform also that the documents described can be reproduced.

Maria Odete Sequeira Martins
Technical Officer

Instituto dos Arquivos Nacionais/Torre do Tombo

Figure 8
Letter from Portuguese National Archives concerning Count Guido de Chayes

Figure 9
Villa Chayes in Livorno

Chapter Eight

Chayes Family Connections

The Drohobycz and Kolomea branches

My great-grandmother Sarah Matel Chayes was born in Kolomea. The search for her pedigree started with a few scraps of anecdotal information and progressed to the study of several Yizkor (Memorial) books, the subscription lists for the publication of rabbinical works, and the chronicles of related families, before concentrating on primary sources such as tombstone inscriptions and the birth, marriage and death records for Kolomea. Some of the latter are only now becoming available on the Internet.

Isaac ben Abraham Chayot, descended from 'the wise men of Provence' was Chief Rabbi of Prague in the sixteenth century and a brother-in-law of Judah Loew.[1] Rabbi Zvi Hirsch Chayes of Zolkiew in the nineteenth century and his grandson Zvi Hirsch Perez Chayes, the Chief Rabbi of Vienna between the two world wars, were among the most distinguished descendants of Isaac ben Abraham of Prague who made their mark in many walks of life. The merchants and bankers of the Italian branch produced a scion who was ennobled by the King of Portugal. The achievements of lawyers, physicians, scientists, men of letters, musicians and chess masters, testify to the many sided talents of this ancient family. My outlines of its history might serve as a preamble to the search for immediate forebears in Kolomea.[2]

This old town by the river Pruth lies about 120 miles south of Lviv [called Lemberg during the period of Austrian rule]. A considerable proportion of Kolomea's population was Jewish, though not as high a proportion as that of Brody, situated about 60 miles east of Lviv. There proved to be family connections with a small town south-west of Lviv called Drohobycz, which experienced a period of affluence when oil deposits began to be developed in the area around the middle of the nineteenth century.

Sarah Chayes married Eliezer Griffel of Nadworna. That town is not very far from Kolomea and the larger town of Stanislau. The *JRI-Poland* Internet records of Nadworna list Sarah Matel, daughter of Isaac Chaim Chayes of Kolomea.[3] Her father's name was passed down to my great-uncle Isaac Chaim Griffel and then to my uncle Edward [Isaac Chaim *ben* David Griffel].

The Brody Memorial Book refers to a Chaim Chayes of Kolomea who was connected to the main branch of the family[4] and the Kolomea Yizkor Book mentions numerous Chayes family members as resident in the town from the beginning of the nineteenth century to the time of the holocaust.[5] In 1833, when Jews were given permission to own land in the area, fifteen Jews applied for the privilege. The first was Yossel Chayes, described as a wholesale wool merchant and leader of the community. Another Chayes was the owner of a distillery. The membership of one of the many synagogues included Zelig Chayes and his sons Zeida and Leibush. Presumably this refers to the period between the two world wars, when Leibush Chayes is mentioned as being one of the leading figures of the 'Society of Traders'.

Our knowledge of the Kolomea branch is complemented by documentation of the Chayes presence in Drohobycz. This is thanks to a genealogical study of the Lauterbach family, who were connected with Chayes by marriage.[6]

R' Jacob Bezalel Lauterbach of Drohobycz (1800–70) and Rahel Mandel (1802–60) had ten children. The second child Hanna (1822–68) married Teyvel (*Tebele=Theophilus*) Chayes. According to Rosenstein, David Tebele Chayes may have been a son of Meir Chayes and thus a brother of R' Zvi Hirsch Chayes of Zolkiew.[7] Hanna and Teyvel had four children, whose descendants are fully recorded in the Lauterbach Chronicle.

The eldest was the learned Zvi Hersch Chayes (1840–1908), who married Haya Bergwerk (1842–1912). She apparently supported her husband by dealing in coral beads and precious stones. The story of her business ties in with the family's long-standing commercial relations between Brody and Livorno, which goes back to the time of Meir Chayes and his father Menachem Manish.[8] The marriage of Herschele's second son, the oil and timber merchant Shaya Chayes (1858–1930), to Berta Seidmann (1858–1919) provides a link to Kolomea. Incidentally, Shaya's daughter, Regina Chayes became the wife of Bernhard Suesser (1872–1929), a son of Salomon Suesser and Salomea Barchau of Cracow. This was the family of Maryla Suesser who married my uncle Zygmunt Griffel. The Suessers were connected with the Wohls of Cracow.[9]

Hanna and Teyvel's second son was Mechel (Michael) Chayes, a merchant who was born in Drohobycz in 1842 and settled in Kolomea, where he died in 1921. He and Suessel Sennensieb had five children. Many members of the family perished in the holocaust, but there are numerous descendants in Israel and America.

The several sources quoted above indicate that Kolomea was the home of a number of distinct Chayes families. They appear to originate from more than one member of the clan. It should be borne in mind that Meir Chayes and his son Zvi Hirsch of Zolkiew had numerous siblings who are not all fully documented.

A learned volume by R' Shmuel Shmelke Horowitz of Nikolsburg prints lists of subscribers from Kolomea who sponsored its publication.[10] The first list includes Reb Isaac Chaim Chayes, while the second contains the names of Reb Isaac Reuven Chayes and his son Eliezer. A book by Rabbi Israel Dov Ber Gelernter published in the same year had a subscription list including several others from Kolomea, namely Ephraim Fischl, Zelig and Yossel Chayes.[11]

References to my great-great-grandfather have now been substantiated from the Kolomea vital records.[12] An outline of the family of Isaac Chaim Chayes is shown in Table 7, with his daughter Sarah and her husband Eliezer Griffel and my descent from them, some of Sarah's siblings and their in-laws, and some connections between branches in Brody, Drohobycz and Kolomea. A part of my great-grandmother's pedigree is shown in Table 8.

Members of the family married girls from prominent families in various Galician towns and went to live there. The Griffels of Nadworna were no strangers to Kolomea, Stanislau or Cracow and neither were the descendants of the Chajes-Lauterbach marriage. Isaac Chaim Chayes settled in Kolomea where the records reveal his death in 1866 at the age of 43 years. Unfortunately the name of his father is not given. However, it is highly probable that Isaac Chaim was a brother or cousin of Zvi Hirsch of Zolkiew and of David Tebele Chayes of Drohobycz. He was certainly not a son of Zvi Hirsch, whose five recorded sons included Chaim Chayes born in Zolkiew in 1830.[13]

Rabbi Isaac Chayes of Skole (the second Isaac in the Chayes line of descent) moved to Drohobycz where he died around 1726. So this town features in the family history at an early date. The fourth Isaac Chayes became head of the community in Brody where he died in 1807.[14] He married a daughter of Nathan Nata, ABD of Brody, whose wife belonged to my father's ancestral line.[15] The fifth Isaac Chayes, the ABD of Brody, was a son of Zvi Hirsch of Zolkiew. His brother Solomon Chayes was the father of Chief Rabbi Zvi Hirsch Perez Chayes of Vienna, who had his uncle Isaac as a teacher. Incidentally, as Table 7 shows, Isaac married Ette Shapiro while Solomon's wife was Rebecca Shapiro. Hirsch Perez remained unmarried.

Our in-laws in Kolomea included the Sternhel and Lichtenstein families. The literature on the Sternhels contains an account of the learned, saintly and wealthy Reb Shaltiel Isaac Sternhel of Kolomea, who retired to the Holy Land in his later years and died in the 1840s and was related to prominent Chasidic rabbis.[16] Another source reproduces a Sternhel family tree and mentions that the author's grandfather R'Yaakov Sternhel (a great-grandson of Shaltiel Isaac) married a descendant of R. Meir Chayes of Tysmienica, who was a mystic to whom wondrous works were attributed and who was greatly praised by the Baal Shem Tov.[17]

Wolf Leib Lichtenstein, the husband of Chana Chayes, was a son of Baruch Bendet and a grandson of Hillel Lichtenstein [1815–91], who came from Hungary and was Rabbi at Klausenburg before becoming Chief Rabbi of Kolomea in 1867. In his day, Hillel Lichtenstein was a leading spokesman of the ultra orthodox school. An outline of his life and work is to be found in the Jewish Encyclopedia.[18] The Lichtensteins claimed descent from great rabbis such as Isaiah Horovitz and Mordecai Yaffe.[19]

Wolf Leib Lichtenstein had one daughter by his first wife Chana Chajes. She was Fanny (Feige) born in Kolomea in 1887. Chana Chajes died in Vienna in 1915.[20] From Wolf Leib's second marriage to Tilla Brettholz there was numerous issue including Chaim Jacob Lichtenstein born in Vienna in 1925, the father of Zeev Judah Lichtenstein.[21] The latter and Reuben Gross[22] have recorded the genealogy of this line. Wolf Leib Lichtenstein worked for Dr Jacob Griffel in the Griffel oil business

Eliezer Griffel of Nadworna and Sarah Chayes had ten children whose families formed a large clan, once strong in Poland and Austria and now dispersed in England, America, and Israel.[23]

It is a chastening thought that while the main stem of the great Chayes family of Brody is reasonably well documented, the genealogy of the side branches has so far remained relatively obscure. The present study of the Kolomea branch illustrates how connections between various Galician towns came about and how a study of these connections can be an integral part of the genealogical methodology.

NOTES

1. B. Wachstein, 'Notizen zur Geschichte der Juden in Prossnitz', *Jahrbuch der Jüdisch-Literarischen Gesellschaft*, xvi (Frankfurt a.M. 1924), pp.167–9.
2. E. Gelles, 'Chief Rabbis in the Genes', *Manna*, 69 (Autumn 2000). E. Gelles, 'A Tale of Two Cities', *The Galitzianer*, 10, 5 (Nov. 2002).
3. http://data.jewishgen.org/jgen/wc.dll?jgproc~jgsys~jripllat [Nadworna].
4. *An Eternal Light. Brody in Memoriam* (Israel: Organisation of former Brody residents, 1994), p.324.
5. Kolomea Memorial Book (Tel-Aviv, Israel: published by from Kolomea residents, 1972), pp.33, 86, 178.
6. L. Lauterbach, *Chronicle of the Lauterbach Family 1800–1991*. Revised and extended by Bernard S. Lauterbach (Jerusalem: The Lauterbach Family Fund, 1961,1968. Revised edn. by Bernard S. Lauterbach, El Paso, Texas: 1992), pp.68–78.
7. Neil Rosenstein, *The Unbroken Chain* (New York, London and Jerusalem: CIS Publishers, 1990), Vol.2, p.806.
8. Gelles, 'A Tale of Two Cities'.
9. E. Gelles, 'The Wohls of Cracow', *The Galitzianer*, 10, 2 (Feb. 2003).
10. R' Shmuel S. Horowitz of Nikolsburg and his son R' Zvi Yehoshua of Trebicz, *Nezir Hashem* and *Semichas Moshe* (Lemberg: 1869).
11. R' Israel Dov Ber Gelernter of Stopesht-Yablonow, *Revid Hazahav* (Lemberg: 1869).
12. http://data.jewishgen.org/jgen/wc.dll?jgproc~jgsys~jripllat [Kolomea].
13. Moritz Rosenfeld, *Oberrabbiner Hirsch Perez Chajes, Sein Leben und Werk* (Vienna: 1933), pp.5–7 (see note to Table 8).
14. Ibid.
15. Louis Lewin, *Die Geschichte der Juden in Lissa* (Pinne, N. Gundermann, 1904), p.204 (see note to Table 8). E. Gelles, 'Gelles Rabbinical Ancestry', to be published.
16. Moshe Yaakov Schwerdscharf of Kolomea, *Hadras Zvi* (Sziget, 1909).
17. R'Yitzchak Sternhel of Baltimore, *Kochvei Yitzchok* (New York: 1979), pp.195–206.
18. Jewish Encyclopedia article on Rabbi Hillel Lichtenstein, http://www.jewishencyclopedia.com/view_friendly.jsp?artid=391&letter=L.

19. L. Rakow, *Tzefunot*, 12 (Bnei Brak, Israel: 1992). Yitzchak Yosef Cohen, *Chachmei Transylvania* (Jerusalem: Machon, 1989), Part 2, pp.142–8.
20. Jewish Community Records in Vienna, courtesy of H.Weiss@ikg-wien.at.
21. Zeev Judah Lichtenstein and Chaim Jacob Lichtenstein, private communications.
22. Reuben Gross, private communication.
23. E. Gelles, 'My Mother's People', *Sharsheret Hadorot*, 16, 4 (Oct. 2002).

Table 7
CHAYES FAMILY CONNECTIONS

The Chayes family spread from their base in Brody to other Galician towns and they also flourished in Tuscany. Meir Chayes was a merchant banker in Brody and Florence and one of his sons was the famous Rabbi Zvi Hirsch of Zolkiew. David Tebele of Drohobycz may have been the latter's brother. Numerous family members in Kolomea included my great-great-grandfather Isaac Chaim Chayes. Two Chayes branches are connected by marriages with the Suesser family of Cracow.

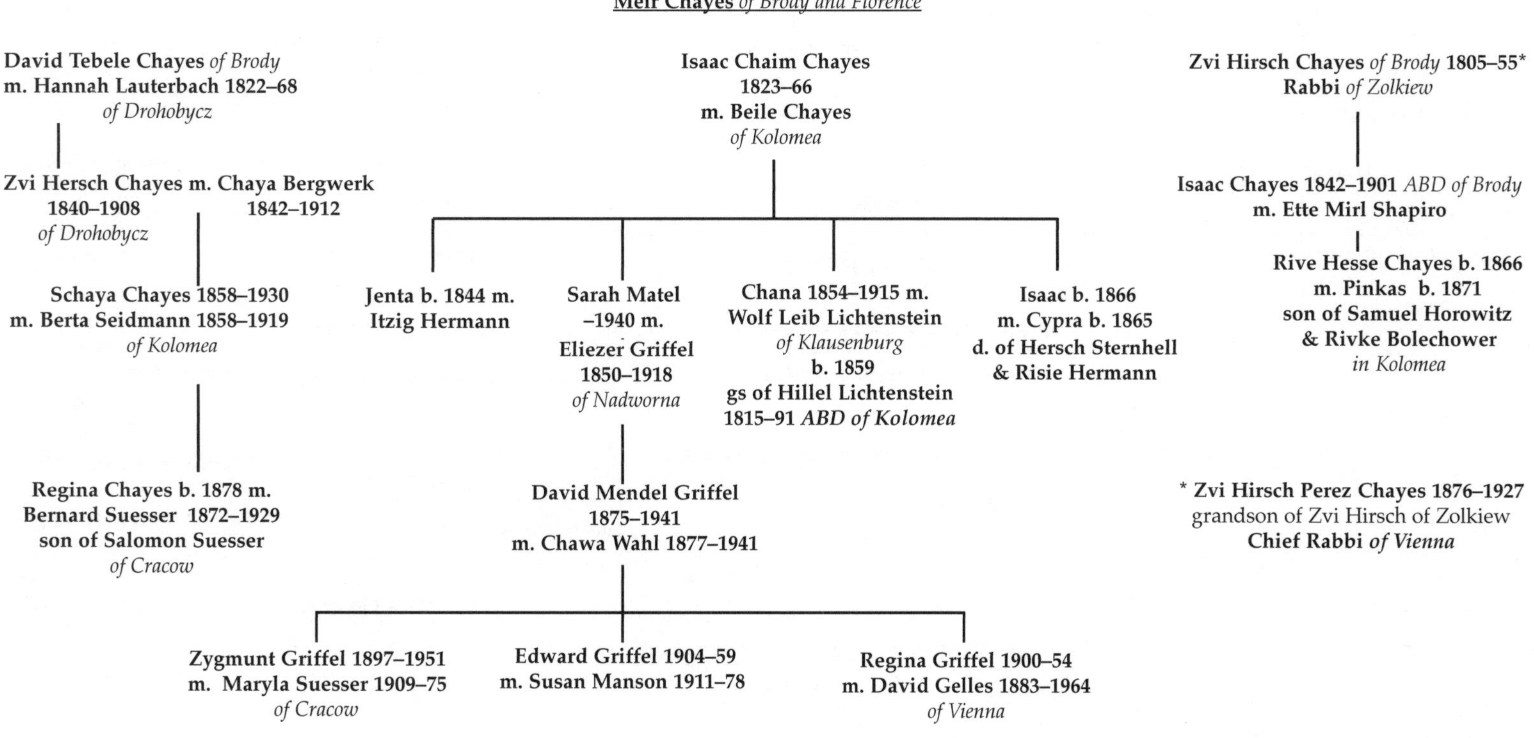

Table 8
ANCESTRY OF MEIR CHAYES

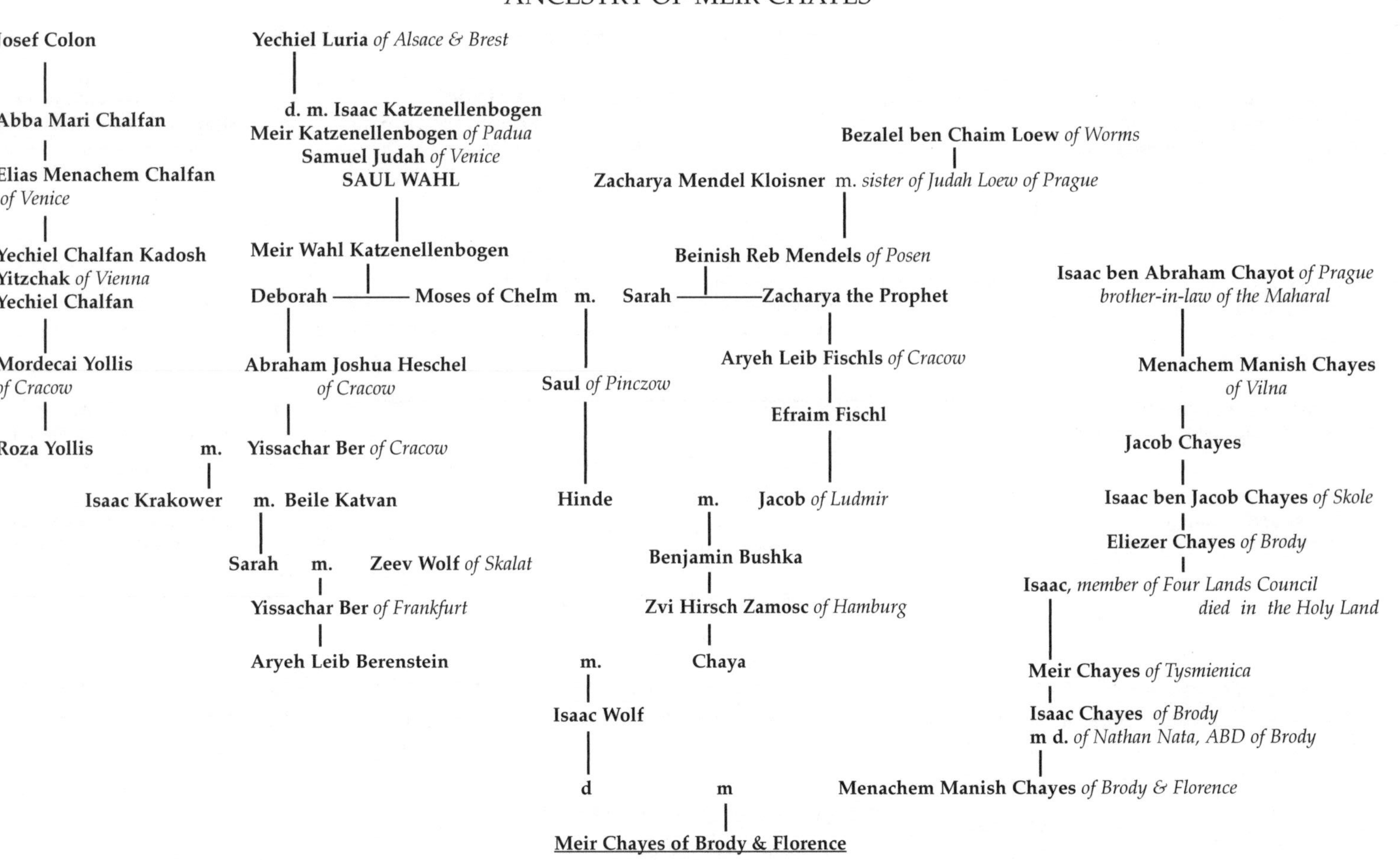

NOTES TO TABLE 8

The ancient Chayes line from Isaac ben Abraham of Prague was joined to the Katzenellenbogen and Kloisners through the marriage of Menachem Manish of Brody and Florence to the daughter of Isaac Wolf, son of Aryeh Leib Berenstein. Their son Meir Chajes reinforced the connection by his marriage to a descendant of Yissachar Ber of Frankfurt. This powerful conjunction of ancient strains evidenced itself in the succeeding generations of Zvi Hirsch Chajes of Zolkiew and his grandson Zvi Hirsch Perez Chajes of Vienna.

The sons of Zvi Hirsch Chayes of Zolkiew were:
Leon [Zolkiew 1828–Vienna 1891].
Chaim [Zolkiew 1830–Lemberg 1886].
Salomon [Zolkiew 1835–Lemberg 1896], father of Zvi Hirsch Perez Ch. [1876–1927]
Isaac [Zolkiew 1842–Brody 1901] Chief Rabbi of Brody.
Wolf [Zolkiew 1845–Danzig 1901]

According to Meir Wunder (*Meorei Galicia* [Jerusalem: Institute for the Commemoration of Galician Jewry, 1978 *et seq.*] Vol. 2, column 1042) Zvi Hirsch Chajes married Hessi Riva (died 1855), the daughter of R. Shlomo Pshivorgarski, a descendant of Rabbi Eleazar Rokeach of Brody and Amsterdam.

The grandfather of Meir Chajes was Isaac ben Meir Chayes of Brody [died 1807]. He married a daughter of Chief Rabbi Nathan Nata of Brody [died 1764]. She was a grand daughter of R' Gershon Vilner of Shklov, who was the grandson of Uri Feivush, Chief Rabbi of Vilna and later Nasi in Jerusalem (see Chapters 34 and 36).

III.

GENEALOGICAL METHODOLOGY

There is no telling what may yet become part of history.
Perhaps the past is still essentially undiscovered

F. Nietzsche, *Die Fröhliche Wissenschaft*

FOREWORD TO CHAPTERS 9–11

A study of the literature including encyclopaedias, genealogical monographs and magazine articles combined with birth, marriage and death records and some tombstone inscriptions had yielded much information on my immediate family. However, much was still obscure. For example, I had not confirmed my grandmother Wahl's birthplace nor found her marriage record. As the following three chapters demonstrate, different approaches via collateral family branches were called for, and the methodology employed will be seen to be of wide applicability.

CHAPTER NINE

Ephemera

A WW1 Postcard from Dr Abraham Low reveals my mother's family connections

This story is about a postcard and how it led to the discovery of hitherto unknown cousins 85 years after it was written.

My mother was born in the Austrian province of Galicia a hundred years ago. On the outbreak of the First World War her parents left their home in the wake of advancing Russian armies and brought their family to Vienna. David Mendel Griffel and Chawa Wahl both came from distinguished Jewish families.[1] Their children were Zygmunt, Edward and Regina. My grandparents perished in the holocaust, and my mother and uncles died in the 1950s.

In the course of my recent studies I came across a card that had lain in a small pile of family papers. The sender is Dr Abraham Loew, a medical officer attached to a battalion of Austrian Infantry Regiment No.1, somewhere on the eastern front, and it conveys cousinly greetings to Miss R. Griffel and her family in Vienna. There is a photograph of Dr Loew on the reverse. The tone of the card is cheerful. The writer appears to be having quite a good time. The date is 23 January 1916 and he announces his intention to go on leave in April. It must have been the calm before a storm, as there was soon to be a renewed Russian offensive under General Brusilov. I don't suppose he got leave in April 1916. Anyway, he survived the war. I remember being told his name and that he had gone to America, but all contact had been lost by the time we fled to England in 1938. I had no idea whether Loew was a cousin on the Griffel or the Wahl side, and indeed what had happened to him since the early 1920s.

When I went through my papers again this year I decided that the clues contained in the card were worth following up. In addition to a date, I had details of his regiment and of the field post office from which the card was sent. So I wrote to the Heeresmuseum in Vienna, and subsequently to the Austrian State Archives.[2] These offices responded with commendable promptitude. The War Archives furnished me with an 'Evidenzblatt' containing essential information on Lieutenant Abraham Loew.

I now had his date and place of birth, and I could surmise that he had studied medicine at Strasbourg. Although I had no idea at this stage how eminent he ultimately became, I felt that it should not be too difficult to trace his later career. And so it turned out. I took my problem to the Wellcome Library for the History and Understanding of Medicine.[3] A month later I had the solution. The *American Medical Directory* (1942) and *Who Was Who in America* (1951–60) gave the same place and date of birth as the First World War records. They stated that he had studied medicine at Strasbourg and Vienna, emigrated to the United States in 1921, practised medicine in New York until 1923 before moving to Chicago, became naturalized in 1927, and was a fellow of the American Medical Association, the American Psychiatric Association, and a member of the Central Neuro-psychiatric Association.

The entries mention his published books including *Mental Health through Will Training*, which has gone through numerous editions. The personal details given include his parents Lazar Low and Blossom Wahl, his marriage to Mae Willett in 1935, the names of his daughters, and the date of his death in 1954.[4] His name Loew had been anglicized to Low and so had his mother's name, Blume.

This is not the place to go further into Abraham Low's contributions to mental health care. He was a pioneer in developing a self-help method of will training which is carried on by Recovery, the community mental health organization based in Chicago.[5] A bibliography of his works is published by the Abraham A. Low Institute.[6] From early childhood in the 1930s I had been aware that I had a cousin called Abraham Loew. Now at last, in August 2000, I knew that he was part of my Wahl heritage. His mother Blume and my grandmother Chawa were sisters. My search has added new buds to an ancient branch of my family tree, and in another chapter I shall have more to say about Abraham Low in a genealogical context.

Seeking my cousins had been a very moving experience for me and the end of this particular quest was now in sight. On 17 August (2000) a good friend in our Genealogical Society posted a message for me to the Jewish Gen Discussion Group on the internet, giving the details I had gathered. Following an almost immediate response, I spoke by telephone to the director of the organization that was founded by Abraham Low. She undertook to pass my message on to his daughters. On 25 August I phoned Phyllis Low Berning in Chicago. On 9 September her sister Marilyn Low Schmitt visited me in London.

NOTES

1. E. Gelles, 'Saul Wahl. A Jewish Legend', *Judaism Today*, 14 (Winter 1999–2000). Gelles, 'The Wahls of Nadworna', *Shemot*, 8, 3 (Sept. 2000); Gelles, 'Chief Rabbis in the Genes', *Manna*, 69, 1 (Autumn 2000); Gelles, 'The Griffels of Nadworna and Stanislau', unpublished.
2. Heeresgeschichtliches Museum, Arsenal, Objekt 1, A-1032 Vienna, Fax : 0043-1-795611770. Oesterreichisches Staatsarchiv, Nottendorfer Gasse 2, Kriegsarchiv,1030 Vienna, Fax: 0043-1-79540-109.

3. Wellcome Library for the History and Understanding of Medicine, 183 Euston Road, London NW1 2BE, Tel.: 020 7611 8888 and Fax: 020 7611 8545.
4. *American Medical Directory* (1942), p.633. *Who Was Who in America* (1951–60), Vol. 3, pp.532–3.
5. Recovery Inc., 802 North Dearborn Street, Chicago, Ill. 60610, Tel.: 001 312 337 5661 and Fax: 001 312 337 5756.
6. Abraham A. Low Institute, 550 Frontage Road, Northfield, Ill. 60093.

Postcard
addressed to Miss R. Griffel, Vienna II, Rote-Kreuz Strasse 5/8.
stamped Imperial & Royal Infantry Regiment 'Kaiser'. Field Post Office No. 72.
address of sender: Abraham Loew, K.u.K. I.R.1, Feldpost 72, Hilfsplatz V, Baon.

Translation of text : 'In the Field, 23.1.16.'

'Dear Cousin,
I have only just learnt of your address, hence this very belated card with a bad photograph which I still have from my stay in Munich. I am very well at the moment.
I have been doctor in charge of our Battalion for the last 2 months. I haven't a lot to do and fill my time with riding, bathing, playing cards, eating and sleeping. I am thinking of going on leave at the beginning of April and will then be sure to visit you.
I hope my dear aunt and uncle and cousins are well and look forward to receiving a longer letter from you. Has your brother joined the colours yet? Please write soon and I shall reply accordingly.
Hearty Greetings to you all, Your, Abraham Loew.'

(My mother's elder brother, Zygmunt was born in 1897. Her brother Edward, born in 1904, would have been too young for military service.)

Evidenzblatt
K.u.K Reserve Hospital Lublin No.3 dated 11 October 1918:
'Reserve Sanitaetsleutnant Abraham Loew (commissioned 1 January 1917) of K.u.K. Infantry Regiment No.1 of the Krakow military district. Joined army in 1912. Born at Baranow in Galizia 1891. Single. Mosaic Religion. Speaks perfect German and good French. Leutnant at the Lublin Reservespital No. 3 since 2 October 1918. Bronze medal for valour. Karl (military) cross. Award (II Class) of the Order of the Red Cross. Peacetime Domicile: Strassburg. Aug. 1914–Jan. 1917 with regiment in the field as under-officer. Jan. 1917–Jun. 1917 garrison hospital No.1 in Vienna. Regimental duties Jun. 1917–Aug. 1917. Aug. 1917–Oct. 1918 based at Lublin.'

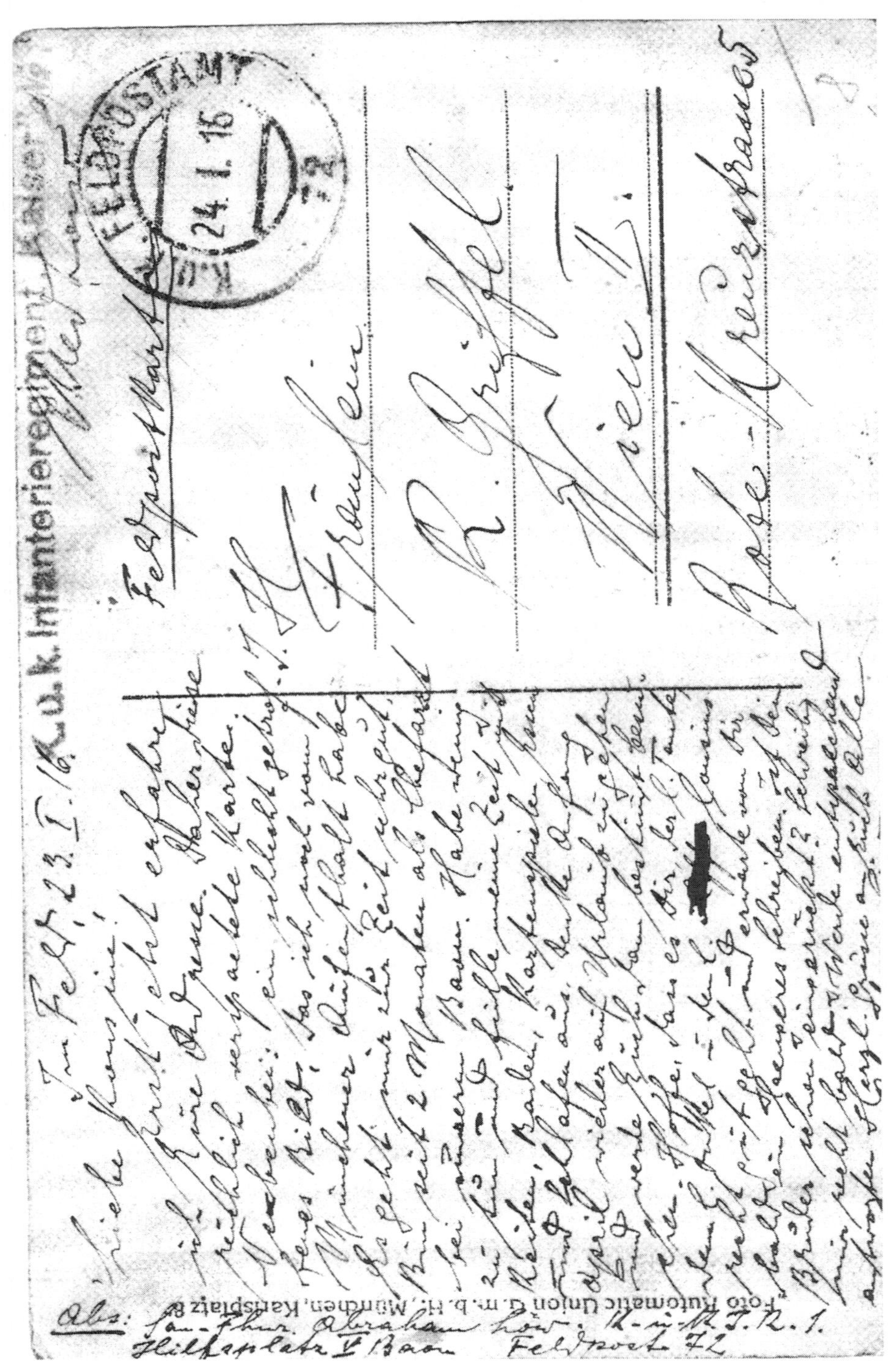

Figure 10
Postcard from Dr Abraham Low to Miss Regina Griffel

Figure 11
Dr Abraham Low (1916)

Chapter 10

Vital Records

How I found the family of my grandmother, Chawa Wahl

Chawa (Eva) Wahl was my grandmother. I dimly recall being taken to see her in Poland when I was a small child in the early 1930s. I knew very little about her family and her ancestry is proving quite a hard nut to crack.[1] The quest started with my parents' marriage certificate, which confirmed that my mother Regina Griffel was born in Nadworna, Austria in 1900, and that she was the daughter of David Mendel Griffel and Chawa Wahl. I obtained data on David Mendel Griffel and his parents from the records kept in the Warsaw archives and also from Rabbi Kolesnik of Stanislau, where my grandparents later lived.[2] The Griffels had been prominent in these two small Galician towns and were also to be found in Lemberg (now called L'viv), Cracow and Vienna. My great-grandfather Eliezer Griffel of Nadworna established the family fortune in the nineteenth century.[3] His wife Sarah was the daughter of Isaac Chaim Chayes of Kolomea, who belonged to the family that was long based in Brody.[4]

I could not find Chawa Wahl in the local records of Stanislau and Nadworna. Various reasons suggested themselves: the records might have been lost, maybe she was listed under her mother's maiden name, or perhaps she was born somewhere else, even though it was customary for Jewish women in the Galicia of this period to go to their mother's home to give birth, especially for their first child. My mother having been born in Nadworna, it seemed reasonable to start with the supposition that Chawa belonged to the family that had furnished the town's Chief Rabbi in the nineteenth century. This was Zvi Aryeh Wahl, and fortunately he wrote about his pedigree to several relatives.[5] Thus, I was able to reconstruct the family tree of the Nadworna Wahls, which had lain for long in the obscurity of rare Hebrew texts.[6] Zvi Aryeh Wahl was a descendant of Saul Wahl, who had played a prominent role in the Polish-Lithuanian State of the sixteenth century, and who was the scion of the Katzenellenbogens.[7] However, any connection between my grandmother Chawa Wahl and the Wahls of Nadworna proved to be elusive.

At this time I re-discovered some Griffel cousins, whom I had not seen for half a century. When at last I located my first cousin Eric Griffel, I phoned him in Washington, DC and said 'Hallo Eric, this is Edward.' He replied 'So it is – I thought you were dead.' We have been in affectionate correspondence since, but these Griffels knew nothing about our grandmother's origins and had not heard of any of her siblings. The family was 'atomised' by the horrific events of our early years in which many relations, including our grandparents, perished.

My genealogical study is a continuing voyage of discovery against a background of the history that shaped our ancestors' lives. My methodology has broadened as I have found new cousins. It started with archive searches in the birthplaces of my immediate family. It has involved family correspondence, recollections and the sifting of legends. More enquiries followed, addressed to communal offices, chambers of commerce, historians, archivists, distant in-laws, friends and strangers, in Europe, America and Israel. I have learned much from the literature dealing with social and economic conditions, and this has gone hand in hand with the uncovering of genealogical data. Patterns of names and occupations appear, which augment and support primary evidence obtained from the archives. Features of character and talent recur. Slowly the family tree is taking shape.

In a recent article I described how I found the family of my cousin Dr Abraham Low and his mother, my great-aunt Blume Wahl.[8] Blume and her husband Eliezer Loew had moved from Austrian Galicia to Strasbourg before the First World War.

The Strasbourg city archives provided documentary evidence that Blume was born at Tarnobrzeg in 1864 and died at Strasbourg in 1903.[9] She had nine children, and many of them later flourished in the United States. None of the grandchildren that I managed to contact appeared to have any documents relating to Blume herself, but suddenly a birth certificate of Selma Low was found by the latter's granddaughter, Judith Ritter. This not only confirmed Selma's parents to be Chaja Blume Wahl and Eliezer Loew, but also gave Blume's parents as Shalom and Sarah Wahl of Tarnobrzeg.

In the meantime, it proved but a short step from the re-discovery of the Lows to that of my Taube cousins who descend from Rachel Wahl, another sister of my grandmother, one whose existence I had surmised but whose name was unknown to me. The Lows knew this great-aunt's descendants, who at first appeared to have no documents at all. When I pressed them, I managed to elicit dimly recalled incidents and family stories which gave me the basis for further enquiries, and I soon began to fill in the picture.

Rachel Wahl was the second wife of Abraham Taube of Lemberg. His young first wife had died in childbirth leaving a son, Shmuel Zygmunt Wittels Taube Yonati. I found his daughter, Bracha Weiser, in Israel and obtained some useful leads from her. Rachel and her husband Abraham apparently were distant cousins. One possible connection might have been within that branch of the Wahl-Katzenellenbogen tree that comes down from Saul Wahl to Moses Katzenellenbogen of Chelm and Saul of Pinszow to the Padua and Padwa families (the two different spellings differentiating two closely-related branches[10]). After Abraham Taube died in 1906, Rachel married an Ohrenstein, whose possible connections require further study.[11] In 1910, a daughter, Lucia, was born from this union.

Blume Wahl was considerably older than her sisters Chawa and Rachel. Not unsurprisingly, the Lows descended from Blume knew nothing about my grandmother, but at least one Taube cousin recollects Rachel speaking warmly of Chawa, with whom she appears to have had a close relationship. Rachel and her children, Rega and Zyga, born in 1903 and 1905, lived at that time in Lemberg, which was not far from Stanislau and Nadworna, and the two young families would have visited each other. The biography of Dr Abraham Low refers to other unnamed siblings.[12] Much work clearly remained to be done, but I was now ready for the next round – to identify the ancestors of my great-aunts and thus come back full circle to my grandmother, Chawa Wahl.

From Nadworna the focus moved to Tarnobrzeg at the other end of Galicia. Its relevance became apparent when I obtained extracts from the Strasbourg municipal archives.[13] This was soon confirmed when Selma Low's birth certificate surfaced and I began to delve into the history of this town. Situated on the Vistula River north-east of Cracow, it celebrated its quatercentenary in 1993. It belonged to the Austrian Empire from the time of the eighteenth-century Polish partitions until Poland was reconstituted at the end of the First World War. The town includes the ancient village of Dzikow, which for a long time had a predominantly Jewish character. An interesting if somewhat biased piece of its social history in the nineteenth century is to be found in the memoirs of Jan Slomka, the long-serving mayor of the town.[14] Among documents of Jewish residence there survive taxation lists for 1814 and 1822. These contain the names of Samuel Wahl, Moses Wahl and Josek Safier.[15] There are continuing references to Wahls and Safiers right down to the Yizkor (Memorial) Book that lists members of both families who perished in the Holocaust.[16]

At this point I felt that I had enough data to make an enquiry at the local archives. The Polish Cultural Institute in London furnished the addresses of municipal and regional offices. They put me in touch with Tadeusz Zych of Tarnobrzeg, whose name had been mentioned to me by the genealogist Michael Honey. I sent Professor Zych the documentary details of Blume Wahl's birth and other information I had gathered. I hoped that he would look up Blume in the town archives and that these would open the door to her ancestral past. In a strange way, he failed in the immediate objective of finding Blume's name, yet he produced vital information. He sent me a list of Tarnobrzeg citizens taken in the 1880 Census and another list of inhabitants from the 1925 Book of Tarnobrzeg. Both are arranged by families and give years of birth. These records are kept in the archives at the nearby town of Sandomierz.[17]

About a dozen Wahl family groups and a similar number of Safiers appear in these publications. The dates span the period from the early-nineteenth to the early-twentieth century. No trace of Blume can be found in either list. However, the 1880 Census includes a Wahl family comprised of Zulim (b.1838), Sara (b.1842), Chaim (b.1869), Moses (b.1873), Sypora (b.187), Chawa (b.1877) and Rachel (b.1879). This certainly looked like my grandmother's family.

Selma Low's birth certificate listed her grandparents as Shulim and Sara Wahl, and Chawa's birth date of 1877 fitted well with the date of my grandmother's first-born child, Zygmunt Griffel, born in 1897. I believe that Chaim, Moses and Sypora must be the missing siblings.[18] The absence of Blume's name could have at least two explanations. We know that she was born in 1864.[19] She may have left home by the time of the 1880 census. Again, if at the time of her birth her parents had not followed a rabbinical marriage with a civil ceremony, Blume would have been called by the name of her mother. This ties in with a hitherto unexplained reference in an old unpublished Low family manuscript to a Blume Safier of the Wahl (Katzenellenbogen) family. Corroboration of the name and family connections now comes from the 1925 Tarnobrzeg Book of Inhabitants, where Chaim Leib Wahl is recorded as the son of Zulim Wahl and Sara Safier. His birth year is given as 1869, in agreement with that in the 1880 Census list.

The Wahls and Safiers go back in Tarnobrzeg-Dzikow at least to the beginnings of the Austrian administration in the last quarter of the eighteenth century. The Leiser Wahl, born in 1815 according to the 1880 Census, was described by Jan Slomka as the wealthiest businessman in Tarnobrzeg.[20] The Griffels, Wahls, Safiers and their in-laws belonged to an ephemeral class of Jewish landowning entrepreneurs who flourished for just a few generations.[21] This class shared a social background and economic interests which naturally led to inter-marriages. They were quite mobile not only within Galicia, but later also in other parts of the Austro-Hungarian Empire.[22]

A realization of these socio-economic circumstances should have alerted me more quickly to the possibility that my grandmother might not have come from Nadworna, in spite of its prominent Wahl family and the fact that my mother was born there.

In the end, I discovered that Chawa came from the Wahls of Tarnobrzeg, and I achieved this by researching her collateral relations. When the road ahead is blocked one has to look for possible detours. I had to find some cousins first, and when I identified their mothers, who were my lost great-aunts, I was on my way to our common great-grandparents. This process has involved the study of Jewish community and municipal records, memorial books, army records, medical directories, all manner of reference works, taxation and census lists, family papers and biographies, genealogical and historical monographs, and much else.

I have now established where and when Chawa Wahl was born and who her parents were. The family background is sketched in. I have found the names of my grandmother's siblings, and in the case of her sisters Blume and Rachel I have a complete map of their descendants. My next task was to bring together the Griffels with the Wahl lines in the matrilineal family tree.

NOTES

1. The name of Wahl given to Saul Katzenellenbogen in Poland is thought by some to refer to his Italian origin – from the medieval German for Italian, as in 'walnut'.
2. Archiwum Glowne Akt Dawnych, 00-263 Warszawa, Ul Dluga 7. For Rabbi Kolesnik's address and other information see Susannah R. Juni, 'Ukrainian Research and Ancestral Travels', *Avotaynu*, XIII, 4 (Winter 1997).
3. *Nadworna (Stanislau District) Memorial & Records* (Israel and US: Landsmannschaft of Nadworna, 1975), pp.25–6. Y.L. Maimon (ed.), *Arim ve-imahot be-Ysrael* (Mother Communities of Israel) (Jerusalem: Mossad HaRav Kook, 1952), Vol.5, pp.63, 212, 213, 219, 233, 311, 314.
4. Edward Gelles, 'Chief Rabbis in the Genes', *Manna*, 69 (Autumn 2000), pp.34–6.
5. Judah Gershon Pickholz, *Chidushei Hagershuni* (Novellae of Gershon) (Kolomea: 1890). Yehiel Michel Fischler, *Chasdei Avoth* (Kindness of the Fathers) (Lemberg: 1880).
6. Edward Gelles, 'The Wahls of Nadworna', *Shemot*, 8, 3 (Sept. 2000), pp.26–9, and 8, 4, (Dec. 2000), pp.31–2.
7. Edward Gelles, 'Saul Wahl. A Jewish Legend', *Judaism Today*, 14 (Winter 1999/2000), pp.36–40.
8. Edward Gelles, 'All Quiet on the Eastern Front', *Avotaynu*, XVI, 4 (Winter 2000), pp.60–1.
9. Strasbourg Archives Municipales, Reference No.30.1.1104/00 GF/BW, dated 5 October 2000, concerning Bluhma Loew, née Wahl, born Tarnobrzeg 15.9.1864 and died Strasbourg 21.5.1903.
10. Neil Rosenstein, *The Unbroken Chain* (New York, London and Jerusalem: CIS Publishers, 1990), Vol.I, p.32. Ibid., Vol.II, pp.844–50.
11. *Weimarer Historisch-Genealogisches Taschenbuch des gesamten Adels Jehudaischen Ursprungs* (Historical-Genealogical Pocket Reference Book for all the Noble Families of Jewish Origin) (Weimar: Kyffhauser Verlag, 1912), pp.395–6.
12. N. and M. Rau, *My Dear Ones* (Biography of Dr Abraham Low) (Chicago: Recovery Inc., 1986), p.2.
13. Strasbourg Archives Municipales.
14. Jan Slomka, *From Serfdom to Self-government. Memoirs of a Polish Village Mayor 1842-1927* (London: Minerva, 1941), pp.98–100.
15. Michael Honey, 'Development of Jewish Family Names in Poland. Demonstrated by Propinacya and Koncygnacya Listings for Tarnobrzeg-Dzikow', *Shemot*, 2, 4 (Oct. 1994).
16. Y.Y. Fleisher (ed.), *Kehilat Tarnobrzeg-Dzikow* (Hebrew) (Tel Aviv: Tarnobrzeg-Dzikow Society, 1973).
17. List of Tarnobrzeg Citizens from the Census of 1880. Book of Tarnobrzeg Inhabitants, 1925. I am obliged to Tadeusz Zych for sending me these lists. His address is: Ul Skarbka 1, Tarnobrzeg, Poland, and the address of the archives is : Oddzial w Sandomierz, 27-600 Sandomierz , Ul. Zydowska 4, Poland (Tel: 832-25-09).
18. Rau, *My Dear Ones*, p.2.
19. Strasbourg Archives Municipales.
20. Slomka, *From Serfdom to Self-government.*
21. C.A. Macartney, *The Habsburg Empire 1770–1918* (London: Weidenfeld & Nicholson, 1968), p.502.
22. Thomas Gasowski, *From Austeria to Manor. Jewish Landowners in Autonomous Galicia.* Polin (Vol.12) (Oxford: Published by the Littman Library of Jewish Civilisation, 1999).

My Dear Ones

The love story of a great physician for his patients

Neil and Margaret Rau

Figure 12
Biography of Dr Abraham Low

Chapter Eleven

A Ship's Manifest

Connecting the Low and Wahl families

Ships' manifests are a well-tried source of genealogical information. A document of this kind proved to be of interest for the light it threw on the connection between families that had been sundered by the aftermath of the First World War.

Dr Abraham Low was a distinguished physician and a pioneer of community mental health care. His achievements are recorded in his writings, in reviews of his work, and in a popular biography. The Institute bearing his name continues to support projects applying his methods and ideas in old and new fields of rehabilitation.[1]

The clues on a postcard written by him to my mother during the First World War led to his parents, Lazar Loew and Blume Wahl.[2] Entries in the Strasbourg municipal records confirmed Blume Wahl's vital details. She was born in Tarnobrzeg in Austrian Galicia and died at a young age in Strasbourg.[3] The fortuitous discovery of her daughter Selma's birth certificate was of significant help, because it gave not only her parents' names but also details of her grandparents, who lived in Tarnobrzeg.[4] Extracts from the 1880 census for that town gave birth dates for Shulim and Sarah Wahl and five of their six children.[5] It emerged that Blume was the sister of Rachel, who married Abraham Taube, and of my grandmother Chawa Griffel.

When I discovered my Loew cousins I found some further records of their ancestral connections.[6] Lazar Loew was the fourth son of Nathan Nata Loew and Malke Katz of Sedziszow. Nathan Nata was president of the Jewish community and mayor of the town (1903–05). The Loews were estate owners and had been in Sedziszow for a long time. Nathan Nata's father, Jacov Shaya Loew, was born there, married Blume Engelhard, and produced seven children. Their eldest son Nathan Nata had nine offspring, and so did Lazar and Blume.

My research prompted Dr Low's daughters to look through their family papers again, and they discovered the ship's manifest, which detailed their father's emigration from Vienna to New York.[7] The genealogically significant details of the manifest are the personal data on Abraham Low, which tie in with the body of information I had previously gathered, the name of his sponsor in America who was his brother Nathan S. Low, and the name of his next-of-kin at the point of departure, his uncle Moses Wahl. The details enabled me to trace the latter, and thus confirm links between the Wahl and Loew families.

In 1914 many Galician Jews, including my mother's immediate family and some of her relations, fled to the safety of the Imperial capital in the wake of advancing Russian armies. Many stayed on in Vienna after the war, some returned to Galicia, which had become part of the reconstituted Polish republic, while others emigrated to America.

My recent researches revealed that Abraham Loew studied medicine at Strasbourg. As an Austrian subject of Galician birth he was called up, and served as a medical officer on the eastern front. At war's end he was in Vienna, where he continued his medical training. It appears that he was in touch with my parents and that his uncle Moses Wahl was also living there, and no doubt so were other relatives as yet unknown to me. It was only recently that I found Moses Wahl in the 1880 Tarnobrzeg census list where the year of his birth is given as 1873. As soon as the details of the ship's manifest came to hand I contacted the Jewish Community Offices in Vienna and obtained confirmation that Moses Wahl died there in 1927 and that he was then 54 years of age.[8] I have also now found a probate application following his death, which gives details including the names of his parents, wife and children.[9]

With the discovery of the ship's manifest he seems to have come alive for me. The details significantly strengthen family connections. As I continue to delve into the past I begin to realize how closely bonded my mother's people once were, and just how that unity was utterly shattered by two world wars and the holocaust. Moses Wahl was not only one of my great-uncles but also the great-uncle of my Taube cousins, of the Low sisters, and of my first cousins on the Griffel side. There are also numerous Safiers who are related to us. So I am assured of the personal interest of some of my future readers. For others, it may serve as an illustration of how much genealogical insight one routine document can provide.

Table 9
DR ABRAHAM LOW

Dr Abraham Low
Baranow 1891–Chicago 1954

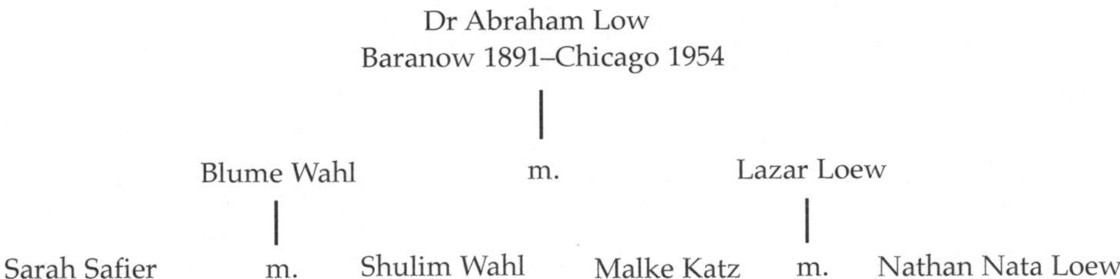

NOTES

1. Abraham A. Low Institute, 550 Frontage Road, Northfield, Il. 60093, USA.
2. Austrian Army *Evidenzblatt* dated Lublin, 11 October 1918 (see Edward Gelles, 'All Quiet on the Eastern Front', *Avotaynu*, xvi, 4 [Winter 2000]).
3. Extract from Strasbourg Municipal Archives (letter dated 5 October 2000, reference 30.1.1104/00GF/BW, including Blume Wahl's birth at Tarnobrzeg 15.9.1864, her death at Strasbourg 21.5.1903, her husband Lazare Loew's birth at Sedziszow 25.12.1861 (the latter date confirmed by Jewish Community records in Vienna, where he died in 1919).
4. Birth Certificate (Vol.II, No.125) issued at Tarnobrzeg on 25.8.1913 recording the birth in that town of Selma Loew on 12.12.1885. Her parents are stated as Lazar Loew and Chaya Bluma, daughter of Shulim and Sara Wahl.
5. Tarnobrzeg Census for 1880 – extract from the lists kept in the archives at Sandomierz. Birth dates for a Wahl family: Shulim 1838, Sarah 1842, Chaim Leib 1869, Moses 1873, Zypora 1875, Chawa 1877, and Rachel 1879. Edward Gelles, 'Searching for Eve – A Methodological Lesson', *Avotaynu*, xvii, 2 (Summer 2001)
6. Information gathered from unpublished MS by Professor Willy Zeev Loew [on whose work the appended Loew family Table of Descent is primarily based], from Dr Abraham Loew's daughters, and from Selma Loew's grand-daughter, Judith Ritter.
7. Details of Ship's Manifest supplied by Marilyn Low Schmitt and Phyllis Low Berning: SS France sailing from Le Havre 9.4.1921 arriving port of New York 16.4.1921. List 12, Passenger No.25: Abraham Loew, 30 years of age, male, single, profession – doctor, Polish nationality, German speaking, Hebrew religion, height 5ft 6 in, skin fair, hair brown, eyes grey, distinguishing marks none, travelling from Vienna. Next-of-kin: Uncle – Mr Moses Wahl, Landstrasse, Vienna, Austria. Sponsor in US: Brother – Nathan S. Low, 44 Avenna Ave, New York.
8. Israelitische Kultusgemeinde Wien, Seitenstettengasse 4, A-1010 Vienna. Jewish Community Burial Records: Moses Wahl of 30 Weintraubengasse, Vienna 2, died on 27 July 1927, at the age of 54 years.
9. Magistrat der Stadt Wien, Abteilung 8, Wiener Stadt u. Landesarchiv, Rathaus, A-1082, Vienna. *Todfallsaufnahme* dated 10.8.1927, in the matter of Moses Wahl deceased 27.7.1927, age 54 years, merchant. His wife is stated as Lea Wahl née Kanner, age 55 years, and his sons as Abraham, 32, of Tigergasse 14, Vienna 8, Isaac, 28, resident in Strasbourg, and Gestar, 20, resident in Paris. The parents of the deceased are given as Sarah and Shulim Wahl.

Table 10
THE LOEWS OF SEDZISZOW

Gen 1:
Yacov Shaya Loew m. Blume Engelhard-Fraenkel

Gen 2 Issue of Gen 1:
1. Natan Nata (Mayor of Sedziszow 1903–05, died 1919) m. Malka Katz
2. Imanuel m. Shprinza Zimels
3. Zeev Wolf (Mayor of Sedziszow, died 1921) m. Diana Waichselbaum
4. Hana m. Tuvia Bloch
5. Gitel m. Moshe Feniger
6. Sara m. Abraham Isaac Lichtman
7. Leah m. Avraham Ritterman

Gen 3 Issue of Gen 2. 1 – Natan Nata Loew and Malka Katz:

1. Baruch
2. Nahum
3. Meir
4. Lazar
5. Feige Bickel
6. Leah Lifshitz
7. Reizel Eckstein
8. Surele Bartfeld
9. Teresa Fuchs

Gen 4 Issue of Gen 3. 4 – Lazar Loew (1861–1919) and Blume Wahl (1861–1903):

1. Ed m. Nelly Stone – issue: Gerald and Bernice
2. Selma (1885–1954 Chicago) m. (1) Moses Kalter (1882–1962) (2) Willy Coteus. Issue from first marriage:
   Henry John Kalter (1907–62) m. Minna Gellert (1909–94) whose daughter Judith Gellert Kalter (born 1934) m. (2) Donald Fale Ritter (born 1925). [*For Selma Low and Moses Kalter see the Jewish Gen Sedziszow Web Site*]
   Issue from second marriage: Robert Coteus (b. 1917) m. Lorraine
3. Nat (1887–1956) m. Dorothy Burland (1899–1976) and had issue:
   Leonard (1924–92) m. Ruth Isaacson, – issue: Nathan and Orli
   Burton (b. 1929) m. Patricia van Runkel, – issue: Ned and Joanna
4. Ben (d. 1953)
5. Abraham (1891–1954) m. Mae Willett (1903–71) and had two daughters:
   Phyllis (b.1936), – issue: Catherine Carey, Bruce, and David Cameron
   Marilyn (b. 1939)
6. Rebecca m. Dr Isaiah Feig; their daughter Shulamit m. Dr Amos Laviel and have issue
7. Sol m. Rosamond Trilling, – issue: John, Richard and Victor (died 2001)
8. Fanny m. Alvarado
9. Theresa (1901–92) m. Jacques Ditteshein (1903–90)

Family Connections

The fourth son of Natan Nata Loew (Gen 2.1) was Lazar Loew (Gen 3.4). He married my great-aunt Blume Wahl. Blume's sister Chawa and her husband David Mendel Griffel were my maternal grandparents. Lazar and Blume's children included Dr Abraham A Low (Gen 4.5) who was my mother's first cousin. The connection of one of Natan Nata Loew's sons with my grandmother's family, the Wahls of Tarnobrzeg, led me to concentrate my researches on this particular branch of the Loew family.

Zeev William Low is a Professor of Physics at the Hebrew University in Jerusalem. He has written about some of the other family branches, including the descendants of his grandparents Zeev Wolf Loew and Diana Waichselbaum (Gen 2.3). Willy Low, born in Vienna in 1922, is the son of Nahum Wolf Loew and Esther (Erna) daughter of Zvi Hirsch Rimalt. He is descended through his mother from the Sternhels of Kolomea and the Heilprins of Brzezany (see Neil Rosenstein, *The Lurie Legacy* [Bergenfield, NJ: Avotaynu, 2004], pp.356–7).

A letter of 6 September 1966 addressed to Max Low by Rabbi Meyer Horowitz touches on ancient roots and diverse family connections. Max Low was a son of Meir Loew (Gen 3.3) and grandson of Reb Nathan Nata Loew (Gen 2.1). The appended copy of the letter (see Figure 13) was made available to me by Professor Marilyn Low Schmitt, daughter of Dr Abraham Low. Rabbi Horowitz was the great-grandson of Rabbi Abraham Horowitz (1823–1905), the first Admur (Chasidic leader or Rabbi) of the Horowitz dynasty of Sedziszow. It refers to the latter's connection by marriage with Rabbi Abraham Zeev Fraenkel of Przeworsk. The forebears of Blume Engelhard – Fraenkel, the wife of Yaacov Shaya Loew (Gen 1), came to Poland from Germany several centuries ago and adopted the name of Fraenkel as indicative of their country of origin. They settled in Przeworsk, Rzeszow and Brody. The family produced some rabbis of note and spread to other Galician towns such as Sanok and Linsk.

Joseph Margoshes, in the memoirs of his life published in Yiddish in New York in 1936, mentions that his sister-in-law Eidel married a Berel Low of Sedziszow. While the Loews were my mother's cousins through the Wahl connection, my father's family had other points of contact with the Margoshes and the Loews. The Gelles and Fraenkels of Brody were in-laws (see Chapter 36), and my paternal grandfather like the Loews adhered to the Czortkow Chasidic connection.

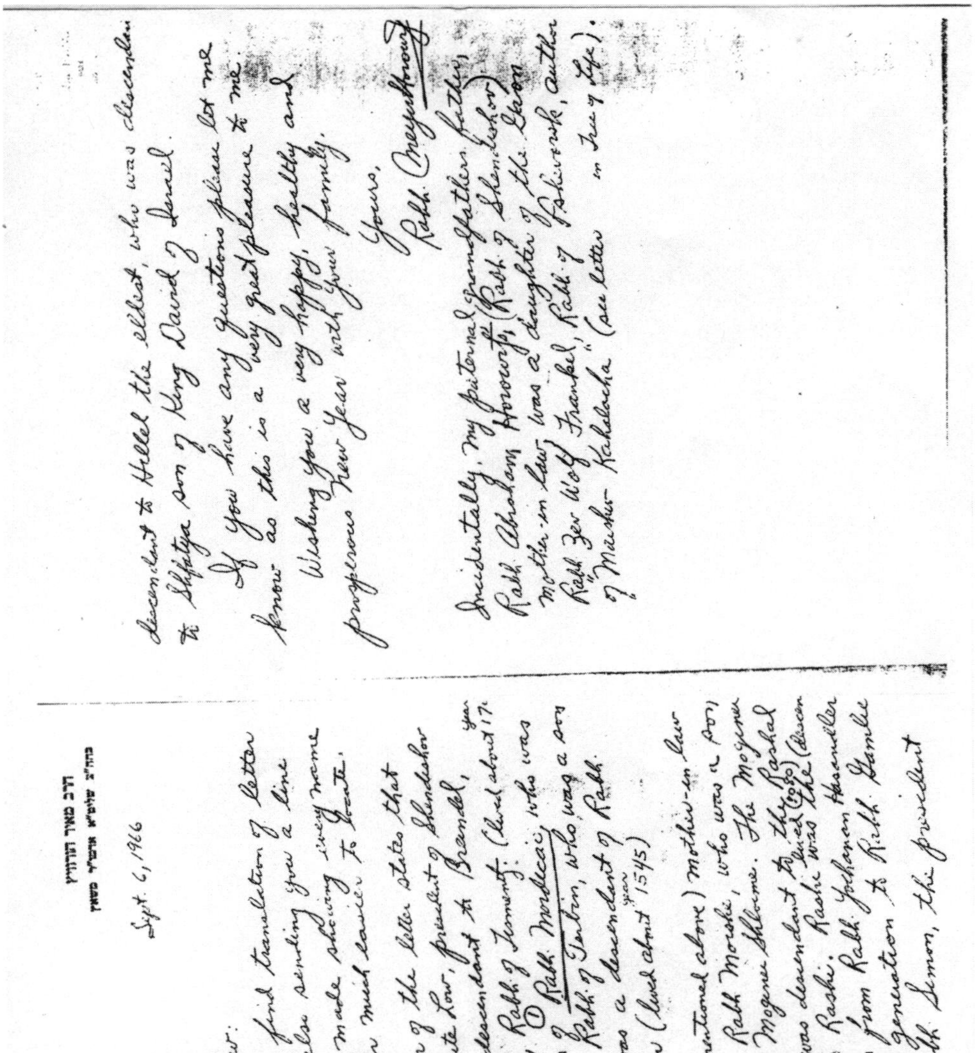

GEDNEY 8-0028

RABBI MEYER HOROWITZ
1846–50TH STREET
BROOKLYN, N. Y. 11204

הרב מאיר הורוויץ
בהה"צ שליט"א אדמו"ר משאנץ

ב"ה

Sept. 6, 1966

Dear Friend Mr. Max Low:

Enclosed you will find translation of letter you sent me. I am also sending you a line of ancestry tree which I made showing every name mentioned in the letter much easier to locate.

In brief the writer of the letter states that your grandfather Reb Nute Low, president of Shendeshov (also mayor) ~~was~~ is a descendant to Brendel, daughter of Rabbi Samuel, Rabbi of Temenitz (lived about 17.. year). Rabbi Samuel was a son of ① Rabbi Mordecai, who was a son of Rabbi Moishe, Rabbi of Terbin, who was a son of Rabbi Samuel, who was a descendant of Rabbi Shachne, Rabbi of Lublin (lived about year 1545)

Rabbi Mordecai's ① (mentioned above) mother-in-law Adele was a daughter of Rabbi Moishe, who was a son of Rabbi Joshua, author of Mogenei Shloime. The Mogenei Shloime (Rabbi Jashua) was descendant to the Rashal who was descendant to Rashi. Rashi (lived 1080) was the (descen[dant]) thirty third generation from Rabbi Jochanan Hasandler who was the fourth generation to Rabbi Gamlie[l] the eldest son of Rabbi Simon, the president descendant to Hillel the eldest, who was descendan[t] to Shfatya son of King David of Israel.

If you have any questions please let me know as this is a very great pleasure to me.

Wishing you a very happy, healthy and prosperous New Year with your family.

Yours,

Rabbi Meyer Horowitz

Incidentally, my paternal grandfathers father, Rabbi Abraham Horowitz (Rabbi of Shendishov) mother-in-law, was a daughter of the Gaon Rabbi Zev Wolf Frankel, Rabbi of Pshevorsk, author of "Maisher Kahalacha" (see letter in Tree of Life).

Figure 13
Letter from Rabbi Meyer Horowitz to Max Low

IV.

MY MOTHER'S FAMILY

Die Herrschaft führen Wachs und Leder
Was willst du böser Geist von mir?
Erz, Marmor, Pergament, Papier?
Soll ich mit Griffel, Meissel, Feder schreiben?

J.W. Goethe, *Faust Part 1*

Griffel – the German word for the writing implement called stylus in Latin

Chapter Twelve

My Mother's People

Introducing the Griffels of Nadworna and their cousins

Figure 14
Regina Griffel and her elder son Ludwig

The 18th day of March in the year 2000 marked the centenary of my mother's birth. I decided to write an article about her to commemorate the occasion, but I lacked knowledge of her family background. I am still finding out much about our ancient ancestry. A brief biographical sketch has turned into a lengthy genealogical study. My parents belonged to a generation of assimilated Viennese Jews, who attached more importance to participation in their contemporary culture than to a study of their family. I had to find my roots largely through my own efforts.

Regina Griffel was the daughter of David Mendel Griffel of Nadworna and Chawa Wahl of Tarnobrzeg. She had an elder brother Zygmunt and a younger brother Edward.

The Griffels were a large clan who had prospered in nineteenth-century Galicia under Austrian rule. The Nadworna line claimed descent from David Halevi Segal, the seventeenth-century Chief Rabbi of Lvov. My great-grandfather Eliezer Griffel built up a commercial empire that went far beyond his native town and gave employment to many members of the clan.

Eliezer married Sarah Chayes of Kolomea. The Chayes family was based in Brody for a long time. It produced distinguished rabbis for many centuries and flourished in Poland and also in Italy. Eliezer and Sarah had ten children including my grandfather. Among his siblings were Isaac Chaim and Zissel, who are shown in Table 11. Isaac Chaim had many children, and other Griffels were also quite prolific, so that even after world wars and the holocaust their issue is more numerous than can be accommodated here.

My grandmother Chawa was one of six siblings. The progeny of three Wahl sisters is shown in the Table. My grandparents had moved from Nadworna to Stanislau when my mother was quite young. At the outbreak of the First World War they sought refuge in Vienna, and in 1921 their daughter Regina married David Gelles, who had established himself as an advocate there. My brother Ludwig and I spent a happy childhood in Vienna between the wars. We came to England shortly after the Anschluss in 1938, and my mother died in London in 1954.

Eliezer Griffel, the patriarch of the Nadworna clan, was known as Zeida (grandpa). He was the head of the Jewish community and dominated its religious, political and economic life. He gave his religious adherence to the Chasidic rabbi of Otonyia. Zeida Griffel was a deeply conservative paternalist, a philanthropist, and an outstanding businessman. He is supposed to have got on well with the Emperor on the latter's visits to his outlying province. They talked mainly about horses. David Mendel and Isaac Chaim Griffel followed him in the family business and represented the ultra-orthodox in local affairs. Isaac Chaim's children remained within the Chasidic fold and so did some other siblings, but David Mendel's children were exposed to Viennese enlightenment at a tender age.

Chawa Wahl's father and mother, my great-grandparents Shulim Wahl and Sarah Safier, had a traditional Jewish background and came from wealthy families.

My uncles Zygmunt and Edward prospered in the timber trade in Lvov and in the export-import business in Warsaw. They often came to visit us in Vienna, and I thought that they cut quite a dash. Edward in particular had been all over the world and his cosmopolitan outlook seemed ahead of his time. Their sons, who are my first cousins, are Eric Griffel of Washington, DC, who had a distinguished career in the US Foreign Service, and David Griffel of Boston, who built up a successful computer software company.

My mother had a number of interesting first cousins. Dr Abraham Low, one of the children of my great-aunt Blume Wahl, became a distinguished psychiatrist in Chicago. His daughter Marilyn Low Schmitt is a professor of art history and worked for the Getty Museum. She and her sister Phyllis are associated with the Institute bearing their father's name.

My great-aunt Rachel Wahl had two children by her first marriage to Abraham Taube: Rega and Zyga ended up in Rio de Janeiro and Los Angeles, and their children are Viola Sachs, a professor of American literature at the University of Paris, and Thaddeus Taube, a Californian businessman who has become a noted philanthropist and benefactor. Rachel Wahl's second marriage to Chaim Simon Ohrenstein produced a daughter called Lucia, who became Countess Tripcovich and a leading light of 1950s Rome café society.

There could not be a greater contrast between my mother's first cousins Lucia Ohrenstein, the socialite, and Dr Jacob Griffel, the deeply religious saviour of thousands of Jews during the Second World War. But then they were from different branches of the family tree. My mother's first cousins included others of Griffel descent, such as Dr Arnold Lam.

These characters and their progeny carry with them the millennial heritage of our people, and more specifically the genetic inheritance of several ancient families. It is tempting to look at some of them in the light of family traits, endeavouring to discern genes from the Griffel, Chayes, Safier and Wahl lines, particularly because of the high degree of inbreeding which must have reinforced certain inherited attributes. For example, Taube and Wahl are related, and indeed there are more or less distant connections of Chayes and Griffel with the Wahl-Katzenellenbogen clan.

I am writing this chapter not only as a tribute to my mother's memory and as a historical record, but also to set out how I began to construct the family tree. I had lost contact with my Griffel cousins in the 1950s. I did not know where my grandmother came from or who were many of my relations. The voyage of discovery on which I embarked a few years ago has given me much historical insight and self-knowledge. I have also made new friends and come across some interesting personalities.

In the appended summary of my findings I refer to articles on family branches or individuals, to documents and other primary sources, and to useful addresses. At the beginning was my parents' marriage certificate obtained from the Jewish Community Offices in Vienna.[1, a] It confirmed my mother's place and date of birth and gave the full names of her parents. I wrote brief outlines of the Wahl and Chayes family histories.[2] The background to the Griffel family since the mid-nineteenth century is to be found in the Nadworna Memorial Book and other sources.[3] Vital records on Eliezer Griffel and David Mendel Griffel came respectively from Rabbi Kolesnik of Stanislau,[b] and from the Warsaw Archives.[c] The Chayes connection with Kolomea is referred to in the Brody Memorial Book and elsewhere.[4] I looked vainly for my grandmother Chawa among the Wahls of Nadworna,[5] and it was not until I had discovered some of her siblings that I found her family in Tarnobrzeg. From a First World War postcard written by Abraham Low to my mother in Vienna the trail led via the Austrian Army Museum[d] and the Wellcome Library for the History of Medicine to Chicago and to the Low cousins, who have flourished and multiplied in America for nearly a century.[6]

The connections with our Wahl family gradually emerged. Abraham's mother, Blume Wahl, is recorded in the Strasbourg municipal archives, where her birth and marriage in Tarnobrzeg are confirmed.[e] Then followed a birth certificate of one of Abraham Low's siblings which stated the full names of her parents and grandparents and located them in Tarnobrzeg.[f] That town's archives are not easily accessible, but through the kindness of the Deputy Mayor I obtained extracts from the 1880 census which confirmed the names and birth dates of most of the Wahl family.[g] I had found my grandmother at last.[7] Furthermore, I now knew who my great-aunts were. I contacted Rachel Wahl's descendants Thaddeus Taube in California and Viola Sachs in Paris, who gave me some additional anecdotal guidance to the fate of other relatives, and particularly to the career of Lucia Ohrenstein. I lost no time in researching her remarkable life story.[8] Abraham Low's daughters then rediscovered their father's ship's manifest of 1921, recorded at the time he emigrated from Vienna to the United States.[h] It contained references to his uncle Moses Wahl. This led me to a probate document in Vienna[i] that had further data on my long-lost great-uncle.[9] The ramifications of the Wahl family are intriguing in their complexity. My great-grandfather Shulim was the son of Leiser Wahl, who in his time was the richest man in Tarnobrzeg, according to the memoirs of the town's mayor.[10] A daughter of Leiser Wahl married a son of Moses Hauser, Count Tarnowski's *Arendar*. The latter's son-in-law Salomon Lamm was connected with the Lamms who later intermarried with the Griffels.[11] Much work remains to be done on the Taube connection[12] and on the Safier family.[13]

I found data for my uncles Zygmunt and Edward Griffel on the Internet, in the Nadworna records of the Baron Hirsch Cemetery on Staten Island.[14] Zygmunt's wife Maryla was the granddaughter of the banker Salomon Meir Wohl of Cracow and Vienna. In this way the Wohls of Cracow are linked to the Wahls of Tarnobrzeg.[15] Edward's wife Susan Manson was connected with the Friedman Chasidic dynasty.[16] So apparently was my father, Dr David Gelles, at least according to his obituary notice in a Viennese newspaper.[17] My paternal grandfather was (almost) the last of an ancient rabbinical line from Brody.[18]

There are innumerable cousins descended from Eliezer and Sarah Griffel. The most noteworthy is Dr Jacob Griffel, whose intellectual and moral qualities and selfless efforts on behalf of his fellow Jews during and after the Second World War merit greater acclaim than he has so far received.[19]

The following generation includes the grandsons of Zissel, Chaya and Iaaac Chaim Griffel, namely the physician Dr Steven Lamm,[20] the psychiatrist Dr Yehuda Nir,[21] and the past president of the American Jewish World Service, Andrew Griffel.[22]

NOTES

1. E. Gelles, 'In Search of My Pedigree', *Shemot*, 8, 2 (June 2000), p.28.
2. E. Gelles, 'Saul Wahl. A Jewish Legend', *Judaism Today*, 14 (Winter 1999–2000), p.36. Gelles, 'Chief Rabbis in the Genes', *Manna*, 69 (Autumn 2000), p.34.
3. Nadworna (Stanislau District) Memorial and Records. Landsmannschaft of Nadworna in Israel and the United States, 1975, pp.25–6. Y.L. Maimon (ed.), *Arim ve-Imahot be-Israel* (Stanislau), Vol.5, pp.63–314. (See extracts from these sources below.)
4. *An Eternal Light: Brody in Memoriam* (Israel: Organisation of former Brody residents, 1994), p.324. Rabbi Chaim Zvi Teomim, *Zikaron Le'Rishonim* (Kolomea: 1913), preface.
5. E. Gelles, 'The Wahls of Nadworna', *Shemot*, 8, 3 (Sept. 2000), p.26, and 8, 4 (Dec. 2000), p.31.
6. E. Gelles, 'All Quiet on the Eastern Front', *Avotaynu*, XVI, 4 (Winter 2000), p.60.
7. E. Gelles, 'Searching for Eve: A Methodological Lesson', *Avotaynu*, XVII, 2 (Summer 2001), p.40.
8. E. Gelles, 'Lucia's Dolce Vita', unpublished. see Chapter 24.
9. E. Gelles, 'Abraham Low's Ship's Manifest', *Shemot*, 10, 2 (June 2002), see Chapter 11. Dr Abraham Low's many works are listed by the Abraham A. Low Institute, 550 Frontage Road, Northfield, Illinois, 60093. The Low family Tree includes my second cousin Dr Victor Low, son of Sol Low and Rosamond Trilling, whose published works include *Three Nigerian Emirates*, 1972.
10. Jan Slomka, *From Serfdom to Self-government. Memoirs of a Polish Village Mayor 1842-1917*, translated by William John Rose (London: Minerva, 1941), pp.90, 94, 98–101 .
11. See Chapters 20 and 21
12. See Chapters 22 and 25, including references to the numerous books of literary analysis and criticism by my second cousin, Professor Viola Sachs.
13. See Chapter 19, The Safiers of Tarnobrzeg,.
14. www.shtetlinks.jewishgen.org/Nadworna/Chrono.htm-17k
15. See chapter 18, The Wohls of Cracow.
16. Neil Rosenstein, *The Unbroken Chain* (New York, London, Jerusalem: CIS Publishers, 1990), Vol.2, p.940.
17. Dr David Gelles, Obituary in *Heruth*, Vienna, 4 Sept. 1964.
18. See Chapter 36, The Gelles Rabbinical Ancestry.
19. Dr Jacob Griffel – see Joseph Friedenson, *Dateline Istanbul* (New York: Mesorah Publications Ltd, 1993); David Kranzler, 'Our Man in Istanbul', in *Thy Brother's Blood* (New York: Mesorah Publications, 1987); and David Kranzler, 'The Istanbul Connection', in David Kranzler and Eliezer Gevirtz, *To Save a World* (New York, London, Jerusalem: CIS Publishers, 1991).
20. Dr Steven Lamm, co-author of *Thinner at Last* (1995), *Younger at Last* (1997) and *The Virility Solution* (1998), published by Simon and Schuster, New York.
21. Dr Yehuda Nir, *The Lost Childhood* (New York: Harcourt Brace Jovanovich, 1989); pages

38 and 41 refer briefly to the Hager rabbinical connection and to the family wealth.
22. Andrew Griffel, 'Remembrance of Things Past, A Lesson for the Future'. http://www.ajws.org/andy.htm

Some Primary Sources

a. Parents' Marriage Certificate. *Israelitische Kultusgemeinde, 1010 Vienna, Seitenstettengasse 4.*
b. Eliezer Griffel birth record. Rabbi Moshe Leib Kolesnik, Pushkina St. 75, Apt.1, Ivano-Frankivsk, Ukraine.
c. David Mendel Griffel birth record. Warsaw State Archives, Archiwum Glowne Akt Dawnych, ul.Dluga 7, 00-263, Warszawa.
d. Evidenzblatt for Lt. Abraham Loew, dated 11 October 1918. Oesterreichisches Staatsarchiv, Kriegsarchiv, 1030 Vienna, Nottendorfergasse 2.
e. Vital Records for Blume Wahl. Strasbourg Archives Municipales, Ref: 30.1.1104/00. GF/BW, dated 5 October 2000.
f. Birth Certificate of Selma Loew giving full names of her parents Eliezer Loew and Blume Wahl and of her mother's parents, Shulim Wahl and Sarah Safier. Issued by the Israelitische Matrikenfuerung in Tarnobrzeg, the copy dated 25 August 1913
g. Town Census of 1880 and List of Inhabitants dated 1925 for the town of Tarnobrzeg. Records kept in the archives, Oddzial w Sandomierzu, 27-600, Sandomierz, ul. Z.ydowska 4, Poland.
h. Dr Abraham Loew's Ship Manifest. S.S. France sailing from Le Havre 9 April 1921 arriving at port of New York 16 April 1921. List 12, # 25.
i. Probate Document for Moses Wahl, died Vienna 26 July 1927. Todfallsaufnahme, Ref.: A 1524/27 with details of his widow, Lea Kanner, b. 1872, and his sons, Abraham, b. 1895, Isaac, b. 1899, and Gestar, b. 1907, domiciled in France. Magistrat der Stadt Wien, Magistratsabteilung 8, Wiener Stadt und Landesarchiv, Rathaus, A 1082, Vienna, Ref MA 8 – A-2021/2001.

Extracts from References in Note 3

Nadworna Memorial Book

In the synagogue of the followers of the Chasidic Rabbi of Otonyia, the leader of the Jewish community Reb Zeida Griffel and his sons and sons-in-law used to pray ... He was the owner of oil wells, refineries and saw mills employing a large number of hands. In spite of his extensive business activities he was meticulous in his religious observances ... As head of the community he ensured that everything was carried out in strict observance of the Torah law. He brought up his sons in the Chasidic tradition. (pp.25–6)

Arim ve-Imahot be-Israel, volume 5 – Stanislau

Isaac Chaim Griffel was a member of the Jewish National Council in Stanislau, 18 May 1919. (p.63)

Isaac Chaim Griffel was elected to the council of the Jewish community on 5 August 1928 representing the *Agudas Israel* party (which was the largest single party holding 6 seats). (p.212)

...all six were wealthy businessmen. (p.213)

David Mendel Griffel was elected to the council of the Jewish community in August 1934 as a representative of *Agudas Israel*. (p.219)

The following Jews were owners of oil refineries and related industries: the Haber brothers with Eliezer Griffel, Eliezer Griffel & Sons (Nadworna), Eliezer Griffel (Pasiecna), Isaac Chaim Griffel at Skavina near Cracow, at Kurneiburg near Vienna in partnership with Herman Adlersberg, and at Kolomea in partnership with Dr Carl Halpern and Iztchak Geller. Eliezer Griffel & Sons owned major saw mills exporting large quantities of timber. Jacob Griffel was also involved in the timber industry. (p.233)

Eliezer Griffel was a great philanthropist whose home was always open to anyone in trouble. (p.311)

he was on the committee of the Yeshiva Or Torah in Stanislau. (p.314)

Table 11
MY MOTHER'S FAMILY CONNECTIONS

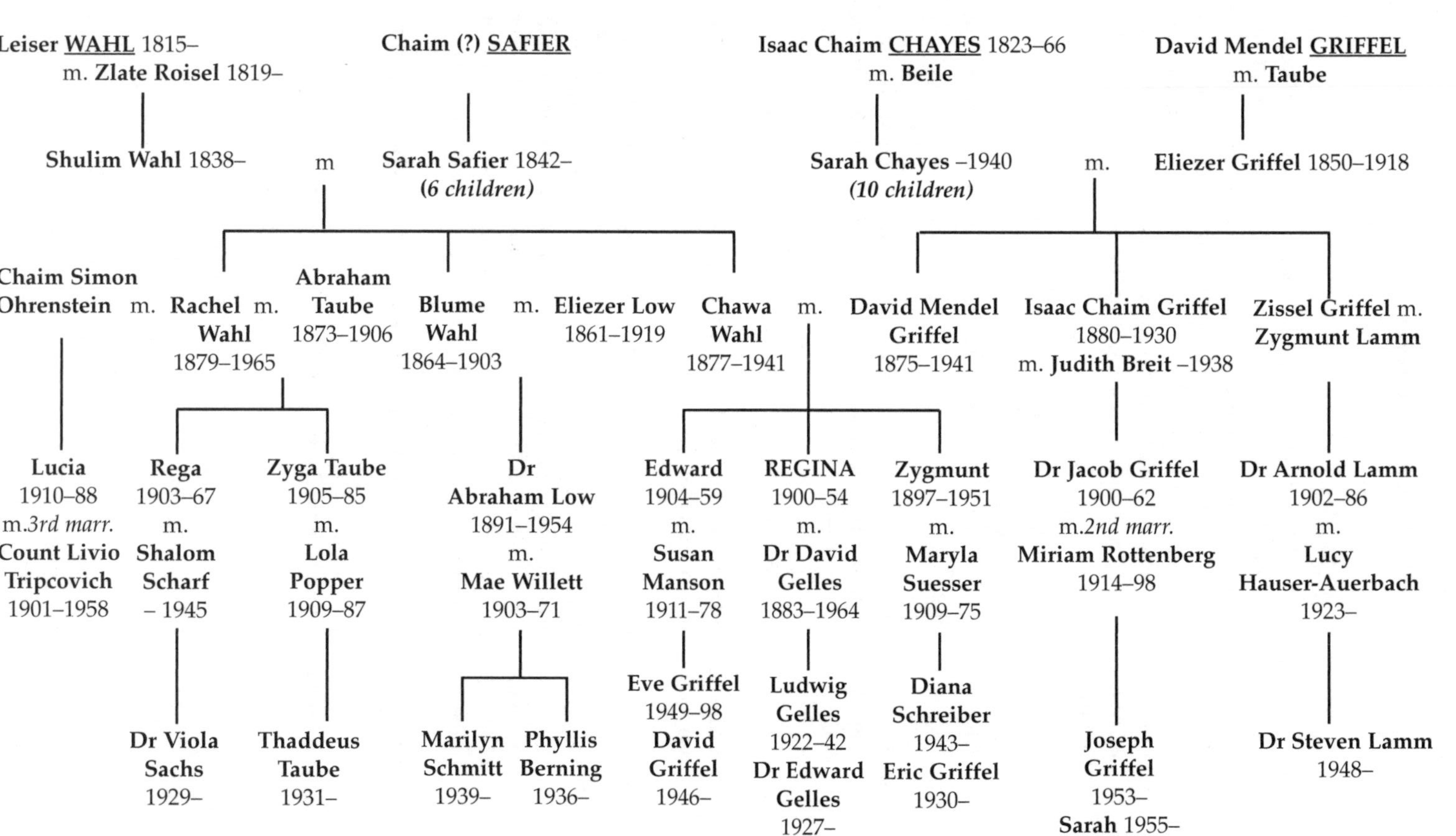

Chapter Thirteen

Three Sisters

Blume, Chawa and Rachel Wahl

The three sisters in this story are the daughters of my maternal great-grandparents, Shalom Wahl and Sara Safier. An account of their lives and of their offspring could be seen as a paradigm for the past 150 years of Jewish history, and I believe that as such it does have some lessons to teach us.

Legend has it that our ancestor Saul Wahl acquired the name Wahl in Poland when he was elected to high office during the interregnum of 1587. Saul had at least eleven children. Distinct Wahl branches developed, not only in Poland, but also in numerous other countries.

My great-grandparents lived in a small Galician town called Dzikow. It was really a large village, which became part of the town of Tarnobrzeg. It was situated on the river Vistula, northeast of the old capital city of Cracow. When Poland underwent a series of partitions in the eighteenth century, the town became part of the Austrian Empire and remained so until the end of the First World War.

During this period of Austrian rule, a relatively liberal regime, a large measure of provincial autonomy, and active encouragement of commerce allowed a certain kind of Jewish entrepreneur to evolve. The Wahls, Safiers, and their in-laws, the Griffels, Taube, Low and Popper families, among others, shared a cultural background and economic interests, and with their inter-marriages they constituted a self-contained group, which flourished for just a few generations. Some of their progeny carried on in the new Poland which was reconstituted after the First World War, but their little world came to an end in 1939. Many escaped in good time and built fresh lives elsewhere, others perished in the holocaust.

These people passed through the darkest days that have ever befallen their kin and the lands they once called home. They were scattered, and they will never be the close-knit family they were in 'the old country', but they are finding themselves again in the 'New World' of the twenty-first century.

Shalom and Sara Wahl had a family of two boys and four girls. Blume was born in 1864, and there followed Chaim (1869), Moses (1873), Sypora (1875), Chawa (1877) and Rachel (1879). We know little of Moses who died in Vienna in 1927. Chaim was still in Tarnobrzeg in 1925, as evidenced by the census of that year. Sypora appears to have dropped out of sight. The three sisters, Blume, Chawa and Rachel left their little traditional Jewish 'shtetl' in the 1880s and 1890s. The story of their lives with all its tragedy and achievement is certainly not unique, but it will be for the reader to judge whether it is worth telling.

Blume died prematurely in Strasbourg (1903) and Chawa perished in the Polish holocaust (1941). Only the toughest sibling, Rachel, was afforded a natural life span, passing away in Rio de Janeiro in 1965. According to the customs of those times the girls married in their teens. Generally alliances were made with families of similar social and economic standing. Business connections or kinship provided the most likely introduction. Marriages between cousins were frequent, the old rabbinical families being particularly inbred. The marriages of Blume and Chawa appear to have been arranged in the usual way.

Blume married Eliezer Loew. He was one of nine children of Nathan Nata Loew of Sedziszow, another small town that was not all that far from Tarnobrzeg. The Loews were wealthy merchants like the Wahls. They owned estates, and Nathan Nata was president of the Jewish community and mayor of the town.

Chawa married David Mendel Griffel, the son of Eliezer Griffel of Nadworna and of Sara Chayes of Kolomea and Brody, whose family had come to Galicia from Portugal via Provence, Italy and Bohemia. By the turn of the century Eliezer Griffel had built up a substantial business. His interests spread beyond Nadworna and Stanislau in Eastern Galicia to Lemberg and beyond. He had ten children, Chawa's new husband and his brother Isaac Chaim Griffel being the most active in the family enterprises and in local politics.

Rachel also married into a prosperous family with rabbinical antecedents. But it came about rather differently. As a teenage girl she went to stay with a cousin, Abraham Taube of Lemberg, to help his young wife, who was awaiting the arrival of her first baby. Unfortunately the mother died shortly after giving birth to a son. Rachel looked after the child and married Abraham. Later she had children of her own by Taube, and when she was widowed, she took Chaim Simon Ohrenstein as her second husband. Abraham Taube was by all accounts a Talmud scholar of independent means.

With the winds of enlightenment and emancipation sweeping to the furthest corners of the realms of traditional orthodoxy, it is not surprising that Rachel at least turned out to be freethinking. She had a strong personality, a good intellect and a biting sense of humour. She was fond of her sister Chawa but described her as being a 'goody-goody'. Chawa was indeed strait-laced and pious as befitted a Griffel bride.

The patriarch of that family, Eliezer Griffel, was the head of the Jewish community in Nadworna, and led his family along the path of fervid religious observance. To this day, one branch of the family has retained its Chassidic loyalties. There was such an age difference between Blume and her sisters, and she married so young, that there could not have been great intimacy between them. Blume made her way to the West whence the winds of change had originally come. Her family maintained their adherence to Jewish traditions, while gradually embracing the assimilation, which was the ethos of the age.

Blume's husband Lazar Loew had a personality problem. He was excitable and subject to fits of violent temper. Unlike his other siblings he could not make a comfortable and stable home for his family in Galicia, and so decided to seek his fortune elsewhere. Blume as a dutiful, old-fashioned wife endured her husband's succession of failures and accompanied him on his westward trek, which ended in Strasbourg. Year after year she bore him children, thirteen in total, nine of whom survived. The youngest child Theresa was born in Strasbourg in 1901. The others came with their parents from Galicia. They were Ed, Selma, Nat, Ben, Abraham, Rebecca, Sol and Fanny. As the new century opened the family looked forward to better days, but then an enemy who killed the entire stock ruined the farm, which they had started, overnight. Lazar was bankrupted. Shortly after, Blume, worn out by childbearing, died of a broken heart at the age of 39. The family was shattered. Four of the children had to go to an orphanage, but Ben and Abraham did complete their studies at the Strasbourg Lyceum. The eldest son Ed went to America to an uncle who had a surgical appliance business, and Nat was to join him a few years later. Lazar returned to Poland where a brother had offered him the management of a large estate. He took Selma, Theresa and Sol with him. He married again and had another son.

A hundred years after Blume's tragic death her descendants are a flourishing tribe in the United States. Generation has succeeded generation. There are now innumerable Low cousins. Their success was due to true grit, hard work and family loyalty of an exceptional order. Ed and Nat saved every cent they could set aside from their wages until they were able to start their own surgical appliance business, which did so well that they could expand and still send regular subsidies to their siblings in Europe. They paid for Ben's training as an engineer and supported Abraham's medical studies. They brought their brothers and sisters over to America, one by one, and nurtured them until they could strike out on their own. The firm of N.S. Low & Co. was incorporated in 1914 and is still going strong under the direction of Nat's son, Burton Low. Meantime, they were briefly in partnership with a cousin Max Low, who later independently became a multi-millionaire industrialist.

Their brother Abraham studied medicine at Strasbourg, served with distinction as a doctor in the Austrian army, and then completed his post-graduate training in Vienna, where he attended Sigmund Freud's courses. He emigrated to America in 1921. Before long he established himself as a psychiatrist in Chicago, abandoning Freudian methods, and developing a system based on professionally guided self-help, group support, behaviour modification, and cognitive therapy. He founded an organization called

Recovery Inc, and thus became a pioneer of communal mental health care. He published many learned articles and books. His popular work 'Mental Health through Will Training' has gone to several editions and is still selling steadily after half a century. His daughters Marilyn, a professor of art history, and Phyllis, married to a prominent lawyer, are involved in the running of the organization founded by their father and of the Abraham A. Low Institute.

The long life of Rachel Wahl was less tragic than Blume's. It had more than its share of tribulation and sorrow, but it was also full of dramatic incident, and she lived to see her children achieve a considerable measure of worldly success.

Brandel Wittels, Abraham Taube's first wife, died in 1895 after giving birth to Samuel Zygmunt Wittels, who later added Yonati, the Hebrew equivalent of Taube, to that name. Rachel was an affectionate stepmother to him. Her own children, Rega and Zyga Taube were born in Lemberg in 1903 and 1905. In the following year she was left a widow. Then she met and married Ohrenstein. They went to live in Cracow where their daughter Lushka (Lucia) was born in 1910. Rachel's second husband was made prisoner by the Russians in 1915 and sent to Siberia. He returned to Cracow after the war but died in the mid-1920s. She must have had a hard time when she was first widowed and left to fend with three children, but her rich sister Chawa Griffel stood by her. Stanislau was not too far from Lemberg, and the young families visited each other. When Rachel was widowed a second time her stepson, who had remained in Lemberg, often came to see her in Cracow. Later, he and his family went to Palestine, but by that time Rega and Zyga Taube were grown up.

Zyga did very well in business from an early age. He married Lola Popper, who belonged to a cultured Cracow family. As the clouds gathered over Poland in the late 1930s he moved to America in good time, taking a substantial fortune with him. He settled in Los Angeles and continued to prosper. Lola's cousin Irene and her husband, on the other hand, were among those who perished in the holocaust. Zyga and Lola rescued and adopted their daughter Ernita and brought her up with their own son Thaddeus. Tad Taube has inherited his father's business acumen and is thriving in northern California.

Rachel was still in Cracow on the eve of war. So was her daughter Rega. Lucia Ohrenstein was living with her husband in Warsaw, where Romeo Puri Purini was director of the Polish office of Reunione Adriatica di Securta, an international insurance company. Rega and her daughter Viola fled with Rachel to Italy and then made their way to Brazil. (Rega's husband Shalom Scharf stayed behind in Poland and perished in 1945.) Lucia was already in Italy where she remained throughout the war. There is a story that when there was a hold up at the frontier, Lucia produced a bundle of love-letters from her husband, whose name was sufficient to gain her family immediate admittance, as Purini's brother was an important official on Mussolini's staff.

Rachel and Rega stayed on in Rio and Rega married again. Viola and her husband Ignacy Sachs returned to post-war Poland for a while. After a few years in India they finally settled in France, where Viola became Professor of American literature at the University of Paris.

Soon after the end of the war, Lucia found herself a widow, and had a great love affair with Oliviero Tripcovich. He was the second son of the founder of a shipping and commercial empire, Diodato Tripcovich, who was born in Dobrota in 1862 and came from a family with deep-rooted seafaring traditions. This Dalmatian family became an important force in post-First World War Trieste under the Italian flag. They were ennobled in 1936. Livio and Lucia had a happy marriage from 1947 until the Count's death in 1958. Lucia did not have issue and died about ten years ago. The present bearer of the name is the distinguished composer Baron Raffaello de Banfield Tripcovich.

This in a nutshell is the story of Rachel and her family. At the end of her eventful life she could look back on the extraordinary and utterly diverse destinies of her progeny.

Chawa Wahl was my grandmother. At the age of 18 she married into the Griffel family. A picture of this family emerges most vividly from the Nadworna Memorial Book and from the Chapter on Stanislau in the well-known work called *Arim ve-Imahot be-Israel*. Great wealth and piety were for a time given to the Griffels in equal measure. Chawa's world revolved around Nadworna and Stanislau, with visits to family and friends in Lemberg and Cracow. Her three children Zygmunt, Regina and Edward were born in 1897, 1900 and 1904. A major break in this provincial existence occurred in 1914 when the family took refuge from the Russian armies advancing into Galicia. They spent the war years in Vienna. After the war, the parents were happy to return to their old life, but the children had very different ideas.

Regina married David Gelles and settled in Vienna. My father established himself as an advocate and they soon started a family, of which I am the sole survivor. My elder brother Ludwig was lost at sea on a return journey from Australia to England during the Second World War.

Zygmunt's wife Maryla was a granddaughter of a merchant banker, Salo Meir Wohl of Cracow and Vienna. The couple had a son Eric and lived in Lvov. Zygmunt had major timber interests and his brother Edward developed an export-import business in Warsaw. Both brothers, as well as my mother, wanted to remember their Jewish past while leading a life appropriate to the era of the 1920s; they had a very modern outlook and inevitably this led to an estrangement from their orthodox parents. By contrast the family of my great-uncle Isaac Chaim Griffel remained close to their ancestral soil and ultra-orthodox beliefs.

I came to England with my parents after the annexation of Austria in 1938. Edward Griffel was already here, but he went on to America a year later. In 1939 Zygmunt and his family also reached the safety of British shores. In the autumn of that year eastern Galicia including Stanislau fell to the Russians in accordance with the provisions of the Molotov-Ribbentrop pact. I have not discovered whether my grandparents stayed put and were slaughtered in 1941 when Hitler invaded the Soviet Union, sweeping through its annexed Polish territories, or whether they had gone to stay with friends in Cracow, in which case they would have perished earlier.

Other Griffels who died included the wife and children of Isaac Chaim's son, Dr Jacob Griffel. He escaped over the Rumanian frontier and made his way to Palestine. He joined a rescue committee in Istanbul in 1943 and played a major role in saving thousands of Jews from Nazi occupied Europe. Several books and articles are beginning to draw attention to his heroic efforts. After the war he settled in America where he raised a second family.

My uncle Edward married late in life. He had two children by his wife, Susan Manson, and his surviving son David has been a successful entrepreneur in the field of information technology. Zygmunt's son Eric moved to America after the war and has had a distinguished career in the US Foreign Service.

This is the story of three sisters and their families. It is about the history of their time, and about genetic inheritance and tradition. I am still working out what moral insights I have gained from a consideration of these lives.

Table 12
THE WAHLS OF TARNOBRZEG

Shulim Wahl 1838–	m.	Sarah Safier 1842–

Their Issue:

Blume (1864–1903)	m.	Lazar Loew (1861–1919)
Chaim Leib (1869–)		
Moses (1873–1927)	m.	Leah Kanner (1872–)
Sypora (1875–)		
Chawa (1877–1941)	m.	David Mendel Griffel (1875–1941)
Rachel (1879–1965)	m.	(1) Abraham Taube (1873–1906) (2) Chaim Simon Ohrenstein

Figure 15
Rachel Taube, née Wahl (1879–1965)

CHAPTER FOURTEEN

Some French Wahls

Including one family from Tarnobrzeg

The progeny of Saul Wahl-Katzenellenbogen were once spread throughout Poland. Now their surviving descendants are to be found elsewhere, notably in France, where families of that name have been established since the seventeenth century. Some came in later times. In the twentieth century, the approach of the two world wars gave an impetus to further migrations.[1]

I looked for my own Wahl ancestors in Austrian Galicia[2] and found them in the old village of Dzikow, which became merged into the town of Tarnobrzeg. In this little town northeast of Cracow, the Wahls flourished under Austrian rule from the time of the eighteenth century Polish partitions to the outbreak of the First World War. A Wahl great-aunt, who married a Loew from the nearby town of Sedziszow, settled in Strasbourg at the close of the nineteenth century. One of her sons, Dr Abraham Loew who was educated in Strasbourg and Vienna, emigrated to America in 1921. A recently-discovered ship's manifest provided valuable information on the connection between the Loew and Wahl families and on a long-lost great-uncle.[3] It pointed to Vienna, where I found a probate document giving vital dates of my kinsman and of his wife and three sons.[4] Moses Wahl was born in Tarnobrzeg in 1873 to Shulim and Sarah Wahl and he died in Vienna in 1927. His wife was Leah Kanner and his sons Abraham, Isaac and Gestar were domiciled in Vienna, Strasbourg and Paris. The sons were stated to be 32, 28 and 20 years of age at the time of their father's death.

The handful of Wahl families in Tarnobrzeg might well have been cousins. It seemed reasonable to attempt a search of Wahl descendants in other countries where some kind of Tarnobrzeg connection could be established.

When I consulted *Who's Who in France* and other reference works, I found numerous distinguished Wahls, but only one mention of Tarnobrzeg.[5] This was in an entry for Jacques Henri Wahl, who has held many high offices in the French Public Service. He is given as the son of Abraham Wahl and Simone Kornbluth, and the father of three children including Muriel Wahl. By coincidence, I had just received an enquiry from the latter via the internet. She was anxious to find out more about her grandfather's antecedents.

The information she gave me was that Abraham Moise had been born in Tarnobrzeg in 1895, that he was called Wahl after his mother, that he came from her first marriage to a Mr Farbmann, and that there was a brother, Pinchas, born in 1897, as well as other siblings. Abraham migrated to France between the two world wars, and settled in Lille where he married Sima Kornbluth. The wartime tragedy, which tore him from his family and ended with his death in Auschwitz in 1942, is recorded elsewhere. His wife and children were saved.

Extracts from the Tarnobrzeg Census Lists for 1880 and 1925 were kindly made available to me by the town's deputy mayor, Mr Tadeusz Zych.[6] On re-examination of the 1925 Census, I found several entries for Abraham Wahl around the year in question, and in some instances it was possible to correlate these entries with data in the 1880 List.

Firstly, Abraham Sulim Wahl is stated to be the son of Moses and Lea and born in Tarrnobrzeg in 1895, while a brother Isaac Naftali is recorded as born at Stanislau in 1898.[7] This ties in with the Viennese document. Moses Wahl is entered as born to Sulim and Sara Wahl in 1873 and variously in 1875. I believe the former to be the correct date. The lists also have Moses' brother, Chaim or Chaim Leib, born in 1869, the parents being given as Sulim Wahl and Sara Safier.

Secondly, the 1925 Census records the birth of a son, Abraham, to Chaim Shimon and Gitel Wahl in 1900. Chaim Shimon's birth is given as 1871 and his wife Gitel is stated to be from Tarnow, where their son Abraham was born. In the 1880 list Chaim again appears with his birth year of 1871 as the son of Shaya and Ester Wahl, who were born in 1844 and 1843.

Thirdly and finally, I found Abraham Moise Wahl and Pinchas David Wahl in the 1925 Census. They are recorded as born in Tarnobrzeg in 1895 and 1897 respectively, as the sons of Taube Hinde Wahl. I looked for her husband in the Tarnobrzeg Death Records covering the years 1904–28. There were three Farbmanns who died in the early years of the century, namely Jacob Josef Farbmann (3/12/1904), Moses Farbmann (12/12/1904), and Salaman Leib Farbmann (27/1/1910).[8] When I contacted Muriel's aunt, Monique, she identified Jacob Josef as her grandmother's first husband.[9] She also told me about her aunt Serala Galitzki, who had a daughter Therese, born in 1930. This particular family tree is thus shaping up as follows: Jacob Josef Farbmann and Taube Hinde Wahl had several children, including Abraham Moise, Pinchas David and Serala. Abraham Moise Wahl and Sima Kornbluth were the parents of Jacques Henri and Monique, who both have issue.

My own great-grandparents Shulim Wahl and Sarah Safier were born in 1838 and 1842. The above-mentioned Shaya Wahl might conceivably be a brother of Shulim Wahl. The dates are not to be completely relied on. In any case, it is quite likely that he was a cousin. His wife Gitel came from Tarnow, and, as was quite usual in those days, she would have gone to stay with her mother to give birth to her child. I noted previously that my great-uncle's second son, Isaac Naftali, was born in Stanislau, which was probably the hometown of his mother Lea Kanner. This is something to look out for in analysing the civil records. Another important point is that orthodox Jews in that period did not necessarily follow a rabbinical marriage with a civil ceremony. In such cases, the children would be entered in the birth records under the name of their mother.

There are evidently more French cousins to be linked to their roots in Galicia and elsewhere in the old Austro-Hungarian Empire.

NOTES

1. http://www.geopatronyme.com/cgi-bin/geopatro/avantgarde.cgi?nom=wahl&submit
2. Edward Gelles, 'Saul Wahl. A Jewish Legend', *Judaism Today,* 14 (Winter 1999–2000), p.36. Gelles, 'The Wahls of Nadworna', *Shemot*, 8, 3 (Sept. 2000), p.26. Gelles, 'All Quiet on the Eastern Front', *Avotaynu,* 16, 4 (Winter 2000), p.60. Gelles, 'Searching for Eve', *Avotaynu,* 17, 2 (Summer 2001), p.40.
3. Gelles, 'Abraham Low's Ship's Manifest', *Shemot*, 10, 2 (June 2002).
4. Magistrat der Stadt Wien, Abteilung 8. *Todfallsaufnahme, 10.8.1927. In the matter of Moses Wahl decd. 27.7.1927.*
5. *Who's Who in France* 2000–2001, pp.1785–6.
6. Tarnobrzeg Census Lists kept in the Archives at Sandomierz, Poland.
7. The Kanners of Stanislau included Rabbi Avraham Shalom Kanner, a wealthy and learned businessman, who having lost his fortune, served on the local Beth Din from 1900 to 1917.
8. Tarnobrzeg Death Records: www.shtetlinks.jewish.gen.org/Tarnobrzeg.
9. Mme Monique Gerlinger, private communication.

WAHL (Jacques, Henri), Inspecteur général des finances. **Né le** 18 janvier 1932 à Lille (Nord). **Fils d'**Abraham Wahl, Commerçant, **et de** Mme, née Simone Kornbluth. **Mar.** le 12 juin 1969 à Mlle Inna Cytrin (3 enf. : Alexandre, Muriel, Olivier-Cédric). **Etudes :** Collège moderne Franklin, Lycée Faidherbe à Lille, Facultés de droit de Lille et de Paris. **Dipl. :** Diplômé de l'Institut d'études politiques de Paris, Diplômé d'études supérieures de droit public, d'économie politique et de sciences économiques. **Carr. :** Elève à l'Ecole nationale d'administration (1959-61, major de sa promotion), Inspecteur des finances (depuis 1961), Chargé de mission auprès du conseiller financier de l'ambassade de France aux Etats-Unis (1965), Chargé de mission à la direction du Trésor pour l'assurance-crédit à l'exportation et les prêts aux gouvernements étrangers (depuis 1966), Secrétaire du conseil de direction du Fonds de développement économique et social (depuis 1967), Conseiller technique au cabinet de François-Xavier Ortoli (ministre de l'Economie et des Finances) (1968-69) puis au cabinet de Valéry Giscard d'Estaing (ministre de l'Economie et des Finances) (1969-71), Sous-directeur du Trésor pour les Affaires internationales multilatérales (1971), Ministre plénipotentiaire, Conseiller financier auprès des ambassades de France aux Etats-Unis et au Canada, Administrateur du Fonds monétaire international et du groupe de la Banque mondiale (1973-78), Secrétaire général adjoint (1978) puis Secrétaire général (1978-81) de la présidence de la République, Ancien maître de conférences à l'Institut d'études politiques de Paris et à l'Ecole nationale d'administration, Inspecteur général des finances (1981), Directeur général (1982), Vice-président du conseil d'administration (1993-97) de la Banque Nationale de Paris (BNP), Président (1993-97) de la BNP Intercontinentale (BNPI), Administrateur et Conseiller du président-directeur général de la BNP, Membre du comité de direction générale de la BNP (depuis 1994). **Décor. :** Officier de la Légion d'honneur et de l'ordre national du Mérite, Commandeur de l'ordre national de la Côte d'Ivoire, Officier de l'ordre national de la République centrafricaine, Chevalier de l'ordre national de Haute-Volta, Grand Officier de l'ordre d'Adolphe de Nassau (Luxembourg), de l'Etoile équatoriale (Gabon), de l'ordre du Mérite de la République fédérale d'Allemagne et de l'Etoile polaire (Suède). **Dist. :** Lauréat de la faculté de droit de Lille. **Adr. :** prof., BNP, 19 bd des Italiens, 75009 Paris; privée, 15 av. de la Bourdonnais, 75007 Paris.

Figure 16
Jacques Henri Wahl (French 'Who's Who')

Chapter Fifteen

The Griffels

A clan spread far and wide

THE BACKGROUND

The Griffels came from Lvov and two small towns lying to the south of that city: Stanislau, where Jews had lived since the Potocki grant of 1662, and Nadworna, which decreased in relative importance during the period of Austrian rule. Nadworna was an early stronghold of the *Chasidic* movement, but from the middle of the nineteenth century the *Haskalah*, and later the Zionist movement, made their impact on these communities. The First World War saw Russian occupation of the region, followed by the authority of a temporary West Ukrainian republic, before the area became part of Poland from 1919 to 1939. In the inter-war period the economic situation for the Jews was improving, there was a thriving cultural life, and the continued hold of the ancient faith was evidenced by the existence of 55 synagogues and prayer houses in Stanislau. This world came to an end in 1939. The area passed under Soviet control. Some Jews managed to flee in time, others were taken away to Russia, and the rest had a brief respite until Hitler's 1941 attack. The towns were occupied by Hungarian troops, the Ukrainians were responsible for massacres, and shortly thereafter came German occupation and the mass murders that are on record. Today there are a mere handful of Jews in Nadworna and Stanislau, which now lie, with changed names, within the Ukrainian republic.

GRIFFEL ANCESTRY

Reb Eliezer Griffel, known as Zeida, was the son of David Mendel and Taube Griffel of Nadworna, where he was born in 1850. He became the patriarch of our branch of the family. According to good authority, he had in his house an ornate tablet inscribed with gold lettering, which set out the family descent from David Halevi Segal (1586–1667), the Chief Rabbi of Lvov.[1] Called the *Taz* after his classical commentary entitled the *Turei Zahav,* he was the son-in-law of Chief Rabbi Joel Sirkes of Cracow.

Zeida Griffel was the head of the Jewish community, and played a leading role in his town's economic and social life. He gave his religious allegiance to the rabbis of the Hager *Chasidic* dynasty. The Nadworna Memorial Book relates that he and his sons and sons-in-law prayed regularly in the synagogue of the Rabbi of near-by Ottynia.[2] There was at least one marriage connecting these two families.[3] The family tree of the Hagers shows their descent from the *Taz* (see note to Table 13). Incidentally, the Hagers also had connections by marriage with another great Chasidic dynasty, the Friedmans of Ruzhyn, and indeed with the family of R' Pinchas Shapiro of Koretz.[4]

Forebears of the Griffels in the eighteenth century include a Rav Leiser Neches of Lemberg and Rav Jacob Leib of the same city. The family in all its diversity developed in Nadworna, Stanislau, Lvov, Cracow, Vienna and elsewhere. Some moved from Nadworna to Stanislau as the nineteenth century progressed. Records of their presence in Lvov and Cracow are increasingly accessible on the Internet.

Zeida Griffel married Sarah Matel Chayes of Kolomea and had a family of ten children, who are recorded in the appended lists. This branch has survived from the mid-nineteenth century to the present day, despite the devastation and anguish of the holocaust in which many, including my own grandparents, perished. After Eliezer, perhaps the outstanding Griffel of the line was his grandson, Dr Jacob Griffel.[5]

OTHER GRIFFEL LINES

Griffels branched out in many directions. There were Griffels in Vienna whose vital records are kept by the Jewish Community Office in that city.[6] From Reb Zeida's cousin, Meir Leib Griffel (b.1828?), there is descent to the Zauderer and Hirsch families via his daughters, while his sisters Lea (1844–1915) and Frieda married Mordechai Wiesner (Weisner) and Fishel Ephraim Wiesel (Weisel). The latters' son, Mendel Wiesel had numerous progeny. These names are to be found on the Nadworna memorial list of holocaust victims. From Lea Griffel there is a line of descent to Louis Wiesner and then to his daughter Rosa Wiesner who married Samuel Kosloff. Louis Wiesner's sister Rachel and Shlomo Schieber were the parents of Sarah, whose husband David was the son of Chaim Yoshua Rose of Stanislau. The latter took the name of Griffel on marrying Gittel Griffel of Nadworna. This David Rose or Griffel worked for my great-uncle Isaac Chaim Griffel, and is not to be confused with my grandfather David Mendel Griffel who, with his brother Isaac Chaim, was the principal successor to their father Zeida's business empire. In 1940 David Rose and Sarah with their boy Max were taken to Siberia. Max was pressed into service with the Red Army and was decorated by the Russians. After the war he studied medicine in Munich, married a Scottish lady, Margaret Urquhart, and settled in New Jersey, where he practised as a physician and brought up his family. I have spoken to him about his experiences.

Some other details obtained from Dr David S. Goldstein[7] tally remarkably well with the rough notes prepared by my late cousin Shmuel Shmelke who was one of the ten children of Isaac Chaim Griffel.[8] His Second World War experiences contrast with those of Dr Max Griffel. Shmuel ended up in a Russian Gulag, from which he was ultimately rescued by his brother Jacob.

The Nadworna branch of the Griffels is mentioned in other chapters.[9] These deal with the three Wahl girls Blume, Rachel and Chawa, who married into the Loew, Taube and Griffel families, with the connections of the Loews and the Friedman Rabbis of Czortkow and of the Nadworna Griffels with the Hager Rabbis of Ottynia, with the inter-marriages of Wahl, Griffel and Lamm families, linking the towns of Nadworna and Stanislau in eastern Galicia with Tarnobrzeg and Cracow in the west of the province, and so on. I mentioned Dr Steven Lamm who is a grandson of my great-aunt Zissel Griffel.[10]

Chaya Griffel was another great-aunt of mine. She and Shlomo Gruenfeld produced a son, Samuel. The latter and Sitka Hager had a boy named Yehuda, who adopted a Hebrew version of the surname. This Dr Yehuda Nir is a prominent psychiatrist in America. His pedigree is shown in Table 13. His autobiography, *The Lost Childhood*, contains references to the connection with the Hager family.

Once the ancient Griffel family was united in their ultra-orthodox faith. Now they are scattered all over the world, but at least one branch clings to their *Chasidic* past. I refer to some of Isaac Chaim's sons, notably Jacob and Shmuel Shmelke Griffel. Their brother, Yehoshua Heshel (Henry) Griffel was also intellectually distinguished. He obtained degrees in law and political science from the University of Cracow, his interests being in constitutional law and jurisprudence. In addition he gained his rabbinical qualification or 'Smicha'. After he brought his family to America in 1946, he took a position as a Conservative Rabbi. From his very orthodox beginnings he became a leading light of ecumenism. For many years he served as President of the New Jersey Interfaith Clergy Council. His son Andrew Griffel, whose charitable work I mentioned in a previous article, took after him in holding to the major tenets of Judaism, acquaintance with the classical Judaic texts, belief in the spiritual strength to be gained from the Jewish religion and the history of the Jewish people, and the duty to help others including those from different religious and ethnic backgrounds.

THE FAMILY OF MY GRANDPARENTS

The descendants of my grandparents, David Mendel Griffel of Nadworna and Chawa Wahl of Tarnobrzeg, came under the influence of Viennese culture at the outbreak of the First World War. My mother Regina and her brothers Zygmunt and Edward were already fairly assimilated and they were at an impressionable age. They continued to have much closer ties with their maternal cousins of the Loew and Taube families, and with Zygmunt's in-laws, the Wohls of Cracow, than with the other Griffels.

Zygmunt Griffel and his wife Maryla Suesser had one son, my first cousin Eric. He attained a high position in the US Foreign service and on retirement owned a bookshop in New Hampshire. He now lives in Washington, DC. My favourite uncle Edward, after whom I was named, was a cosmopolitan globetrotter. When he married much later in life we had been separated by the vicissitudes of war and ill fortune. My first cousin David Mendel (named after his grandfather) was Edward Griffel's only son. He studied at M.I.T. and became a successful entrepreneur in Boston, Massachusetts. Through his mother Susan, and her rabbinical forebears, the Manzons, he is descended from Israel Friedman, the founder and head of the great Ruzhin *Chasidic* dynasty. (For Gelles connections with the Friedmans of Czortkow see chapters 35 and 36.)[11]

Figure 17
Zygmunt Griffel

NOTES

1. Boruch Griffel, Jerusalem (son of Shmuel Shmelke Griffel), private communication.
2. Nadworna Memorial Book (Landsmannschaft of Nadworna in Israel and the United States, 1975), p.26.
3. Dr Yehuda Nir, *The Lost Childhood* (New York: Harcourt, Brace, Jovanovich, 1989).

Figure 18
Edward Griffel

4. Dr N.M. Gelber, 'TheVishnitz Zaddikim-Dynasty', in Hugo Gold, *Geschichte der Juden in der Bukowina* (Tel Aviv: Olamenu, 1958), pp.89–90.
5. Edward Gelles, 'Jacob Griffel's Rescue Missions' (unpublished article). See also David Kranzler, *Thy Brother's Blood* (New York: Mesorah, 1987) and (with Eliezer Gevirtz), *To Save a World* (New York, London, Jerusalem: CIS, 1991); and Joseph Friedenson, *Dateline Istanbul* (New York: Mesorah, 1993).
6. Israelitische Kultusgemeinde, Wien 1010, Seitenstettengasse 4. For instance, Jacob Griffel (Buczacz 1863–Vienna 1926) and his wife Chaye Etel Zierler (Stanislau 1869–Vienna 1930) had a son Joseph Griffel (1907–89). The latter and his wife Klara Fischer (Poland 1908– ?1964) were the parents of Leonard Michael Griffel and Jack Griffel (Vienna 1938–) who married Marsha Zakheim (New York 1942–).
7. Dr David S. Goldstein, Baltimore, Maryland (cousin of Dr Max Griffel), private communication.
8. Shmuel Shmelke Griffel (son of Isaac Chaim Griffel), private notes.
9. Edward Gelles, 'My Mother's People', *Sharsheret Hadorot*, 16, 4 (Oct. 2002).
10. See Chapters 20 and 21.
11. Neil Rosenstein, *The Unbroken Chain* (New York, London, Jerusalem: CIS Publishers 1990), Vol.2, p.940 whose entry is: 'wife of Griffel. Their son David Griff' this should read 'Susan Manzon, wife of Edward Griffel. Their son David Mendel Griffel'.

Table 13
GRIFFEL FAMILY CHARTS

CHILDREN OF ELIEZER GRIFFEL (1850–1918) AND SARAH MATEL CHAYES (d. 1940)

(Birth Dates from JRI-Poland Records of Nadworna and Krakow)

1. David Mendel Griffel (1875-1941) m. Chawa Wahl (1877-1941)
   Chawa was a daughter of Shulim Wahl and Sarah Safier
   Issue: Zygmunt, Regina (Rivka), and Edward (Isaac Chaim)
   see above and Chapter 12 (My Mother's People)
2. Machla Griffel (b. 1876) m. Benzion Wilner
3. Zissel Griffel (b. 1878) m. Zygmunt (Shalom) Lamm
4. Isaac Chaim Griffel (1880-1930) m. Judith Breit (d. 1938)
   Judith was a daughter of Moses Breit (b.1856) and Rebeka Freilich (b.1855)
   Issue: see following table
5. Shaya Griffel (b. 1883) m. Adela Englard
6. Leibish Griffel (b. 1885) m. Ziporah
7. Benjamin Griffel (b. 1887) m. Chana Kahan
8. Rivka Griffel (b. 1888) m. Berish Rapaport

9 Rachel Griffel (b. 1892) m. Bonya (Abraham) Ohrenstein

10. Chaya Griffel (d. 1918) m. Shlomo Gruenfeld

CHILDREN OF ISAAC CHAIM GRIFFEL AND JUDITH BREIT

1. Jacob Griffel (1900–1962) m(1) Feiga Freilich (d.1942),
   m(2) Miriam Devora (Dora) Rottenberg (1914–1998)
   Issue: see Chapter 16 (Jacob Griffel's Rescue Missions)
2. Taube Griffel m. Shmuel Rosenbaum
3. Machla Griffel
4. David Mendel Griffel (1902–) m. Leah Aichenbaum
5. Rachel Griffel m. Zalman Horowitz
6. Beila Griffel
7. Shalom Griffel m. Rega Fortgang
8. Yehoshua Heshel (Henry) Griffel (1910–1968) m. Pola (Sura-Perl) Werchaizer (1918–2000)
   Issue: Andrew (Israel Isaac) and Judy (Yehudis) Griffel

9 Shmuel Shmelke Griffel (1913–1999) m. Chana Rosefeld
   Issue: Yitzchak Isaac Chaim, Boruch Elimelech, Yudith Miriam, Moshe Eliezer, and Rivka Sarah Griffel

10 Rivka Griffel (1918–)

Pedigree of Dr Yehuda Nir

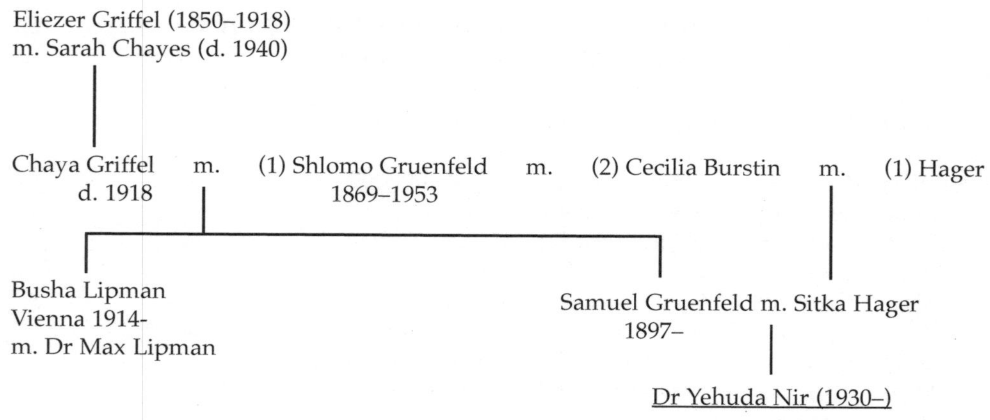

Descendants of Gittel Griffel and Chaim Yoshua Rose

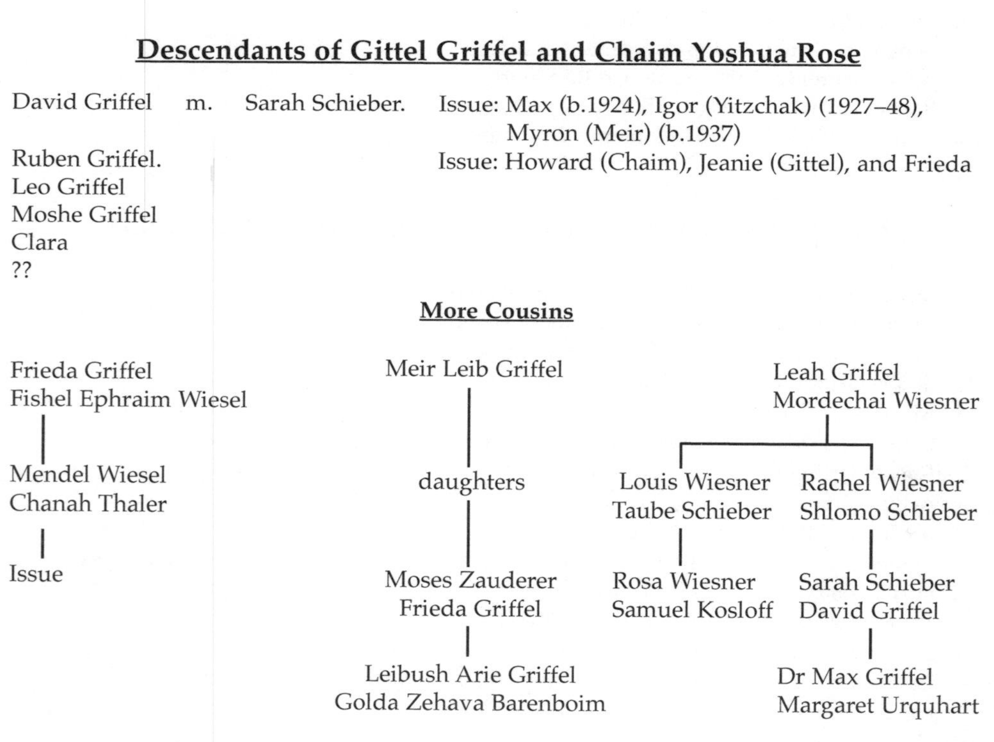

Figure 19
Judith Breit, wife of Isaac Chaim Griffel

ADDITIONAL NOTES

Leah Griffel (1844–1915). Mendel Wiesel, born Nadworna circa 1870. Rosa Wiesner (Czernowitz 1901–New York 1990). Samuel Kosloff (1894–1954). Sarah Schieber (Roumania 1901– ?1987). David (Rose) Griffel (Stanislau 1889–New York 1970). Dr Max Griffel (Nadworna 1924–). Margaret Urquhart (Scotland 1926–). Leibush Arie Griffel (Nadworna 1907–Haifa 1961). Golda Zehava Barenboim (1910–2001).
Yigal Griffel, the one-time acting mayor of Tel Aviv, deserves more than this brief mention.

A Griffel-Babad Connection

Rivka Griffel, a sister of Eliezer (Zeida) Griffel, married Chaim Brandwein. Their daughter Yente Babad was the mother of Reb Yakov Babad, who owned the well-known Babad Hotel in Jerusalem. The widespread Babad family descended from Isaac 'Krakower', the son of Yissachar Baer, who was a son of the distinguished scholar Abraham Joshua Heshel of Cracow (1596–1663). The latter was descended from the Maharam of Padua on both his father's and mother's side.

Ancestral Connections of the Hager Family

R' Jacob Kopel ben Nehemia Feiwel of Kolomea was a pupil of the founder of the Chasidic movement, the Baal Schem Tov. The mother of Kopel's wife Chaya was a descendant of R' David Halevi Segal of Lvov. R' Kopel's second son, R'Menachem Mendel (1768–1826) started the Kossow dynasty. He was succeeded by his son R' Chaim (1795–1854), who married Zipora, a granddaughter of R' Pinchas Shapiro of Koretz. Their eldest son took over the Kossower dynasty while their youngest son, R' Menachem Mendel Hager married Miriam, daughter of the Ruzhyner Zaddik, and founded the Vishnitz dynasty. He died in 1885. His son R' Baruch (1845–93) had many children. The latter's second son R' Chaim Hager settled in Ottynia, but moved to Stanislawow in 1919 and died there in 1932. (N.M. Gelber, 'The Vishnitz-Zaddikim Dynasty', in Hugo Gold, *Geschichte der Juden in der Bukowina* (Tel Aviv: Olamenu, 1958), pp.89–90).

The Galician Oilfields

The principal activities of Eliezer Griffel were connected with timber and oil. Reference has already been made to the numerous entries in the Nadworna Memorial Book and *Arim ve-Imahot be-Israel* (vol.5. Stanislau). Members of the Griffel family were involved in these large scale enterprises for three generations. An outline history of the Galician oil industry is given by Valerie Schatzker ('Oil in Galicia', *The Galitzianer*, 9, 4 (Aug. 2002), pp.6–9 – 'From the middle of the nineteenth century, the area around Drohobycz, Boryslaw, Tustanowice, Schodnica and other towns in the Drohobycz administrative district became known as the Galician California … At the turn of the century Galicia was fourth in the rank of oil producers in the world ... after 1910 … production started to slow down'). Eliezer's grandson, Dr Jacob Griffel, was actively involved in the oil business and lived for a time at Boryslaw.

Figure 20
Dr Jacob Griffel (1900–62)

CHAPTER SIXTEEN

Jacob Griffel's Rescue Missions

A life of heroic faith and service

Two of Eliezer Griffel's children were principally involved in his inheritance. They were my grandfather David Mendel and his brother Isaac Chaim. My mother Regina and her first cousin Jacob were born in the same year 1900. At the dawn of the twentieth century all seemed set fair for the large Griffel clan with their widespread business empire. With the First World War and Eliezer's death in 1918, the family drifted apart. Some remained in the new Polish republic and loyal to their orthodox persuasion, others stayed in Vienna or migrated further west, seeking their fortunes in more liberal climes. My mother and her two brothers were by that time quite assimilated, while Jacob and some of his siblings kept tenaciously to their *Chasidic* way of life.

Jacob Griffel's life started so auspiciously, was marred by great tragedy, and ended prematurely, but with a large measure of fulfilment. He found his mission and obeyed its call to the last. From the time his first wife and their children perished in Poland to the end of his days he devoted himself to saving and helping his fellow Jews. He was truly a servant of his God.

Unusually for such a devout Jew, Jacob sought a secular education at the Universities of Cracow and Vienna. He became a doctor of law and involved himself in the family oil business. He married Feiga, the daughter of Chaim Freilich of Cracow. At the outbreak of war in 1939 he sent his wife with their two children, Zipora and Eliezer, to the presumed safety of central Poland, where they were engulfed by the German *Blitzkrieg*. He never saw or heard from them again, and they supposedly perished in 1942.

Jacob had stayed in the southeastern corner of the country near the oil fields, and managed to slip over the border into Roumania, ultimately making his way to Palestine. He immediately threw himself into the work of helping Jews in Nazi-occupied Europe. In 1943 he was sent to join the Committee of Rescue in Istanbul, where he worked day and night with the Jewish leadership in Palestine, through all available diplomatic channels, and with the Jewish underground, rallying worldwide political opinion, arranging permits, supplying travel documents, raising funds for rescue work, and lending a hand to those who were bargaining with their persecutors for Jewish lives. There is no doubt that he was instrumental in saving many thousands of souls. After 1945, his efforts did not cease. He threw himself into helping displaced persons and rescuing Jews caught up in the Soviet Union. He managed to extract one of his brothers from a Russian Gulag.

Later on, he made great efforts to bring orphaned and adopted Jewish children back into the fold. He went to live in the United States in 1950, where he married Miriam Devora (Dora) Rottenberg and raised a second family, his surviving children being Joseph Isaac Chaim and Sara Rivka Griffel. He died in 1962.

The full horror of Jewish oppression in Nazi occupied Europe did not become apparent until 1942. Even then, the priorities of the Allied war effort, of the Catholic Church, and even of some Jewish organizations delayed effective action for too long. The Zionist leadership in Palestine wished to concentrate their resources on securing and building up their base in the Holy Land and bringing in enthusiastic young people of working age, while the ultra-orthodox party were anxious to help any persecuted Jews. Finally, the Jewish Agency got together with various political groupings to set up the Committee in Istanbul, chaired by Chaim Barlas of the Agency, and including Venia Pomerantz of Mapai, Menachem Bader of Hashomer Hatza'ir, Jacob Klarman of the Zionist Revisionists, and Jacob Griffel associated with Agudath Israel.

Jacob Griffel was uniquely qualified for the work to which he devoted himself with his immense energy. He was reported to have installed a bed in his office so that he should never miss any message or allow even an hour's delay in any possible rescue attempt. He was a *Chasidic* Jew with the highest educational qualifications and wide secular culture. He had a commanding presence and charisma. He could talk with equal facility to orthodox rabbis, Marxist Zionists, American diplomats, and Papal nuncios, and gain the respect and trust of these as well as of the Jewish underground leaders in occupied Europe. His legal training and wide business experience also served him well. His passionate aim was to use any means to save any Jew of whatever religious or political hue. Griffel maintained contacts with the authorities in Palestine, with America, with diplomats in neutral countries, and with many committed rescue workers.

To quote Dr David Kranzler, they were such as Israel Chaim Eis in Switzerland and the Sternbuchs, who frequently relayed messages to New York, forwarded funds to him, and generally worked together on several major rescue efforts. He communicated with R' Eliezer Hager, the Rebbe of Vishnitz, and R' Sucha Portugal, the Admur of Skulen, who passed on vital information on the condition of Roumanian Jewry. Most importantly, he kept in touch with Rabbi Michael Dov Weissmandel in Slovakia, who knew he could trust Griffel more than anyone else on the Jewish Agency's Istanbul delegation. Weissmandel sent him the coded message calling for the bombing of the railway lines to Auschwitz from the post office in Bratislava.

Undoubtedly the best-known rescue efforts of this period were Weissmandel's negotiations with Dieter Wisliceny, the SS officer who was deputy to Eichmann, which achieved a substantial delay in the deportation of Slovakian Jewry, and the daring attempt of the Hungarian Joel Brand to barter with Eichmann himself for the lives of a million Jews in return for ten thousand trucks.

Griffel was also involved in much work that did not hit the headlines, but it may well be that the relative neglect of his great services is due to the undoubted strains between the ultra-orthodox and those who differed on aims and methods. A fresh assessment will surely be added in due course to the literature on the subject.

NOTES

1. John Mendelsohn, *The Holocaust: Relief and Rescue of Jews from Nazi Oppression 1943–45* (Garland, New York 1982), pp.47–51.
2. Abraham Fuchs, *The Unheeded Cry* (New York and Jerusalem: Mesorah Publications, 1983).
3. David Kranzler, *Thy Brother's Blood* (New York: Mesorah Publications, 1987).
4. David Kranzler and Eliezer Gevirtz, *To Save a World* (New York, London, Jerusalem: CIS Publishers, 1991), Ch. 4.
5. Joseph Friedenson, *Dateline Istanbul* (New York: Mesorah Publications, 1993).

Numerous references on the Internet include the evidence submitted by Dr Griffel at the Eichmann trial, as well as differing Orthodox and Zionist assessments of the period.

Chapter Seventeen

Andrew Griffel

Representing the next generation of Griffels

Dr Jacob Griffel's life and work is now part of the history of the holocaust and its aftermath. The eventful history of the Griffel family remains to be written. There are many heroic and tragic tales to tell. Some of them concern the families of Jacob's siblings. Yehoshua Heshel (Henry) Griffel was Jacob's younger brother, who survived the war in Poland and then brought his family to America, where he became a Conservative Rabbi. His son Andrew was born in 1942 in the Polish town of Radom, while the 'Final Solution' was in full force and the Nazis were liquidating the ghetto and sending Jews to the Treblinka concentration camp. Half a century later, Andrew wrote

> The Polish workers in my grandfather's leather factor smuggled my mother from the ghetto to the factory where she gave birth in hiding; 20 of the Polish workers stood guard and then whisked me away to safety. Barely a day old, I was immediately handed over to a Polish family who raised me as their own child for the next three years. My parents escaped from a Nazi labour camp and were taken a hundred miles north to Warsaw where they were hidden in the basement of a Polish family's house for the duration of the war. We all miraculously survived, and at war's end we were reunited. We lived in a displaced person's camp for a year and came to America in 1946. Tragically and sadly, however, most of our near relations perished.

It is not altogether surprising that Andrew's father, who had enjoyed as orthodox an upbringing as Jacob, became increasingly interested in ecumenical affairs. For many years he served as the President of the New Jersey Interfaith Clergy Council.

Andrew Griffel learned from his early experiences that Jews and non-Jews can live together and help each other. So many Polish Catholics risked their own lives to save him and his parents. His attitude was reinforced when he lived in Israel in a part of Jerusalem that was next to Arab neighbourhoods. His service in the Israeli Army as a Military Judge in the West Bank and Lebanon showed him, ironically perhaps, that Jews and Arabs do not have to be enemies. Thus, after a 'first' career as an international lawyer and economic consultant, he chose to devote himself to charitable work. He was President and Chief Executive Officer of the American Jewish World Service, an international humanitarian agency, and was on the Executive Board of InterAction, a consortium of over two hundred humanitarian organizations of all faiths. He founded the Jewish Volunteer Corps, which sends skilled professionals to the developing world. He has helped the poor and underprivileged people in Africa, Latin America and Asia. Recently, he has been working with Palestinians in the West Bank/Gaza and Arab citizens of Israel to help improve their economic conditions with the hope that this will give them a greater incentive and stake in maintaining a peaceful coexistence with Israel.

His activities can be followed on the Internet, which carried a report of Andrew recently joining the Harvard University-affiliated Center for Middle East Competitive Strategy as its Executive Director.

The tragedy that robbed Andrew of his first wife Anita and Tali of her mother is related on the web page of *Americans for Peace Now.* In October 1985 Anita and Tali, who was then 5 years old, went on a vacation to Sinai. The group of Israeli tourists was suddenly attacked and massacred by a crazed Egyptian soldier. Tali was the only survivor of the attack because her dying mother sheltered her with her body.

Tali is a brave young woman. After attending Brown University in America she served for two years in the Israeli army. Then she went to the Hebrew University in Jerusalem and subsequently devoted herself to the cause of Arab-Israeli reconciliation. She is now engaged in helping victims of terrorism at the Hadassah hospital.

NOTES

www.ajws.org/andy.htm
www.peacenow.org/publications/int_ag.html
www.bronfman.org/newsletters/2003springnewsletter.pdf

Chapter Eighteen

The Wohls of Cracow

Kinsfolk of Wahl descent

When I was a child in Vienna I often heard the story that my maternal grandmother's family was descended from Saul Wahl, the community leader, royal adviser, and legendary 'One-day King of Poland'.

The genealogy of Saul's family, the Katzenellenbogen rabbis of Padua and Venice, and their descendants has been the subject of much study.[1] Not least among those claiming a connection with the Katzenellenbogens are the Samuel family, whose chronicler published some interesting material just before the First World War. He referred to one Meir Wohl of the Cracow banking house, A. Holzer & Co., who was supposed to have an unassailable pedigree going back to Saul Wahl.[2] I knew that we had a cousin called Artur Wohl, who had a private bank in Zurich in the 1930s. But it was not until many decades later that I established my own links with the Wohl mentioned by J. Burnford Samuel in 1912. We do not know what documentary evidence of Wahl descent was available to the author at that date, referring as he does to an unpublished manuscript, but his book at least confirms that these claims had been around for a long time.

When I found my long-lost cousin Eric Griffel recently, he told me that his mother was the granddaughter of Meir Wohl and Feigla Holzer of Cracow. By this time I knew about the genealogical records of the *JRI-Poland* project.[3] I searched the Internet and managed to dovetail findings in the birth and marriage records of Cracow with anecdotal information from my cousin. Thus the connection between the two separate Wahl families became apparent, one based in Cracow and the other in the little town of Tarnobrzeg, to the northeast of the capital city. The story illustrates the scope of this kind of Internet search.

Meir Wohl married Feigla Holzer, who was heiress to a large fortune.[4] He took over the running of the Cracow family bank, which established a branch in Vienna some time before the First World War. His son Artur Wohl inherited his father's business acumen. He became a partner in the Zurich bank, Wohl und Landau. After the Second World War his family moved to Brazil, where his son Steven Wohl still lives. Salomon and Feigla also had three daughters Sidonie, Anna and Eugenia.

The Cracow records, which are available on *Jewish Gen* sites, have many gaps, and their interpretation often requires knowledge of contemporary Jewish customs and civil regulations. Thus we have an entry for the marriage of Salomon Meir Wohl and Feigla Holzer in 1893, and also a record for the birth in 1881 of a Sarah Wohl/Holzer. The marriages are listed of Sarah Wohl, Anna Wohl and Eugenia Wahl (*sic*) for the years 1899, 1914 and 1921 respectively. There is no mention of a Sidonie Wohl or Holzer in the available birth or marriage records.

The explanation must be that Salo and Feigla had a rabbinical marriage around 1880, and that their eldest child was recorded under her Jewish name of Sarah and described as Wohl/Holzer. She was the issue of this marriage and the civil ceremony came much later. This was not an uncommon occurrence at that time. The indicated date of the parents' religious marriage is compatible with that of Feigla's parents, Aaron Holzer and Rachel Karmel of Cracow, which is given as 1850.

We gather from the marriage records that Salomon Meir was the son of Moses Wohl and of a Malka Cypres of Cracow. His eldest child Sarah (Sidonie) married Bendet or Benedikt Suesser of Cracow and they had several children including Maryla, born in 1909. The Suessers were a prominent Jewish family in Cracow. Maryla married Zygmunt Griffel and their offspring is my first cousin Eric Griffel of Washington, DC.

Salo and Feigla's only son Artur married firstly Teresa Mieses, and secondly Gisa Stieglitz, having issue from both unions. Artur's sister Anna perished in the holocaust with her husband Leon Wald. The youngest sibling, Eugenia married Leon Raab and their surviving children are Stefanie Mach of London and Riane Gruss of New York.

The Griffels descended from Eliezer Griffel of Nadworna spread to Stanislau, Lemberg, Cracow and beyond. My grandfather, David Mendel Griffel of Nadworna, married Chawa Wahl. There were Wahls in Nadworna whose lineage undoubtedly went back to sixteenth century Padua, but Chawa turned out to be from Tarnobrzeg.[5] It is not surprising that descendants of Saul Wahl were to be found in many Polish towns, as this ancient clan multiplied over the centuries. We shall see in Chapter 20 that there were close family ties between Nadworna and Tarnobrzeg.

As for the genealogy of the Samuel family, in connection with which Salo Meir Wohl first came to my attention, this is in a process of reassessment since the publication of an article by Neil Rosenstein and Dov Weber.[6]

The Samuels were essentially of the Halpern clan and adopted the name Pulvermacher (manufacturer of gunpowder). Thus Moses Samuel (1741–1839), the son of Samuel Pulvermacher of Krotoschin, who became a very rich and well-connected pillar of the Jewish community in London, claimed descent from Saul Wahl.[7] The Halperns and Katzenellenbogens touch at several points in the complex family tree, but the pedigrees put forward by earlier writers including Hirsch Edelman and Burnford Samuel have to be revised in several important respects.

NOTES

1. Neil Rosenstein, *The Unbroken Chain* (New York, London, Jerusalem: CIS Publishers, 1990).
2. J. Burnford Samuel, *The History of the Samuels*, Philadelphia: Lippincott, 1912).
3. JRI-Poland Web Site for Cracow Civil Records http://data.jewishgen.org/jgen/wc.dll?jgproc~jgsys~jr.
4. Aaron Holzer and Rachella Karmel had a large family. Feigla Holzer Wohl had five brothers, Isaac, Elias, Leon, Adolph and Sigmund, whose later descendants flourished in England, America and elsewhere. One branch (from Elias' son Ludwig) became very wealthy in Mexico. Lolek Holzer, grandson of Sigmund, who lives in London has provided me with a family tree of the Holzer family.
5. Y.L. Maimon (ed.), *Arim ve-imahot be-Ysrael* (Mother Communities of Israel) (Jersualem: Mossad HaRav Kook, 1952), Vol.5 (Stanislau), pp.63, 212, 213, 219, 233, 311, 314. Nadworna Memorial Book (Landsmannschaft of Nadworna, Israel and the United States, 1975), pp.25–6. Edward Gelles, 'The Wahls of Nadworna', *Shemot*, 8, 2 (Sept. 2000), pp.26–9 and 8, 4 (Dec. 2000), pp.31–3. Gelles, 'Searching for Eve: A Methodological Lesson', *Avotaynu*, xvii, 2 (Summer 2001).
6. Neil Rosenstein and Dov Weber, 'The Edelman Hoax and the Origins of Anglo-Jewish Aristocracy', *Avotaynu*, xiv, 2 (Summer 1998).
7. Cecil Roth, *History of the Great Synagogue* (London: Edward Goldston & Son Ltd, 1950), p.194.

Table 14
WAHL OF TARNOBRZEG AND WOHL OF CRACOW

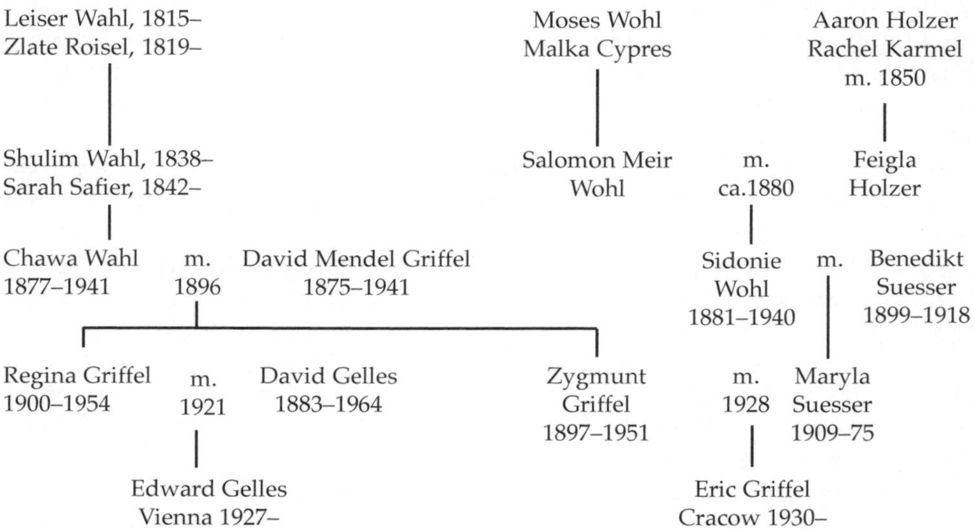

Chapter Nineteen

The Safiers of Tarnobrzeg

My great-grandmother's family with Wahl and Taube connections

The names Saphir, Sapir, Safier and other variants may hark back to one kind of precious stone that adorned the breastplate of the ancient high priests. The Safiers of Dzikow, who spelled their name in this way, were possibly related to other Safiers in Cracow, Opatow and elsewhere in Austrian Galicia.

The story is told that a Safier of Dzikow had been a court jester in eighteenth-century Prussia. A Josef Safier is recorded in the Tarnobrzeg inventory of 1791.[1] Wahls and Safiers were in Dzikow-Tarnobrzeg for a long time and rose to considerable affluence in the nineteenth century. These families of my great-grandparents, with their in-laws from various parts of Galicia, were involved in the management of land and its natural resources, in the timber trade and ownership of forests, and in other commodities.[2]

Moses and Samuel Wahl and Josek Safier appear on the Tarnobrzeg taxation lists of alcohol sellers for 1816 and 1822.[3] Licences or concessions for such business were obtained from the overlords, the Counts Tarnowski, and often formed the starting point to the making of some individual fortunes. One generation might be innkeepers, the next were timber merchants, and the third owned estates and carried on a merchant banking business. Thus Leiser Wahl, who was born in 1815, appeared in the town records as a timber merchant, but his son Shulim, born in 1838, is described as a capitalist.[4]

Shulim's wife Sarah Safier was born in 1842. The Census Lists for 1880 and 1925 give her and her husband's names and their years of birth, as well as the names and birth years of their children, Chaim Leib 1869, Moses 1873, Ziporah 1875, Chawa 1877 and Rachel 1879. I have not found a record of Sarah's parents. However, there is considerable information on other Safiers right up to the eve of the Second World War. The Yizkor Book for Dzikow mentions the brothers Chaim and Elimelech (Meilech) Safier, who were among the wealthiest in the town. They owned forests and had other business interests. Chaim died just before the war, but Meilech and his wife Gitel perished in the holocaust.[5]

According to the Census Lists, Chaim was born in 1868 and Meilech in 1872. I have also identified their parents as Moses and Szysia Safier, born in

1843 and 1845 (see Table 15). Further details are given in the appended Notes.

I recently turned up hitherto unknown cousins in America and Australia on the Internet. Dr Emil Safier of Los Angeles is a grandson of Meilech,[6] and Dr Marcel Safier is descended from Chaim.[7]

Emil's father, Isaac Safier was born in Tarnobrzeg in 1903. He and his wife Sabina Zamorje lived there until the outbreak of the Second World War. They fled eastwards to the USSR and spent most of the war in Siberia. Eventually Isaac joined the British army and Sabina became a nurse. They wound up in Jerusalem where Emil was born in 1944. In the 1950s they emigrated to America. Isaac died in 1978, but his sister Carola, who survived the war in Berlin under an assumed Christian identity, lives in Florida and has a flourishing progeny. Emil Safier obtained a doctorate in theoretical physics. Later he settled in Los Angeles where he has built up a computer software company. Dr Marcel Safier is an Australian physician descended from Chaim Safier via his daughter Klara. His family web page provides leads to several other Safier descendants. Particularly interesting from the point of view of my own family tree was my discovery of the Welners. They were not only descendants of Chaim Safier of Tarnobrzeg but also had a Taube ancestry. My great-aunt, Rachel Wahl of Tarnobrzeg, had married Abraham Taube of Lemberg. Starting with my Wahl-Safier ancestors and Wahl-Taube alliance, there now suddenly appeared a Safier-Taube marriage to enter into the family nexus.

Isaac ben Chaim Safier married Sarah Taube. One of their youngest daughter's sons, Dr Michael Mark Welner, is a prominent forensic scientist.[8] When I managed to contact Barbara Welner, I heard that her father Isaac Safier had been a prosperous timber merchant. He was also a learned Talmud scholar, who had obtained his *Smichah*, or rabbinical diploma, and an accomplished violinist, who had studied at the Vienna Conservatoire. His wife Sarah was the daughter of Feivel Taube and Golda Ginsberg of Lemberg. Both of Sarah's parents came from orthodox Jewish families, which included several rabbis. One of Sarah's brothers was Rabbi Mordechai Taube of Lvov. Isaac's father-in-law Feivel was a major property developer with land near Przemysl, and that is where the young couple made their home. Barbara was only a child when she escaped from the catastrophe that overtook Polish Jewry and most of her family. She lived in England for a while, met her husband Nick Welner, who was a civil engineer, became a nurse, went to Canada, and finally settled in the United States. The Taube family was mainly from Lemberg (Lvov) and included estate owners and merchants. Some were followers of the Belzer Rebbe, from the ancient town lying between Lemberg and Lublin.

There were only a handful of Wahl and Safier families in Tarnobrzeg linked by various degrees of kinship. It is striking that since the beginning of the nineteenth century there have been numerous estate owners by the name of Taube in Belz and later in Lemberg. They were not indigenous to Tarnobrzeg, but now that I have identified contemporaneous marriages between Taube and both Safier and Wahl of Tarnobrzeg, a degree of order is beginning to appear in the old family tree, reflecting the underlying social connections of my ancestors' families.

Table 15
SAFIER–WAHL–TAUBE

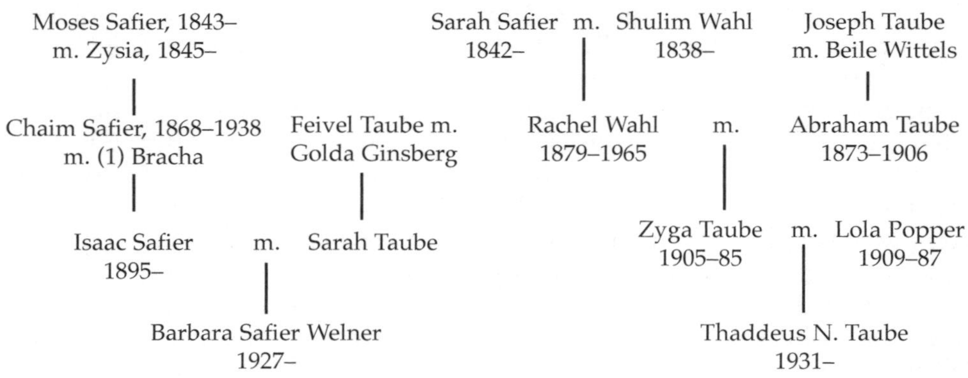

Table 16
BIRTH RECORDS FOR SAFIER FAMILIES FROM THE 1880 AND 1925 CENSUS LISTS

Moses, 1843	**Chaim**, 1868	**Meilech**, 1872
Szysia, 1845	Beila, 1875	Gitla, 1872
|	|	|
Metka, 1867	Regina, 1901	Efroim, 1896
Chaim, 1869	David, 1902	David, 1898
Meilech, 1872	Simon, 1906	Moses, 1902
Chaya, 1875	Aaron, 1908	Isaac, 1903
Rachel, 1880	Efraim, 1909	Aaron, 1908
	Pinek, 1916	Szysie, 1915

From Dr Marcel Safier's Website and Mrs Barbara Welner
Chaim Safier (1868–1938) married (1) Bracha. Their Issue :

a. Isaac Safier born 1895 m. Sarah Taube.
   their three daughters were Bracha (Bronislawa), Shoshana (Rusa), and Barbara (Shifra)
b. Klara (1897–1943) married (circa 1915) to Moses Gewurz, born 1897, having issue:
   Bronya Gewurz (1919–43) and Oscar (Yehoshua) Gewurz (1925–93), the father of Dr Marcel Safier

Chaim Safier married (2) Eve (Beila in the Census List)
Issue of the second marriage not quite tallying with the census details:

Regina, David Leib, 1900, Simon, 1903, Bianka, Aaron (died 1938), Efroim (married Dora), Paul (Pinek).

Simon (1903–84) escaped to Siberia, and made his way to France, finally reaching New York. His two children are Henry L. Safier, who is a gastroenterologist in New York, and Felicia Safier.

Elimeilech Safier (1872–1942?) Issue included :

a. Isaac Safier (1903–78) married (circa 1939) to Sabina Zamojre, one of the six children of Samuel Zamojre (1884–1939) and Sophie Dingelthal (1885–1940), Sabina was born 1914. Isaac and Sabina's son, Emil Safier, born 1944, has two children, Isaac M. Safier (1982–) and Chloe L. Safier (1984–).
b. Carola Safier

For details of other Safiers see Marcel Safier's web page (see note 7).

NOTES

1. Tarnobrzeg City Inventory for 1791 Website: http://www.shtetlinks.jewishgen.org/Tarnobrzeg/html.
2. Edward Gelles, 'Searching for Eve: A Methodological Lesson', *Avotaynu*, xvii, 2 (Summer 2001); Edward Gelles, 'Capitalists and Rabbis', *The Galitzianer*, 9, 2 (Feb. 2002). List of Alcohol Sellers, Tarnobrzeg Website, as above.
3. List of Alcohol Sellers, Tarnobrzeg Website, as Note 1.
4. Michael Honey, 'Propinacya and Konsygnacya Listings from Tarnobrzeg/Dzikow', *Shemot*, ii, 4 (Oct. 1994).
   Extracts from Tarnobrzeg Census Lists kindly made available to me by Mr Tadeusz Zych, Oddzial w Sandomierzu, 27-600 Sandomierz, ul.Zydowska 4, Poland.
5. Y.Y. Fleisher (ed.), *Kehilat Tarnobrzeg-Dzikow* (Tel-Aviv, 1923).
6. Dr Emil Safier, http://www.quantumfilms.net/QF_main/qf_aqf.htm.
7. Dr Marcel Safier, http://members.ozemail.com.au/~msafier/Safier/msafier.html.
8. Dr Michael Mark Welner, http://www.forensic panel.com/media.

V.

BACKGROUND TO FAMILY LINKS

And if one prevail against him,
two shall withstand him, and
a threefold cord is not quickly broken

Ecclesiastes, 4: 12

CHAPTER TWENTY

Family Connections Spanning Austrian Galicia

Griffel–Wahl–Safier–Taube and Griffel–Wahl–Hauser–Lamm

A study of a handful of Jewish families suggested that the pattern of their marriages was a natural concomitant of their religious adherence, social status and economic interests. These families flourished in Austrian Galicia from the late-eighteenth century to the eve of the First World War. They were to be found across the breadth of the province, from Krakow in the west to Lemberg and beyond in the east.

The Wahls and Safiers of Tarnobrzeg made their appearance in earlier chapters. Connections emerged between these two families and the Taube family of Lemberg.[1] My mother's family, the Griffels, who were a clan with ancient Lemberg connections, were also strong in the towns of Stanislau and Nadworna to the south of Lemberg.[2]

I must now introduce two new families to join these kinsfolk. They are the Lamms of Stanislau and the Hausers of Tarnobrzeg. This connection started with a marriage between Shlomo Lamm and Bracha, the youngest daughter of Moshe Hauser of Tarnobrzeg. The families of Moshe Hauser and Leiser Wahl were already linked. In the following generation, David Griffel of Nadworna married Chawa Wahl of Tarnobrzeg.[3] His sister, Zissel Griffel, became the wife of Zygmunt Lamm of Stanislau. Their son married a descendant of the Tarnobrzeg Hausers. Thus a Lamm went 'west' to marry a Hauser, and two generations later a Hauser came 'east' to marry a Lamm.

The Wahl-Hauser, Hauser-Lamm, Lamm-Griffel and Griffel-Wahl marriages illustrate in microcosm the unity of a certain class, their mobility in pursuit of business opportunities and of suitable marriage alliances, their adaptability to changing economic circumstances, and their resilience in the face of political adversity. These folk were orthodox Jews for the better part of the period, as are some of their descendants to this day. A few indeed were followers of the great Chasidic rabbis, such as the Hagers of Otonya, the Friedmans of Czortkow, and the Rokeach of Belz. Over the course of a few generations quite a few of them became very wealthy. Thus, Feivel Taube was a man of property and head of the community of Belz at the beginning of the nineteenth century. His descendants included estate owners in and around Lemberg. Some of our Loew cousins were presidents and mayors of Sedziszow and owned estates in that area.

Eliezer Griffel (1850–1918) was the social leader and economic arbiter of the community in Nadworna. The Griffels owned oil wells and saw mills as well as other businesses. The timber trade had largely contributed to the rise of others in this family nexus.[4] Leiser Wahl made his fortune in timber and then went into merchant banking. His son Shulim is described in the Tarnobrzeg records as a capitalist. He married Sarah Safier, whose family were also timber merchants and estate owners.[5]

Leiser Wahl's contemporary, Moses Hauser, was *Arendar* to the lords of Dzikow, the Tarnowskis. Studies of the Polish *Arenda* system include a recent account of its eighteenth-century history.[6] Hauser held licence and monopoly rights covering a variety of business activities arising from the management of the Count's property. In the process of these activities he acquired two separate estates. The memoirs of Jan Slomka, a mayor of Dzikow, would be more valuable as a piece of social history if it were not for the author's obvious bias. The original text has more about Leiser Wahl and Moshe Hauser than the English translation and it also refers to Hauser's son-in-law. It mentions that Shlomo Lamm augmented the family fortune through holding a licence for operating distilleries.[7] Lamm and his brothers eventually had a variety of businesses, including sugar refineries. This was in the days of the Tarnowski Counts Jan Dzierzyslaw (1838–94) and Jan Zdsislaw (1862–1937).[8] Moshe Hauser and his great wealth are also mentioned in the memoirs of Joseph Margoshes.[9]

A common thread for this group of families was their connection with landed property and the exploitation of its natural resources. As I have indicated, the most frequent path to affluence was through the timber trade, which might lead to the ownership of forests and estates. Oil and sugar beet were also of considerable importance. An interest in the primary products of the land led to industrial undertakings such as distilleries, sugar refineries, leather production, and so on. Surplus funds might then find their way into merchant banking. This varied commercial activity required constant movement of people and goods across the province. Even before the coming of the railways these folk travelled frequently to attend family gatherings or even to visit their favourite rabbis. This is the shared background to the marriages that were arranged between families from either end of Galicia.

Given my interest in the Wahl and Lamm families I was pleased to find references to Hauser links on Michael Honey's historical chart.[10] Some of these are based on interviews with a very aged Tarnobrzeg survivor who recalled personalities from pre-First World War days. The chart shows Frieda as the daughter of Leiser Wahl and married to Hirsch, the youngest son of Moshe Hauser. The latter's daughter Bracha was allied to Shlomo Lamm, who in due course succeeded his father-in-law as the last *Arendar* before the First World War.

THE TARNOBRZEG CENSUS OF 1880

These families were quite prolific. Moshe Hauser had at least eight children, while Hirsch and Frieda had seven or more. Some details given in the appended notes come from the Tarnobrzeg Census, kindly supplied with other information by Mr Tadeusz Zych.[11] In due course, the full census list will no doubt appear on the Tarnobrzeg Web Site, but the data are not easily accessible at the present time. Continuing progress in the publication of archival material for this town can be followed on the Internet.[12]

The town censuses for 1880 and 1925 list names with places and dates of birth arranged in family units. Sometimes house numbers are noted, which can often provide valuable clues. For example, Honey's historical chart gives Leiser Wahl as the father of Frieda Wahl who married Hirsch Hauser, so it was interesting to see that the census list gave Hirsch and Frieda as living next door to Leiser Wahl. The census data on my Wahl, Safier, Lamm and Hauser families dovetailed neatly with the anecdotal information from the other quoted sources.

LAMM DESCENDANTS: PERSONAL CONTACTS AND INTERNET SEARCHES

During my study of the Griffel family I heard that Dr Steven Lamm was a prominent physician in New York. With the help of the local telephone directory it was quite easy to track down Dr Lamm and to make contact with his mother. Lucy Lam confirmed that her late husband, Dr Arnold Lam, was the son of my great-aunt Zissel Griffel and of Zygmunt Lamm of Stanislau. When I discovered that Lucy's maiden name was Ludwica Hauser-Auerbach I had found an ideal starting point for further enquiry. Lucy was born in Krakow in 1923 and her parents were Raphael Auerbach and Caroline Hauser of that city. I was curious to find out if Caroline was related to the Tarnobrzeg Hausers. The family had no record of her marriage, but I was assured that it had taken place shortly after the end of the First World War. Lucy also remembered that her mother was born in 1902. She was not immediately forthcoming about any Tarnobrzeg connection, a mere backwater compared to the great city of her birth. However, I was not put off the scent. I myself was never told about Tarnobrzeg in my younger days, and when I started on my researches a few years ago I had to dig deep to discover my Wahl grandmother's birthplace. It was one of many provincial towns that the next generation, who lived in Cracow, Vienna or Rome, preferred to forget!

There is much more information on the Internet for the city of Krakow than for some of the small shtetls.[13] but even there the marriage records are somewhat fragmentary. However, the JRI – Poland records for Krakow did reveal a marriage in 1899 between Baruch Mordko Hauser of Tarnobrzeg and Chawa Auerbach of Krakow. I thought this couple could be Caroline Hauser's parents.

Lucy confirmed my supposition and that her parents were indeed first cousins. The records state that Baruch Mordko Hauser was the son of Chaim and Cyna Hauser of Tarnobrzeg and his wife Chawa was the daughter of Chaim and Keila Heindla Auerbach of Krakow. I had found Lucy's great-grandparents and established the Tarnobrzeg connection!

Lucy's son, Dr Steven Lamm, is not my only Griffel cousin in the American medical profession. The psychiatrist Dr Yehuda Nir is a grandson of Chaja Griffel, a sister of Zissel and of my grandfather, David Mendel Griffel.[14]

The movements between Galician towns as revealed by the vital records throw light on how roots could become transplanted and how family branches proliferated during the period under review.

NOTES

1. Edward Gelles, 'The Safiers of Tarnobrzeg', *Shemot*, 10, 3 (Sept. 2002).
2. Gelles, 'My Mother's People', *Sharsheret Hadorot*, 16, 4 (Oct. 2002).
3. Gelles, 'Searching for Eve', *Avotaynu*, xvii, 2 (Summer 2001).
4. Gelles, 'Capitalists and Rabbis', *The Galitzianer*, 9, 2 (Feb. 2002). Gelles, 'Economic Background to some Family Links', *The Galitzianer*, 9, 3 (May 2002).
5. Tarnobrzeg town records kept in the Sandomierz Archives, Oddzial w Sandomierzu 27-600, Sandomierz, ul. Zydowska 4, Poland.
6. M.J. Rosman, *The Lord's Jews* (Boston, MA: Harvard University Press, 1990).
7. Jan Slomka, *From Serfdom to Self-government. Memoirs of a Polish Village Mayor 1842–1917* trans. William John Rose (London: Minerva, 1941), pp.90, 94, 98–101.
8. Adam Tarnowski, 'History of the House of Tarnow', Unpublished MS by last Austro-Hungarian Ambassador to the United States
9. Joseph Margoshes, *Memoirs of my Life* (New York: Posy-Shoulson Press, 1936), p.251.
10. Michael Honey, 'The Jewish Historical Clock', *Avotaynu*, xvii, 3 (Fall 2001), pp.10–15. The Megale Amukot Diagram includes material from the Hauser, Lamm and Engelberg families of Tarnobrzeg
11. Professor Tadeusz Zych is the Deputy Mayor of Tarnobrzeg. The address of the Town Council is Urzad Miasta, ul. Mickiewicza 2, 39-400, Tarnobrzeg, Poland. Gelles, 'Economic Background to some Family Links'.
12. For Tarnobrzeg records see http://www.shtetlinks.jewishgen.org/Tarnobrzeg/html/2nd%20level/source.htm.
13. JRI – Poland web site for Cracow Civil Records: http://data.jewishgen.org/jgen/wc.dll?jgproc~jgsys~jripllat.
14. Dr Yehuda Nir, *The Lost Childhood* (New York: Harcourt, Brace, Jovanovitch, 1989).

Hirsch Hauser and his wife Frieda Wahl lived at house No.109 (next door to her father, Leiser Wahl at No.108). They were born in Tarnobrzeg in 1843 and 1844 and their children's births are recorded as Aaron (1862), Gitla (1867), Zaja (1869), Lisel (1872), Jankel (1873), Cypra (1878) and Frajda (1880). Shlomo Lamm and his wife Brucha Hauser were born in 1858 and 1856 respectively. They lived in house No.302 and the births of some of their children are recorded as Szulim (1876), Yechiel (1877) and Markus or Mordechai (1879). Shlomo's occupation (at the age of 22) is modestly given as shopkeeper and counting-house owner. These census details are complimented by entries in the weekly Hebrew newspaper *HaMagid,* which reported on 12 August 1897 a donation of 50 z'l to the newsletter from Mordechai and Shulim Lam, and on 5 August 1898 a donation of 20 z'l from Mordechai Lam in honour of his brother Yechiel's engagement. It might be noted at this point that Shlomo Lamm's son Szulim or Shulim may well have been a first cousin of Zygmunt Lamm of Stanislau (whose Jewish name was Shulim). The family connections are outlined in Table 17.

From the late-eighteenth century to the eve of the Second World War there were many Hausers recorded for Krakow, as well as many marriages connected with Tarnobrzeg. The *Arendar* Moses Hauser and his wife Edel were actually born in Tarnobrzeg in 1816 and 1828.

Table 17
CONNECTIONS BETWEEN NADWORNA AND TARNOBRZEG

Griffel–Wahl–Lamm–Hauser

Leiser Wahl of Tarnobrzeg, 1815–
m. Zlate Roisel of Nisko, 1819–

- Shulim Wahl, 1838–
  m. Sarah Safier, 1842–
  - Chawa Wahl, 1877–1941 Tarnobrzeg
    m. David Mendel Griffel, 1875–1941
    Nadworna
- Frieda Wahl, 1844– m. Hirsch Hauser, 1843–1935

Moshe Hauser of Tarnobrzeg, 1816–
Arendar of Count Tarnowski

- Hirsch Hauser, 1843–1935 (m. Frieda Wahl)
- Bracha Hauser, 1856–
  m. Shlomo Lamm, 1858–
  Arendar

Zissel Griffel, Nadworna, 1878– m. Zygmunt Lamm, Stanislau

- Dr Arnold Lamm, Nadworna 1902– New York 1986
  m. Lucy Hauser-Auerbach, Cracow, 1923– *from* Tarnobrzeg *Hausers*

CHAPTER TWENTY-ONE

Galician Socio-Economic Conditions

Capitalists and rabbis: economic background to some family links

Two articles published under the titles of 'Capitalists and Rabbis' and 'Economic Background to some Family Links' are combined here in shortened form, as a summary and recapitulation of the family connections established at this stage of my studies.

Generations of my maternal ancestors flourished in small towns such as Brody, Stanislau, Nadworna, Kolomea, Tarnobrzeg and Sedziszow, as well as in the cities of Lemberg and Cracow. The political and economic regime during the greater part of the nineteenth century encouraged commercial development. Galician Jews shared in the enlightenment and emancipation that continued its pan-European progress. Traditional orthodoxy was the norm, but as the century progressed enlightenment ideas made themselves increasingly felt in education and other areas of culture. On the other hand, the Chasidic rabbis retained their hold on devoted flocks throughout the period. A number of their dynasties established themselves in various centres, and the more famous of these attracted followers from far and wide. Branches of families were often found in more than one town. Marriages were frequently arranged on the basis of kinship or business connections that might span the entire province.

The strength of these Galician entrepreneurs seemed to derive from a high degree of religious, social and economic cohesion. They thrived on inbreeding, hard work and frugal living, and using all their resources, including family manpower, to the full. They were capable businessmen, but no doubt luck also played some part in their success. They managed to maintain their positions through the ups and downs of political, social and economic change to the eve of the First World War, and indeed in some instances well into the interwar years.

Factors determining the economic fortunes of Galician Jewry were manifold. First, the Polish partitions, which led to a century-and-a-half of Austrian rule. Second, the geography of the region and its natural resources. To the south were the Carpathian mountains, to the west and east the rivers that could serve as political boundaries and that were vital trade routes. The timber of the great forests, iron and coal, grain and salt, sugar beet and oil were some of the commodities with which our ancestors were involved for centuries. Favourable taxation to encourage trade, the pace of industrialization, and the coming of the railways all have to be considered in their influence on the fortunes of regions, individual towns and different industries.

The border town of Brody at the eastern extremity of the province flourished as an entrepot for the Russian trade and was favoured with the status of a 'free city'. The town of Tarnobrzeg on the Vistula in western Galicia had some basic industries such as sulphur mines. There was an active trade across the river into Russian Poland, which became very profitable whenever punishing duties on commodities such as sugar could be evaded. The river was also the lifeline along which quantities of timber were floated down to the Baltic coast for export. As the nineteenth century progressed, the oil fields of southeastern Galicia were increasingly exploited; they brought wealth to the Griffels of Nadworna and Stanislau.

The Griffel, Wahl, Safier, Loew and Taube families had close connections with the land, in the sense that they were involved in the management of estates or dealt in landed property. Jews were not permitted to own freeholds until the second half of the nineteenth century, but there were several categories of exceptions to this rule. For example, a Taube family based at one time in Belz, not far from Lemberg, owned substantial estates in the early 1800s. In any case, Jewish merchants who had accumulated some capital from trading with farmers or managing the estates of aristocratic landowners became increasingly involved with the exploitation of the land's natural resources, such as timber, oil and minerals. They would lease land, negotiate concessions, buy the standing wood, and so on. They would plough back the profits from their activities into loans to estate owners. Some remained timber merchants and the like, others went on to acquire estates of their own; in due course their mortgage lending might grow into more broadly based merchant banking.

THE WAHLS

Tarnobrzeg received a royal charter during the reign of Zygmunt III in 1593. This was in the heyday of Saul Wahl, the Jewish community leader, who played a leading role in the Polish-Lithuanian state at the time. Wahls are recorded in the Tarnobrzeg archives from the beginning of the nineteenth century. Families descended from Saul Wahl were to be found in numerous Galician towns. Nadworna, the stronghold of the Griffels, had a chief rabbi in the nineteenth century called Zvi Aryeh Wahl, who had a recorded pedigree going back to Saul Wahl and his Katzenellenbogen forebears.

Leiser Wahl was born in Tarnobrzeg in 1815. We gather from the town archives and the memoirs of the mayor, Jan Slomka, that Leiser obtained a liquor monopoly from Count Tarnowski and later began to deal in timber, buying the standing forest and shipping the wood by raft to Danzig. He was able to set up his sons and give his daughters dowries of tens of thousands of gulden. He remained banker to many tradesmen in trouble, and the probate to his will came in at 300,000 gulden, mostly in mortgages on peasant and gentry properties.

THE SAFIERS

There are scattered references to the Safiers of Tarnobrzeg from the eighteenth century and the census of 1791 to the Second World War and the memorial records of holocaust victims. A Safier is listed in the taxation records of 1822. There are about a dozen families of this name in the census lists of 1880 and 1925, and numerous entries in the birth and death records kept in the nearby town of Sandomierz, in the records of high school graduates up to 1939, and in the Dzikow-Tarnobrzeg Memorial Book. The latter refers to the two brothers, Chaim and Elimelech Safier, who were among the wealthiest in the town during the period between the two world wars. They owned forests and other property and were prominent in the timber trade, as indeed had been their forebears a century earlier.

A collection of Chasidic stories includes the tale of Reb Ahron Safier, a timber merchant from Cracow, whose commercial ventures thrived on a blessing from Rabbi Yechezkel Halberstam of Siniawa. The Radzichow Memorial Book refers to an Isaac Safier who owned an estate at Shtruvitz and was a follower of Rabbi Yehoshua Rokeach of Belz. There were also a number of Safiers in Opatow, a town not very far from Tarnobrzeg.

Three daughters of Sarah Safier and Shulim Wahl married into families who were involved in the same kind of merchant venturing and had a similar social background. The Loew, Griffel and Taube families were linked by the marriages of the three sisters Blume, Chawa and Rachel Wahl.

THE LOEWS

Sarah Safier's eldest daughter, Blume Wahl, married Lazar Loew, a son of Nathan Nata Loew, who owned estates and was head of the Jewish community of Sedziszow. He and his brother were successively mayors of that town. Their father Jacob Yoshua Loew was already well established there. As leaders of the community they would have many poor families to dine with them on Saturdays and festival days. Their paternalism was also evidenced by marrying off orphan girls of the community at their expense. Although the Rabbi of Sedziszow was a Horowitz who had distant family connections, the Loews gave their religious allegiance to the Rabbi of Czortkow of the famous Friedman dynasty of Ruzhin, Sadagora and Czortkow. Old Loew used to take his carriage with four horses, flying the Ruzhin flag, to drive to the Rabbi for the festivals. In the days of his sons, the Rabbi visited the area of Sedziszow with his entourage, and the Loews bore the entire cost of the visit.

THE FRIEDMANS

The majority of the Chasidic rabbis adopted a simple lifestyle. The Friedmans by contrast lived in great splendour, in quasi-regal style supported by their ecstatic followers. Some rabbis of the Gelles family had collateral connections with the Czortkow 'wunder-rabbis and also with the celebrated sage Pinchas Shapiro of Koretz.

My grandfather and the Czortkover Rebbe Israel Friedman coincidentally both died in Vienna within months of each other in 1933/34. Rabbi Nahum Uri Gelles had many responsa addressed to him by leading rabbis of his day. One of these refers to him as a judge of a rabbinical court at Sedziszow. The Czortkov connection probably had something to do with that appointment.

THE GRIFFELS AND THE CHAYES

Another of Sarah Safier's daughters was my grandmother, Chava Wahl. Her husband David Mendel Griffel was the eldest son of Eliezer Griffel of Nadworna and Sarah Matel Chajes of Kolomea.

The Chayes family were a family of established wealth in Brody, but it was in eighteenth-century Livorno and Florence that they became rich in the coral trade and in merchant banking.

The Griffel oil interests extended beyond the areas of Nadworna, Stanislau, Kolomea and Pasiecna, to Austria, at Korneuburg near Vienna. Many family members worked in one or other of Leiser Griffel's enterprises, in oil and timber, and in expanding interests that at one time included a merchant bank. A grandson, Dr Jacob Griffel, who later became famous for his wartime rescue efforts, was an oil expert who lived at Boryslaw in the Galician oil fields. Eliezer Griffel was a follower of the Chasidic Rabbis of Otoniya, who were of the Hager family. The Griffels and Hagers were also linked by marriage. David Mendel and Isaac Chaim Griffel, and their children, succeeded to different parts of the family enterprises. The family was for long ultra-conservative in religion, paternalist in community affairs, and monarchist in their sentiment towards Austrian rule.

THE LAMMS AND THE HAUSERS

My great-aunt Zissel Griffel married Zygmunt Lamm of Stanislau. Their son Dr Arnold Lamm of Nadworna was the husband of Lucie Hauser-Auerbach of Cracow, who was descended from the Hausers of Tarnobrzeg.

Moses Hauser of Tarnobrzeg was *Arendar* to the local overlords, the Counts Tarnowski. He was a prototype of a successful *Arendar*, and would even have founded a dynasty but for the coming of the First World War. At any rate he was the patriarch of a clan that survived in Tarnobrzeg until the Second World War.

Leiser Wahl's daughter Frieda married Hirsch, one of Hauser's numerous sons, while his youngest daughter, Bracha Hauser, became the wife of Shlomo Lamm who hailed from the Lamms of Stanislau and Nadworna. Shlomo settled in Tarnobrzeg and in due course succeeded his father-in-law as *Arendar.*

THE TAUBE FAMILY

The Taube family became rich through the possession of land and this was the basis of their prosperity for many generations. As late as the 1930's there were numerous forest and estate owners of that name in the Lvov area.

A Feivel Taube of Lemberg flourished as a property developer in Przemysl in the later-nineteenth century and his family was linked to the Safiers through the marriage of his daughter Sarah to Isaac, the son of Chaim Safier of Tarnobrzeg. Isaac Safier was a timber merchant like many of his family. His grandfather Moses Safier was a cousin or perhaps even a brother of Sarah Safier, the wife of Shulim Wahl and mother-in-law of Abraham Taube. There was clearly a close triangular relationship between the Wahl, Safier and Taube, as well as quadrilateral connections between the Wahl, Griffel, Lamm and Hauser families.

CONCLUSION

These entrepreneurs flourished for a brief period. The pillars of support were a benevolent Imperial regime and a social cohesion backed by strong Chasidic faith. The economic climate was favourable at times, but I believe that my ancestors had the resilience and adaptability to cope in less propitious circumstances, as some of their surviving descendants proved. The pillars crumbled at the time of the First World War. Economic and political circumstances were very different in the Poland of the inter-war years. The intellectual currents of the nineteenth and early-twentieth centuries, the rise of nationalism, assimilation, and Zionism, weakened the hold of the ancestral faith, although some branches of these families have maintained their unqualified Chasidic adherence. Their descendants have entered the twenty-first century as inheritors of a historical tradition, with the chance of full integration into our great western culture to which their ancestors contributed so much. It is surely our duty to preserve the memory of this almost forgotten world of faith, kinship and community.

Table 18
SOME FAMILY LINKS

S=Safier, T=Taube, W=Wahl, H=Hauser, G=Griffel, L=Lamm
Wahl and Safier families of Tarnobrzeg , Taube of Lemberg and Cracow, Hauser of Tarnobrzeg and Cracow, Griffel and Lamm families of Nadworna and Stanislau

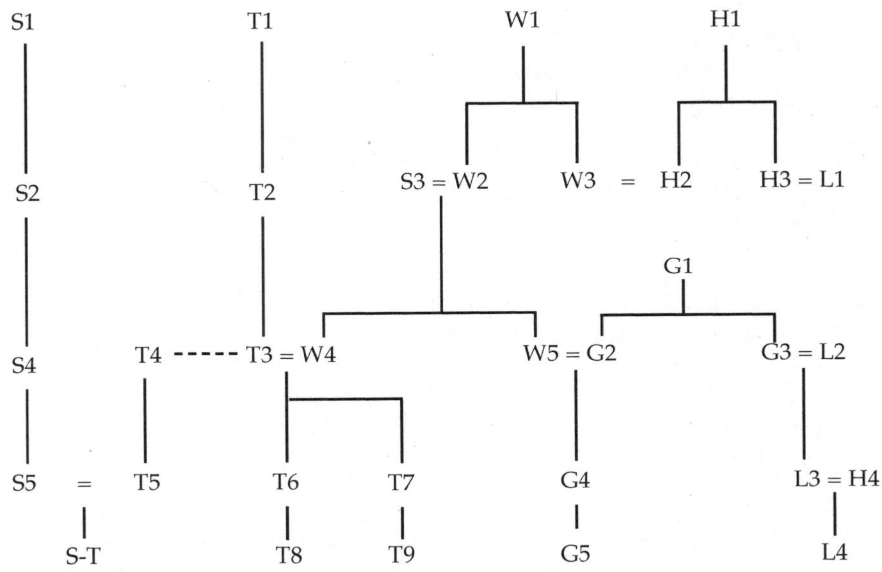

SAFIER:	S1 – Father of S2 (and possibly of S3) so far unidentified
	S2 – Moses Safier, b. 1843
	S3 – Sarah Safier, b. 1842, (from her 6 children, Blume, Chaim, Moses, Zypora, Chawa, and Rachel Wahl, there are many Wahl, Griffel, Taube, and Loew descendants, such as her grandson Dr Abraham A. Low (Baranow 1891–Chicago 1954) belonging to the LOEW family of Sedziszow
	S4 – Chaim Safier (1868–1938)
	S5 – Isaac Safier (1895–1941), born in Tarnobrzeg & lived in Przemysl – married Sarah Taube, T5
	ST – Barbara Welner, joining Safier and Taube lines, b. 1927, mother of Drs Michael and Alan Welner
WAHL:	W1 – Leiser Wahl, b. 1815
	W2 – Shulim Wahl, b. 1838
	W3 – Frieda Wahl, b. 1844
	W4 – Rachel Wahl (1879–1965), b. Tarnobrzeg & lived in Lemberg and Cracow
	W5 – Chawa Wahl (1877–1941, b. Tarnobrzeg & lived in Stanislau
HAUSER:	H1 – Moshe Hauser, b. 1816
	H2 – Hirsch Hauser (1843–1935)
	H3 – Bracha Hauser, b. 1856
	H4 – Lucy Hauser-Auerbach, b. Cracow 1923 & lives in New York
LAMM:	L1 – Shlomo Lamm (Tarnobrzeg), b. 1858
	L2 – Zygmunt Lamm (Stanislau)
	L3 – Arnold Lamm (Nadworna 1902–New York 1986)
	L4 – Steven Lamm, b. Rome 1948 & lives in New York
GRIFFEL:	G1 – Eliezer Griffel of Nadworna (1850–1918) married Sarah Chayes of Kolomea (–1940), descendant of the CHAYES family of Brody
	G2 – David Mendel Griffel of Nadworna & Stanislau (1875–1941)
	G3 – Zissel Griffel, b. 1878
	G4 – Regina Griffel (Nadworna 1900–London 1954) married Dr David Gelles of Vienna (1883–1964), descendant of the GELLES family of Brody
	G5 – Edward Gelles, b. Vienna 1927 & lives in London
TAUBE:	T1 – Simon Taube of Krystynopol
	T2 – Josef Isaac Taube of Lemberg (1843–)
	T3 – Abraham Taube of Lemberg (1873–1906) – a cousin
	T4 – Feivel Taube of Lemberg
	T5 – Sarah Taube, b. Przemysl 1894
	T6 – Rega Taube (Lemberg 1903 – Cracow – Rio de Janeiro 1967)
	T7 – Zyga Taube (Lemberg 1905 – Cracow – Los Angeles 1985)
	T8 – Viola Sachs nee Scharf, b. Cracow 1929 & lives in Paris
	T9 – Thaddeus N. Taube, b. Cracow 1931 & lives in California

VI.

TAUBE COUSINS AND THEIR CONNECTIONS

Taube – a female proper name
[Old Saxon = Dubva, English = Dove]
A bird of the family of columbidae
[Columba, Colombe, etc.]
[Polish = Golab, Hebrew = Yonah]

Chapter Twenty-Two

The Taube Family

Their history and ancient links

Tad Taube has been involved in a variety of enterprises among which his real estate business is particularly noteworthy, because its success is very much in the style of his ancient forebears. His Taube ancestors were not noted for their philanthropy, but Tad has become a major benefactor in California and supports many educational and cultural projects in his home state, in his native Poland, and elsewhere.

Our great-grandparents, Shulim Wahl and Sarah Safier, lived in Tarnobrzeg, a little town in Austrian Galicia. They brought up a family of six children.[1] The two youngest were Rachel (1879–1965), who married Tad's grandfather Abraham Taube of Lemberg (1873–1906), and Chawa (1877–1941), who became the wife of my grandfather, David Mendel Griffel of Nadworna (1875–1941). The two sisters named their boys Zygmunt and their daughters Regina. Tad's father was called Zyga for short and my mother was Regina. At that time there was clearly some cohesion to the family. I remember Tad's aunt Rega coming to visit us in Vienna in the 1930s. After the dispersals of two world wars and half a century of separation the search for my kinsfolk became quite a challenge.

Our ancestors exhibited certain qualities that have been passed down the generations. The contributions some of them made to the cultural and social life of their communities in the course of centuries must in some measure be due to these qualities. Tad Taube is acknowledged to be a highly successful businessman. I had no preconceived ideas about inherited traits, but Tad does seem to have derived some of his undoubted acumen from forebears on both sides of his family. His mother's people, the Poppers, produced successful entrepreneurs, while the Taube ancestors were men of property, going back to a time when Jews were generally barred from owning land. The family was in the ancient town of Belz for several centuries. In the nineteenth century they spread to neighbouring towns and then to Lemberg (Lvov) and ultimately Cracow. Many perished in the holocaust, but those who escaped in time or managed to survive made new homes for themselves and their descendants overseas.

TAUBE FAMILY ORIGINS IN BELZ

The town of Belz is situated to the north of Lvov, about half way between that city and Lublin. The Jewish community dates from the middle of the sixteenth century and attained importance in the nineteenth century when the town became the seat of the Rokeach Chasidic dynasty.

The Taube family had ancient local roots. Their forebears were in Belz in the early seventeenth century when they were supposedly involved in a dispute with the Rabbi, Joel Sirkes. During the eighteenth century they became one of the wealthiest Jewish families in Belz.[2] The head of the community at the beginning of the nineteenth century was Yossel Taube. He was primarily responsible for the appointment of the first Rebbe of the dynasty. Rabbi Shalom Rokeach moved from Sokal to Belz and was acclaimed *Zaddik* in 1815. Yossel Taube's son Feivel succeeded his father as community head around that time.

DISPUTE WITH THE BELZER CHASIDIM

There is no doubt that the Taube family were orthodox Jews, but in later generations most of them did not follow the Belzer Rebbe. There developed a doctrinal schism and it also appears that their wealth aroused a degree of envy. In the longstanding dispute that began during the reign of the second Belzer Rebbe they got a bad press. The well-known author Josef Margoshes (1866–1955) published some articles on the Rabbinical Court of Belz which appeared in the *Lemberger Togblatt* in the 1920s. He repeated some of the aspersions made by opponents of the Taube family. We know about these aspersions from Yosef Falk, whose writings contain a vigorous defence of the Taube family.[3] Their opponents referred to the Taube landowners as *sons of gentiles* or *Belzer Goyim*,[4] the latter being a play on the letters BG sometimes appended to the Taube signature. This suffix apparently signified a privilege or distinction granted by the authorities. GB (written in Hebrew letters from right to left) might conceivably have stood for *Gutsbesitzer*, an entitlement to own estates at a time when Jews were not generally allowed to possess freeholds.[5] These Taubes continued as substantial landowners for several generations. A branch that claimed descent from the famous talmudist Rabbi Meyer Margolioth maintained a Chasidic allegiance. However, by and large, the Taube family were too go-ahead and progressive for the Rabbis of Belz.

REB FEIVEL TAUBE OF BELZ AND HIS FAMILY

Yosef Falk recounts that Reb Feivel had five sons and one daughter and that he arranged fine marriages for all of them as befitted a wealthy man of his standing. One of his sons and Nachman Krochmal married two sisters of a distinguished Zolkiew family. Feivel's daughter became the wife of Reb

Lippa Vassilover, who left a large portion of his estate to the Belzer Rebbe, surely a sign that the Rokeach dynasty was held in high esteem by some of the Taube family. 'Feivenyu' and his sons were the leading businessmen in the area and used to lend money to the gentile landowners on interest. One of them is recorded as leaving two estates.

TAUBE–KATZENELLENBOGEN CONNECTIONS

In the course of the nineteenth century the Taube family formed several marriage connections with the Katzenellenbogens, the great and diverse clan descended from the sixteenth-century Rabbis of Padua and Venice, whose scion was Saul Wahl (1545–1617).[6] His descendants included the family of Abraham Joshua Heschel, an important Chief Rabbi of Cracow, and Rabbi Saul Katzenellenbogen of Pinczow, a son of Moses Katzenellenbogen of Chelm. There were Taube marriages with these two rabbinical branches.[7] The later marriage of Abraham Taube and Rachel Wahl of Tarnobrzeg united two families with a shared ancestral background.[8]

BELZ, KRYSTYNOPOL AND LEMBERG

In the early decades of the nineteenth century the doves began to spread their wings. Simon Taube was an ancestor of Tad Taube's immediate line. He lived in Krystynopol, which is only a few miles from Belz. Throughout the nineteenth century there were Taubes in Krystynopol as shown by the vital records on the JRI – Poland website,[9] and in the twentieth century those that escaped the holocaust were dispersed to Israel, America and elsewhere.[10]

From the days of Feivel Taube, the head of the Belz family, many of the clan moved to Lemberg where they multiplied and flourished. We do not know how many siblings Feivel had, but his six children could alone account for the dozens of the family name found in the Lemberg records in the period up to the Second World War. As the nineteenth century progresses references to estate owners and owners of forest land begin to give way to property developers, merchants and members of the professions. There are rabbis, doctors, lawyers and civil servants among them.[11]

Galician Jews were drawn to the Imperial capital up to the outbreak of the First World War. The Viennese Jewish community records contain details of numerous members of the Taube family, some of which can be identified as coming from Lemberg.[12]

THE FAMILY OF JOSEF TAUBE

Josef Isaac Taube was a son of Simon and Mariam Taube of Krystynopol. He married Beile Wittels, the daughter of Leib Wittels and Biene Selzer of

Lemberg. Beile was the eldest of twelve children. The Wittels were prosperous merchants. Their name, which may be a matronymic, could derive from 'the quick-witted one'. Rabbis of that name included Simcha, Dov Berish and Jacob Wittels. The latter was a *Dayan* (judge) in Lemberg. The appended charts show that Joseph and Beile had at least seven children. The basic genealogical data on the Taube and Wittels families were found in the Lviv archives.[13]

The youngest child Abraham was born in 1873. He married a cousin, Brandel Wittels. Information on Abraham and his marriages came from a variety of sources, including his granddaughter, Bracha Weiser.[14] Joseph Taube was a successful jute merchant whose activities extended throughout the Austro-Hungarian Empire. Some of his children followed him in the business, but Josef allowed his youngest son, Abraham, to pursue a life of Talmudic study.

Table 19 which shows Josef Taube's family is being extended to take in data that is appearing on the JRI – Poland website: Frederica (Fradel) Taube-Wittels (b.1872) married Isaac Nuta Jaworower and Samuel Taube (b.1870) may be the husband of Ruchel Losch of Botosany.

Table 19
THE FAMILY OF JOSEF TAUBE OF LEMBERG

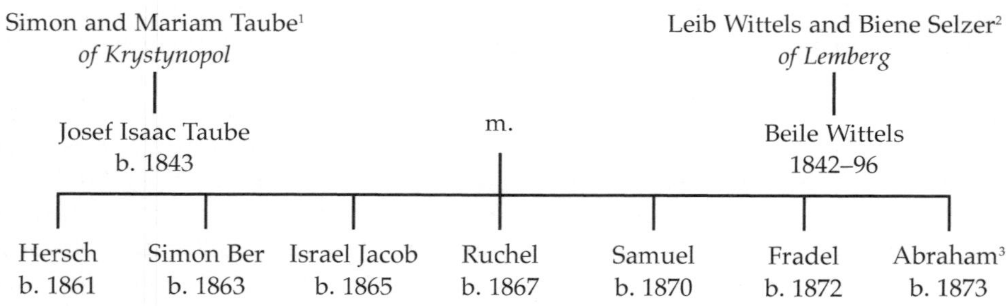

Notes:

1. Krystynopol is just a few miles from the town of Belz. Josef Taube may have moved to Lemberg on his marriage to Beile Wittels.
2. The children of Leib Wittels and Biene Selzer were Beile (b. 1842), Riwka (b. 1844), Mordche (b. 1846), Chane (b. 1849), Mayer (b. 1850), Ruchel (b. 1852), Sarah (b. 1853), Feige (b. 1856), Ziwye (b. 1857), Schlomcze (b. 1858), Jacob (b. 1859), and Moses Hersch (b. 1861).
3. Abraham Taube was the youngest surviving child of Josef and Beile Taube. He married firstly, Brandel Wittels, whose father Ahron Leiser Wittels appears to have been his mother's cousin. Brandel died in childbirth and Abraham married secondly Rachel Wahl.

ABRAHAM TAUBE AND THE WAHL CONNECTION

Abraham Taube's first wife Brandel Wittels died in 1895 just after giving birth to a baby boy. At that time Rachel Wahl was a young girl who had come to stay in Lemberg with her mother Sarah Safier. She looked after the motherless child of her kinsman and in due course became his second wife. The JRI – Poland records show a child born to them in 1898, but it did not survive. However, in 1903 and 1905 Abraham and Rachel had a girl, Rega and a boy, Zyga to join their stepbrother Shmuel Zygmunt (who later added the Hebrew name Yonati). After Abraham died in 1906 Rachel married again and moved to Cracow. Her second husband was Chaim Simon Ohrenstein by whom she had a daughter, Lucia, in 1910, only to be widowed not many years later. Lucia Ohrenstein's adventurous life is described in Chapter 24. Shmuel Wittels Taube remained close to his step-mother until 1935 when he moved to Israel. His two daughters and their families continue to flourish there. Taube family connections are set out in Tables 19–24.

FEIVEL TAUBE AND THE SAFIER CONNECTION

Abraham Taube's mother-in-law Sarah Safier came from an old Tarnobrzeg family who successfully combined commercial and cultural pursuits. They were landowners and timber merchants. They were linked by marriage with the Wahl and Taube families.[15] Some present-day Safier descendants can be found on Marcel Safier's family web site.[16]

Feivel Taube of Lemberg was a cousin of Abraham Taube. He was a substantial property developer, who owned land round Przemysl where he built an entire quarter called after him, the *Golembianka.* He also had a large business as an importer of Brazilian nuts and raisins. He and Golda Ginsberg had a number of children including Rabbi Mordecai Taube of Lemberg, Chana, whose two children survive in Israel, Sarah ,who married Isaac Safier of Tarnobzeg and perished in the holocaust, Mendel, Nussan, Zipporah and Jacob (Leopold). The marriage of Sarah Taube and Isaac Safier united the two families. Barbara Safier Welner is a child of this marriage.[17]

SOME FAMILY LINKS

Table 18 shows connections between the Safier, Taube and Wahl and of the Wahl, Hauser, Lamm and Griffel families. Moshe Hauser of Tarnobrzeg was *Arendar* to the local overlord, Count Tarnowski. One of Hauser's sons married a daughter of Leiser Wahl and a daughter, Bracha Hauser, married Shlomo Lamm. The Lamms came from Nadworna and Stanislau where the Griffels also had their base. Shlomo Lamm succeeded his father-in-law as the last *Arendar* at Tarnobrzeg before the First World War.

Leiser Wahl and Moshe Hauser were the two richest Jews in Tarnobrzeg. Leiser Wahl's son Shulim married Sarah Safier. Their children included the wives of David Griffel and Abraham Taube. The latter's cousin Feivel Taube was the father-in-law of Isaac Safier. The Griffels were linked with the Lamm as well as the Wahl families. Arnold Lamm, whose mother was a Griffel, married a Hauser descendant.[18]

This brief sketch of one branch of the Taube family through three centuries demonstrates how some of their ancient roots were shared by families who were related to them by marriage.

THE HOLOCAUST

The memory of millions who perished in the holocaust is kept alive not only by their immediate families but by Yad Vashem and other centres, and also by the Yizkor Books of hundreds of Jewish communities. The memorial books of Tarnobrzeg and Nadworna give an inkling of the devastation wrought in such families as the Safier, Taube, Wahl and Griffel. The original home of the Taube family, Belz, suffered grievously. Dr Leon Taube, the leader of the Belz community who had served as an officer in the Austrian army in WW1, committed suicide rather than obey Nazi orders to supply quotas of Jews for the death camps.[19]

THE FUTURE

Those who survived the greatest tragedy of our long history have made new lives for themselves and for their families in many parts of the world. We carry with us collective memories of our sufferings and of our ancestors who believed in ultimate redemption and justice.

NOTES

1. Edward Gelles, 'Searching for Eve. A Methodological Lesson', *Avotaynu,* xvii, 2 (Summer 2001).
2. Joel Sirkes (1561–1640), also known as the *Bach* from his magnum opus *Bayis Hadash,* was Rabbi of Belz before becoming Chief Rabbi of Cracow. His son-in-law, David Halevi Segal (1586–1667), known as the *Taz* after his *Turei Zahav,* was Chief Rabbi of Lvov, and reputedly an ancestor of my Griffel line.
3. Yosef Falk, *Mivchar Kethavim.* Collected writings, edited and introduced by Dov Sadan (Tel Aviv: Yosef Shimoni-Mefitz Hasefer, 1974), pp.107–9. Reb Feivel Taube and his family were in dispute with the Belzer Court during the reign of Shalom's son, Rabbi Yehoshua Rokeach and of the latter's son Rabbi Yissachar Ber.

   The dispute began when Rabbi Yehoshua removed a member of the [Taube] family from an honourable position in the Beth Hamedrash, and the family was offended by this action. The climax of the dispute occurred when a member of the family outbid the Rebbe's attendants from holding on to the privilege of supplying alcoholic drinks in the town … The epithet *goyim* that was applied to the family had nothing to do with this but stems from jealousy of their wealth … in fact Reb Feivel Taube was an ardent follower of Rabbi Shalom and was a 'man of the shtiebel'.

4. Avraham Adler, *The Righteous Man and the Holy City*. Aharon of Belz – Stories of Jerusalem (Jerusalem: Jerusalem Library), pp.94 et seq.

   One of the wealthiest families in Belz were the Reis-Tobe clan, otherwise known as the *sons of gentiles*. It seems that this name was earned by the founder of the clan, one Herini, who was a rich landowner but not particularly diligent in the observance of his religious duties ... Between this wealthy family and the Adorim of Belz there existed a state of continuous strife. They [Taube] were the founders of the *Yishrei Lev* congregation, established during the days of Issachar Ber's excommunication of his opponents. Being extremely wealthy, the rumour got around that they kept barrels of Maria Theresa dollars in their cellars. They engaged the best tutors in Galicia for their daughters, including the great scholar Reb Ben-Zion'dl Diamant, who was also the teacher of Reb Aharon'u.

5. I am indebted to Akiwa Padwa for this anecdote. Mr Padwa is a Padwa-Katzenellenbogen (see Note 7, below). Rabbi Meyer Margolioth of Lemberg and Ostrog was the author of *Meir Nessivim*, published in 1774.
6. E. Gelles, 'Saul Wahl. A Jewish Legend', *Judaism Today*, 14 (Winter 1999–2000).
7. Rosenstein, *The Unbroken Chain* (London, New York and Jerusalem: CIS Publishers, 1990), pp.821–4. Saul Loewenstam (son of Abraham Joshua Heschel, the Chief Rabbi of Cracow, who died in 1663) married Esther (daughter of Aryeh Leib Fischls aka der Hoicher Rebbe Leib, also a Chief Rabbi of Cracow, who died in 1671). Their son Aryeh Leib (1690–1756) married Miriam Ashkenazi (daughter of the Chacham Zvi Hirsch Ashkenazi (1660–1718) and Sarah Mirls). Their son was Rabbi Zvi Hirsch Berlin (1721–1800), known as Hirschel Levin on the Continent and as the Reverend Hart Lyon in England where he was Chief Rabbi for a time before returning to the Continent. One of his sons was Rabbi Abraham David Tebele Berliner of Piotrkow who married Zlate, daughter of Eli, son of Hirsch Parnes. He died in 1831. His son Rabbi Aryeh Lieb Berliner was known as Liebish Reb Tebeles. One of the latter's sons was Rabbi Efraim Berliner of Lublin who married Hinde, daughter of Rabbi Abraham Finkelstein. One of their daughters married a Feivel Taube of Belz. This Feivel lived in the later nineteenth century and may be a descendant of the head of the Belz community at the beginning of the century.

   Ibid, pp.31–3: Rabbi Saul Katzenellenbogen (1617–91), ABD of Chelm and Pinczow was the progenitor of a line through Saadia Isaiah, ABD of Holleschau (d. 1726), to Aaron of Brest-Litowsk (d. 1837). The latter Rabbi and Sheine Halevi were the parents of Rabbi Chaim Padua of Brest (d. 1837). His daughter Bracha (1799–1848) married Israel Meir Hakohen. This family used the surname of Padwa. They lived in Brody and later in nearby Busk. Their daughter Breine married Samuel Taube and the issue kept the name Padwa but were of Taube stock. One son was Rabbi Eliezer Wolf Taube Padwa of Belz (1875--1971), a direct descendant of Reb Feivel Taube who had been the head of the Belz community at the time of Rabbi Shalom Rokeach's appointment. One of Eliezer Wolf's sons was Hanoch Dov Padwa (b. in Busk 1912–d. in London 2000), who was Chief Rabbi of the Union of Orthodox Hebrew Congregations leaving numerous and distinguished progeny.

   Personal communication from Akiwa Padwa of London. He is the son of R. Joseph Padwa and Riva Rumpler, and the grandson of Rabbi Hanoch Dov Padwa and Chanah Gitel Gottesman (who was a descendant of the First Belzer Rebbe, Shalom Rokeach).

8. E. Gelles, 'My Mother's People', *Sharsheret Hadorot*, 16, 4 (Oct. 2002).
9. Miscellaneous items on the JRI – Poland data base include the marriages in 1897 of Shmelke Reis of Belz, son of Nuchim Reis and Chaja Taube to Roza Tilles of Cracow and of Suessel Taube, daughter of Isaac and Chaya Taube of Belz to Benjamin Wolf Schoenblum. Abraham Taube of Krystynopol and Feige Fraenkel as the parents of

Anczel Taube (b.1855), who married Hinde Lea Fadenknecht (b.1860) at Brzezany in 1882. We also have birth dates for Neche Dine at Zloczow in 1881 and of Betti at Lemberg in 1896 to Rafael Tauber and his wife Szarlotte (Scheindel) Taube of Krystynopol.

10. Pinchas ben Moses ben Asher Taube informed me of numerous kinsfolk in Sao Paulo-Brazil. His parents were from Krystynopol, who managed to escape to Israel where they and their friends formed an organization to help Krystynopol victims.
11. Some data from Lemberg (Lviv) found for me by Professor Jacob Honigsman provided valuable background material for the Taube archive, but as they do not seem to be relevant to the genealogy of my immediate family, only a brief summary is appended here. The information comes from address books, business directories and official lists. It includes Taube and also some Wittels, a family with whom Taube was related by marriage over at least two generations. Some births include Salaman (1893), Mina (1893), Rozalia (1894), Sacher (1902), Genia (1901), Feivel (1905), Genia (1912), Genia (1919), Mendel (1925), Manisch and Michel Taube (1932). Various sources mention Chaim (councillor at Sasow) and Maurycy Taube (Doctor of Medicine) in 1877, Samuel Wittels (court offical) and Leon Taube (railway official) in 1905, an advocate Markus Taub and Dr Leon Taube, community leader in Belz (1912), Abraham, Chaim and Anselm Taube, estate owners, and Ignatz, Isaac, Jacob and Zygmund Wittels, businessmen (1916). In 1927, there are Taube references to Abram, Baruch, Berisch, Edward and David as businessmen, Adolf, Chaskel and Majer as estate owners, Anselm Taube owner of forests, the advocate Bernard Taube, as well as the Rabbis Juda and Hersch Taube. Numerous other bearers of the name are listed as traders of one kind or another.
12. Burial Records of the Israelitische Kultusgemeinde Wien: Brane Taube , born 1858 and died Vienna 1916; Baruch Taube from Lemberg, born 1888 and died Vienna 1929; Filip Taube, born 1863 and died Vienna 1936; Feivisch Taube, born 1882 and died Vienna 1938.
13. Data from Lviv Archives searched by Alexander Dunai including Lemberg Register of Births 1837–44, 1844–49, 1849–58,1858–63 and 1863–72 giving details of the families of Leib Wittels and Biene Selzer and of Josef Isaac Taube and Beile Wittels:

    Marriage Record 7 June 1866:
    Groom: Josef Taube, unmarried, son of Simon and Mariem Taube from Krystynopol, born 1843; Bride: Beile, unmarried, daughter of Leib Wittels and Biene Selzer of Lemberg, born 1842. Note for bride: died 15 February 1896. Announcement of marriage 3, 10 and 18 February 1866 in Krystynopol, 10, 17 and 24 March 1866 in Lemberg.

    Fragment from a Register of Property Documents 1829–39:
    mentions a testament of an Abraham Taube dated 1812 leaving property to his daughter Rachel Taube, and an affidavit relating to property in the Rynek, half of which belonged to Abraham Taube and the other half to Chaya Taube Fraenkel and her sister Sprince Taube, who inherited it from Samuel Taube.

    The names of Taube and Reisz, Reiser or Reisser come up together in early property transactions. Reisz and Taube had close family ties [see Avraham Adler, Note 2, above].
14. Bracha Weiser wrote:

    My grandmother Brandel Wittels died on 5th June 1895, one week after my father's birth [Shmuel Zygmunt Wittels Taube]. The family came to Israel in 1935 and my father later had a deep-freeze factory. We translated the name Taube to the Hebrew Yonati. I heard from my late father that Rachel and my grandfather were related. She lived in his house before his wife's death. Later she took care of his orphan son – my father – and soon married him ... I found the birth certificates of my grandfather and of my father. When I was six years old in 1928, Lusia, Rachel's daughter spent a whole summer vacation with us. Maybe her father was already dead [Chaim Simon Ohrenstein was a prisoner of war in Russia during WW1. He contracted TB and died a few years after returning to Cracow]. My mother was Reisie Henie [Shoshana], daughter of Baruch and Pesia Lea Altschuler-Stark who lived in Brzezany. The names of my grandmother's parents were Aharon Leiser and Sarah Chaya Wittels. Sarah died in 1933 and her husband Aharon died before the First World War.

15. E. Gelles, 'The Safiers of Tarnobrzeg', *Shemot*, 10, 3 (Sept. 2002).
16. Marcel Safier, members.ozemail.com.au/~msafier/Safier/msafier.html.
17. The Przemysl records now available on the JRI – Poland website reveal the birth dates of Sarah, Cypora, and Nussan Taube – children of Feivel Taube and Golda Ginsberg – as 1894, 1897 and 1899. Barbara Safier Welner, daughter of Sarah Taube, is the mother of American medical specialists Drs Michael and Alan Welner. She has intimated that her Taube family in Lemberg looked to Belz for their origins and inspiration.
18. E. Gelles, 'Economic Background to Some Family Links', *The Galitzianer*, 9, 3 (May 2002).
19. *Belz Sefer Zikaron* [Belz Memorial Book]. Published by Belz Societies in Israel and America. Tel Aviv, 1974, pp.408–9 and 533–4.
20. See chapters 29 and 30, this volume. E. Gelles, 'Finding Rabbi Moses Gelles', *Avotaynu*,18, 1 (Spring 2002).
21. See Chapter 16, this volume.
22. Joseph Friedenson, *Dateline Istanbul* (New York: Mesorah, 1993), p.119.

Table 20
THE FAMILY OF SHULIM WAHL OF TARNOBRZEG

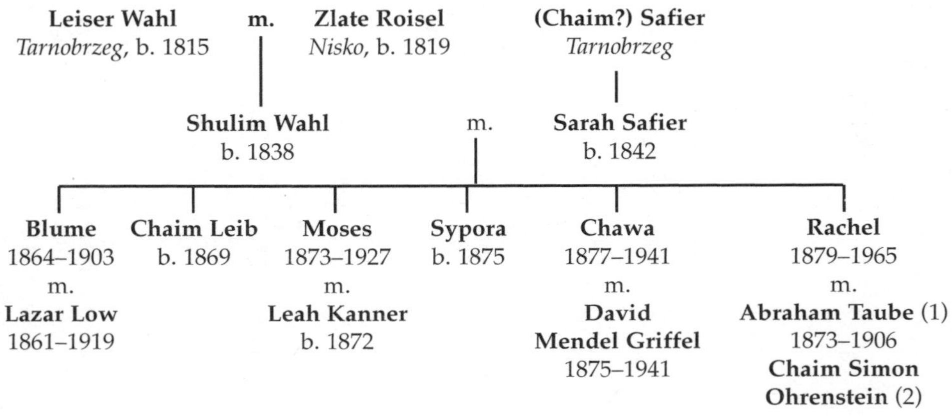

Table 21
THE FAMILY OF LEOPOLD POPPER OF BIELITZ

Moritz Popper d. ca.1886
Isaac Goldberg 1814–1902 m. Jetti Wischnitzer 1826–1902

Leopold Popper 1843–1916 m. Wilhelmine Goldberg

Honoria 1872–86

Artur Henryk Popper m. Clara (Chaya) Weinberg
- a. Jacques 1902–[1] m. Anna Kaplan
- b. Irene 1907–42[2] m. [1] Marceli Liebeskind [2] Dr Leon Schorr 1887–1942
  - Ernita (Nita) Schorr Taube[3] 1933–
- c. Erika[2]

Elizabeth Popper 1878– m. Armin Wittmann 1872–
- Bogod 1902 m. Herta Pipesberg
- Geza 1903 m. Alice Argoud
- Tibor 1905 m. Maria Hortola
- Ernest m. Ruth Bowden

Rudolf Popper 1880s– m. Ernestine Weinberg
- Lola 1909–87 m. Zyga Taube 1905–85
  - Thaddeus 1931–
  - Nita Schorr[3] (adopted)

Isidor Moritz Popper 1891– m. Regina Zweig

Armin 1895–90

Notes:
1. Jacques had another marriage in Cracow (1931) to Marta, daughter of Alfred Holzer and Liebe Silberberg of Borgentowna.
2. Irene and Erika were adopted by Rudolf and Ernestine when quite young following the premature deaths of their parents.
3. Following the deaths of Leon Schorr and Irene in the holocaust, their child Nita was rescued and adopted by Irene's first cousin Lola and her husband Zyga Taube.

Table 22

THE FAMILY OF ARIEL NUTA AND NATALIE WEINBERG OF BUCAREST

Albert m. Zitta	Wilhelm Maritza	Moritz Anette	Josef Otilie	Marcus[1] Rosa Filip	Deborah Isidor Loebl	Matilde Josef Halpern	Clara Artur Popper	Ernestine Rudolf Popper	Rosa Witzling
issue: five	three	two	two	three	two	four	three	one	
			Georges[2]	Robert Paula Justin Lester			Jacques Irene Schorr[3]	Lola Taube[3]	

Notes:

Ariel Nuta Weinberg (1810–1902) and his wife Natalie (ca 1815–1911) had a large family and their descendants flourished in Rumania, Austria, and Germany.

1. Marcus Weinberg (born 1868) married Rosa Filip Leibovici (1880–1944), sister of Simon Filip, Minister of Communications under King Carol of Rumania. Their son, Robert , born 1900, was a lawyer and landowner, and lived in Bucarest until 1941. He married Mina Josipovici, born 1912. He built up a Jewish Sports Association in Rumania. Later, he emigrated to Israel and in 1947 was sent to Paris as Israeli envoy. Robert's sister, Paula Kerschen, born 1922, moved to Canada with her daughter Vera, and has left some notes on the Weinberg family.
2. Georges, a chemical engineer and gifted musician, became Rumanian Minister for the Petroleum Industry, and also emigrated to Israel.
3. The lives of Irene Schorr and Lola Taube, of their parents, and of their children were closely interwoven.

Table 23
TAUBE FAMILY CONNECTIONS

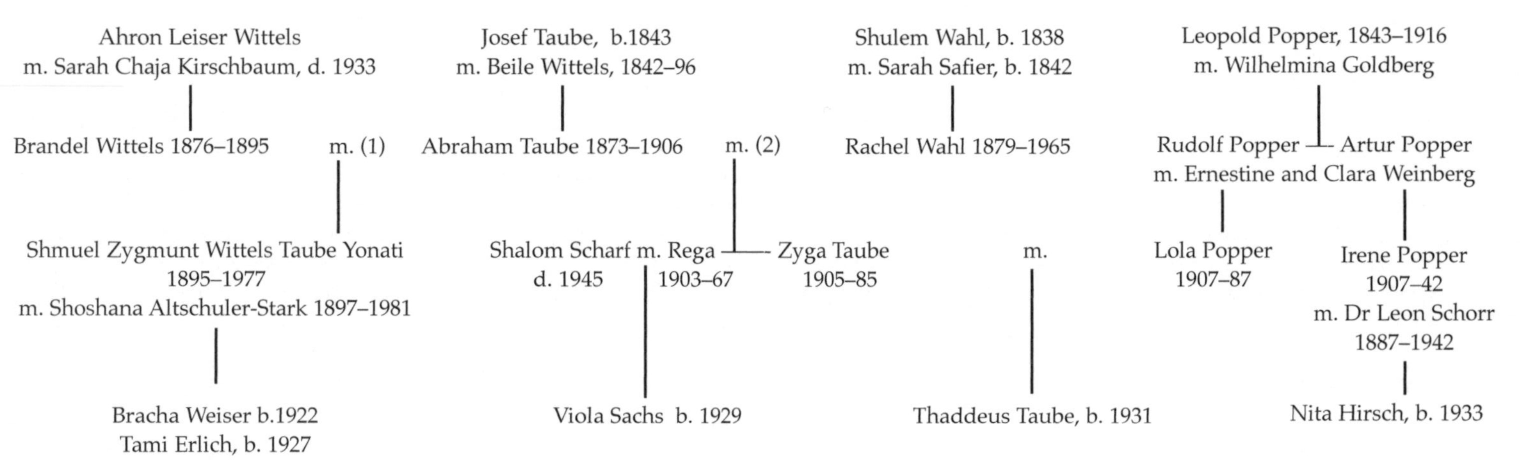

Josef Taube of Lemberg, son of Simon and Mariam Taube of Krystynopol, near Belz.
Shulem Wahl of Tarnobrzeg, son of Leiser and Zlate Roisel Wahl of Tarnobrzeg.
Shulem's daughter Chawa Wahl was the mother of Regina Griffel (who married Dr David Gelles of Vienna).
Rachel Wahl was the mother of Rega and Zyga Taube and through her second marriage to Chaim Simon Ohrenstein, of Lucia 1910–1988 (who married Count Livio Tripcovich 1901–1958).
Shmuel Zygmunt Wittels Taube, the half-brother of Rega and Zyga Taube, adopted the additional Hebrew name of Yonati. His wife Shoshana Altschuler-Stark was the daughter of Baruch and Pesia Leah of Brzezany.
Zyga and Lola Taube lived in Cracow, where their son Thadeus was born. They escaped to America just before the outbreak of WW2 and made their home in California. Ernita (Nita) Schorr lost her parents in the holocaust and was adopted by Lola Popper and her husband Zyga Taube.
Viola Taube Scharf married Ignacy Sachs in Brazil and they now live in Paris.

Table 24
THE FAMILY OF THADDEUS N. TAUBE

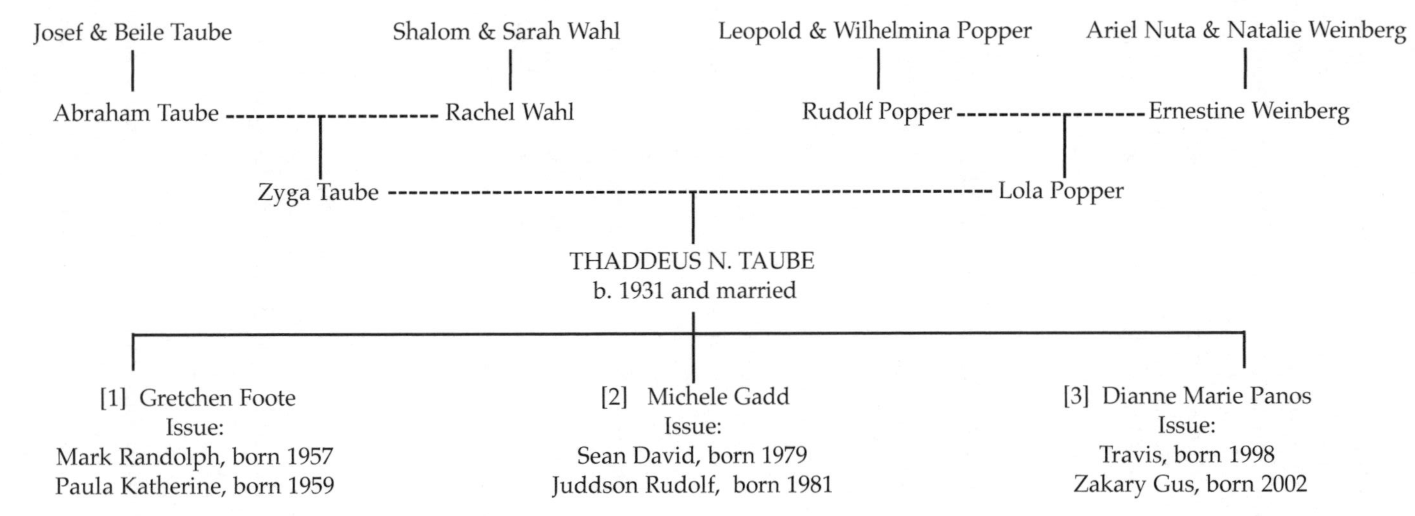

FAMILY CONNECTIONS WITH THE ROKEACH GRAND RABBIS OF BELZ

The involvement of our Taube cousins with the Rokeach dynasty in its early days at Belz certainly had its ups and downs. The Gelles family of Brody, descending from the eighteenth-century scholar Moses Gelles, appear to have a cousinly connection with Shalom Rokeach, the first Belzer Rebbe. Rabbi Yehuda Leib Zundel Ramraz, also a scholar of the Brody Klaus, was the grandfather of Shalom Rokeach as well as of his wife Malka. This Zundel Ramraz may be the Rabbi Yehuda Zundel who was the grandfather of Moses Gelles aka Levush, a great-grandson of the first Moses Gelles.[20]

THE BELZ CHASIDIC DYNASTY

Shalom Rokeach (1779–1855) m. Malka, daughter of Issachar Ber of Sokal, son of Yehuda Zundel Ramraz of Brody*
Joshua Rokeach (1825–94)
Issachar Dov Rokeach (1854–1927)
Ahron Rokeach (1880–1957)**
Issachar Dov Rokeach (1948–), son of Ahron's brother Mordecai Rokeach (1882–1949) m. Sarah, daughter of R. Moses Hager, leader of the Vishnitzer Chasidim

* Sarah Bathya (d. 1826), a daughter of R. Yehuda Zundel, married R. Mordecai Levush, grandson of Moses Gelles of Brody.

** In his later days Ahron Rokeach supported the Agudas Israel movement, which his father had strongly opposed. Jacob Griffel was actively involved with Agudas Israel. The Griffel family had long-standing ties with the Hagers of Otonyia.

I have written about my mother's first cousin, Dr Jacob Griffel, who was prominently involved in the rescue of thousands of Jews from Nazi occupied Europe.[21] These included the fourth Belzer Rabbi Ahron Rokeach and his brother Mordecai, the Rebbe of Bilgoraija. To quote from *Dateline Istanbul:*[22]

> Dr Griffel had as a matter of fact a significant part in the rescue of the revered leader of the Belzer Chassidus. It was he who obtained the necessary emigration papers the Rebbe needed to go to Palestine, and then with not much time to spare to leave Budapest before the Germans occupied Hungary [whence he had fled from Poland with much difficulty and with the tragic loss of his family]. He also played an active part in the preparations for the Rebbe's arrival in Turkey [on his way to Palestine] He obtained with great effort the necessary transit visas ... due to his intervention two prominent functionaries from

the Jewish Agency accompanied Rabbi Rokeach for the entire fateful journey. He personally arranged that the then Chief Rabbi of Israel, Rabbi Herzog, should travel to Aleppo through Syria and Lebanon and personally greet the Rebbe and welcome him upon his rescue.

Chapter Twenty-Three

Tad Taube

Portrait of a philanthropist

The preceding sketch outlines the Taube history and genealogy from the beginning of the seventeenth century to the outbreak of the Second World War. During these three centuries the family lived in a corner of Europe that was part of Poland, but was incorporated into the Austro-Hungarian Empire in the later eighteenth century. Many of them flourished mightily in a material sense, but their spiritual life was certainly not without its periods of stress. They were leaders of the Jewish community in Belz and they went on to prosper in Lemberg and elsewhere in Austrian Galicia before the storms of two world wars and the holocaust wrought havoc with their ancient way of life.

The marriage of Abraham Taube of Lemberg with Rachel Wahl of Tarnobrzeg united two old families, who according to contemporary testimony were already distant blood relations. The millennial Katzenellenbogen clan is very much part of their ancestral background. Simon Taube of Krystynopol was the father of Josef Isaac Taube of Lemberg. The latter's youngest son Abraham had two children by his second wife Rachel. These were Rega and Zyga, who were born in Lemberg in 1903 and 1905. Following the premature death of their father in 1906 and their mother's remarriage to Chaim Simon Ohrenstein of Cracow in 1909, the family settled in that old capital city, where they were joined in 1910 by a little stepsister, Lucia Ohrenstein. They kept in close touch with a step-brother Zygmunt Wittels Taube, who was the son of Abraham Taube's first marriage. He had been brought up by his stepmother Rachel and remained devoted to her and the family. In the mid-1930s he emigrated to Israel, where he left two married daughters.

Zyga Taube grew up in the troubled times after the First World War. He was a very bright boy who studied law in Cracow before going into business. He married Lola Popper of Cracow. Lola came from a well-to-do family whose origins lay in Bohemia, Moravia and Silesia during the period of Austrian rule which ended in 1918. Zyga and Lola were living in the town of Torun in northern Poland before their son's birth in 1931. Lola went back to her mother in Cracow to have her child. Thaddeus first saw the light of day there on 1 April 1931, but the family soon moved to Warsaw. Zyga Taube was doing well in business as the clouds of war again began to gather. Unlike so many of their relatives who perished in the holocaust, Zyga took his family to America before the outbreak of war. He was thus able to salvage his financial assets. After a difficult time in New York the family finally settled in California. Lucia Ohrenstein was already in Italy in 1939 and was in a position to help Rachel and Rega gain entry to that country on their way to Brazil, where they settled in Rio de Janeiro. Rega lost her husband in the holocaust, but she brought up her daughter Viola in Brazil. Viola married the economist Ignacy Sachs and in her peripatetic career collected four degrees before settling in Paris as a University Professor of American literature. Many close relatives were not so lucky. Lola's cousin Irene Popper and her husband Dr Leon Schorr were murdered, but their daughter Ernita Schorr survived and at the end of the war she was rescued by Lola and Zyga, who adopted her and brought her to California to become Tad's beloved step-sister.

Before the war the Poppers lived in Cracow and Bucarest and had ancient connections with Prague and Vienna. Tad's childhood days were spent against this cosmopolitan background. His father Zyga, who had been left fatherless as a baby when Abraham Taube died, could not tell Tad much about the history of the Taube family in Galicia. The potency of that heritage is revealed in the preceding chapter, but Tad could not have been greatly attracted to the Taube story as recounted by his grandmother Rachel. She would have dwelt on her turbulent and unsettled times rather than on ancient religious concerns and achievements. By contrast the Poppers offered the stability of a cultured upper-middle-class family with wider European horizons. Tad's emotional attachment to his mother's people is a significant factor in understanding his character.

HISTORY OF THE POPPER FAMILY

The Poppers may have taken their name from a Slovakian town and the river on which it lay. They were a large tribe who flourished in Austrian Bohemia and Moravia. Benjamin Wolf Popper of Bresnitz (1685–1767) became head of Bohemian Jewry. His son Chaim moved to Prague and followed him in that high office. He prospered in business, profiting particularly from his share in the tobacco concession. He was distinguished for his charitable works, for services to the Prague community, and to the Emperor, and was ennobled as Joachim Edler von Popper in 1790. Subsequent generations spread further afield. In the nineteenth century a number had taken up residence in Vienna. The most successful in various walks of life were ennobled in the course of the next two centuries, before the First World War brought the Austrian Empire to an end. The most distinguished bearers of the Popper name were undoubtedly the two outstanding thinkers, Josef Popper-Lynkeus (1838–1921) and Sir Karl Popper (1902–1994). Both descended from Jewish families of Bohemian origin and spent a part of their lives in Vienna.

The family of Tad's mother had connections going back to Prague and Vienna but their immediate origin is to be sought in Moravia. The Poppers of Bruenn were among the earliest industrialists in that city. In 1840–48 it had seven textile factories. Three were in Jewish hands and one belonged to the Popper brothers.[1]

At about that time a Moritz Popper had established himself in the town of Bielitz in Austrian Silesia. This town had prospered over the centuries as it lay on an important trade route from Cracow to Cieszyn (Teschen) and through the Moravian basin straight to Vienna. Bielitz became noted early for its cloth weaving, thanks to the plentiful supply of sheep wool and mountain streams for powering the mills. In the eighteenth century there was an influx of Prussian weavers and the town continued to grow during the Napoleonic wars, which gave an impetus to industrialization, particularly of cloth manufacture. Polish and Moravian Jews came to the town as merchants, especially for the wool trade, but restrictions on rights of residence and occupational activities deterred Jews from settling there in appreciable numbers until 1848. From the middle of the nineteenth century Jews were participating increasingly in the textile industry. Following the break-up of the Austro-Hungarian Empire in 1918, Bielitz became part of the newly reconstituted Polish Republic under the name of Bielsko. Later it was joined to the town of Biala, which lay just across the Biala River. The provinces of Moravia and Slovakia were merged with the ancient land of Bohemia to create the Czechoslovak Republic.

I found an entry on the JRI – Poland website for Jewish vital records from Cracow which referred to a Leopold Popper and Wilhelmine Goldberg of Bielsko.[2] A booklet on *The History of the Jews from Bielsko-Biala* gives a brief historical account of the Jewish community and makes reference to a Leopold Popper as a pioneer of the modern textile industry. It also mentions his wife's family.[3] This entry is echoed in other sources.[4] The author of a book on the Jewish tombstones of Bielsko was able to supply me with photographs of Leopold Popper's stone and also that of Isaac Goldberg and his wife Jetti Wischnitzer.[5] From the epitaphs, some fragmentary Bielsko civil records, and my search of the Jewish Genealogy JRI – Poland database, an outline of Leopold Popper's family has emerged.[6] The Register of Companies kept in the archives of Cieszyn contributed further information on the business activities and relationships within the family.[7] The Register reveals that the Poppers were in the textile business as manufacturers and merchants from the middle of the nineteenth to the beginning of the twentieth century. At one time or another they had family connections in Bruenn and elsewhere and maintained branches in that Moravian city as well as in Prague and Vienna. From the records it seems that Moritz Popper may have been Leopold's father. He was actively involved in more than one firm and died around 1886. Adolf Popper was Leopold's brother. Heinrich and Samuel Popper, of the same generation, also appear as partners in the business register. These records point to the Poppers of Bielitz as belonging to the family who were among the earliest industrialists of Bruenn.

Figure 21
Tombstone of Leopold Popper of Bielitz (1834–1916)

At the dawn of the twentieth century Leopold Popper of Bielitz was the head of an old established, prosperous and well-integrated Jewish family. The expanding cultural horizons of his children led them to seek a higher education further afield. Artur and Rudolf embarked on professional careers in Cracow. When Artur went to Rumania on business he met Clara Weinberg. She was one of the ten children of Ariel Nuta and Natalie Weinberg of Bucarest. The Weinbergs were another prosperous old family. The available vital records of Bucarest have proved even sparser than those of Bielsko,[8] but when dovetailed with reminiscences of Paula Kerschen and others,[9] a family tree began to take shape.

Artur Popper and Clara Weinberg married in Bucarest and lived there for a while. Their first child, Jacques, was born in 1902. The young Poppers moved back to Cracow, where their second child Irene was born in 1907. There was another little girl, Erika, who died at the age of 8 or 9 years. Around this time, Clara's sister Ernestine came to visit them in Cracow. She met Artur's brother Rudolf, a chemical engineer. They fell in love and married soon afterwards. Their daughter Lola was born in 1909. When Irene and Erika were orphaned at a tender age Rudolf and Ernestine took them under their wing. Irene and Lola were thus not only first cousins but also stepsisters.

Jacques Popper first married Marta Chaya Holzer and, secondly, Anna Kaplan. Irene's first husband was Marceli Liebeskind, who may have been related to the famous latter-day architect of that name. Her second marriage was to Dr Leon Schorr whose parents were from Tarnopol. The young couple lived at Radlow near Tarnow and had a daughter, Ernita, born in 1933. Dr Schorr studied medicine in Germany. At the beginning of the war he was called up to the Polish army and posted to Lvov. He was shot by the Germans at Tarnow in 1942. His sister and wife were taken to a ghetto and perished in the same year. Ernita Schorr survived the war in a convent. Lola Popper lost her father in Auschwitz. When the war ended Lola and Zyga came from America to look for their family. They found Ernita and took her back to their new home in Los Angeles. Nita Schorr Taube married Bob Hirsch and they are flourishing in Southern California.

TAD TAUBE'S LIFE AND WORK

Zyga was a successful and well-respected businessman. He and Lola brought up their son and stepdaughter. They had a good family life. He gave his son a secure and loving home and the best available education. Tad learned at an early age about the tragedy and grandeur of his family's history. A respect for scholarship and learning was inbred. His ancestors were mostly men of property, but there were also rabbis and scholars. His grandfather Abraham was a learned man. Tad's student years at Stanford must have been very happy ones. He has been a most loyal and generous alumnus. As for his business talent, something of his father's acumen was no doubt passed on by example, and certainly via the Taube genes. To my mind, the secret of Tad's success is not entirely in his genetic inheritance, but is at least partly attributable to certain family characteristics. Life in Galicia a couple of hundred years ago was not easy. To acquire and maintain wealth for generations required rare qualities of toughness in mind and body. The old Taube folk were undoubtedly very smart and worked very hard. For Tad, hard work and self-reliance are great virtues. The compassion and generosity comes from the influence of his mother and her family and from long reflection on the tribulations through which his family has passed. Add a great respect for one's roots and the urge to give something of oneself back to the community and we have a very American philosophy – a conservative Judeo-Christian work ethic and moral world view.

Innumerable articles and entries on the Internet describe the career and achievements of Tad Taube. We know that he studied at Stanford University, where he obtained his B.S. and M.S. degrees in 1954 and 1957 in industrial engineering and management. In 1999 he was given an honorary doctorate in philosophy from the Pacific Graduate School of Psychology. He served as an officer in the US Air Force before embarking on a career which encompassed the fields of engineering, the textile business, and the development of his real estate investment and management interests. He founded the Woodmont Group of property companies in 1968. Success brought him increasingly into the social, cultural and economic life of his University and community. His intense loyalties and social conscience also led him inevitably to support Jewish cultural projects in his home state and further afield. Increasing affluence gradually allowed him to back his passionate involvement in this multitude of projects with munificent financial donations, through his own Taube Family Foundation and through other charities that eagerly sought his advice. His business association with Joseph Koret ultimately led to Tad becoming President of the Koret Charitable Foundation which, under his guidance, has disbursed many millions in good causes. Contributions to his *alma mater* included the endowment of the Taube Center for Jewish Studies, the University Institute for Economic Policy Research, and his involvement with the Hoover Institution as a member of its executive board. His intense belief in free enterprise economics and other socio-political matters has also found expression in his support for major projects in Israel. Expanding his commitment to the furtherance of Jewish scholarship and education, he more recently set up the Taube Foundation for Jewish Life and Culture in San Francisco. He is also doing great things for the cause of preserving the records of past Jewish culture in his native Poland and he has been hailed for his efforts in bringing about warm relations of understanding and friendship between Jewish and Polish institutions. His support of the Judaica Foundation in Cracow and of the Jewish Historical Institute in Warsaw are part of this continuing process. In addition to his largesse to so many good causes he freely gives of his time by serving as chairman or in other senior positions on innumerable boards and committees. He has been a Trustee or Governor of several Universities including the Hebrew University in Jerusalem. He has been very much involved in community work in the Bay area. In 1998 United Way appointed him as Chairman of its Community Leadership Council His interest in sport has found expression in the gift of the Taube Family Tennis Stadium at Stanford and in his service on the University Athletics Board. He has also been a supporter of football in a number of ways. Many honours and distinctions are outlined in the appended notes.[10]

THE HOOVER INSTITUTION

Among his many and varied interests Tad has attached a special importance to his association with the Hoover Institution. As a long-time member of its Board of Overseers he has worked hard and contributed generously to translate his personal philosophy into the public good. This philosophy is based on the principles of individual, economic and political freedom, private enterprise and representative government. The Institution's mission is to further these principles 'by collecting knowledge, generating ideas, and disseminating both. The Institution seeks to secure and safeguard peace, improve the human condition, and limit government intrusion into the lives of individuals'.[11]

Four hundred and twenty years ago a certain Chaim Gans, also known as Joachim Gaunse, was the first professing Jew to set foot on American soil. His close kinsman was David Gans of Prague, the famous renaissance man of science and letters – rabbi, historian, mathematician and astronomer. The ancestral background of this family, which over the centuries moved from Germany to Prague and then to Poland, is close to that of my forebears.[12] Joachim Gaunse was a distinguished mining engineer who was sent to America by Sir Walter Raleigh to assess the mineral wealth of this new land. He was undoubtedly a disciple of Georg Bauer, known by his Latin name *Agricola*, who wrote the great treatise *De Re Metallica*, a work that was in due course translated by another famous mining engineer, Herbert Hoover, the founder of the Hoover Institution at Stanford University and 31st President of the United States of America.

CONCLUSION

As Table 24 indicates, Tad is the father of six children. His third wife Dianne has given him two baby sons, Travis and Zakary Gus. Regrettably, the story of their generation is outside the scope of this book.

My study has been of the past and present that contain the seeds of the future. I have not attempted a rounded biography of Tad Taube. Any special qualification that I have to comment on the Taube history is by virtue of my broad study of numerous related families.[13] An understanding of this background of family relationships over a long period of time must have a bearing on the fields of genetic, historical and philosophical enquiry.

NOTES

1. Sigmund Mayer, *Die Wiener Juden* (Wien and Berlin: R. Loewert Verlag, 1917), p.435.
2. Krakow progressive marriages 1919–39. JewishGen JRI – Poland database, [ref. 499/1009].
3. *History of the Jews from Bielsko-Biala* (Tel Aviv: Irgun Josei Bielsko-Biala, 1987), p.3. 'Among the pioneers of the textile industry were Leopold Popper .... the Goldberg brothers' brush factory was the second largest in the whole of Poland between the two world wars' p.4.
4. Pinkas Hakehilot, *Poland,* Volume 3, Bielsko-Biala, p.79. Leopold Popper is referred to as a pioneer of the modern textile industry.
5. Jacek Proszyk, *The Jewish Cemetery in Bielsko-Biala* (Bielsko, 2002). Leopold Popper was born in Lipnik-Biala in 1843, married Wilhelmine Goldberg in 1873, and died in Bielitz in 1916 on his 73rd birthday. His wife was the daughter of Isaac, son of Samuel Goldberg, He was born in Rajcza (District of Saybusch-Zywiec) in 1814 and died in Bielitz in 1902. His wife was Jetti Wischnitzer, born in 1826, the daughter of Meir Wischnitzer from Galicia. She died in Bielitz in the same year as her husband.
6. *From the Vital Records of Bielsko*:
   Adolf Popper (a brother of Leopold Popper) married Cecilie Grauer
   Leopold Popper and Wilhelmine Goldberg's children included:
      Armin, born 1885 and died 1890 in Bielitz
      Honoria, died 1886 in Bielitz
      Isidor Moritz, born 1891 in Bielitz
   JewishGen JRI – Poland database:
   Krakow Births:
   Helena Popper b. 1885 [Ref. 634/1895666]
   Szymon Popper b. 1889 [Ref. 211/1895667]
   Krakow Progressive Marriages:
   In 1920, Isidor Moritz Popper, son of Leopold Popper and Wilhelime Goldberg of Bielsko, m. Regina Zweig, daughter of Moses Aaron Zweig and Gitla Markheim of Podgorze [Ref. 499/1009]. In 1931, Jacob (Jacques) Popper, son of Artur Henryk Popper and Chaya Weinberg of Bucarest m. Marta Holzer, daughter of Alfred Holzer and Lieba Silberberg of Borgentowna [Ref. 918/1010]. Note: Jacques had issue from a second marriage to Anna Kaplan.

   In 1927, Irene Popper, daughter of Artur Henryk Popper and Chaya Weinberg of Krakow m. Marceli Liebeskind, son of Juda-Wolf Liebeskind and Anna Betta Ripp of Krakow [Ref. 804/1009]. Note: this marriage was dissolved and Irene Popper married secondly Dr Leon Schorr. A child of this union is Ernita (Nita) Hirsch née Schorr of Los Angeles California.
7. *The Register of Companies trading in Bielitz* is kept in the Archives of Cieszyn: Archiwum Panstwowe w Cieszynie Zespol: Sad Okregowy w Cieszynie – Rejestr Firm Lag. Nr. 224 (1817).
   Sheet 45. Firm 23. Reg. 9. 2. 1864. A. Popper Soehne & Latzko. Bielitz and with a branch in Vienna. Adolf, Leopold and Samuel Popper (formerly resident in Pesth), Latzko *et al.* Further entries involving Dr Adolf Engelsmann, Gottlieb Bendiener, Heinrich Popper and another Popper.
   Sheet 85. Firm 43. Reg. 7. 3. 1870 Wilhelm Schaeffer & Co. Bielitz with branches in Vienna

and Prague Wilhelm and Victor Schaefer and a Popper.
Sheet 127. Firm 63. Reg, 24. ?. 1872 Popper et Wiedmann of Bielitz Moritz Popper & Robert Wiedmann. Dissolved 12.4.1886 on death of Moritz Popper.
Sheet 171. Firm 85. Reg. 11.2. 1875 Leopold Popper & Co. Bielitz. Woollen Cloth Manufacturers. Agreements between Loepold Popper and Dr Adolf Engelsmann, Heinrich Latzko and further entries 25.3.1875 re branch in Bruenn and 12 June 1876 re branch in Vienna. 24.2.1881 retirement of Dr Engelsmann and 21.8.1885 and 23.?.1886 liquidation of company.
Sheet 231. Firm 107. Reg. 30.5.1879. Heinrich Popper Cloth Merchants Bielitz. Henrich and his wife Josefine Popper. Closure 6.10.1886.
Sheet 328. Firm 146. Reg. 16.7.1886. Leopold Popper & Co. Woollen Cloth Manufacturers. Leopold Popper, manufacturer of Bielitz and Berta Popper née Barthfeld, wife of manufacturer in Bruenn. Closure for family reasons 6.10.1886
Sheet 354. Firm 156. Reg. 24.7.1888. Leopold Popper & Co. Wool Merchants Bielitz with branches in Bruenn and Vienna. Loepold Popper, manufacturer of Bielitz and Theodor Pollak, merchant of Bruenn.Further enties 8.9.1888, 17.3.1889, 4.3.1890, 6.8.1892, 17.4.1895, 4.2.1897, Closure 18.6.1902.

8. Dr Lladislau Gyemant of Cluj-Napoca, Rumania. E-mail address: gyemant@zortec.ro.
Register of Births, Bucarest:
Birth certificate of Robert Marcus Weinberg, born on 27.4.1900 in the house of his parents on Filaret Street 35, Bucarest, son of Marcus Weinberg, 32 years old, clerk, and Rosa Weinberg born Leibovici, 20 years old, housewife [No. 3075/1900].
Register of Marriages, Bucarest:
Marriage certificate of Arnold Kirschen, 26 years old, merchant, born in Braila, resident in Bucarest, Schitu Maegureanu Street 1760, son of Leon Kirschen and Fanny, born Segal, residents in Bucarest, with Paula Weinberg, 20 years old, housewife, born and resident in Bucarest, Cales Victoriei Street, daughter of Marcus and Rosa Weinberg of Bucarest. There was no marriage contract. The witnesses declared that the parties were not related. The marriage took place on 23 August 1922 [No.3621]. Marriage certificate of Robert Weinberg, born 27 April 1900, 34 years old, born and resident in Bucarest, Cales Victoriei Street 61, son of Marcus Weinberg and Rosa, born Leibovici, residents in Bucarest, with Mina Iosipovici, born in Iassi, 2 June 1912, housewife, resident in Bucarest, Alexandru Street 5, daughter of Innus Iosipovici from Bucarest and Rosa, born Marcusohn from Iassi. There was no marriage contract and the witnesses declared that the parties were not related. The marriage took place on 16 May 1934 [No. 432].

9. Paula Kirschen (a grand-daughter of Ariel Nuta and Natalie Weinberg):
Notes on the Weinberg Family (1812–1989):
Strunuta and Natalie Weinberg of Bucarest had ten children. The Weinbergs were very wealthy and all the children had governesses, went to the best schools, and were taught German, French and English.
   i. Albert. Married Zitta and had five children including
      a. Martin who had two children
      b. Jean, a philosopher, who also had two children and lived in Alexandria, Egypt
      c. Frederick, whose wife was a niece of Theodor Herzl
      d. Carl lived in Vienna with his family
      e. Mariette who married a Dr Schwartz and lived in Bucarest
      Albert was mayor of Craiova but moved with his family to Vienna after WW1.
   ii. Wilhelm was the author of several books and his wife Maritza was an accomplished musician whose three children were all concert players.
   iii. Deborah married Isidor Loebel and their two children, Martin and Alfonso, studied in Leipzig. Isidor was a very rich and successful businessman. Deborah had a beautiful coloratura voice and studied at the Vienna Conservatoire.

iv. Moritz and his wife Anette had two daughters, Coca who married Witzling (?) and Beatrice who married Paul Hecht. Anette was a great beauty and an accomplished pianist.
v. Josef and his wife Otilie had two sons, Georges and Henry Georges, a chemical engineer, became Minister for the Petroleum Industry in Rumania and later left for Israel, where he settled in Tel Aviv. Henry also emigrated to Israel.
vi. Mathilde married Josef Halpern, a very successful businessman, and had four children.
vii. Marcus married Rosa Filip and had three children:
    a. Robert married Mina Josipovici
    b. Paula married Arnold Kirchen
    c. Justin married Trude Lirmer.

    The brothers of Rosa Filip [Leibovici] had distinguished careers in the Rumanian public service and were decorated by King Carol. Emilian Filip, who was a lawyer and magistrate, drafted an important Land Reform Law, and his younger brother Simeon Filip, an engineer, became Minister of Communications. Robert Weinberg created the first Sport Association for Jewish children in Rumania along the lines of *Makkabi*. In 1941 he left for Israel, and in 1947 he was sent to Paris to become that country's spokesman to all French-speaking lands. [More on Paula Kirchen below] but she noted that she lost two little boys, that she moved to Canada in 1963 with her daughter Vera, who had married Alfons Profeta of Bucarest, and whose daughter Miky became a librarian and the wife of a chartered accountant, William High Wylie. Vera had two university degrees and so has her daughter Miky. Justin and Trude had four children of whom more below.
viii. Clara (Chaya) married Arthur Popper, a chemical engineer, who came from Poland to Bucarest on business. They married and lived for a while in Bucarest and had their first child, Jacques, who was born there in 1902. Then they moved back to Cracow and had another child, Irene. Their third child, Erika, had a most beautiful singing voice. She died at the age of eight or nine years.
ix. Ernestine married Rudolf Popper. When Artur and Clara had moved to Cracow they invited Ernestine to visit them. Artur's brother Rudolf fell in love with Ernestine, they were married and had one daughter, Lola.
x. Rosa Weinberg married a Witzling. She had no children and died in Bucarest at a young age.

Family Notes on Marcus Weinberg:

Marcus Weinberg married 1898/99 in Bucarest to Rosa Filip (1880–1944).

Children:

i. Robert, born 1900, a lawyer and big landowner, married in Moldavia to Mina Josipovici (1934–92) in Paris. Lived in Bucarest until 1941 when arrested by the Communists. Moved to Israel and died in Paris.
ii. Paula, born 17 April 1902, interior designer, married in Rumania, 27 August 1922 to Arnold Kerschen, business man (1887–1949). Paula moved to Canada in 1963 with daughter Vera (born 1924) who married Alfons Profeta in Bucarest but later divorced and remarried to become Vera Profeta-Nistor. Vera's daughter Miky married William Hugh Wylie, C.A. and their children are Andrew (born 1983) and Sean (born 1985).
iii. Justin Lester, born 1905, married Trude Lirmer and their children are Sandi (born 1952), Dany and Gary (twins), and Linda Lester.

Sketch of the Popper-Goldberg Family based on the notes of Tibor Wittmann.

10. Awards made to Tad Taube:
    - Torch of Learning Award, Hebrew University, Jerusalem 1982
    - Scopus Award of the Hebrew University 1985

- President's Club Award of the State of Israel 1991
- Glide memorial United Methodist Church 1994
- Economic Freedom Award of the Institute for Advanced Strategic & Political Studies, Jerusalem 1996 (for advancing the cause of freedom and democratic values)
- Distinguished Community Service Award of the Anti-defamation League, 1998 (in recognition and appreciation of your community activism in promoting and advancing the cause of human rights, dignity, education, and equal opportunity)
- Alexis de Tocqueville Award of United Way, 1998
- Polish Government Medal, 1999 (for leadership in repatriating Polish archives taken from the Polish people in World War 2)
- Arthur Ashe Award of the Youth Tennis Advantage Program, 2000 (for bringing healthy sports activity to disadvantaged young people)

11. http://www-hoover.stanford.edu/Main/brochure/mission.html.
12. E. Gelles, 'David and Chaim Gans of Prague', *Shemot,* 12, 1 (March 2004).
13. E. Gelles, unpublished articles on other family links.

Figure 22
Thaddeus N. Taube

Chapter Twenty-Four

Lucia's Dolce Vita

The adventurous life of an Italian cousin

Among the unusual and diverse life stories of my mother's first cousins is that of Lucia Ohrenstein, whose very existence was unknown to me until quite recently. Lucia was a girl from a once-orthodox Jewish family in Poland who became an Italian Countess and a leading light in post-war Rome café society. She died over a decade ago, and it was by no means easy to gather the barest facts on her life.

My quest started in Vienna where I was born. The state archives, including the Austrian army records, led me to the family of a cousin who had become a leading psychiatrist in Chicago and a pioneer of modern community mental health care. His mother's records in the Strasbourg municipal archives pointed to an origin in the little town of Tarnobrzeg northwest of Cracow in what was then part of Austrian Galicia. From the archives in Lviv and Sandomierz I finally arrived at a picture of my great-grandparents, Shulim Wahl and Sarah Safier of Tarnobrzeg. Shulim and Sarah had six children including my grandmother Eva and my great-aunt Rachel.[1]

Rachel Wahl's first husband was Abraham Taube of Lemberg. I learnt from my newly-discovered cousins that Rachel married again after being widowed and had a child called Luska. Little information was forthcoming on her second husband. His name was Ohrenstein, He was taken prisoner by the Russians in Lemberg during the First World War and sent to Siberia. He returned to Poland after the war but died in the 1920s. Lucia, as she was called later, was reportedly born in Cracow around 1910 and became the wife of an Italian businessman in Warsaw whose name sounded like Purini. I heard that she fled to Italy on the outbreak of war in 1939, and that she had met and later married a Count Livio Tripcovich belonging to a Dalmatian shipping family.

I began my search for Lucia by telephoning the London offices of major Italian companies and the trail led finally to the Reunione Adriatica, where Romeo Puri Purini was confirmed as the head of the Polish branch of this leading insurance company during the years leading up to the Second World War.[2] The library of the Italian Cultural Institute in London's Belgrave Square provided some of the background to the Tripcovich family.

Several books referred to the family's historical involvement with Trieste.[3] I proceeded by contacting the appropriate ministries in Rome and town offices in Trieste and Venice.

My requests for information on Lucia Ohrenstein and Livio Tripcovich invariably elicited courteous replies. Some were negative but directed me elsewhere. The Trieste town office wrote that a Livio Tripcovich was unknown, and it only occurred to me later that I should have quoted his full name Oliviero. The Central State Archive in Rome sent me copies of the relevant extracts from the Golden Book of the Italian Nobility with details of the honours conferred on members of the Tripcovich family. Livio's elder brother Mario held the hereditary title, while the honours of Count Livio and his sister Maria were personal.[4]

It was actually the Trieste Chamber of Commerce that provided me with the lead to their heir, the composer Raffaello de Banfield. In reply to my enquiry he suggested that I might find some records in Bologna.[5] That city's archives did indeed confirm that Lucia and Livio had married there in 1947, and I received a certificate giving their names, ages and places of birth. I then managed to obtain a death certificate from the Trieste municipality which states that Oliviero, son of Diodato Tripcovich and Ermenegilda Pozza, was born in Trieste in 1901 and died in 1958, and that his widow Lucia was the daughter of Chaim Simon Ohrenstein and Rachel Wahl. This document confirms Lucia's date and place of birth as 10 June 1910 in Cracow. It also gives the full name of Lucia's father, which I had been unable to obtain from surviving relatives.[6]

With this information I could now turn to the Internet, where the websites sponsored by Jewish genealogical societies provide a substantial body of data on the old capital city of Cracow. The city's marriage banns on Jewish Gen, JRI Indexing – Poland had the following details: Chaim Simon Ohrenstein married Rachel Wahl in 1909. The groom was born in Cracow to Moses Leib and Reizle Ohrenstein and the bride was born in Tarnobrzeg to Shulem and Sura Wahl. The Cracow cemetery records give the location of the graves of Chaim Simon and his father.

I was told that sometime after Livio's death Lucia met Morton Llewellyn and that they lived in Rome. I could not find any records of Morton there and I drew a blank from a consultation of the available reference works. I suspected that he might have some connection with the prominent Welsh family of that name, and so I decided to write to the family. I thought they might have heard of him but the response to my letter exceeded my expectation. When I ultimately made contact with Sir Dai Llewellyn, the 4th Baronet, I was gratified to receive his personal recollections of my cousin.[7] I thus learned a lot about Lucia from the relatives of the men in her life, and their letters were most complimentary. Combining these reports with the genealogical data, I was at last able to form a picture of Lucia.

The story goes that Lucia helped her family gain entry to Italy at the outbreak of war when she produced a bundle of love letters from her husband. Then the frontier gates swung open. Purini's brother was a member of

Mussolini's personal staff and his name was the magic password. Lucia herself was protected during the war by her brother-in-law's influence. She had also adopted the Catholic faith.

She had met Livio Tripcovich through her husband. When Purini died at war's end, a romance blossomed between the young widow and the Dalmatian Count. Livio and Lucia married and lived happily together until his untimely death.

Diodato Tripcovich had founded a shipping company before the turn of the century. It expanded and diversified and became a major player in the development of Trieste under the Italian flag after the First World War. After his sons, Counts Mario and Livio, his daughter Maria's husband, Baron Goffredo de Banfield, took over the running of the business. His son, Baron Raffaello de Banfield-Tripcovich, is now the bearer of the family name. He is the nephew of Countess Lucia and holds her in affectionate memory.

Lucia and Livio enjoyed a decade of La Dolce Vita in Rome, Venice and Trieste. They entertained lavishly and Lucia mixed her aristocratic friends with stage and screen idols. Her cousins from the New World were warmly received. She and Livio often visited Monte Carlo, where they knew Princess Grace and befriended various celebrities.

Lucia was alone for some time after Livio's death. Then she met Morton Llewellyn, an investment banker in Rome, who numbered the Vatican among his distinguished clients. He was a cousin of the late Sir Harry Morton Llewellyn, the well-known Olympic show jumper. By the 1960s his friendship with Lucia was firmly established, but they did not marry until much later because Lucia was reluctant to give up her title and the perquisites that came with it. They continued to be prominent members of Rome café society until they retired to the South of France.

Sir Dai Llewellyn first met them in Rome in the 1960s, and later he used to see them at the house of Princess Maritzina Odescalchi in Cap d'Ail, where the Princess gave receptions on the Sunday night after every Grand Prix de Monaco. Maritzina, who was one of Lucia's closest friends, bore the family name of Innocent XI, a great Pope, described by Lord Acton as a rare and original figure. Such a description would also be apt for Lucia's ancestors from Padua and Venice. In a strange way Lucia's journey to Italy was like coming home to roost.

NOTES

1. E. Gelles, 'My Mother's People', *Sharsheret Hadorot*, 16, 4 (Oct. 2002). E. Gelles, 'All Quiet on the Eastern Front', *Avotaynu*, xvi, 4 (Winter 2000). E. Gelles, 'Searching for Eve', *Avotaynu*, xvii, 2 (Summer 2001).
2. Letter dated 23 February 2001 from Milan office of Reunione Adriatica di Securta confirming that Romeo Puri Purini was in charge of the independent branch office in Warsaw in 1941.
3. Elio Apih, Trieste. Editore Laterza 1988, pp.215–16; http//www.tripcovich.com /storia.htm.

4. Archivio Centrale dello Stato, Rome. Extract from the Libro d'Oro della Nobilta Italiana (No.12097) for Count Oliviero Tripcovich – see vol. xxiv, p. 110 re Letters Patent dated 1 October 1936.
5. Baron Raffaello de Banfeld, private correspondence, 12 March 2001. Commune di Bologna, Estratto dei Registri degli Atti di Matrimonio. Atto No. 71, parte 1, anno 1947.
6. Commune di Trieste, Cert. No. 16639 dated 28 November 1958 http://data.jewishgen.org/jgen/wc.dll?jgproc~jgsys~jripllat.
7. Sir Dai Llewellyn, private correspondence, 15 May 2001.

B

Stato: REPUBBLICA ITALIANA
Etat:
Staat:
Stade:
Estado:
Staat:
Devlet:

Comune di: BOLOGNA
Commune de:
Gemeinde:
Municipality:
Municipio de:
Gemeente:
Köy veya mahâlle:

ATTO N. 71 parte 1° anno 1947

Estratto dai registri degli atti di matrimonio
Extrait des registres de l'état civil concernant un mariage
Auszug aus dem Eheregister
Extract of the register of marriages
Extracto del registro de matrimonios
Uittreksel uit de registers van de burgerlijke stand omtrent een huwelijk
Evlenme kayit hülâsasi sureti

a) Luogo di celebrazione del matrimonio — lieu du mariage — Ort der Eheschliessung — place of marriage — lugar del matrimonio — plaats van huwelijksvoltrekking evlenme yeri	BOLOGNA
b) Data della celebrazione — date du mariage — Datum der Eheschliessung — date of marriage — fecha del matrimonio — datum van het huwelijk — evlenme tarihi	09.08.1947
c) Cognome del marito — nom de famille du mari — Familienname des Ehemannes — surname of husband — apellido del marido — familienaam van de man — kocanin soyadi	TRIPCOVICH
d) Prenome del marito — prénoms du mari — Vornamen des Ehemannes — christian names of husband — nombres de pila del marido — voornamen van de man — kocanin adi	OLIVIERO
e) Data di nascita o età del marito — date de naissance ou âge du mari — Geburtsdatum oder Lebensalter de Ehemannes — date of birth or age of husband — fecha de nacimiento o edad del marido — geboortedatum of leeftijd van de man — dogum tarihi; yas	di anni 46
f) Luogo di nascita del marito — lieu de naissance du mari — Geburtsort des Ehemannes — place of birth of husband — lugar de nacimiento del marido — geboorteplaats van de man — kocanin dogum yeri	TRIESTE
g) Cognome della moglie prima del matrimonio — nom de famille de la femme — Familienname der Ehefrau — Surname of wife — apellido de la mujer — familienaam van de vrouw — karinin soyadi	OHRENSTEIN
h) Prenome della moglie — prénoms de la femme — Vornamen dei Ehefrau — christian names of wife — nombres de pila de la mujer — voornamen van de vrouw — karinin adi	LUCIA
i) Data di nascita o età della moglie — date de naissance ou âge de la femme — Geburtsdatum oder Lebensalter der Ehefrau — date of birth or age of wife — fecha de nacimiento o edad de la mujer — geboortedatum of leeftijd van de vrouw — dogum tarihi veya yasi	di anni 37
j) Luogo di nascita della moglie — lieu de naissance de la femme — Geburtsort der Ehefrau — place of birth of wife — lugar de nacimiento de la mujer — geboorteplaats van de vrouw — karinin dogum yeri	CRACOVIA
k) Scioglimento o annullamento — dissolution ou annulation — Auflösung oder Nichtigerklärung — dissolution or nullification disolución o anulacion — ontbinding of nietigverklaring — seval veya butlan	XXXXXXXXXXXXXXXXXXXXX

NON ESISTONO ANNOTAZIONI

Data in cui è rilasciato l'estratto con firma e bollo dell'ufficio — date de délivrance, signature et sceau du dépositaire — Ausstellungsdatum, Unterschrift und Dienstsiegel des Registerführes — date of issue, signature and seal of keeper — fecha de expedición firma y sello del depositario — datum van afgifte, ondertekening en segel van de bewaarder — verildigi tarih, nüfus (ahvali sahsiye) memurunum imzasi ve mührü

BOLOGNA, li 30/03/2001

Timbro dell'Ufficio

L'ufficiale dello stato civile

Figure 23
Lucia Ohrenstein's marriage record

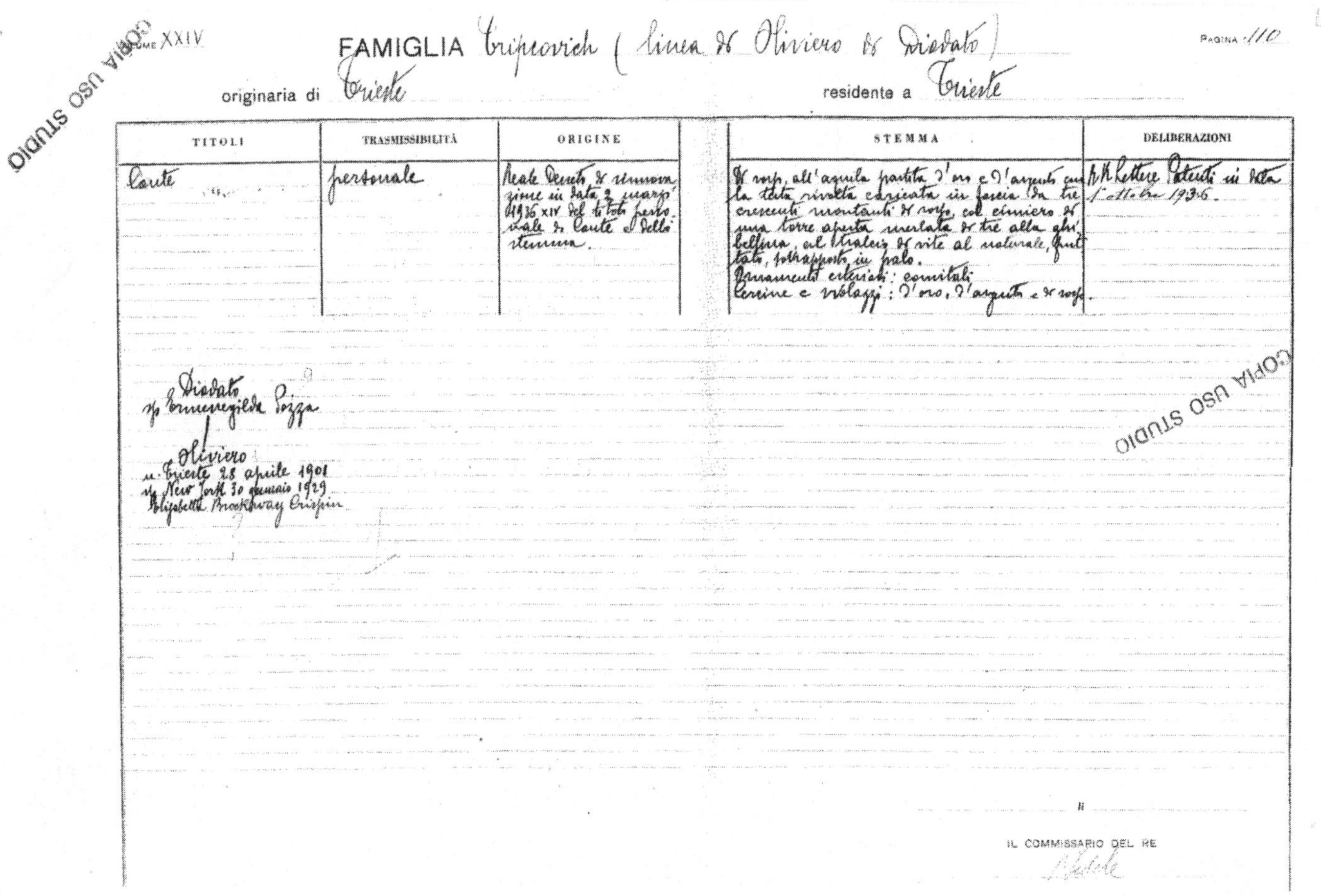

TOMO XXIV

PAGINA 110

FAMIGLIA Tripcovich (linea di Oliviero di Diodato)

originaria di Trieste residente a Trieste

TITOLI	TRASMISSIBILITÀ	ORIGINE	STEMMA	DELIBERAZIONI
Conte	personale	Reale Decreto di rinnovazione in data 2 marzo 1936 XIV del titolo personale di Conte e dello stemma.	Di rosso, all'aquila partita d'oro e d'argento con la testa rivolta caricata in fascia da tre crescenti montanti di rosso, col cimiero di una torre aperta merlata di tre alla ghibellina, col tralcio di vite al naturale, fruttato, sottapposto in palo. Ornamenti esteriori: comitali. Cercine e svolazzi: d'oro, d'argento e di rosso.	RR Lettere Patenti in data 1 ottobre 1936.

Diodato
m. Ermenegilda Pozza

Oliviero
n. Trieste 28 aprile 1901
m. New York 30 gennaio 1929 Elisabetta Brockway Crispin

IL COMMISSARIO DEL RE

Figure 24
Tripcovich record of ennoblement

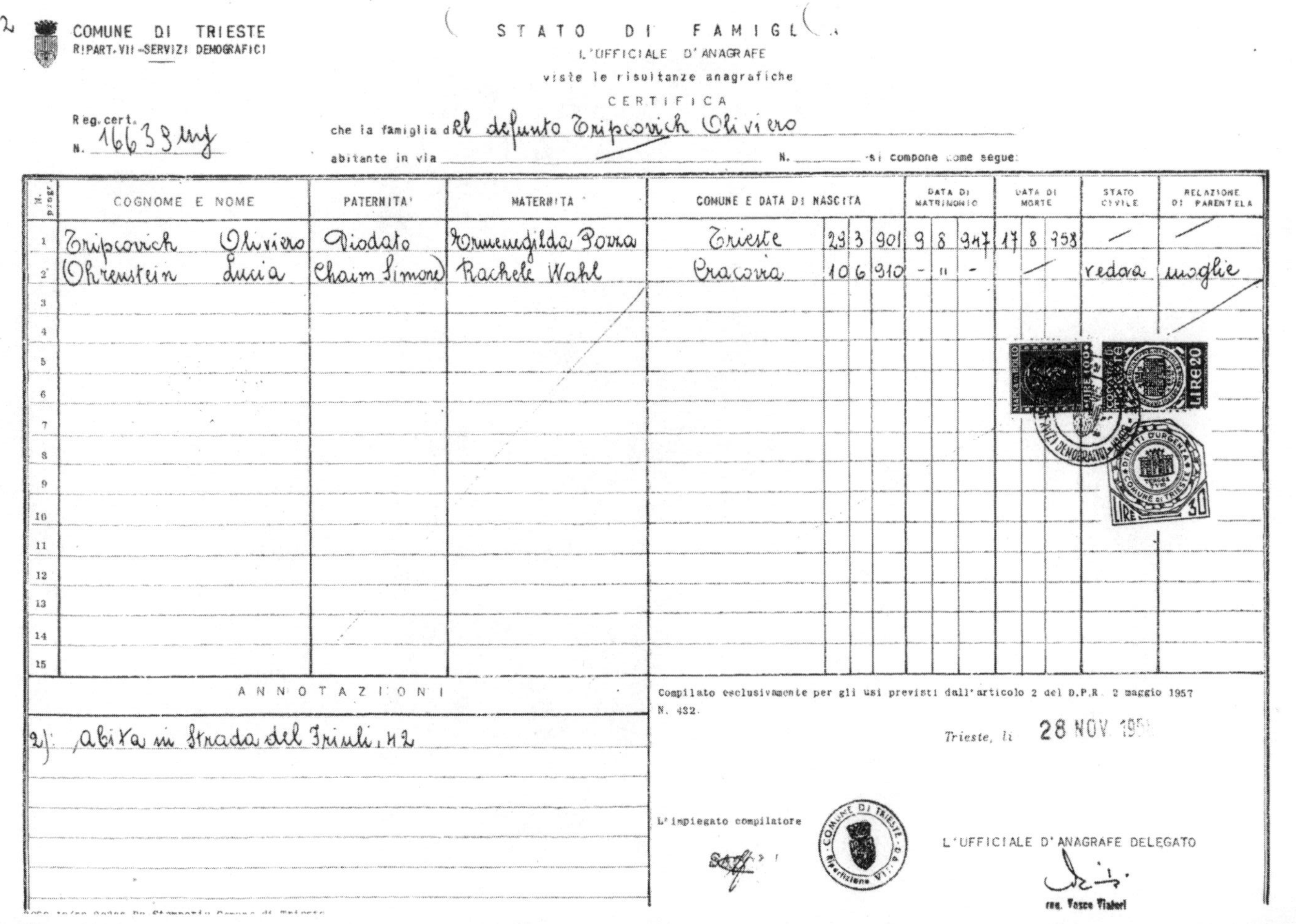

12 COMUNE DI TRIESTE
RIPART. VII - SERVIZI DEMOGRAFICI

STATO DI FAMIGLIA

L'UFFICIALE D'ANAGRAFE
viste le risultanze anagrafiche
CERTIFICA

Reg. cert.
N. 16633 my

che la famiglia del defunto Tripcovich Oliviero
abitante in via ______ N. ______ si compone come segue:

N. d'ord.	COGNOME E NOME	PATERNITA'	MATERNITA	COMUNE E DATA DI NASCITA				DATA DI MATRIMONIO			DATA DI MORTE			STATO CIVILE	RELAZIONE DI PARENTELA
1	Tripcovich Oliviero	Diodato	Ermenegilda Porra	Trieste	23	3	901	9	8	947	17	8	958	/	/
2	Ohrenstein Lucia	Chaim Simone	Rachele Wahl	Cracovia	10	6	910	-	"	-	/			vedova	moglie
3															
4															
5															
6															
7															
8															
9															
10															
11															
12															
13															
14															
15															

ANNOTAZIONI

2): abita in Strada del Friuli, 42

Compilato esclusivamente per gli usi previsti dall'articolo 2 del D.P.R. 2 maggio 1957 N. 432.

Trieste, li 28 NOV 195

L'impiegato compilatore

COMUNE DI TRIESTE Ripartizione VII

L'UFFICIALE D'ANAGRAFE DELEGATO

rag. Vasco Viatori

LIRE 100 MARCA DA BOLLO · LIRE 20 · LIRE 30 DIRITTI D'URGENZA COMUNE DI TRIESTE

Figure 25
Death record of Count Livio Tripcovich

Figure 26
Count and Countess Livio Tripcovich

Chapter Twenty-Five

Viola's Quest for Identity

Another cousin's intellectual odyssey

Most people derive a feeling of identity from the circle of their immediate family and from their tribal associations. Their connection with the past may not go much further than an acquaintance with the lives of their grandparents. As for a place in the cosmic scheme, most continue to rely on received religion. The consolations of philosophy are reserved to the few, but the search for roots is becoming an increasingly popular pastime. Those engaged in this hobby are no doubt fuelled by hopes of gaining a better understanding of themselves, and it is certainly one of the paths I have followed in the pursuit of self-knowledge.

It required a measure of serendipity to find my great-aunt Rachel Wahl.[1] She was born in Tarnobrzeg in Austrian Galicia in 1879 and died in Rio de Janeiro in 1965. Her three children were Lucia Ohrenstein who became an Italian countess, Zyga Taube who prospered in California and Rega Taube who spent her later years in Brazil and had a daughter Viola.

When I discovered this branch of my family, I was amazed to find that my cousin Viola had been engaged on an identity quest of a very different kind for half a lifetime. Mine is through genealogical and historical study, while hers has been a journey of the literary imagination.

Viola's parents were Shalom Scharf and Rega Taube. She was born in 1929 and spent her early years in Hamburg, Brussels and London before going back to Poland. In 1939 she escaped with her mother and widowed grandmother and found refuge in Brazil. Her father did not get away. Viola grew up in Rio where she married the economist Ignacy Sachs. They returned to Poland after the war, and then they were in India for several years before settling in France.

From her schooldays Viola has had a passionate interest in American literature. She gained master's degrees and doctorates in this field from Universities in Brazil, Poland, India and France, and she has been Professor at the University of Paris for several decades. Her first doctoral dissertation was on Walt Whitman's *Leaves of Grass*. She has written works on Faulkner, Hawthorne and Melville, as well as Twain, Fitzgerald and, above all, on recurrent patterns and trends in American literature. A book published in

Poland in 1966 sold 30,000 copies and has since been issued in a revised edition.[2] The direction of her more recent studies is indicated in a *Festschrift* dedicated to her in 1996. It deals with the impact of other cultures, particularly the black and red, on the white Puritan American culture.[3] Her engagement with Melville's *Moby Dick* has been a long one. She delved into the symbolic world of this American masterpiece in such books as *Le Contre-Bible de Melville: Moby-Dick déchiffré* and *The Game of Creation*.[4]

Her interpretation of Melville's world-view draws on a wide range of literary criticism, biblical hermeneutics, the Cabbala, including the symbolic interpretation of letters and numbers, subjects such as astrology and alchemy, and others of an occult nature. Depth psychology, sociology, anthropology, the history of art, and the history of ideas are some of the disciplines contributing insights into the work of great American writers. With *Moby-Dick,* Viola believes that Melville is attempting to write a new sacred scripture for nineteenth-century America. The hidden message is steeped in myth and cipher. This is about Ahab who 'thou knowest was a crowned king' and Ishmael the castaway, and other deeply symbolic characters in the crew. Moby Dick is the cosmic womb to which one has to return for ultimate revelation. In this sense he is Jonah's fish, the Right Whale, through the mouth of which Jonah, according to Ishmael, seems to have passed. Yet Moby Dick is simultaneously Job's Leviathan – the primordial chaos. The dichotomy between the two levels of Melville's 'scripture' corresponds to the dichotomy between Christian civilization and pagan wilderness that lies at the roots of the New World and inspired the Puritan literary imagination.

To quote again from *The Game of Creation*:

> the apparent text with its linear time, realistic whaling details, precise historical and geographical references, logical sequence of ideas and Aristotelian poetics can be compared with the one superficial western world which Columbus discovered – the different levels of the text correspond to numberless unknown worlds; contrary to Columbus' singular limited world, they are indeterminate. Numberless, like the great enigmas of life, they will never be encompassed by man – Melville's conception of his book as a backwards quest in time and space to primordial origins shapes the book's very language.

I should like to think that Viola Sachs, who grew up with a dim and distant awareness of her forebears, had an inherited disposition to become enthralled with the mysticism and symbolism of Melville's work, which draws so heavily on the Judeo-Christian tradition while 'turning it on its head.[5] I would imagine that many readers must be very sceptical about her involvement in numerology and the alleged codes in Moby Dick but this should not detract from her more solid contributions to American literary scholarship.

Viola and I had a common great-grandfather, Shalom Wahl. Our grandmothers Rachel and Eva Wahl were siblings from a once united family. Rachel was married twice. Firstly, to her distant cousin, Abraham Taube, and secondly, to Chaim Simon Ohrenstein. Abraham Taube was the son of a wealthy jute merchant and a gentle Talmud scholar. He died when his daughter Rega was 3 years old, so Viola has no recollections of him. Her grandmother Rachel, on the other hand, was a dominant, or even domineering, character who lived to a ripe old age, and exerted a powerful influence over Viola in her formative years. Viola's affection and respect centred rather on her uncle Zyga Taube, who sprang from the union of Wahl and Taube.

The biblical tale of Jonah and the whale has been a recurrent theme in western literature and art, but it became of particular prominence in nineteenth-century American literature, and continues to fascinate depth psychologists and writers to this day

My fanciful thoughts were stimulated by one of Viola's precursors in American literary criticism. In *The Power of Blackness: Hawthorne, Poe and Melville,* Harry Levin talks about the so-called *Jonah Complex,* of the reluctant prophet brought to recognize his responsibilities through his prayerful ordeal inside the whale, forced out to propound unwelcome truths, and treated without honour by his compatriots and contemporaries.[6] The passage from darkness into the light, from the unconscious to the conscious, from discord to peace, is a theme taken up by American writers since their Civil War. The sin of slavery and the virtue of its abolition, as a black and white duality, weighs on the minds of those in the title of Levin's book and haunts their successors, such as James and Faulkner, O'Neill and Ezra Pound.

Against this background, I begin to understand how Viola's literary studies led her to focus on the role of the black, red and white in the American psyche, and to her later concern with sociological questions about the Negro in American society.

NOTES

1. E. Gelles, 'All Quiet on the Eastern Front', *Avotaynu,* xvi, 4 (Winter 2000); 'Searching for Eve', *Avotaynu,* xvii, 2 (Summer 2001).
2. Viola Sachs, *Idee przewodnie literatury amerykanskiey* (Warsaw: 1966 [revised 1992]).
3. Viola Sachs, 'African American Components of Mid-Nineteenth Century American Identity. Moby Dick; or The Whale: a Case-Study', *Letterature d'America* (Rome, Bulzoni Editore, 1996), xvi, No.65.
4. Viola Sachs, *The Game of Creation* (Paris: Editions de la Maison des sciences de l'homme, 1982).
5. David Lodge, *Changing Places* (London: Penguin, 1978), Ch. 5: 'Walt Whitman who laid end to end words never seen in each other's company before, outside of a dictionary, and Herman Melville who split the atom of the traditional novel in the effort to make whaling a universal metaphor.'
6. Harry Levin, *The Power of Blackness: Hawthorne, Poe and Melville* (London: Faber and Faber, 1958), Ch. 7.

VII.

MY FATHER'S FAMILY

I shall light a candle of understanding in thine heart
which shall not be put out

II Esdras, 14:25

Chapter Twenty-Six

Three Generations: Grandfather, Father and Son

Where did I come from and where am I going?

Figure 27
Dr David Gelles in Jerusalem, 1922, and lecturing in Vienna, 1955

COPIA.

Q. F. F. F. Q. S.

SUMMIS AUSPICIIS AUGUSTISSIMI IMPERATORIS AC REGIS

FRANCISCI IOSEPHI I

IN UNIVERSITATE LITTERARUM VINDOBONENSI

NOS

ADOLPHUS MENZEL

IURIS DOCTOR IURIS PUBLICI PROFESSOR PUBLICUS ORDINARIUS IMPERATORIS AUSTRIAE A CONSILIIS AULAE

H. T. UNIVERSITATIS RECTOR

FRIDERICUS LIBER BARO DE WIESER

IURIS DOCTOR OECONOMIAE POLITICAE PROFESSOR PUBLICUS ORDINARIUS
IMPERATORIS AUSTRIAE A CONSILIIS AULAE EQUES ORDINIS CORONAE FERREAE CL. III
CAES. ACADEMIAE SCIENTIARUM VINDOBONENSIS SOCIUS

H. T. IURIS CONSULTORUM ORDINIS DECANUS

Aemilius nobilis Schrutka de Rechtenstamm
iuris doctor processus civilis austriaci professor publicus
ordinarius imperatoris austriae a consiliis aulae

PROMOTOR RITE CONSTITUTUS

IN

VIRUM CLARISSIMUM

Davidum Gelles

e Kudrynce in Galicia ortum

POSTQUAM EXAMINIBUS LEGITIMIS LAUDABILEM IN UNIVERSO IURE DOCTRINAM PROBAVIT

DOCTORIS IURIS NOMEN ET HONORES IURA ET PRIVILEGIA

CONTULIMUS IN EIUSQUE REI FIDEM HASCE LITTERAS UNIVERSITATIS SIGILLO SANCIENDAS CURAVIMUS

VINDOBONAE, DIE *XIII. m. Novembris* MCMXV.

A. Menzel mp. *F. Wieser mp.* *Ae. Schrutka mp.*

L. S.

Copiam cum originali in charta signo publico instructa

Figure 28
Dr David Gelles, Doctor Juris

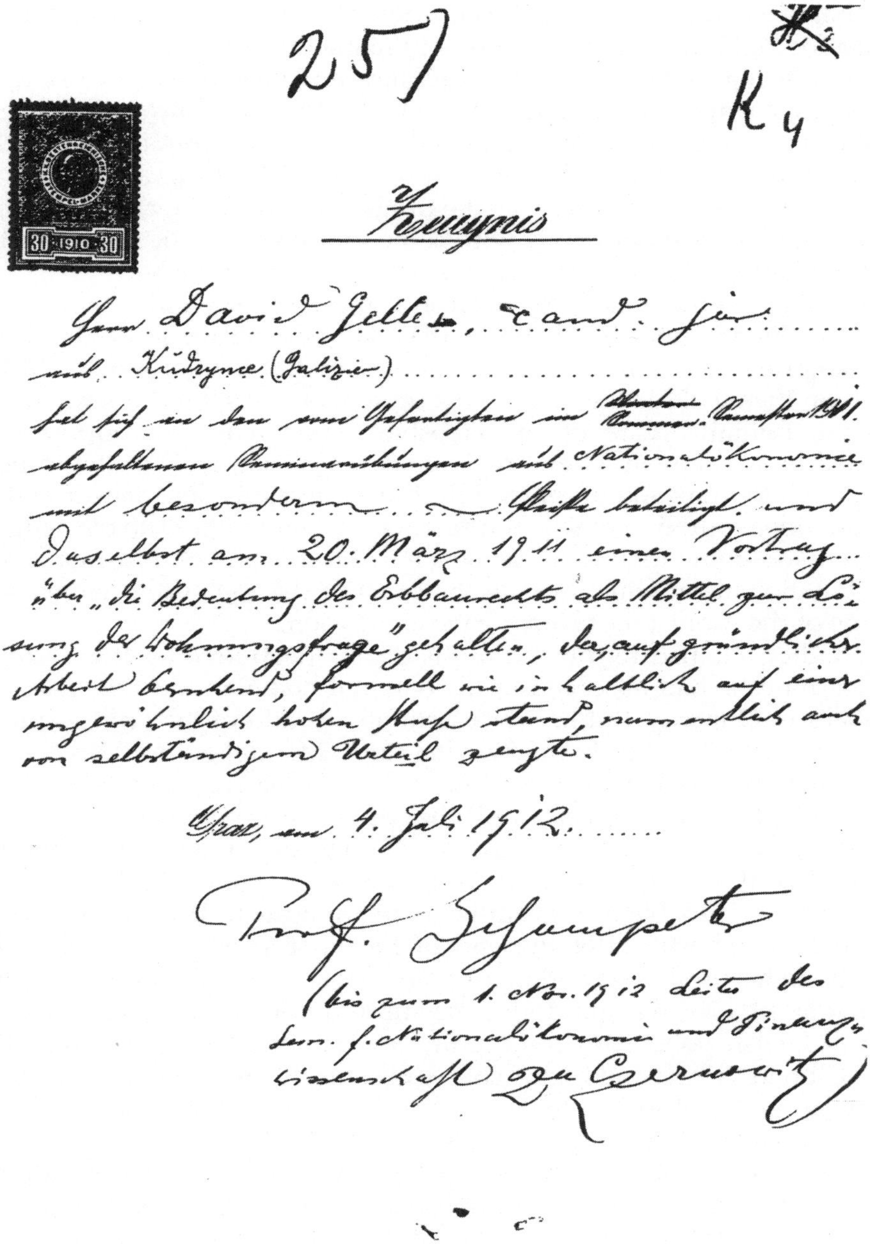

257

K 4

30 1910 30

Zeugnis

Herr David Geller, cand. jur. aus Kudrynce (Galizien) hat sich an den vom Unterfertigten im Sommer-Semester 1911 abgehaltenen Seminarübungen aus Nationalökonomie mit besonderem Fleiße beteiligt und daselbst am 20. März 1911 einen Vortrag über „Die Bedeutung des Erbbaurechts als Mittel zur Lösung der Wohnungsfrage" gehalten, der, auf gründlicher Arbeit beruhend, formell wie inhaltlich auf einer ungewöhnlich hohen Stufe stand, namentlich auch von selbständigem Urteil zeugte.

Graz, am 4. Juli 1912.

Prof. Schumpeter

(bis zum 1. Nov. 1912 Leiter des Sem. f. Nationalökonomie und Finanzwissenschaft zu Czernowitz)

Figure 29
Testimonial from Professor J. Schumpeter

Nahum Uri Gelles was born 150 years ago in a Galician village called Narayow, at a time when the province was part of the Austro-Hungarian Empire. His family came out of Germany in the middle ages. Later they were based in Brody for several centuries. My grandfather was a rabbi in Galicia for nigh on 60 years. He died in Vienna in 1934 and is buried in that city. He was highly respected for his learning and piety. There are numerous references to responsa addressed to him by leading East European rabbis on questions of Jewish law. His eighteenth-century ancestors included Chief Rabbi Samuel Hillman of Metz and Moses Gelles, who was a noted scholar of the Brody *Klaus*. The latter was the progenitor of several rabbinical lines. There were Gelles connections with some famous Chasidic rabbis such as Pinchas Shapiro of Koretz and the Friedmans of Czortkow.

My father David Gelles was born in Galicia in 1883 and practiced as a lawyer in Vienna until his death in 1964. He took refuge in England from the time of the Anschluss until just after the end of the Second World War. The main theme of his life, next to his profession, was the Zionist cause.

In the twilight years of the Habsburg monarchy, the opportunities afforded by a relatively liberal regime drew Galician Jews to the Imperial capital, where they sought entry into the professions, journalism and the arts, or endeavoured to make their fortunes in commerce. The old religious ties were loosening their hold, while a new kind of anti-Semitism evoked a Jewish nationalism, which was in the spirit of the age and to which some strands of the Zionist movement gave expression.

My father retained to the end of his days a deep love for the traditions and learning he had absorbed in his parental home and in the *yeshivah* at Munkacz in Hungary. But he was essentially a child of the Enlightenment. In Czernowitz the study of Lessing and Mendelssohn, Voltaire and Rousseau replaced that of the Talmud. His formative years fell into the period of Russian *Pogroms* and the publication of Theodor Herzl's *Judenstaat.* He shared the enthusiasms of his Jewish student contemporaries.

From Czernowitz he moved to Vienna where he obtained his degree of *Doctor Juris* in 1915. He was admitted as an advocate in 1916 and started his legal practice shortly after the end of the First World War. He reached maturity in his profession and in his political beliefs at that time. The *Balfour Declaration* of 1917 was no doubt the stimulus for his continued involvement in Jewish politics on community and national levels. He joined the Herzl Club in Vienna and in due course became its president. He was at one time vice-president of the Jewish community council, and served on the world council of the General Zionists.

At the time of his death he was president of the Zionist Federation of Austria. His obituary in *Heruth* published in Vienna on 4 September 1964 and a note in Hugo Gold's *Geschichte der Juden in Wien* give some biographical details. My father supported his younger brother and sister during their legal studies, and they both received their doctorates from the University of Vienna. Max Gellis practiced as an advocate and wrote a book on Austrian company law, which, in a revised edition, is still a standard work on the subject. Lotte Gelles was also a Zionist and went to live in Palestine in the 1930s. Max died in 1973 and Lotte in 1984. They are buried in Tel-Aviv.

I spent the first ten years of my life in Vienna. I was brought up as an Austrian with a Jewish background. Zionism was for me a part of Jewish history, and this I have tended to see as part of a universal history. In 1938 we fled to England, where I have made my home, and which has nurtured me ever since. I was educated here and my political loyalty is entirely with this country. A study of my family background has taken me back to France, Germany and Italy. My ancestors made their home in Europe for more than a thousand years, and I believe that my cultural roots are to be found in the heartland of the medieval Holy Roman Empire. This is not the place to discuss the complexities of my family tree and the influence of my mother and her ancestors. I deal with genealogy and genetic inheritance elsewhere. The question for this chapter is how were three generations of my family shaped by the history of the past century and a half.

My grandfather was a student and exponent of Jewish law. He was a teacher and a judge. Many Ashkenazi Jews with ancient rabbinical roots thought of their lineage as going back to the distant past, perhaps to the great commentator Rashi of Troyes, who lived in the eleventh century and influenced generations of Christians and Jews. Their cultural interaction in the middle ages is evident and is particularly marked in German Jews, even after centuries of sojourn in Poland. If my grandfather represented the age-old Jewish traditions, my father was typical of those who made the transition from East to West. His generation sought to escape from aeons of oppression in assimilation and nationalism. Some even tried to combine the two, as in the Jewish National Party, which put up candidates for the Austrian Parliament in the inter-war years. For this generation, assimilation proved to be a cruel disappointment when Hitler came to power. It was particularly devastating because Viennese Jews like my father had such a deep attachment to their city and to German culture.

My grandfather looked backward to our patriarchs and prophets of old. My father to some extent rejected the past in favour of new prophets like Theodor Herzl. Like my father and grandfather, I too am bound by my place and time. I see nationalism slowly losing its earlier grotesque forms. Religious fanaticism is still with us. At least racialism, while still virulent, has been exposed as the evil that it is. Slowly the world is coming together, and a tolerant and ecumenical spirit may still triumph over divisive and obscurantist forces. We have survived the slings and arrows of outrageous fortune thanks to our adaptability to external circumstances. Our outer shell has changed, but the spirit of our ancestors endures in the Jewish tradition of law and ethics, which is at the foundation of our civilization.

Figure 30
Rabbi Nahum Uri Gelles (1852–1934)

Chapter Twenty-Seven

The Family of Rabbi Nahum Uri Gelles

Including my father and his grandfather, Rabbi David Isaac Gellis

Nahum Uri Gelles was born at Narayow 1852 and died in Vienna 1934. He was a son of Rabbi David Isaac Gelles (ca.1790–1870) by his wife Sarah[1] and married Esther Weinstein (1861–1907), daughter of Rabbi Zvi Aryeh Weinstein of Solotwina, who died in 1884. Nahum Uri became Rabbi of Kudrynce (Kudryntsy) in 1877 and of Solotwina near Stanislau in 1884. Nahum Uri and Esther had issue:

1. Philip (Ephraim Fishel), born 1879. Trained as a Rabbi, but died young. His (second?) wife belonged to the Leifer family of Nadworna, descended from the noted Chasidic Rabbi Meir of Przemyshlany. Philip's sons were
   a. Leo (Ahron Leib), who died New York in 1973.
   b. Joseph, who became a Rabbi.[2]
2. Bertha (Feiga Rivka) (1881–1965). Emigrated to America in 1910. Married Nathan Resnick (1888–1979), bookstore owner.[3] Their children are:
   a. Isidore, b. 1915. Issue: 1. Anita, b. 1943, who is married to a computer consultant; 2. Richard, b. 1948.
   b. Edythe, b. 1916. Married Murray (Moshe) Rothenberg, who died in 1982. Issue: 1. Dr Stuart Rothenberg, b. 1948, married Joan Singer and has a daughter, Jenny, b. 1975; 2. Dr Robert Rothenberg, b. 1951, married Dianne Locke and has two sons.
   c. Oscar (1921–2002). Issue: 1. Arlene, b. 1943, who has four children by two marriages; 2. Philip, b. 1947, Lt.-Col. US Air Force (retd), married with two adopted children, and lives in Kentucky.
3. David Isaac, born at Kudrynce 1883 and died Vienna 1964.[4] Doctor of Law and Advocate in Vienna. President of Zionist Federation of Austria etc. Married Regina Griffel (1900–54). Two Sons:
   a. Ludwig Friedrich (1922–42)
   b. Edward, b. Vienna 1927. In England since 1938.
4. Rosa, died in holocaust.
5. Lotte, born at Solotwina 1895. Doctor of Law of Vienna University. Her

marriage to lawyer, Dr Ostrer, was dissolved. She emigrated to Palestine in the 1930s. Her second marriage was to physician, Dr Kurt Kallmann of Berlin. She died in Tel Aviv in 1984.

6. Max, born at Solotwina 1897. Doctor of Law and Advocate in Vienna.[5] Died in Tel Aviv in 1973. The only child of his marriage to Nellie Leinkram (1906–91) was Elsa, b. Vienna 1929. Married Walter Schmaus (b. 1920), jewellery designer, and lives in New York. Issue: Dr Peter Howard Schmaus, orthopaedic physician and specialist in rehabilitation medicine, b. 1959, married Phyllis Chinitz, b. 1959, their three children are Matthew David, Gregory Harrison and Jaclyn Nicole.

REFERENCES TO RABBI NAHUM URI GELLES IN CONTEMPORARY RESPONSA

I recently located and spoke by telephone to Rabbi Elimelech Ashkenazi, sometime Chief Rabbi of Sao Paulo and Melbourne, who was born in Stanislau in 1915 (Rosenstein, *The Unbroken Chain*, p.274). He vividly remembers meeting my grandfather and described him as a distinguished figure of striking appearance.

Rabbi Nahum Uri Gelles corresponded with many well-known halachic authorities of his day. All address him with great respect for his opinions and some, such as Rabbi Steinberg of Brody, refer to him in terms of particular friendship. According to Ohalei Shem, Nahum Uri was the author of manuscript works including collections of responsa and sermons.

There is an enquiry from Rabbi Moshe Teomim addressed to Nahum Uri and to his brother-in-law Rabbi Dov Berel Brenner (ca. 1840–1910) at a time when both were young men studying under their father-in-law Rabbi Weinstein in Solotwina. (Rabbi Dov Berel Brenner was the son of Rabbi Yaakov Brenner [ca 1810–80]. Rabbi Dov Berel served as Dayan in Solotwina, Kremnitz, and then in Czernowitz. His name appears in responsa together with Rabbi Hirsch Leib Wohl of Nadworna in 1859 and 1863. In *Sheilath Shalom* (v.i.) he is referred to as the son-in-law of the Rabbi of Slotwina.)

Rabbi Steinberg of Brody writes to Nahum Uri regarding the identification of a man found murdered between Czortkow and Proskorow. This might provide another indication of Nahum Uri's Czortkow connection. His correspondents, Rabbi Abraham Menachem Steinberg and Rabbi Meyer Arik, were also followers of the Rabbi of Czortkow.

Oriyan Telisai, by Rabbi Moshe Teomim, ABD of Horodenka (Lemberg: 1880), Ch.80.
Imrei Yosher, by Rabbi Meyer Arik, *ABD* of Jaslowitz, Buchach and Tarnow (Cracow: 1925), Part 2, Ch.59.
Harei Besamim, by Rabbi Aryeh Leibush Horowitz, *ABD* of Stanislau (Lemberg: 1897), Vol.2, Ch.205.

Machazeh Avraham, by Rabbi Abraham Menachem Steinberg, *ABD* of Brody and later of Vienna (New York: 1964), Vol.2 *Even Haezer*, Ch.15 and 40.
Minchas Yechiel, by Rabbi Alter Yechiel Nebenzahl, *ABD* of Stanislau (Bilgoraj: 1933 and Stanislau: 1939), Vol.1, Ch.5-10 and Vol.2, Ch.95.
Minchas Pittim, by Rabbi Meyer Arik, *ABD* of Jaslowitz, Buchach and Tarnow (Munkacz: 1898) *Yoreh Deah*, p.28b.
Minchas Shay, by Rabbi Shmuel Yitzchak Shorr (Jerusalem: 1911), Vol.2, Ch.19, 41 and 101.
Maharsham, by Rabbi Shalom Mordechai Schwadron, *ABD* of Berezhany (Warsaw, Piotrkow, Szatmar, Jerusalem: 1902, 196?), Vol.2, Ch.190; Vol.3, Ch.175; Vol.4, Ch.97; Vol.5, Ch.69, 70; Vol.6, Ch.95; Vol.7 Ch.162.

LETTERHEAD USED BY RABBI NAHUM URI GELLES

Nuchim Ire is a vernacular rendering of Nahum Uri. The family name of Gelles or Gellis was variously transliterated through several generations. The German title of Nahum Uri Gelles was Bezirks-Rabbiner or District Rabbi and the Hebrew abbreviation ABD' K stands for Av Beth Din of the Kahal, that is, head of the Rabbinical Court or Chief Rabbi of the community of Solotwina and surrounding villages.

The letter heading is taken from a letter in the David Simonson archive at the Royal Library in Kopenhagen, kindly supplied by Dr Eva-Maria Jansson.

Nuchim Ire Gellis
Bezirks-Rabbiner
Solotwina (bei Stanislau)

Telegramme :Gellis, Solotwina.

נחום אורי געללים אבד"ק
סאלאטווינא.

Solotwina, den [illegible] 1901

Figure 31

NOTES

1. Rabbi David Isaac Gelles was buried in Brody, where rabbis of this family can be traced back to the eighteenth century scholar Moses Gelles. My grandfather's birth at Narayow suggests that his mother Sarah may have come from a rabbinical family of that town. Jacob Isaac Fraenkel-Teomim was ABD of Narayow from 1850 to 1865. See Meir Wunder, *Meorei Galicia* (Jerusalem: Institute for the Commemoration of Galician Jewry, 1978 *et seq.*), Vol.4, p.330, and Neil Rosenstein, *The Unbroken Chain* (New York, London, Jerusalem: CIS Publishers, 1990), pp.307, 312. His wife Beila was the daughter of Eleazar Horowitz, ABD of the nearby town of Rohatyn, and of Esther Rivka, whose father Rabbi Efraim Fischel Horowitz became ABD of Munkacz in Hungary. He was a half brother of Rabbi Yehuda Aaron Horowitz of Solotwina (see Table 25 and chapter 28).
2. Joseph was the son of Ephraim Fischel Gelles of Solotwina. He studied at the Yeshivah established in Lublin in 1930 by Rabbi Meir Shapira, author of *Imrei Da'as* (Israel: Bnei Brak, 1990), containing a list of the Yeshivah students. Joseph appears to have perished in the holocaust.
3. Nathan's father, Asher Resnick, had three children by his second wife Golda. A son, Eliezer, went to Palestine in the 1920s, and one of the latter's daughters, Ofira (1936–93) became a clinical psychologist, won a Miss Israel beauty title, and married Isaac Navon, b. 1921, the fifth President of the State of Israel (1978–83). There are two children from that marriage.
4. My father's birth and other details are to be found in the records of Melnitsa-Podolskaya (near Kudrynce) as well as the Austrian State and the Viennese Jewish community records. He studied at the Yeshiva in Munkacz and then at the University of Czernowitz before going on to the University of Vienna. There appear to have been family connections in Munkacz and in the Bukowina.
5. Dr Max Gellis wrote a book, *Kommentar zum GmbH-Gesetz*, published by Linde Verlag, Vienna and Eisenstadt, 1st edition 1960. In a revised 5th edition this is still an authoritative reference book on Austrian Company Law. Max was an amateur chess champion whose games have been quoted in chess literature.
6. Hirsch Leib, died at Kudrynce in 1886 at the age of 2 months [named after his grandfather who had pre-deceased him in 1884]. The infant's death record was found at Skala [1886, signature 1111, Act 101]. Kudrynce births of my aunt Bertha (1881) and my father David Isaac (1883) were recorded at the nearby town of Melnitsa Podolskaya: 1881 (signature 874, Act 113), and 1883 (signature 874, Act 224). Nahum Uri is given in the records as 'of Kudrynce' and Esther Weinstein as 'of Bukowina'. Esther Weinstein was born in 1861, presumably at the home of her maternal grandparents, who had moved to the Bukowina (see Chapter 28 on Rabbi Zvi Aryeh Weinstein and his family). Esther died in 1907, and Nahum Uri survived her until 1934. According to prevailing custom the town rabbi was expected to be married, so it did not come as a complete surprise when recently-discovered letters in the Solotwina file kept at the Central Archives of the History of the Jewish People in Jerusalem revealed a second wife, Malka Chaye Gelles, who following Nahum Uri's death in November 1934 appealed to the local authorities about the inadequacy of her widow's pension (P65/3/36).

The Herald, Saturday, June 14, 1947
MELBOURNE

CONTEMPLATIVE STUDY of Dr. Max Gellis, representing Australia in the radio chess match with Canada, conducted at Australia-Soviet House today. His opponent in this game is Yerhoff, of Canada.

CONSIDERING CHANCES OF CHECKMATE

Figure 32
Dr Max Gellis

Figure 33
Ludwig Gelles, Dr Max Gellis, his daughter Elsa, and Dr Lotte Gelles

Table 25
RABBIS EFRAIM FISCHEL AND YEHUDA AARON HOROWITZ

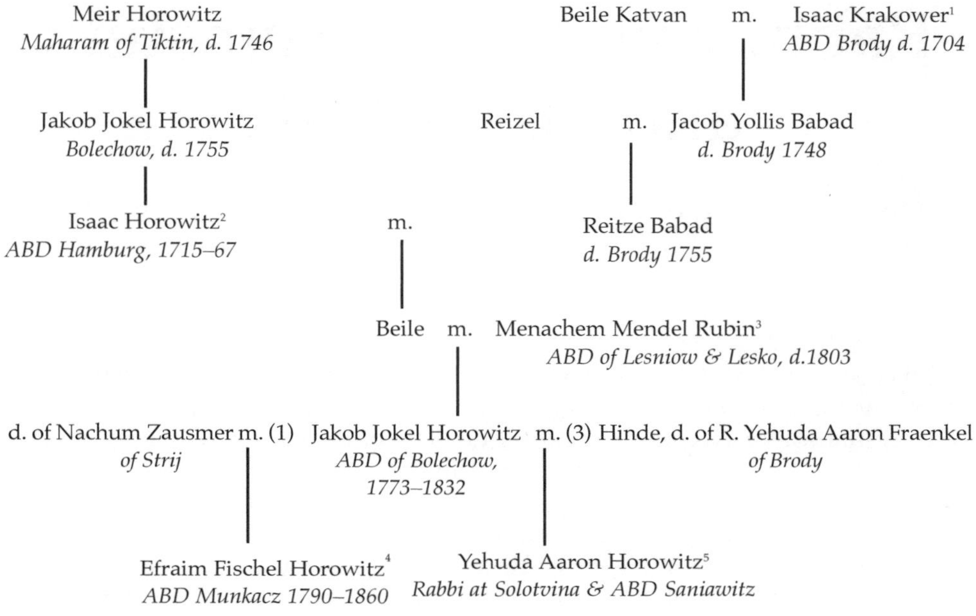

NOTES

1. Isaac Krakower was a son of Yissachar Ber, President of the Council of the Four Lands and a grandson of Chief Rabbi Abraham Joshua Heschel of Cracow. He was the head of the Rabinowitz–Babad family [Babad being an acronym of the sons of the Av Beth Din i.e. Chief Rabbi].
2. Isaac '*Hamburger*' Horowitz was the father of Eleazar, whose son Aryeh Leib, 1784–1843, was the first of a line of Horowitz Rabbis of Stanislau
3. Menachem Mendel Rubin was also the father of Naftali Zvi Rubin, 1760–1827, founder of the Ropshitz dynasty.
4. Efraim Fischel Horowitz was Rabbi at Bolechow, Mariampol and Linsk, moving to Munkacz in Hungary in 1841 where he was ABD until 1860. His wife was a daughter of David Horowitz of Leshnov. His daughter Esther Rivka married Eleazar Horowitz, ABD of Rohatyn, and this couple's daughter Beila was the wife of Joshua Heschel Fraenkel-Teomim, ABD of Narayow (near Rohatyn). Efraim Fischel's son Yehoshua served as ABD of Rohatyn. Eleazar Horowitz had a son David who ultimately became ABD of Stanislau and married a daughter of Haim Babad, the ABD of Mikulince.
5. Yehuda Aaron Horowitz was Rabbi at Solotwina until 1858/59. He then moved to Saniawitz in the neighbouring province of Bukowina, where his son R. Naftali succeeded him in the Rabbinate. His place at Solotwina was taken by Rabbi Zvi Aryeh Weinstein, the father-in-law of Rabbi Nahum Uri Gelles.
   (See N. Rosenstein, *The Unbroken Chain* [New York, London, Jerusalem: CIS Publishers, 1990], pp.761,764–5,1016. M. Wunder, *Meorei Galicia* [Jerusalem: Institute for the Commemoration of Galician Jewry, 1978 *et seq.*], vol.2, pp.124–5, 176–7, 220, 235–6, 295. Z.H. Horowitz, *Letoldoth Hakehilot Bepolin* [Jerusalem: Mosad Horav Kook, 1978], p.110.)

Chapter Twenty-Eight

Rabbi Zvi Aryeh Weinstein and His Family

Including my grandmother, Esther Weinstein

Zvi Aryeh (Hirsch Leib) Weinstein was Rabbi of Solotwina near Stanislau, where he died in 1884. The *Encyclopaedia of Jewish Communities in Poland* (Vol. 2) includes a chapter on Solotwina. The entry is unfortunately incomplete and inaccurate, but it does provide some historical background to a little town where, in the later nineteenth century, Jews made up half of the population of about 4,000. *Meorei Galicia,* the Encyclopaedia of the Galician Rabbinate by Dr Meir Wunder of Jerusalem, gives numerous references to Rabbi Weinstein in contemporary responsa.[1] He had a connection with the Chasidic Rabbi of Vizhnitz, who was of the Hager family. The Weinsteins had kinsfolk in Czernowitz and other towns in the neighbouring province of Bukowina. Rabbi Weinstein appears to have held the position of *Dayan* in Solotwina. He became ABD (*Av Beth Din*) at about the time Rabbi Yehuda Aaron Horowitz left Solotwina to become ABD of Saniawitz in the Bukowina. It is an intriguing possibility that Weinstein married a daughter or kinswoman of the departing rabbi.

Nahum Uri Gelles and Dov Berel Brenner studied under Rabbi Weinstein. My grandfather married his daughter Esther and in turn became *Av Beth Din* on the death of his father-in-law. A sister of Esther's married Rabbi Dov Berel Brenner (ca.1840–1910), who was the son of Rabbi Yaacov Brenner. Hirsch Leib had a son Chaim, whose issue included a son, Hirsch Leib, named after his grandfather. This grandson and some of his siblings emigrated to America on the eve of the First World War.[2] Malka (Molly) Weinstein married a Mr Eckstein. They had two sons, called Harry and Philip. Molly's brothers, Jake and Sam, married Clara and Gussie Spiegel, two sisters who also hailed from Solotwina. Jake and Clara had a son, Phillip. Sam and Gussie's children included (1) Nancy who married Charles Rosenfeld; (2) Philip, born in 1922, an attorney in New York. He married Molly Rencoff who died in 1990. She became a professor of philosophy at Queens College, NY;[3] (3) Howard, born 1923, also a lawyer, who married Ruth Framer.

REFERENCES TO RABBI ZVI ARYEH WEINSTEIN IN CONTEMPORARY RESPONSA

Zvi Aryeh corresponded with some of the best-known halachic authorities of his day. He seems to have been particularly close to Rabbi Sosnitzer of Brody and Rabbi Ettinger of Lemberg. Those of the responsa that are dated were written between the years 1857 and 1879.

Eretz Zevi, by Rabbi Zvi Teomim (Lemberg: 1880), Part 2, ch.7 and 16; Part 4, ch.16.
Beth Shlomo, by Rabbi Shlomo Drimmer, ABD of Skala (Lemberg: 1878–91), *Yoreh Deah* Part 1, Ch.138; Part 2, Ch.11, 87, 88 and 194. *Choshen Mishpat*, Ch.2.
Bar Livai, by Rabbi Meshulam Yissachar Horowitz, ABD of Stanislau (Lemberg: 1861 and 1872), Vol.2, *Even Haezer*, Ch.55.
Devar Moshe, by Rabbi Moshe Teomim, ABD of Horodenka (Lemberg: 1864), Vol.2, Ch.78.
Oriyan Telisai, by Rabbi Moshe Teomim, ABD of Horodenka (Lemberg: 1880), Ch.141.
Harei Besamim, by Rabbi Aryeh Leibush Horowitz, ABD of Stanislau (Lemberg: 1883), Ch.67.
Maharya Halevy, by Rabbi Yitzchak Aharon Ettinger, ABD of Lemberg (Lemberg: 1893), Vol.1, Ch.38.
Sheilath Shalom, by Rabbi Shmuel Shmelke Taubes, ABD of Botosani (Lemberg: 1883), Vol.2, ch.100.
Shoel Umeishiv, by Rabbi Yoseph Shaul Nathansohn, ABD of Lemberg (Lemberg: 1869–90), Vol.1, Part 1, Ch.165; Vol.2, Part 4, Ch.1; Vol. 4, Part 2, Ch.149.
Shaarei Deah, by Rabbi Chayim Yehuda Leib Sosnitzer, Dayan and Rosh Yeshiva of Brody (Przemysl: 1884), Vol.2, Ch.84.

NOTES

1. Meir Wunder, *Meorei Galicia* (Jerusalem: Institute for the Commemoration of Galician Jewry, 1978 *et seq.*).
2. US immigration records (accessed through *Searching the Ellis Island Database EIDB in one Step*) include Samuel Weinstein, 1906 (age 14 years) and Hirsch Leib Weinstein, 1909 (age 25 years), both of Solotwina, Austria.
3. Philip Weinstein and Molly Rencoff had issue including (1) a son, David, born 1951, a lawyer who lives in Boston and married Clare Villari; and (2) a daughter, Elaine Beth, born 1955, who married Richard Bolack, a musician, born 1951. They live on Lummi Island, Washington.

Figure 34
Descendants of Rabbi Zvi Aryeh Weinstein
(Howard, Nancy and Philip Weinstein)

VIII.

GELLES RABBINICAL ANCESTRY AND CONNECTIONS

Some people have to be born so that they can carry out but one special good deed in the course of their entire lives

Rabbi Pinchas Shapiro of Koretz, *Midrash Pinchas*

Chapter Twenty-Nine

Finding Rabbi Moses Gelles

Tombstones and house numbers reveal a distinguished ancestry

My ancestor Moses Gelles of Brody turned out to be a man of many names. His identification involved the study of a variety of primary sources including rabbinical, vital and property records. The latter are especially useful for the late-eighteenth to early-nineteenth century period when family names were still in flux and a single individual was often known by different ones in different circumstances.

My father's people were rabbis from earliest times. I have found a reference to a Rabbi S. Gelles of Brody going back to the beginning of the eighteenth century. His daughter married Rabbi Menachem Levush, who assumed his father-in-law's name, as was sometimes the custom in those days. Gelles or Gellis has an ancient matronymic meaning: child of Geyle – the fair or fair-haired. Such matronymics were often retained in lineages long before the adoption of hereditary family names. Long ago, patronymics and trade sobriquets were the rule, although some families took their names from places of origin, such as the Katzenellenbogen from the eponymous town in Hesse-Nassau, Halpern from Heilbronn, and Shapiro from Speyer.

The bustling little market and frontier town of Brody was under Austrian rule from the time of the eighteenth century Polish partitions until the end of the First World War, but even before that period a Jewish community flourished there. For much of the eighteenth century it was essentially a Jewish town. Scottish missionaries who visited in 1839 reported that it had three churches and 150 synagogues.[1] A picture of its rich cultural life emerges from the writings of N.M. Gelber and others,[2] while no one has captured the soul of the shtetl better than Joseph Roth.[3]

RABBINICAL RECORDS

A fragment of the records of the Brody rabbinical court (*Beth Din*) dating from 1808–17 contains some interesting information about the late Rabbi Menachem Levush and his family.[4] The family owned a chandlery. They had a concession from the community for making candles. It was the inheritance of the sons of Rabbi Moses Gelles. These included Rabbi Joseph Gelles who is referred to by the Yiddish/Polish sobriquet of Vaskievonie, meaning the waxworks. A Reb Moshe Gershon Gelles was one of the latter's sons. A house at the edge of the chandlery grounds is reported as belonging to Reb Mordechai Gelles. Reb Michel is stated to be a son of Rabbi Menachem Levush (the son-in-law of Rabbi S. Gelles). He is also referred to as Michel Gelles, son of Rabbi Moses Gelles. It appears from the entries that the names of Levush and Gelles were used interchangeably, and that there was some ambiguity concerning Rabbi Menachem Levush and Rabbi Moses Gelles. They might have been one and the same person. There are, however, definitely two separate Rabbis Mordechai. One in the Beth Din records is Rabbi Moredechai Levush, son of Rabbi Michel Gellis or Levush. Another Rabbi Mordechai Gelles of Brody is mentioned in a Hebrew genealogical monograph as the son of Moses Gelles.[5] In a chapter of this book dealing with the family of Rabbi Pinchas Shapiro of Koretz, the author states that Rachel Sheindel, the daughter of Rabbi Pinchas, married Rabbi Samuel, son of Rabbi Mordechai, son of Moses Gelles, one of the scholars of the Brody Klaus, whose epitaph refers to him as 'Moses the Servant of God'. The Klaus of Brody was a study circle for distinguished Talmudists.

Rabbi Shmuel Dov Gelles, who died in 1811, was the progenitor of a long line of rabbis who are chronicled by his descendant Rabbi Shimson Ahron Polonski.[6] The latter was the son of Abraham Isaac Polonski, son of Menachem Nachum, son of Elyahu Pinchas, son of Ahron, son of Shmuel of Kolibolet (the son-in-law of Rabbi Pinchas of Koretz), son of Mordechai Gelles of Brody, son of Moshe Gelles, a member of the famous Brody Klaus. Another monograph dealing with these connections was written by Matityahu Yechezkiel Guttman of Jassy, who was a Gellis on his mother's side, and married a daughter of Rabbi Mordechai Dov Shapiro. Both were direct descendants of Rabbi Pinchas of Koretz, Guttman being seven generations from Rabbi Pinchas and eight generations from Moshe Gelles of Brody.[7]

TOMBSTONE DATA

Only a handful of Jews survived World War II in Brody. The old cemetery was destroyed, but many tombstones remain from the 'new' cemetery, which dates from 1830.[8] Among these is the stone marking the grave of my great-grandfather Rabbi David Isaac Gellis. The inscription gives his father as Rabbi Moshe, who may have been a grandson of the eighteenth-century scholar of the same name. David Isaac's children included my grandfather Rabbi Nahum Uri Gelles, who died in Vienna in 1934. He was buried in that city, and his tombstone states that the Gelles family hailed from Brody. Another Brody tombstone records the death of Lea, daughter of Abraham, in 1894, and the inscription confirms that she was 'a descendant of Rabbi

Moshe Gellis, a scholar of the Brody Klaus'. The civic records give Lea, born in 1838, as the daughter of Abraham Gelles. Abraham can be identified from the vital records as the son of Rabbi Moshe Gershon Gelles, the son of Rabbi Joseph Gelles, son of Rabbi Moshe Gelles.

VITAL AND PROPERTY RECORDS

The data obtained from the tombstones, genealogical literature and the Beth Din records provided the background to an extended search of the birth, marriage and death records from about 1815 to 1861 and of the land registers and other property records from 1780 to 1844.

Brody civil records are preserved in the archives of Lviv. Much is fragmentary, and marriage records have almost no details about the families of wives, but the documents do include house numbers and other valuable data. The archive address and the categories of records which have been consulted are given in the appended Notes. The birth records generally give details of the year and date of birth, the house number, name and sex of child, and name of father. The marriage records state the date, house number, and details of the couple. The death register has date, house number, name of deceased, name of parent or parents, sometimes the cause of death, sex and age (indicated as one of eight categories from 1 for an infant to 8 for over 100 years). The various types of property records often accompany the house number and name of owners at a given date with a description of the property. The Josephine and Franciscan land registers, named after the then-reigning Austrian Emperors, indicate changing ownership of properties over a period of 60 years. A detailed comparison of information from these different types of records can be very revealing, as for example, when a particular house stays in the family for generations, but with different names clearly referring to father and son, or to one and the same person.

Analysis of the house numbers has allowed me to draw some lines of descent with a measure of confidence. In fact, the use of property records is of general applicability, particularly appropriate for a time and in a social milieu where patronymic and matronymic names, trade sobriquets, and other means of identification of every kind were in a state of flux. From a very large database, I have selected a few salient features.

The (Josephine) land register of 1780 lists the owner of house No. 122 as Moysze Knot (Polish for Wick), while the (Franciscan) land register of 1820 gives the name Gershon Gelles as the owner of the same house. The land register for 1784–89 lists Mendel Wax as the owner of No. 49. Moses Gershon Gelles was a son of Joseph of the Waxworks, who was the son of Moses Gelles. Having previously concluded that Moses Gelles was one and the same person as Moses Levush (and Moses Menachem Mendel Levush) we are confronted with the possibility that the same man might also have been known as Moysze Knot or Mendel Wax. It is even conceivable that the latter two names referred to one and the same chandler (candlemaker). Clearly, various names were in use by or for the same person at the same time, depending on the ethnic, linguistic or social character of a given situation.

Saul Woskoboynik (Russian for waxmaker) owned house No. 26 in 1820. The land register for 1844 lists the owner as Osias Woskoboynik, and the vital records give Osias Gelles as living in the house of that number. The descent from Moses to Joseph, to Saul and then to Osias is clear. There are many candlemakers or chandlers in that branch of the Gelles family. Given the several sobriquets in the Polish, Yiddish and Russian vernacular alluding to that trade, and the evidence that the established family business was a chandlery, it becomes extremely unlikely that the Hebrew name of Levush refers to a trade or occupation.

We can trace the occupants of house Nos. 45 and 46 for several generations. A Reisel Lowe died at No. 45 in 1839 at an advanced age, the stated category 7 referring to the age group 80–100. She could have been related to Moshe Menachem Levush. The latter's grandson, Rabbi Mordechai Levush aka Marcus Lewish or Luwicz, lived at No. 45 and owned house No. 46 in 1820, and his son Moses Levush was recorded as the owner of No. 46 in 1844 under the name of both Levush and Gelles. Details of this Levush branch were given in the Beth Din records. House No. 27 also features prominently in the family records. In 1820 it belonged to Moshe Gershon Gelles; his brother-in-law Rabbi Meir Frankel owned it in 1844. Several family members lived there at one time or another, including Moshe Gershon's son, Rabbi Abraham Gelles, and Nathan Gelles, who was the father of Rabbi Chaim Naftali Gelles (born at No.139). The tombstones of some of the latter's children tell of 'descendants of a distinguished family'.

In a way, the most interesting of Moses Gelles' progeny was the line of descent from his son Rabbi Mordechai, but documentation is not to be found in Brody. Mordechai died too soon for the birth records there, and his children had moved elsewhere. His son Rabbi Shmuel Dov is of the branch related by marriage to Rabbi Pinchas of Koretz and to the Friedmans of Czortkow. The possible connections of my great-grandfather, Rabbi David Isaac, and my grandfather, Rabbi Nahum Uri Gelles, will be dealt with in a following chapter.

The name Levush recalls the epithet of the great Rabbi Mordechai Yaffe, known as HaLevush, from the title of his magnum opus 'The Rabbinical Robes of Learning'. The connection of rabbis bearing this name with the author of the *Levushim* has been made before, as in the instance of Rabbi Nehemia Levush of Svierz and later of Vilna, whose tombstone gave his father as Rabbi Zvi Levush, and whose descent from Rabbi Mordechai Yaffe is affirmed in contemporary records. These Lithuanian rabbis bearing the Levush name may have a connection with Rabbi Abraham Levush of Kostiokowitz, son of Rabbi Meir Heller (1804–77), who was a judge at Vilna, Rabbi of Troki and Kostiokowitz, and a descendant of the famous Rabbi Yomtov Lipman Heller, the author of *Tosafot Yom Tov*.[9]

In summary, I believe that a matronymic of medieval German origin became, in due course, our family name of Gelles, that the Hebrew epithet

Levush might be a reminder of Yaffe ancestry, and that the sobriquets in the Jewish, Polish and Russian vernacular were for common use in everyday social and commercial life in earlier times. Moses Menachem Mendel Levush, known as Moses Gelles, was in any case of ancient distinguished lineage, a progenitor of learned and holy rabbis, wax chandler, scholar and, in the words of his epitaph, a Servant of God.

NOTES

1. A.A. Bonar and R.M. McCheyne, *Narrative of a Mission of Inquiry to the Jews from the Church of Scotland in 1839* (Edinburgh: William Whyte, 1842), 2nd edn, pp.266–75.
2. *Toldot Yehudei Brody 1584–1943* (Jerusalem: Mosad HaRav Kook, 1955). Nathan Michael Gelber, 'Brody: The Jerusalem of Austria', in *An Eternal Light: Brody in Memoriam* (The Organisation of Former Brody Residents in Israel, 1994). For quotations from pp.22–6 see Footnote at end of article.
3. Joseph Roth, *The Wandering Jews* (London: Granta, 2001).
4. Records of the *Beth Din* of Brody 1808–17, MS 4037, Jewish Theological Seminary, New York.
5. Rabbi Levi Grossman, *Shem U'She'erit* (Name and Remnant) (Tel Aviv: 1943), p.92. A list of Chasidic leaders and their descendants.
6. Rabbi Shimson Ahron Polonski, *Chidushei Horav MiTeplik* (The Novellae of the Rabbi of Teplice) (Jerusalem: 1984).
7. Matityahu Yechezkiel Guttman, *Rabbi Pinchas MiKoretz* (Tel Aviv: 1950).
8. Dr Neil Rosenstein and Rabbi Dov Weber, Brody Tombstone Project, progress of which will be found on the Internet in due course at www.shtetlinks.jewishgen.org./Brody/Brody_cemetary_project.htm.
9. *Jewish Encyclopaedia*, 1904 ed. Articles on Yaffe family. S.J. Fuenn, *Kiryah Ne'emanah* (Vilna: 1860), p.216. Nathan Zvi Friedman, *Otzar Harabbanim* (Bnei Brak: 1973), Nos.510, 1282 and 1543.

BRODY RECORDS IN THE LVIV ARCHIVES

Address: Tsentralnyi Derzhavnyi Istorychnyi Archiv, u.m. Lviv; Ploshna Soborna 3a, Lviv 290008, Ukraine.

- Extracts from the registers of births, deaths and marriages for the period 1815 to 1861, initially for Gelles and variant spellings of that name, and later for variants of Levush and Woskoboynik.
- Lists of homeowners from the (Josephine) Land Register of 1780 and the (Franciscan) Land Register of 1820.
- Extracts from additional lists of landowners for 1784–89 and for 1820–22 (including a card file of Brody landowners 1820).
- Register of Landowners' Incomes 1821, extracts from the Brody Land Register 1844 and the Register of Realty Owners of Brody 1844.

RECORDS OF THE BRODY BETH DIN (1808–17)

- 1808. Rabbi Michel, son of Rabbi Menachem Levush (son-in-law of Rabbi S. Gellis) signed and sealed to his wife Feiga, daughter of Rabbi Yehoshua Heshel HaKohen.
- 1810. A contract between Leah, the daughter of Rabbi Gershon, and her husband Rabbi David Hertz, the son of Rabbi Ahron Benish, and the two brothers-in-law, Rabbi Meir Fraenkel, the son of Rabbi Dov Baer, and Rabbi Moshe Gershon Gellis, son of Rabbi Joseph.
- 1810. Sale between Chaya, daughter of Rabbi Henoch, and her husband Rabbi Abraham Yonah Reich, son of Rabbi Joseph, son of Rabbi M. Gellis. Half of this house belongs to the couple in partnership with his brother, Rabbi Hirsch Jacob Feigang, son of the above-mentioned Rabbi Joseph, and their brother-in-law, Rabbi Meir Shlomo Fraenkel, son-in-law of the said Rabbi Joseph, which they inherited from their father.
- 1810. Sale between Bonna, daughter of Rabbi Menachem Nachum, and her husband Rabbi Simcha, son of Rabbi Ahron Benyosh, the two other halves of the portion belonging to the two brothers-in-law, Rabbi Meir Fraenkel and Rabbi Moshe Gershon Gellis, the son of Rabbi Joseph Gellis. The said couple also sold their two halves of the portion to the above-mentioned brothers-in-law, Rabbi Meir Fraenkel and Rabbi Moshe Gershon Gellis.
- 1811. This place (or square) is bordered by the Vaskivonie of the heirs of the deceased Rabbi Moshe Gellis.
- 1812. After it, on the south side, is the house of Reb Mordechai Gellis.
- 1813. Sale between the wealthy Finkel, daughter of Rabbi Dov Baer, and her husband the learned Rabbi Benyamin Z. Wolf Bolchover, son of Rabbi Yaakov, who sold it for the purpose of honouring the deceased, in memory of the soul of the late Feiga, daughter of Reb Yehoshua Heshel HaKohen, the wife of Rabbi Michel, son of Reb Moshe Gellis.
- 1814. Deed of sale between Sarah Bathya, daughter of Rabbi Yehuda Zundel, and her husband, Rabbi Mordechai Levush, son of Rabbi Michel Gellis, to their son, Rabbi Moshe Levush.
- 1815. Contract by Chaya, daughter of Rabbi Aryeh Leib, widow of Rabbi Shmuel Gellis; half of this site had been left to her by her late husband, Rabbi Shmuel Gellis.
- 1817. Abraham (a bachelor), son of Rabbi Moshe Gellis, son of Rabbi Joseph Vaskivonie, married Taube, daughter of Rabbi Joseph Kalischer, son of Rabbi Berach Margoshes, the marriage contract mentioning the bridegroom's father, Rabbi Moshe (living) and the bridegroom's brother Rabbi Yankel Gellis. (This Rabbi Moshe is identifiable from an analysis of house numbers in the vital records as Rabbi Moshe Gershon Gellis, son of Rabbi Joseph Gelles).

SOME DESCENDANTS OF RABBI MOSES GELLES OF BRODY

Moshe Menachem Levush (Moses Gelles of the Brody Klaus) married a daughter of Rabbi S(amuel) Gelles of Brody. Their issue included:

1. R' Michel Levush or Gelles, married Feige (died ca. 1808–13), daughter of Rabbi Yehoshua Heshel HaKohen:
   a. Mordechai Levush (Marcus Luwicz or Lewish), married Sarah Bathya (who died in 1826), daughter of Rabbi Yehuda Zundel
      i. Their son, R' Moshe Levush or Gelles, (died 1851)

2. R' Joseph Gelles Vaskivonie:
   a. R' Moshe Gershon Gelles (died 1824), married Rose (died 1820)
      i. Rabbi Abraham Gelles, married (1817) Taube, daughter of Rabbi Joseph Kaliszer, son of R' Berach Margoshes. Their daughter Lea was a 'descendant of Moses Gelles of the Brody Klaus'
      ii. R'Yankel Gelles (or Jacob Leway ?) married (1818) Hinde Gelles
      iii. Possibly, R' Nathan Gelles who married Sarah Berman (died 1852); their son, Rabbi Chaim Naftali Gelles, was born in 1838
      iv. Leah married R' David Hertz, son of Ahron Benish
   b. Daughter married Rabbi Meir Fraenkel
   c. Saul Woskoboynik (died 1831) married Beile (died 1831)
      i Their son, Osias Woskoboynik aka Osias Gelles (1804-1854) married Scheindel Schreiber
   d. R' Abraham Yonah Reich married Chaya, daughter of R' Henoch Reich
   e. R' Hirsch Jacob Feigang

3. Rabbi Mordechai Gelles
   a. Rabbi Shmuel Dov Gelles (died 1811), married Sarah Rachel Scheindel (born 1772), daughter of Rabbi Pinchas of Koretz (1726–91) for issue see notes 6 and 7
   b. ? Rabbi Moses Gelles
      i. Rabbi David Isaac Gelles (ca.1790–1870) married Sara, and their son, Rabbi Nahum Uri Gelles (1852–1934) married Esther (1861–1907), daughter of Rabbi Zvi Aryeh Weinstein (died 1884).

QUOTATIONS FROM THE MEMORIAL BOOK FOR BRODY

In Brody proper and in its 14 dependent settlements there were, in 1765, 15 leasing agents, 3 distillery owners, 4 taverners; of 737 providers... 147 were in trade, with a hand in practically every branch of business in Brody at that time (such as marketing wines and liquors, grain and flour, iron, furs, horses and cattle, fabrics, spices, books, and more); 5 in industry (of whom 4 manufactured soap and 1 made candles).

One of the more interesting chapters, both in the history of the community of Brody, and of the scholars and scholarship in all Poland at the time is that of the 'Wise Men of the Kloiz of the Holy Community of Brody'. Over a period of almost 80 years [from the 1730s to the end of the eighteenth century] the learned of Brody, or rabbis and scholars from the towns of the area, sat learning steadily from Sabbath to Sabbath in the large 'bait midrash' called a Kloiz [from Klaus, cf. Latin claustrum], a smaller, more informal house of worship and study near the old synagogue. These scholars enhanced the honour of the Torah through their writings and by dint of study, debate and exchange of opinions with the greatest Torah scholars in the world of their time. Among the scholars were those who knew the Kabbalah, and they had their own 'Shtibl' [small house of prayer] near the Kloiz. The community of Brody took care of the material needs of the scholars of the Kloiz, establishing a fund from the contributions by the rich men of Brody.

[I suggest that the Gelles chandlery may have enjoyed some form of monopoly, conceivably in recognition of Moses Gelles as a meritorious member of the Klaus or of his family connections.]

CHAPTER THIRTY

Jewish Community Life in Brody

From the Beth Din Records of 1808–17

A fragment of the Brody Beth Din Records from the early-nineteenth century has survived and I obtained a copy of this manuscript through the courtesy of the Jewish Theological Seminary in New York.[1] It has proved to be an invaluable source of genealogical and sociological material for a town within the Austro-Hungarian Empire, which had a large Jewish community and was also for a considerable time an important centre of Jewish learning. For ten years from 1808 to 1817 the Records detail all manner of transactions that make up the warp and weft of the social fabric, such as the purchase and sale of houses, land, and other property, wills and bequests, marriage contracts, and much else.

The names of people and the details involved in these transactions, when combined with the civil records of births, marriages and deaths, and the registers of landed property, throw much light on family connections and the life of the community.[2]

The procedure followed in the study of the Gelles family is of general applicability, and so are some of the conclusions. For example, Moses Gelles of Brody was a scholar of the study group called the Brody *Klaus* around the middle of the eighteenth century.[3] He was variously referred to as Gelles and Levush. I suggested that the epithet *Levush* recalled a descent from the sixteenth-century Rabbi Mordecai Yaffe of Prague and the title of his magnum opus, the *Levushim*. This Hebrew epithet is noted in four generations and is quite distinct from vernacular trade soubriquets, such as *Woskoboinik* (wax chandler or candle maker) used by some members of the Gelles family. There is evidence of other Levushs who were known to be descendants of Mordecai Yaffe. A perusal of the Beth Din Records reveals that, at least in this place and period, it was general practice to refer to men of distinguished ancestry by adding the ancestor's epithet or the title of his major work of scholarship.[4] This custom of recalling famous forebears clearly provides useful pointers in rabbinical genealogy.

It also indicates the importance attached to lineage (*yichus*) and to standing in the Brody community, in which learning tended to take precedence over wealth in determining social position. Families like the Babad, Chayes,

Margolioth, Shapiro and others combined ancient lineage, intellectual distinction and wealth. The balance between lineage and learning on one hand and more material attributes on the other was delicately struck in arranged marriages. The leading rabbis featured prominently in the social hierarchy.

The Gelles family owned some land, several houses, and a chandlery (Vaskievonia). They appear to have had a monopoly for the supply of candles to the community. From the mid-1700s to the early 1800s, a part of which is covered by the Beth Din Records, the family was quite prosperous. Membership of the *Klaus* certainly carried considerable prestige. This is the period for which there are records of marriage alliances with the families of Brody Rabbis Heschel Hakohen, Meir Fraenkel, Yehuda Leib Zundel, Berach Margoshes, and others. Our connections with Rabbi Pinchas Shapiro of Koretz are documented and discussed elsewhere.

A marriage contract (*Kethuba*) from the year 1817 between the Gelles and Margoshes families contains several points of interest, viz. the relative status of the participating families, the apparent youth of the bridegroom, the use of the Russian rouble, among other currencies, in a town which was an entrepot between the Austrian and Russian Empires, and an undertaking by the bridegroom's brother to carry out the *chalitza* ceremony.[5]

The community was strong in its religious faith, the winds of enlightenment blowing from post-revolutionary France not yet having made much impact in this distant outpost of the Austrian Empire. The synagogue was central to the life of the community and there were many smaller houses of prayer to cater for special groups. Synagogue seats were bequeathed, sold and rented. A good example is provided by Finkel, a daughter of R. Dov Ber Fraenkel and the wife of Reb Wolf Bolechower, who purchased 35 seats, later selling some or using the funds from their rental for charitable purposes.[6]

Many houses and plots of land stayed in the same family for several generations and the numerous entries for property transactions refer to owners passing property to their heirs, and to later subdivisions. An analysis of names, property numbers and dates of transaction has confirmed a number of family links.

Moses Gelles had died before the period covered by the Beth Din document. His property was divided between his children and in-laws and then went to their children and grandchildren. Their houses and parcels of land were therefore often adjoining to one another or to the land on part of which stood the family *Vaskievonie* or waxworks.

In the short span of ten years the Beth Din Record encompasses information on four generations of related families. Several entries show that Moses Gelles of the *Klaus* was one and the same person as Menachem Levush and that his sons Michel Levush or Gelles, Joseph Gelles *Vaskievonie*, and Mordecai Gelles had numerous issue known by various names. R. Moshe Gershon, a son of Joseph Gelles, sometimes referred to as R. Moshe, can be distinguished from the R. Moshe Gelles, whose name is given on the Brody tombstone of his son, Rabbi David Isaac Gellis. This R. Moshe was probably a son of the above-mentioned R. Mordecai Gelles, who was a *mechutan* (in-law) of Rabbi Pinchas of Koretz. More light is thrown on other in-laws. Thus, Rabbi Yehuda Zundel, grandfather of another Moshe Levush or Gelles, appears to be identical with the Rabbi Yehuda Leib Zundel Ramraz, who belonged to the circle of the wise men of Brody and died in 1804. Reb Berach Margoshes' granddaughter married a Gelles and Berach's wife may have been the daughter of R. Shmuel Gelles. The family of Reb Ahron Benish seem to be connected through the wives of Ahron's sons, Reb Simcha and Reb David Hertz. The two couples sold their separate interests in two houses to the brothers-in-law Meir Fraenkel and Moses Gershon Gelles.[7]

The prosperity of the Gelles family declined as candles gave way to gaslight, and as Brody suffered from the siting of the new railways, the decline of its importance as a trading centre, and the loss of its status as a Free City. Many Jews left their ancient hometown. Some, like the Brodskys, flourished in Odessa and elsewhere in Russia. In the closing decades of the nineteenth century the influx of refugees from Russian pogroms led to overcrowding and poverty in Brody, but by that time many of the old families had been dispersed throughout Galicia, Austria and beyond.

NOTES

1. Records of the Beth Din of Brody 1808–17. MS 4037, Jewish Theological Seminary, New York.
2. E. Gelles, 'Finding Rabbi Moses Gelles', *Avotaynu*, 18, 1 (Spring 2002).
3. Nathan M. Gelber, 'Brody: The Jerusalem of Austria', in *An Eternal Light: Brody in Memoriam*, (The Organisation of former Brody residents in Israel, 1994), Footnote on the Brody *Klaus*.
4. *Epithets:* Instances are entries No.1116 for R. Zalman Margoshes *Shach* [descendant of the *Shach* – an acronym for Rabbi Shabbatai Katz], and No.1172 for Chaim Zvi Hersh, son of R. Moshe Efrayim *Chacham Zvi* [descendant of Chacham Zvi Ashkenazi]. Records of the Beth Din of Brody 1808–17.

   More relevant to the interpretation of the *Levush* name, as referring to descent from Rabbi Mordecai Yaffe and to the title of his book, are instances of other epithets derived from famous rabbinical works, namely Nos.1132, 1138, 1278 for Reb Mendel *Tevuos Shor,* Reb Alexander Chaim *Tevuos Shor*, and Reb Yosef, Yisrael *Tevuos Shor* [members of the Shor family descended from the author of *Tevuos Shor*], and No.1350 for Leah, daughter of R. Avrohom Yitzchak Halevy *Turei Zahav* [after his ancestor David Halevy Segal, the author of the book *Turei Zahav*]. The case for the derivation of the epithet *Levush* is certainly strengthened by these examples from the Beth Din Record. The civil birth, marriage and death records of Brody confirm that Gelles and Levush were alternative or additional names in the family for several generations. There is a previous record of this epithet attached to known progeny of the Levush. The tombstone of a R. Nehemia Levush of Svierz and later of Vilna has an inscription stating that his father Rabbi Zvi Levush was a descendant of Rabbi Mordecai Yaffe; see note 2.
5. No.1420. Kethuba of Abraham (a bachelor) son of Rabbi Moshe Gelles, son of Reb Joseph *Vaskievonie* [a], married Taube, daughter of Rabbi Josef Kalischer, son of R. Berach Margoshes, on Friday 6th Tammuz 5577 [July 1817]. Reb Moshe Gelles promised to pay

the sum of 450 Russian roubles, support the couple for the first three years of their marriage [b], and pay for their clothing, as well as tuition fees [c]. Reb Josef Kalischer gave the sum of 100 Russian roubles. The bridegroom's brother Reb Yankel Gelles gave an undertaking to carry out the *chalitza* ceremony if necessary [d].

[a] owner of the waxworks and one of the sons of Moses Gelles – Levush of Brody.

[b] other marriage contracts of the period refer to varying sums of money and years of support. Thus, in entry No.277, the marriage of Yitzchak, a son of Reb Benjamin Zeev Bolechover, which took place in 1808, was endowed with 1,980 *reinish* and a promise of five years' support by the father of the bridegroom and separately by the mother of the bride. Entry Nos.1391, 1395, 1397 and 1412 refer to 2,700 silver roubles and six years' support; 675 roubles and three years' support from the bride's father; 1,425 new roubles with each side supporting the couple for four years; and 1,125 Russian roubles with support of two years from the bride's father and five years from the bridegroom's father. While the most common currency of the period was the Russian rouble, Austrian ducats [*Kaiserliche dukaten*] are mentioned in entry No.1258 dated 1814, Prussian currency [*Preussisch*] in No.447 dated 1808, and Dutch coinage [*rendelech Hollander*] in Nos.424 and 429 in 1808. See Note 8.

[c] the provision for the payment of tuition fees may indicate the extreme youth of the bridegroom.

[d] the *chalitza* ceremony involves release of a childless bride by the brother of the bridegroom in the event of the bridegroom's death.

6. No.394. Finkel, daughter of R. Dov Ber Fraenkel and wife of Reb Wolf Bolechower, purchased 35 seats in the Synagogue. No.1133:

> A sale by the wealthy Finkel ... of a seat in the women's section of the New Synagogue ... in memory of the soul of the late Feiga, daughter of Reb Yehoshua Heshel Hakohen, the wife of Rabbi Michel, son of Reb Moshe Gelles ... so that this should be an everlasting memorial to her soul, never to be sold. The rental income from the seat is to be used to pay for a Yahrzeit lamp [candle lit on the anniversary of the deceased' death] and the remainder to be distributed to the local poor on the day of her Jahrzeit. She appointed a Trustee ... Ellul 5573 [September 1813].

Finkel was the sister of Rabbi Meir Fraenkel, a son-in-law of R. Josef Gelles *Vaskievonie*, who was a son of R. Moses Gelles.

The husband of the above-mentioned Feiga is identified in No.270. Reb Michel, son of Reb Menachem Levush (son-in-law of Reb S. Gelles) signed and sealed to his wife Feiga, daughter of Rabbi Yehoshua Heshel, that if she passes away before him, he is obliged to return to her heirs, or to whoever she instructs, half of the value of her *shterentuchel* [the customary jewelled head-dress], and all clothing, bedding etc, immediately after her death....27th Tishri 5568 [Oct. 1808].

Menachem Levush in No.270 is thus one and the same person as Moses Gelles in No.1133. An entry in 1808 gives the value of a *shterentuchel* as at least 200 *rendelech Hollander*, and an entry for the wedding in 1813 of Benjamin Wolf, son of Zvi Hirsch Schonblum of Lvov, to Rikel Landau, daughter of R.Yosef ben R. Shachna, refers to a *shterentuchel*, earrings and pearls being worth at least 900 Russian roubles.

No. 401. Gittel Malka, the widow of Reb Todros be Ramraz [of the Zundel family] sold a seat on the eastern wall in the women's section, next to the seat belonging to Malka Margoshes ... Iyyar 5568 [May 1808]. No.1308. Sale by Chaya, widow of R. Shmuel Gelles, of half a seat in the women's section of the Synagogue to Ektish, wife of the wealthy R. Yehoshua Margalioth ... 28th Menachem [Av] 5575 [August 1815].

7. Parts of houses and parcels of land were conveyed very frequently between the heirs of Moses Gelles and their descendants. These transactions involved Leah and Bonna, and

their in-laws of the Benish family [Nos.713, 813, see also Nos.1064,1067], Reb Moshe Gershon Gelles, a son of R. Joseph Gelles *Vaskievonie* and his brother-in-law Rabbi Meir Shlomo Fraenkel [Nos.713, 786, 813], the latter's wealthy sister Finkel and her husband Reb Benyamin Wolf Bolechover [Nos.574, 922], and other sons of R. Joseph Gelles, namely Reb Yaakov Hersh Feigang and Rabbi Abraham Yonah Reich with the latter's in-laws of the Reich family [No.786].

These two Gelles were referred to by the names of their fathers-in-law, which was a common custom at the time. Yonah Reich is perhaps identifiable as the father of R. Isaac Reich who married a granddaughter of R. Joseph Landau, ABD of Zolkiew and later head of the Brody *Klaus* (see Note 8). R. Moshe Gershon Gelles was probably Bonna's brother. Reb Mordechai Gelles, a brother of Reb Joseph *Vaskievonie* is mentioned [Nos.762, 1035] and Reb Shmuel may be a kinsman of Moshe Gelles of the *Klaus* [Nos.481, 530, 953]. His daughter married Reb Berach Margoshes. The Margoshes also had marriage links with the Shapiro family [Nos.860, 863]. The identity of Rabbi Yehuda Zundel whose daughter Sarah Bathya married Mordecai Levush, son of R. Michel Gelles, is indicated by the entries for a property sale to their son Reb Moshe Levush in March 1814 [No.1194] and the entries relating to land belonging to the heirs of the late R. Zundel Ramraz [No.1131], and again to the heirs of Reb Zundel son of R.M. Reb Zelig's in December 1814 [No.1260]. Rabbi Yehuda Leib Zundel carried the epithet *Ramraz,* an acronym for Rabbi Moshe Reb Zelig's. The details of Zundel's daughter Sarah Bathya (Bassie) as given in the Beth Din Record are corroborated by the civil records for Brody housed in the Lviv archives that give the year of her death as 1826.

8. Neil Rosenstein, *The Unbroken Chain* (New York, London, Jerusalem: CIS Publishers, 1990), pp.755–7.

Currencies

The use of a variety of coins was widespread in this period and by no means confined to Brody. For a century from 1779 it was a 'Free City' with a flourishing trade between eastern and central Europe. Money in the above-mentioned documents included the Rhenish, a term for the contemporary German or Netherlandish gulden (guilder). References to Dutch coinage might have been to the ryder, worth 14 guilders (see, www.giacomo-casanova.de/catour16.htm. This web page contains interesting information drawn from various sources including Casanova's *Memoirs,* Thomas Nugent's *Grand Tour,* and other writings). In the late eighteenth century the pound sterling was worth about eleven and a half Dutch guilders and about five and a half Russian roubles, which were of similar value to the rixdollar. The new Russian silver rouble, introduced under Tsar Alexander I in 1810, was clearly popular in Brody. The money settlements in the quoted marriage contracts were in the range of a few hundred to a few thousand roubles or the equivalent in other currencies. Among the few indications of the low price and wage levels in this period is a record of the fee of one rouble per week paid to the part time prayer leader of the New Synagogue (Entry No.1275, in March 1815).

Table 26
GELLES OF BRODY

Partial family tree showing some rabbinical connections

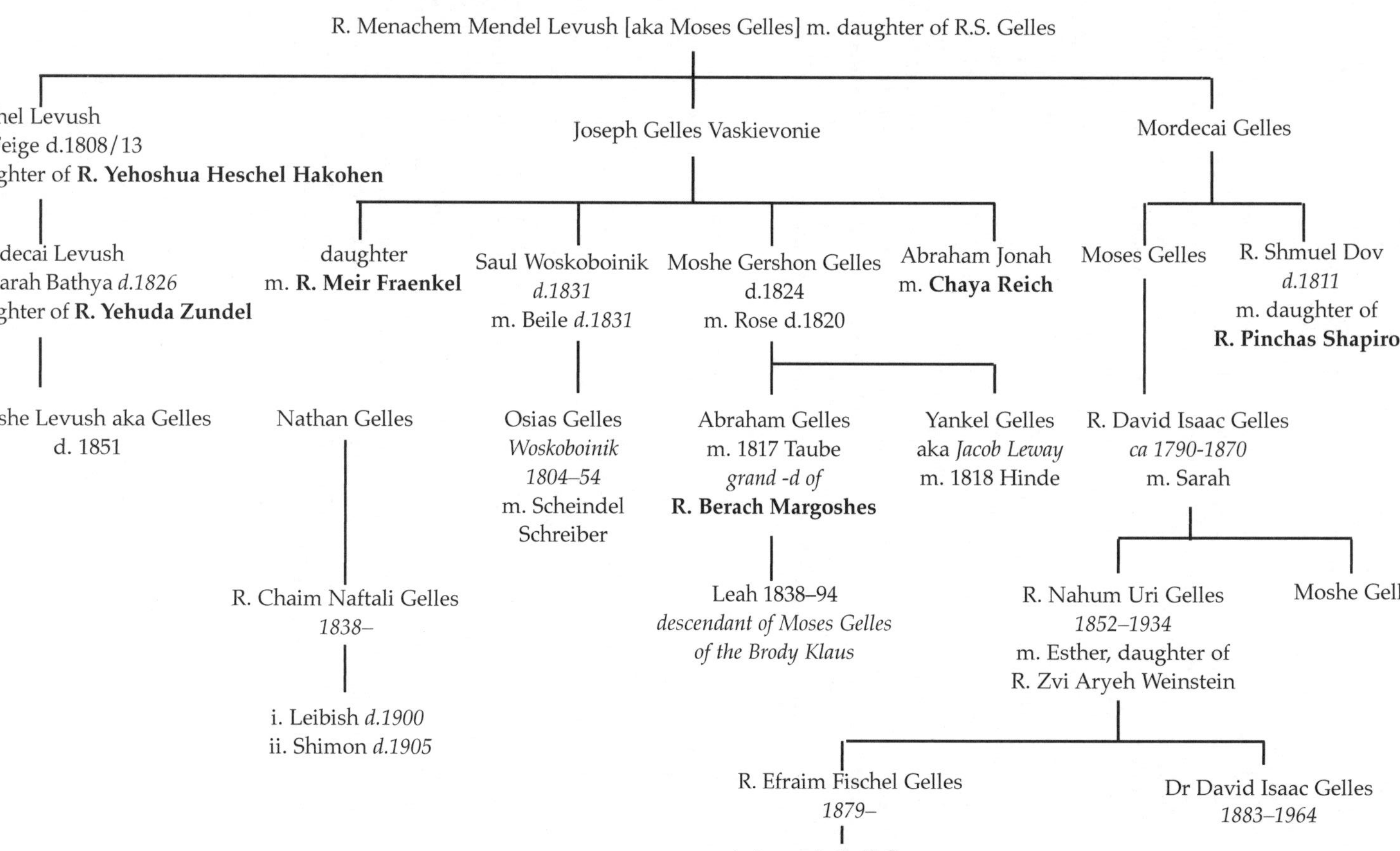

Table 27
ZUNDEL RAMRAZ

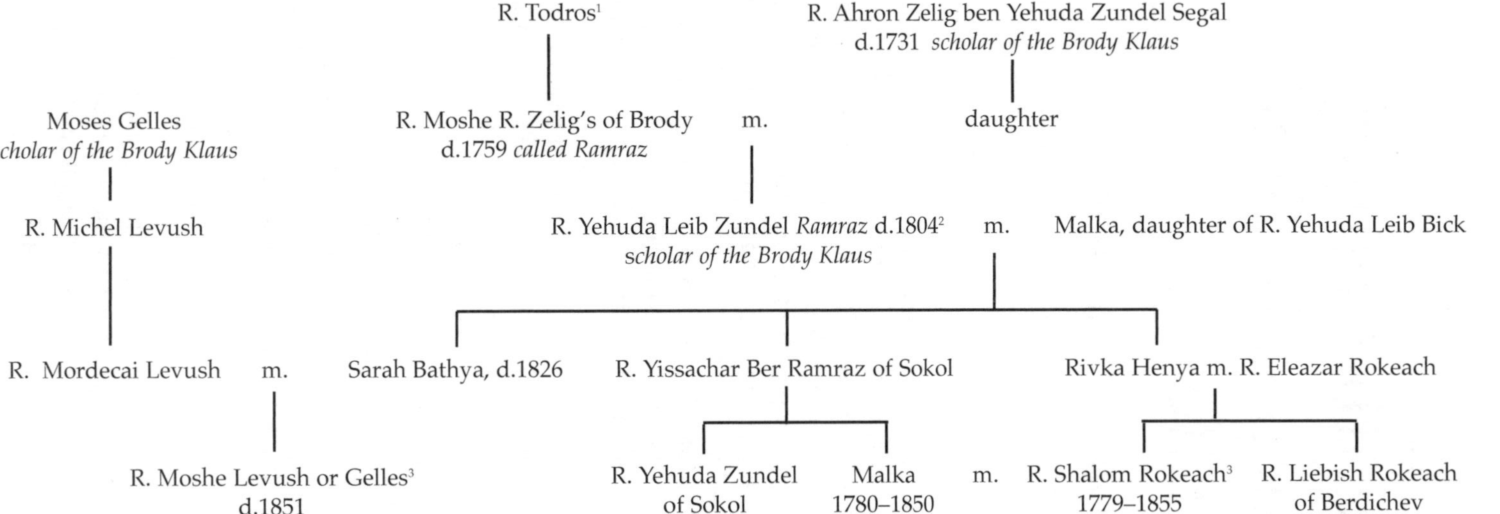

Notes:

1. R. Todros was a descendant of R. Todros Abulafia, of the family distinguished as scholars and courtiers in thirteenth- and fourteenth-century Spain.
2. R. Yehuda Zundel of Brody may have been married (secondly) to Frieda, daughter of R. Yitzchak of Sokol, who was a descendant of many famous rabbis. Rabbi Yehuda Zundel, like his grandfather was a scholar of the Brody Klaus, and so were Moses Gelles and Jacob Horowitz. The latter married Sarah, a daughter of R. Todros Zundel Ramraz (nephew of the above Yehuda Leib Zundel). Jacob's son Rabbi Todros Zundel Horowitz (d.1866) of Brody and Busk, author of *Shoresh Miyakov*, was thus a cousin of one of our Gelles lines. Other Horowitz connections are shown in later charts.
3. Some descendants of Moses Gelles of Brody and of the Rokeach Grand Rabbis of Belz also share a Zundel Ramraz ancestor. Chaya, a granddaughter of R. Liebish Rokeach of Berdichev, married Israel Brodsky (1823–89).

Sources: E. Gelles, 'Finding Rabbi Moses Gelles', *Avotaynu*, xviii, 1 (Spring 2002).
N.M. Gelber (ed.), *Arim Veimahot Beisrael* (Jerusalem, 1952 and later), vol.6 (Brody), pp.54, 56, 69–70.
Meir Wunder, *Meorei Galicia* (Jerusalem: Institute for the Commemoration of Galician Jewry, 1978 *et seq.*), vol.4, pp.844–907 and 967–9.
Yitzchak Shlomo Yudlov, *Sefer Yichus Belza* (Jerusalem: Machon, 1984), pp.25–35 and 311–15.
Neil Rosenstein, *The Unbroken Chain* (New York, London, Jerusalem: CIS Publishers, 1990), pp.806–7 and 1103–4 for Brodsky connections.

CHAPTER THIRTY-ONE

A Nineteenth-Century Pictorial Record of Brody Life

The decline of an old Jewish town in Austrian Galicia

Brody was a quintessentially Jewish town that flourished within the Austrian Empire for more than a century. It lay on the border with Russia, and through its ancient trading connections it was exposed to cultural influences from peoples of many ethnic origins. In the mid-eighteenth century, Brody had the largest Jewish population of any town in the Polish Kingdom and (while Jews were temporarily expelled from Prague) second only to Amsterdam in the whole of Europe.[1] The records of the Gelles family indicate that the period from about 1760 to 1830 was one of relative prosperity and cultural cohesion.[2] Political, economic and demographic factors contributed to the gradual decline of the town's fortunes in the later nineteenth century.

The American artist Joseph Pennell made drawings of the town during his tour of Eastern Europe in 1891. A number of these were included in a book he published in the following year.[3] The pictures are of some quality and historical interest. It is a pity that Pennell did not stick to his art, but ventured to accompany it with a deplorably biased text.

A few of the drawings are reproduced below. The first is of the cemetery with long rows of tombstones which the artist described as '8 to 10 feet high, decorated in the most fantastic fashion, one side is gilded elaborately and covered with Hebrew characters, though the other, perfectly plain, save for a tiny inscription, is unhewn and rough'. It should be noted that the old cemetery of Brody was totally destroyed during the Second World War. Tombstones of the new cemetery dating from 1830 onwards are being catalogued at the present time.[4]

Another drawing has a concourse accompanied with the comment 'the Jews seemed to have no amusement except going to the synagogue ... the chief synagogue in Brody is a huge square building, with a large square hall for the men in the centre, and on either side, like side aisles in a church, two smaller rooms for the women'.

The synagogue and many small prayer houses and study groups did play a significant part in an active and varied Jewish cultural life, as we know, for example, from the more sympathetic account written half a century earlier, when the community was relatively better off and more at ease with itself.[5]

Market and street scenes, sketches of figures, including an Austrian officer in a café, and some Jews sitting on a park bench, convey the late-nineteenth-century atmosphere of a community hovering between life centred on ancient pieties and traditions and the embrace of the modern world and pan-European horizons.

NOTES

1. Jonathan I. Israel, *European Jewry in the Age of Mercantilism, 1550–1750* (Oxford: Clarendon Press, 1985), p.241.
2. E. Gelles, 'Finding Rabbi Moses Gelles', *Avotaynu*, xviii, 1 (Spring 2002).
3. Joseph Pennell, *The Jew At Home. Impressions of a summer and autumn spent with him in Russia and Austria* (London: Heinemann, 1892).
4. The Brody Tombstone Project is being undertaken by Dr Neil Rosenstein and Rabbi Dov Weber.
5. A.A. Bonar and R.M. McCheyne, *Narrative of a Mission of Inquiry to the Jews from the Church of Scotland in 1839* (Edinburgh: William Whyte, 1842).

Figure 35
The Jewish Cemetery, Brody

Going to the Synagogue, Brody

Figure 36
The Main Synagogue, Brody

Figure 37
The Market, Brody

CHAPTER THIRTY-TWO

Prague at the Crossroads

Loew and Yaffe, Mordecai Yaffe (the Levush), David and Chaim Gans

The spirit of the Renaissance spread from Italy across a large part of the continent, taking on a local flavour in different places. The sixteenth century was a great period for European culture generally, and in particular for Prague and for Jewish history. That city was a most important staging post. Many descendants of its great Rabbis such as Judah Loew, Mordecai Yaffe and David Gans were found in Poland and Lithuania in later centuries. A few examples illustrate the geographical and genealogical aspects of their journey.

JUDAH LOEW, YAFFE AND OTHERS

The most famous Rabbi of this period is surely Judah Loew (ca. 1520–1609), known as *der Hohe Rabbi Loew* or *Maharal*. He came to Prague in 1573. His family stemmed from Worms in Germany. His uncle, *der Kaiserrabbiner,* or Chief Rabbi of the German communities, was Jacob of Worms. The Loews formed alliances with Yaffe, Katzenellenbogen, and other families. Isaac ben Abraham Chayot, the progenitor of the Chayes rabbinical line, alternated with Judah Loew in the Chief Rabbinate of Prague and was his brother-in-law.

The Yaffe family was in Bologna and Mantua in the middle ages, and from those who moved to Bohemia sprang the scholar Mordecai Yaffe (1530–1612). He took refuge in Venice in 1561 when the Jews were expelled from Prague – one of a series of temporary expulsions recurring over a period of over two centuries. From Venice Mordecai moved to Poland where he became a great community leader. He was also a true Renaissance scholar who wrote about astronomy, social and political matters and other subjects from an essentially Jewish viewpoint, although his principal work was of course the commentary the title of which earned him the epithet *HaLevush*.

His contemporary in Venice was Rabbi Samuel Judah ben Meir Katzenellenbogen (1521–97), son of the *Maharam of Padua* (1483–1565) and father of Saul Wahl (ca. 1545–1617). Saul's mother was of Yaffe's family. A cousinly branch of the Yaffes acquired the name of *Kalamankes* from Kalonymos, the name borne by some of their forebears. Some members of this line distinguished themselves in the field of printing and book publishing.

The path of scholarship, both sacred and profane, stretched from Padua in Italy, to Prague in Bohemia, to Cracow and the Yeshivahs of Poland-Lithuania. Padua attracted classical scholars from far and wide, while seekers after Jewish learning were drawn to the famous Rabbis such as Moses Isserles of Cracow, and Saul Wahl's kinsman Shlomo Luria, the *Maharshal of Lublin*.

On the historical map of Jewish migrations Prague in the Renaissance period stood at the crossroads between Germany and Italy and the rising centres of learning in the east. This golden period came to an end with the thirty years war and the Chmielnicki massacres.

The main source for Judah Loew's family tree is the work by R' Meir Perels.[1] For the Yaffe family tree, reference is made to the *Jewish Encyclopaedia*.[2] There may be a connection to the Kalamankes-Senderlich family that originates from Sender Loeb Kalamankes, a son of Kalonymus of Lublin.[3] Aaron Yaffe of Uman was born in Prague, and his son Ephraim was a noted rabbi in that city. A younger son, Israel ben Aaron Yaffe Saba, became a distinguished rabbi of Shklov. He wrote a number of books, and one of these has numerous approbations including that of the Rabbi of Minsk, who refers to Israel Yaffe as a relative.[4] Moses Zeev Wolf of Minsk was a son of R'Yudah Yudel of Kowel, a descendant of Zvi Hirsch Saba of Prague and his wife Tilla Loew, a daughter of the Maharal.[5] Israel Yaffe, but not his father Aaron, is sometimes referred to by the name of Saba. A connection with Prague and possibly to the family or Judah Loew is of intrinsic interest. Israel was also related by marriage to the Teomim and Heschel families, and these connections lead from Prague to Cracow and further afield.

RABBI MORDECAI YAFFE AND DESCENDANTS IN LITHUANIA AND GALICIA

Some Yaffes migrated from Italy to Bohemia in the late fifteenth century. Abraham of Bohemia had two grandsons: they were respectively the grandfathers of Rabbis Joel Sirkes of Cracow and Mordecai Yaffe of Prague.

Mordecai was born around 1530. He studied in Poland under Solomon Luria and Moses Isserles, and then returned to Prague as head of the yeshiva. He had family connections with the Katzenellenbogens of Padua. After a lengthy Venetian interlude, Mordecai answered the call of Jewish communities in Poland, becoming head of the yeshiva and the rabbinical court at Grodno in 1572. He also served in Lublin and in Kremenetz. He returned to Prague in 1592, where he succeeded Rabbi Judah Loew, finally settling in Posen, where he remained as Chief Rabbi from 1599 until his death in 1612.

His codification of the law on which he worked for decades is entitled *Aseret Levushim* and after this magnum opus he was called the Levush. While he was a great Talmudic scholar, his enthusiasm for the Cabbala influenced his approach, which tended to reconcile the Talmudists and Cabbalists. In several of the *Levushim* ('garments' or rabbinical robes of learning) he dealt with social, economic and political questions, skilfully interpreting traditional teaching to take account of conditions and practices in different Jewish communities, his approach being quite liberal in the spirit of the times.

This is not the place to expand on his numerous scholarly works, but if a single quotation might be allowed, he wrote on civil law 'only that government is legitimate in which the king's seal of authority is voluntarily acknowledged by his subjects; otherwise he is not their king but a robber gathering imposts by force whose edicts have no legal value'.

He wrote learnedly on astronomical matters and the calendar, and his mind was open to the intellectual movements of his day. He was strongly opposed to usury in any form.

Mordecai Yaffe's judgments and responsa were greatly valued in his lifetime. He was one of the founder members of the Council of the Four Lands, the semi-autonomous governing body of the Jewish communities in Poland-Lithuania. Having established his reputation in Grodno, he was chosen to be a judge in Lublin, which was one of the country's major commercial centres and attracted many Jews from neighbouring countries to its fairs.

Disputes growing out of their transactions required adjudication by an authority of more than local standing, and Mordecai Yaffe's role increased his influence in the Council, so that even after his return to Prague he was recognized as one of its leaders.[6]

Mordecai Yaffe had two sons and three daughters. Bella married the physician Jechiel Michel Epstein, son of Rabbi Abraham Epstein of Brest. A line of descent from this couple involving the Chayes and Heilprin families comes into the story of the Wahls of Nadworna.[7] Another daughter, Walka, married a Wahl, and the third was the wife of Benjamin Wolf Guenzburg. Among the progeny of Mordecai's son Perez was Abraham Aberl of Nikolsburg, who was the father and grandfather of Joseph Yaffe of Posen and of Mordechai of Plungian. The latter had an interesting life. Born in 1721, he was caught up as a child in the War of the Polish Succession (1733–35), when he was taken prisoner by a band of soldiers and held to ransom. The wealthy Enoch Zundel, who subsequently gave him his daughter in marriage, saved him. Some of their progeny adopted the name of Zundel. Such a custom was not uncommon among Polish Jews in that period. Zundels crop up in the Yaffe family tree from that time. Joseph ben Mordechai ben Joseph became president of the Lithuanian council and Moses ben Mordechai ben Joseph was the father of Zundel Halfon, the grammarian.

The connection of rabbis bearing the Levush name with the author of the *Levushim* has been attested for a Rabbi Nehemia Levush of Svierz and later of Vilna who died in 1804. He was the son of Rabbi Zvi Levush, as stated on his tombstone, and his descent from Mordechai Yaffe is confirmed in contemporary records.[8] Rabbi Nehemia is listed in *Otzar Harabbanim* (No.15963).[9] He might be related to Rabbi Abraham Levush of Vilna (No.510), son of Rabbi Meir Heller (1804–77), who was dayan in Vilna and Rabbi of Trocki.[10]

The connections of the Gelles family of Brody with Mordecai Yaffe through Menachem Mendel Levush aka Moses Gelles are discussed in Chapters 29 and 30. It appears very plausible that we can number Mordecai Yaffe among the Gelles ancestors.[11]

Gelli(e)s and Yaffe (Yofe) spread out over a wide area of Lithuania with an epicentre at Grodno, where the Levush had once been Chief Rabbi. Gellis families, not necessarily related to the Brody line, had Yaffe connections that are relevant in the study of the migration pattern from Prague to Lithuania, to Silesia and further west, and south to Galicia, and to Hungary and Austria. For example, there was a line of 12 Rabbis of the Yofe family in Gorzd including R. Zev Yofe who died in 1848, his son R Moshe Yaffe who succeeded him as Rabbi there and served from 1848 to 1855, and his son R. Joseph Yaffe (1846–97), who became Rabbi of Münster, and then of Manchester, England in 1893.[12] According to Sefer Gorzd there was a tradition that this Yofe family descended from the Levush. Joseph Gellis, who wrote an article on the Yofe family, was a descendant of the above-mentioned Rabbi Moshe Yaffe.[13] Several Gellis families were based at Gorzd and nearby Kretinga in the Kovno Gubernya of Lithuania (Chapter 38).

DAVID AND CHAIM GANS

Most visitors to Prague will have come across the name of David Gans. He is a famous figure in the history of the city and of its Jewish community. Few will have heard of his near kinsman Chaim Gans, whose adventurous life and work is better known to students of the history of science in England and America. The common thread is their background of Talmudic study and their ready engagement with the new ideas of the renaissance. A few genealogical digressions help to show their sixteenth-century world hovering between old and new philosophies and continents.

Several Jewish families of their name emerged from Germany in the middle ages. David Gans was born in the Westphalian town of Lippstadt in 1541. His family developed branches at Leipen and Bischitz in Bohemia.[14]

David was the son of Solomon ben Seligman Gans. His teachers included Eliezer Treves in Frankfurt and Moses Isserles in Cracow. He also studied under Judah Loew in Prague where he finally settled in 1564. He took an active interest in mathematics, astronomy and geography and also wrote a history, the *Zemach David*, which transcended the scope of the usual Jewish

ספר

לבוש חבוץ וארגמן

והוא הלבוש הרביעי מלבוש המלכות אשר חבר הגאון מוהר״ר
מרדכי יפ״ה נקרא ופ״ה וקרא שמו לבוש הבו״ץ וארגמ״ן
על שם הפסוק ומרדכי יצא בלבוש מלכות וגומר ותכריך בוץ
וארגמן וגומ׳ והוא כולל כל דיני סדר נשים המבוארי׳
בטור אבן העזר כמבואר בהקדמה ראשונה
הנדפסת עם שני לבושים הראשונים
אשר המה לבוש התכלת
ולבוש החור
ע״ש:

נדפס פה ק״ק פראג

תחת ממשלת אדונינו הקיסר רומי פרדיננדוס יר״ה ותתנשא מלכותו חכי״ר

על ידי הר״ד משה בן מהר״ר יוסף בצלאל כ״ץ דצ״ל מהוקק

היום יום ג׳ ח׳ אייר שנת שפ״ג לפ״ק

Figure 38
Title page of the *Levushim* by Rabbi Mordecai Yaffe

history and earned the description of *Historia Chronologica Sacra et Profana*.[15] His circle of friends in Prague included the great Rabbi Judah Loew and the astronomers Kepler and Tycho Brahe. David was a true Renaissance scholar in a city that at the time stood at the crossroads between Germany and Italy and the centres of Jewish learning in Poland. He died in Prague in 1613. His tombstone is decorated with the Shield of David (the title of one of his many books) and also with the familiar emblem of a goose. The name of Gans (goose) derived in typical medieval German fashion from a house name and shield. The migration of this family over the centuries from towns in Germany, and specifically from Frankfurt to Prague, and then to Cracow and beyond, followed a common pattern among Ashkenazi Jews.

David Gans had children and relatives who lived in these cities and further afield. His brother was Yoshua Seligman and his children included Yisrael Gans of Cracow (died 1619), Yoshua Seligman Gans of Bischitz (died Prague 1638), and a daughter who married Wolf Fleckeles. The eighteenth-century Rabbi Eleazar Fleckeles of Prague was their descendant.

David's father-in-law Samuel Rofe (a doctor) was credited with devising a cure for syphilis with less dangerous side effects than the quicksilver treatment then generally employed. His first cousin Nathan Nata Shapiro of Grodno (died 1577) is mentioned in the *Zemach David*. He was the author of several books and reportedly had 'a vast knowledge of the Hebrew language and grammar'. He belonged to the Shapiros who go back to the Spiro son-in-law of Mattityahu Treves, the medieval Rabbis of France, and thence to Rashi of Troyes, the biblical scholar and commentator of the eleventh century. Nathan of Grodno was the grandfather of the Rabbi of Cracow of the same name (1585–1633) and the line continued to Rabbi Pinchas Shapiro of Koretz (1726–90) and to Rabbi Yehuda Meir Shapira (1887–1934). The Gelles rabbis of Brody had links of descent, marriage and friendship with the Shapiro line.

The records of Frankfurt hint at a possible connection of the descendants of Geyle, who died there in 1634 and is identified as a daughter of Rabbi David Gans, with the rabbis bearing the Gelles matronymic in Prague.[16]

Hock's transcriptions of the Prague tombstones include numerous entries for the Gans family covering the period from 1598 to 1776. For example, No. 5395 [1634] is for Seligman, son of the pious Rabbi David of Bischitz. A footnote refers to a Rabbi Seligman Gans of Prague and also mentions the name of Chaim Gans, the metallurgist who developed copper mining in England. The Prague burial lists also contain many entries for Gelles from 1632 to 1745, including an entry for 1651 for the honourable Rabbi Mendel, son of Salman Gelles, 'emissary of the Beth Din'.[17] It is noteworthy that while there were Gelles next to Seligman and Gans in Prague in the seventeenth century, a Gellis family was also in Grodno where a contemporaneous Gans–Shapiro connection has already been noted. However, there is no firm evidence that the Gelles of Prague were closely related to Gans or indeed to the Gellis family from Grodno, who may have taken their name from a different lady by the name of Gele.

Chaim Gans was David's near kinsman, perhaps a nephew. His family background was one in which the traditional Talmudic learning was combined with that of the new science. Interest in Jewish arcane lore such as the Cabbala, astrology and alchemy remained intense. Chaim's interest in metallurgy was also not unconnected with the proximity of the so-called *Erzgebirge* at the borders of Bohemia and Saxony, which had long been exploited for its wealth of minerals. Here and in the Austrian Tyrol were the prime areas of European metal production. Following the publication in 1556 of the classic work *De Re Metallica* by Georg Bauer [Agricola], the above-mentioned regions far surpassed that of the rest of Europe in the sophistication of mining and metallurgy.

Chaim Gans was an expert in his field. He came to England in 1581 and made an outstanding contribution to the development of the mining industry. He took part in an expedition to the New World and appears to have been the first professing Jew to set foot in English-speaking North America. He has been regarded by some as one of the pioneers of the modern scientific method.

Chaim, known here as Joachim Gaunse, enjoyed the patronage of some of the most important men in Elizabethan England. Sir Francis Walsingham was the principal patron of his work for the Society of the Mines Royal at Keswick. It revolutionized English copper production and was just in time to give English ships the advantage of good bronze cannon to pit against the cast iron guns of the Spanish Armada. Sir Walter Raleigh recruited him for his expedition of 1584–86 which established a base on Roanoke Island, Virginia. The site at which Gans carried out metallurgical tests has been described as 'America's First Science Center'. Fort Raleigh National Historic Site in North Carolina preserves relics of his work. The ship that took Gans and his team of German miners to America was captained by Sir Richard Grenville. When supplies failed, the survivors of the expedition were brought back to England by Sir Francis Drake. It has been suggested by Lewis S. Feuer that Joachim Gaunse was the model for Joabin, the Jewish innovator of scientific enquiry, in Sir Francis Bacon's *New Atlantis*.[18]

Gans introduced procedures for treating minerals and producing copper in which the lengthy and repeated roastings of ores was replaced by a much less time consuming and less costly treatment of the powdered material, alternating with repeated washings by means of which metal sulphates and impurities were gradually removed. The iron and copper sulphates thus extracted were put to use in the dyeing of textiles. Gans further developed his method for smelting ore at Neath near Swansea, and it has been suggested that some Cornish mines were re-opened at his instigation. As the leading 'metal man' of his day it is no wonder that he was sought out to search for minerals and to explore the potential for metal production in America.

For a few years Gans was near the centre of the great Elizabethan Renaissance. But this was a time for religious as well as scientific revolution. In this great period of transition there were boundless opportunities as well as great dangers. The Elizabethan state in its life and death struggle with Catholic Spain did not tolerate any expressions of religious dissent. Gans was accused of denying the divinity of Christ. As a professing Jew he could not be accused of heresy, but a charge of blasphemy may have been enough to enforce his departure from these shores, and he probably returned to Bohemia, but all trace of him appears to have been lost around 1590.

Some Bohemian Jews like David and Chaim, whose minds had been sharpened through Talmudic study over the generations, took readily to the new science and the emerging spirit of empirical enquiry. This family played an interesting role in the process that ultimately led from astrology to modern astronomy and from alchemical lore to modern chemical science.

SUMMARY OF PRAGUE CONNECTIONS

The families of the great Rabbis of sixteenth century Prague had diverse origins. Judah Loew's forebears hailed from Worms, David Gans came to Prague via Frankfurt. The Yaffes originated in northern Italy. The Chayes and Altschulers were Sephardim from Provence. The Horovitz family who took their name from the town in Horovice were also of ancient Sephardic origin. These great families of Prague, as well as the Meisels and less well-known ones such as that descended from the Katz (Kohen-Zedek) son-in-law of Judah Loew, and the Gelles, later flourished in Poland, Lithuania and Galicia, where the thread of their connections emerged again (see Chapter 36 and Table 49).

There was also a continual movement from Prague to rabbinical appointments in Western Europe. Thus, my ancestor Shmuel Helman came from Silesia to study in Prague under Abraham Broda at the beginning of the eighteenth century (see Chapter 33). Both were later Chief Rabbis of Metz in Lorraine, and indeed the succession of incumbents in Metz included a number of others with links to Prague.

NOTES

1. R' Meir Perels, *Megillath Yuchasin Mehral miPrag* [German translation in *Jahrbuch der Jüdisch-literarischen Gesellschaft*, Frankfurt, vol.20, 1929]. See also David Nachman Rutner, Beth Ahron Veyisrael (18:2), Jerusalem pp.170–5 referring to a work by Rabbi Yair Chayim Bacharach in a periodical *Bikurim* published in Vienna 1865, clearly identifying Judah Loew's first wife as the sister of Rabbi Isaac Chayes, son of Rabbi Abraham Chayes of Prague. The Maharal married secondly – at the age of 32 – Perel, daughter of Schmelke Reich, and her descendants were known by the surname of Perels. (Rabbi L. Rakow, *Keren Yisrael*, London and Jerusalem: 2000, pp.57–66.)
2. *Jewish Encyclopaedia* 1904 edn, articles on Yaffe including the Kalamankes branch.
3. R' Chaim U. Lipschitz, *Jewish Press*, 30 March 1984, p.24 on the Kalamankes-Senderlich family. Aviva Neeman, a descendant of Israel Yaffe, has confirmed some of the details on the Kalamankes-Senderlich family given in this reference.

4. Israel Yaffe, *Or Israel* (Frankfurt-on-Oder: 1703); attached approbations include one by Moses Zeev Wolf, Rabbi of Minsk, in which he refers to Israel Yaffe as his relative.
5. Neil Rosenstein, *The Unbroken Chain* (New York, London, Jerusalem: CIS Publishers, 1990), p.265 and tables opposite pp.251 and 464.
6. *Jewish Encyclopaedia*, Article on the Yaffes.
7. E. Gelles, 'The Wahls of Nadworna' *Shemot*, (Sept. and Dec. 2000).
8. *Jewish Encyclopaedia*, Article on the Yaffes. S.J. Fuenn, *Kiryah Ne'emanah* (Vilna: 1860), p.216.
9. Rabbi Nathan Zvi Friedmann, *Otzar Harabbanim* (Bnei Brak, Israel: 1973).
10. Ibid.
11. E. Gelles, 'Finding Rabbi Moses Gelles', *Avotaynu*, xviii, 1 (Spring 2002). See Chapter 29. *Idem*, Jewish Community Life in Brody (see Chapter 30).
12. Y. Alperowitz (ed.), *Sefer Gorzd* (Tel Aviv: 1980), p.191; 'The Gorzd Rabbis', p.194; Prof. Joseph Gellis, 'The Yofe Family', and other relevant chapters.
13. Ibid. Prof. Harold Gellis, private correspondence. Rabbi Joseph Yaffe has an entry in the *Jewish Encyclopaedia* (1904 edn).
14. Ludwig Herz, *Die Sechshundertjährige Geschichte der Familie Gans 1330-1930* (Wiener Library, London: Microfiche WLMF 89151 [MFBK503]). Shlomo Berman, *Otzar Israel*, ed. Eisenstein (New York: Menorah Publications, 1974),Vol.iii, pp.233–4.
15. David Gans, *Zemach David* (Prague: 1592), paragraph 5367 [1507].
16. Alexander Dietz, *The Jewish Community of Frankfurt. A Genealogical Study 1349–1849* (Cornwall: Vanderher Publishing, 1988), pp.126, 131–3, 446, 447, 511, 551. Marcus Horovitz, *Die Inschriften des alten Friedhofes der Israelitischen Gemeinde zu Frankfurt a.M.* (Frankfurt: Kauffman, 1901), No.626. F.W. Ettlinger, 'Ele Toldot' (Manuscript at the Leo Baeck Institute, New York).
17. Simon Hock, *Die Familien Prags nach Epitaphien des Alten Jüdischen Friedhofes* (Pressburg: Adolf Alkalay, 1892).
18. State Papers, Domestic, Elizabeth I, London, vol.152, item 88, March 1582; vol.226, item 40, 1589. Cecil Roth, *A History of the Jews in England* (Oxford: Clarendon, 1964), but see entries in the *Jewish Encyclopaedia* by I. Abrahams, in the *Encyclopaedia Judaica* by C. Roth and Grassl, *loc cit* who places Chaim Gans with the Leipen branch of the family. Gary C. Grassl, 'Joachim Gans of Prague. The First Jew in English America', *American Jewish Historical Society Quarterly Publication*, 86, 2 (June 1998). Lewis S. Feuer, *Francis Bacon and the Jews. Who was the Jew in the New Atlantis?* (pamphlet originally published in the Transactions of the Jewish Historical Society). Lewis S. Feuer, *The Life and Work of Joachim Gaunse, mining technologist and first recorded Jew in English-Speaking North America* (Cincinnati: The American Jewish Archives, 1987), No.8.

Figure 39
Tombstone of Rabbi David Gans

Chapter Thirty-Three

Rabbi Shmuel Hillman of Metz

Pan-European family connections

For centuries rabbis moved about Europe from one appointment to another, but few can have been more peripatetic than Shmuel Hillman of Metz and his family. References to him and to his distinguished rabbinical connections are scattered about in Hebrew, German, French and English texts. It is high time that this corpus of information is brought together, not only to direct the different branches of this widespread family to their source material, but also to throw light on a number of gaps and questionable links.

Shmuel Helman of Metz was a prominent Rabbi in his time, whose first name was later adopted in the form of Hillman as a family name.[1] He was born in Krotoschin in the province of Posen around 1670 and lived to a ripe old age. His extensive family provides a paradigm for the pan-European character of the eighteenth-century Ashkenazi rabbinate. Helman is remembered for the great influence he acquired through his many years in important posts at Mannheim and Metz, for his learning, his initiative in matters of education including the setting up of a Hebrew printing press at Metz, and for his part in the Eibeschuetz controversy which rocked the mid-eighteenth-century rabbinical world. The emphasis of the present work is on the genealogy of his family, highlighting the continent-wide links between the Jewish communities of his time.

Helman studied in Prague under Rabbi Abraham ben Saul Broda in the early years of the eighteenth century.[2] He went on to become Rabbi of Kremsier in Moravia in 1720 and Chief Rabbi of Mannheim in 1727.[3] In 1751 he moved to Metz in Lorraine where he held the Chief Rabbinate until his death in 1764.[4] His first wife came from Glogau in Silesia, not far from Krotoschin. When she died, her wealthy father supported Helman while he continued his studies at Prague until a younger daughter came of age to take her place. That was not a particularly unusual custom at a time when so many young wives died in childbirth (see extract in Note 2). Helman's wife Sarah, who outlived him by ten years, was his second or possibly third spouse.

Glogau became the Helman home base. Not only was at least one of his wives from that town, but also his son Uri Feivush was the son-in-law of the locally prominent Saul Parnes.[5]

Helman's grandson, Naftali Hirsch Katzenellenbogen, married Rachel, daughter of a Feivel of Glogau.[6] Helman's son Moshe, a leading member of the community, was always known as Moshe of Glogau.[7] One of the latter's daughters, Chana, married Yechiel Michal Segal, son of Asher Lemel Halevi, the Chief Rabbi of Glogau and Eisenstadt.[8] Yechiel Michal succeeded his father as Chief Rabbi of Eisenstadt in the Burgenland and continued a rabbinical line there.

Moshe of Glogau was also a forebear of my grandfather Rabbi Nahum Uri Gelles.[9] This Gelles rabbinical line flourished for long in Galicia, but there were other Gelles elsewhere in Poland and Hungary, and specifically in Eisenstadt and its associated villages of the so-called 'Seven Communities'.[10]

Helman's son Uri Feivush, became in turn Chief Rabbi of Hanau, Lissa, Bonn and Cologne.[11] He died in his prime during a visit to his father's grave in Metz.[12] Uri's wife was Chaya Jutlé (Chaya Ittel Parnes). Details of four of their children and later progeny are to be found in the records of Metz.[13] One daughter, Hinde, married a son of the distinguished Chief Rabbi of Prague, Ezekiel Landau, who delivered a funeral oration on the death of Shmuel Helman.[14]

Helman's daughters included (i) Jached, wife of Eliezer Katzenellenbogen of Alsace, who was Rabbi of Bamberg and Hagenau, (ii) Beila, wife of Juda Leib Fraenkel of Dessau, son of David Mirels Fraenkel, the noted Chief Rabbi of Berlin,[15] and (iii) Deborah, wife of Isaac Rappoport of Hanau.[16] Deborah's tombstone inscription has been recorded at Nikolsburg in Moravia.[17]

Jached Helman's son, Naphtali Hirsch Katzenellenbogen of Frankfurt-on-Oder and Winzenheim, became Chief Rabbi of the Palatinate. Also known to the French as Naphtalie Lazare Hirsch, Grand Rabbin Président du Consistoire Israélite, he was a member of the Grand Sanhedrin called together by the Emperor Napoleon in 1806. His grandson, Isidor Lazare, became Chief Rabbi of France in 1867.[18]

An interesting deed of provision for their daughter Jached drawn up by Shmuel Helman and his wife Sarah in 1749 shortly before they left Mannheim for Metz provides some confirmation of their wealth and Sarah's independent means.[19]

ANCESTRY OF SHMUEL HELMAN

The Metz tombstones of Shmuel Helman and his wife Sarah have not survived. Neither have full records of their inscriptions.[20] Passages dealing with Helman and his parentage found in some German texts are quoted in translation in the chapter notes below. Particularly relevant is the History of the Jews of Kremsier (see Note 3) which quotes an entry from the town's *Pinkas* (Jewish records) reading 'son of Feivel of Krotoschin', apparently referring to a Rabbi Samuel Helman.

The ancestry of Shmuel Helman of Metz has for long been taken on the authority of *Da'at Kedoshim*[21] and other reference works, which rely on primary sources such as a memorandum written by a relative, Eliezer Lipman Zak, shortly before Helman's death.[22] The traditional view is that Shmuel Helman was a member of the rabbinical Halpern clan and that he was the son of Israel Halpern, the descendant of Rabbi Moses Halpern of Lvov, author of *Ahavat Zion*, who was the son of Zebulon Ashkenazi Halpern. According to Meir Wunder's *Elef Margoliot* the latter traced his lineage back to Isaac of Dampierre in the twelfth century.[23] Rabbi Israel Halpern of Krotoschin was married to Lifsha, a daughter of Chief Rabbi Nathan Nata Spiro of Cracow, author of the Cabbalistic work *Megaleh Amukot*. The Spiro line goes back to Rashi of Troyes via the nexus of the Spiro, Luria and Treivish families.

There are some scholars who have interpreted the entry in the *Pinkas* of Kremsier as meaning that there were two rabbis of the name of Shmuel Helman from Krotoschin, and that the one who became Rabbi of Metz was not the son of Israel Halpern. This is the line taken by David Leib Zinz in *Gedullath Yehonathan*.[24] The argument is discussed by Rabbi Dov Weber in his book *Kol Todah*.[25] However, Zinz himself quotes an approbation by Shmuel Helman of Benjamin Katzenellenbogen's work *Or Chachamim* (published at Frankfurt-on-Oder in 1752) in which Helman refers to the author with a midrashic expression meaning that he is a member of his (Helman's) father's family. The approbation is included in Leopold Loewenstein's *Index Approbationum* for 1753.[26] The traditional view that Helman's father was Israel Halpern of Krotoschin fits in with the existence of previous connections between the Halperns and Katzenellenbogens and the marriages that Helman's children contracted with prominent families. These are certainly compatible with Helman himself being of Halpern parentage. However, it would not necessarily have to be the particular Halpern in question. There is a document from the Council of the Four Lands signed in 1692 by 'Samuel Helman, son of Israel Halpern of Krotoszyn',[27] that would make the Rabbi of Metz a very young man at the time or suggest that his birth might be earlier than the accepted date of 1670. Furthermore, in the Minutes of the Council of the Four Lands there is an entry for 1692 referring to Shmuel Helman of Krotoschin as one of three Elders or *Juden-Ober-Ältesten in Polen*.[28] This casts doubt on Shmuel Helman of Metz having been one of the signatories in 1692. The evidence of the aforementioned contemporary Heilprin document (see Note 22), taken together with passages in *Yesh Manhilin* written by Helman's kinsman, friend, and fellow student, Phineas Katzenellenbogen (see Note 2), is to be set against a possibly misleading entry in the Kremsier records, and one wonders whether the Rabbi Uri Feivush mentioned there might not be Helman's father-in-law. Relevant entries in *Ohalei Shem* are largely based on information supplied around the publication date of 1912 by the rabbis concerned. The entry for my grandfather has already been mentioned.[29] Another instance is the pedigree given for Rabbi Eliyahu Chaim Meisels of Lodz, whose mother was descended from Rabbi Eliezer Lipman of Chelm, a brother of Rabbi Shmuel Helman of Metz, stated to be the son of Rabbi

Israel Halpern, called 'Charnash', of Krotoschin.[30] On balance, the traditional view of Helman's Halpern descent may prevail to the extent that his father is to be found within the nexus of Halpern and Katzenellenbogen, as discussed above.

SHMUEL HELMAN'S ACHIEVEMENTS

Helman was considered a great Talmud scholar in his time, but few of his writings were published. One of his novellae appeared in *Kol Yehuda* by Rabbi Yehuda ben Chanina Selig of Glogau. During his long sojourn in Mannheim he did much to further Torah education and to encourage literary activity. Other noteworthy achievements included the setting up of a flourishing Hebrew printing press in Metz in the 1760s.[31] He was involved in a long drawn out controversy centered on the prominent Rabbi Jonathan Eibeschuetz whom he succeeded in the Metz Rabbinate in 1751. Suspicions had been aroused that Eibeschuetz was a secret Shabataian (that is a follower of the false Messiah, Shabatai Tzvi), and in 1752 Helman joined with the Rabbis of Frankfurt, Amsterdam and Hannover in pronouncing a ban on Eibeschuetz. Incidentally, the latter was, like Helman himself, a descendant of Nathan Nata Spiro of Cracow. A list of approbations from Helman's time in Mannheim and in Metz is appended (see Note 26).

Helman became the patriarch of an extended family spread over Lorraine and Alsace, Germany, Poland, Austria and Hungary. Many close relatives held senior rabbinical appointments, and a few were rabbis of some consequence. As the respected leader of an important and wealthy community and at the centre of continent wide Jewish affairs, Helman exerted considerable influence on doctrinal matters, rabbinical appointments, and by arranging marriages with other prominent rabbinical families.

RABBINICAL CONNECTIONS

Shmuel Helman was the father-in-law of Eliezer of Alsace, who was a son of Moses Katzenellenbogen of Anspach (1670–1733). Eliezer's mother was a daughter of Eliezer Halpern (Heilprin) of Fuerth (1649–1700), a cousin of Helman's ancestral line.

Moses of Anspach (near Schwabach) was a direct descendant of Meir Katzenellenbogen, known as the Maharam of Padua, via Meir Wahl Katzenellenbogen of Brest. Rabbi Abraham Joshua Heschel of Cracow (1596–1663) was a grandson of the latter.

Abraham Joshua Heschel was a great-great-grandfather of the Chief Rabbi of Prague, Ezekiel Landau (1713–93). Helman's granddaughter Hinde married Ezekiel's son, Samuel Landau.

Ezekiel Landau was the grandson of Rabbi Zvi Hirsch Witeles Landau of Opatov (1643–1714), who according to David Tebele Efrati was the brother-in-law of Rabbi Gershon of Vilna.[32] The latter was a grandfather of Rabbi David Tebele of Lissa who died in 1792. Rabbi Tebele was a Gelles cousin and also a cousin of Ezekiel Landau.[33]

SOME OF SHMUEL HELMAN'S DESCENDANTS

Helman's two sons and three daughters, as shown on the accompanying chart, had a numerous progeny, which is still largely unexplored. We have French records relating to the Katzenellenbogen descendants of his daughter Jached and to the offspring of his son Uri Feivush. There are some German references to the family of his daughter Beila. The family of his daughter Deborah must be sought in Germany and Moravia.

Details of the life of Helman's son Moshe are very sparse indeed. Little assistance could be gained from works on the Jews of Silesia and of Glogau,[34] but I have managed to gather a sufficient number of other references to show that Moshe was a leader of the Jewish community in Glogau, and that he was a learned and well-respected figure. His only recorded daughter Chana married the Rabbi of Eisenstadt whose family came from Glogau. An outline of this rabbinical line in the Burgenland community is given in the chart.

The gaps in the available records make it well nigh impossible to discover Moshe of Glogau's other issue. Another, as yet unidentified, daughter may be the link with my family. The entry on my grandfather Rabbi Nahum Uri Gelles in Ohalei Shem (see Note 9) states that Moshe Hillman was ABD at Glina, and *Otzar Harabbanim* has it that he was at Glina in 1780.[35]

My great-grandfather Rabbi David Isaac Gelles, from the Brody rabbinical family of that name, studied at Glina under Rabbi Meir Krasnipoler (ca.1740–1820), who later became ABD in Brody (see Note 9). There is also a reference to David Isaac Gelles in the Memorial Book of Glina.[36] From David Isaac's tombstone in Brody we know that he died around 1870 and that his father was Rabbi Moshe. From the birth records of my grandfather at Narayow we know that his mother was called Sarah, but no records have as yet been found identifying the families of David Isaac's wife or mother. However, from the Eisenstadt records we know that Moshe of Glogau's daughter Chana died in 1805 at a relatively young age. Moshe of Glogau might have been born in the period 1700–20. We do not know when he died, although Stuart Steinberg has argued from the dates of his grandson, Moshe Halevi, that it must have been not later than the 1760s.[37] The births of David Isaac Gelles and of his father Moses can be put in the 1790s and 1760s. The conjunction of Moshe of Glogau's supposed sojourn in Glina, my great-grandfather's study there under Meir Krasnipoler, the connection by marriage between the Krasnipoler and Kallir families of Brody and with Moshe of Glogau's Halevi in-laws in Eisenstadt, and what we know about the Gelles family,[38] forms the background to the links of my Gelles line with Moshe of Glogau.

A brief word is in place here about the ancient connections between Glogau in Silesia, Brody and neighbouring towns in Galicia, and Eisenstadt in the Burgenland, which was for a long time in Hungary but later became part of Austria. In earlier centuries German and Austrian Jews sought refuge at various times in Silesia where Breslau was the principal centre, and in Cracow whence they would have found their way to eastern Galicia and elsewhere. Some Jews expelled from Vienna in 1670 went to Eisenstadt where they enjoyed the protection of the Esterhazys. Following the expulsion of the Turks from Hungary in 1686, Jews were forced to leave Ofen (Budapest) and many joined those who had settled earlier in the so-called 'Siebengemeinde'. During the first half of the eighteenth century there was an influx of Moravian and Galician Jews into Hungary. Eisenstadt grew at that time into a notable centre of Jewish learning.

Other descendants of Moshe Helman were to be found in Poland, Lithuania and Russia as well as in Austria-Hungary before the first world war.[39]

Among those who joined the flow of emigration to America was Sidney Hillman (1887–1946), who received a rabbinical education in Lithuania, fell foul of the Tsarist government when he became involved in the trade union movement, but rose to prominence in America as a leader of the Congress of Industrial Organisations, a member of Franklin Roosevelt's Labor Advisory Board, and an influential figure in the Democratic Party. At the time of his death he was vice-president of the World Federation of Trade Unions.[40]

After two and a half centuries, descendants of Shmuel Hillman are flourishing in America, Israel, England and elsewhere. A few years ago more than a score attended a Hillman Reunion in America. Among descendants with an active interest in the history of this family are Harold Rhode in Washingtom, DC and Stuart Steinberg in California. Dr Harold Hillman, who is resident in England, is the grandson of Samuel Isaac Hillman, who was born in Lithuania in 1868 and held appointments as Chief Rabbi of Glasgow in Scotland and judge of the Rabbinical Court in London before finally settling in Jerusalem, where he died in 1953. The latter's daughter Sarah married Yitzchak Halevi Herzog, Chief Rabbi of Dublin and subsequently Chief Rabbi of Israel. Their son Chaim Herzog (1918–1997) was a distinguished diplomat and politician who became the sixth President of Israel in 1983.

Harold Rhode, whose extensive family website can be easily accessed under his name has also written much about Lithuanian Hillman descendants.[41] He has noted the personal recollections of Sarah Hillman, embracing numerous kinsfolk and including the afore-mentioned Sidney Hillman who turned out to be her second cousin.[42]

NOTES

1. Helman = *seer* or *prophet* – for example, Samuel – hence frequent association of the two names as Shmuel Helman. It should be noted that there are references to more than one

Rabbi of that name. Charnash, a name applied to Israel Halpern, is an acronym of 'son-in-law of Rabbi Nathan Shapiro' (see the Glossary for terms like Av Beth Din, abbreviated as ABD, mechutan etc.).

2. Phineas ben Moses Katzenellenbogen (ca. 1691–1765), *Yesh Manhilin* (Jerusalem: Machon Hatham Sofer, 1984), pp.84–5, 109, 192–3, 195, 197, 208, 219, 311–12, 375:

> I remember that my master and uncle [Rabbi Saadya Yeshaya Katzenellenbogen] came to Prague in August 1709 ... The scholars of the town came to see him, and among them was my *mechutan* and friend Reb Hillman, who is now one of the great rabbis of our generation, the ABD of Metz, and also the late Rabbi Aaron Kempner. When my uncle saw Reb Aaron he said 'I recognize your face from somewhere but I cannot remember when I saw you, did you perhaps study at the Yeshiva of my father Rabbi Shaul in Pinczow?' He confirmed that 25 years earlier he had indeed studied in Pinczow. (pp.84–5)
>
> [in 1722] I presided at a big financial case at Reinitz [Rechnitz?] together with my Beth Din from Leipnik ... and Rabbi Hillman, who was then Rabbi at Kremsier, was also there with us. (p.109)
>
> In the Yeshivah of Prague in the winter of 1708–9 ... those students who studied under our master the Rosh Yeshiva [Rabbi Abraham Broda] are currently the exceptionally great rabbis of our generation: Rabbi Hillman who is now my *mechutan* and friend, the ABD of Metz and Mannheim and the father-in-law of my brother Rabbi L(eizer) [Eliezer of Alsace]. (pp.192–3)
>
> The great one of our generation who is now ABD of Metz, my *mechutan* the Gaon Rabbi Hillman and his wife were from Glogau, and at that time in 5469 [1709] was in Prague and was my close friend. He was a widower at the time, after the death of his [first] wife, and his father-in-law from Glogau was supporting him while he waited a few years before marrying her younger sister, who was still very young at the time. He told me that the wife of the Rabbi of Glogau wished me to come there and to find me a good *shidduch* [arranged marriage] as is befitting to my distinguished ancestors and in particular her late husband (my great-uncle) the martyr Rabbi Pinchas, after whom I was named. Rabbi Hillman also attempted to bring me to Glogau, trying to persuade me to come there and suggesting fine marriage proposals. But everything is from Above and his words did not enter my ears and I placed my trust in G-d. (p.208)
>
> Referring to the case on p.109 and a halachic ruling he heard from Rabbi Hillman on that occasion, the author describes him as 'my *mechutan*, the elderly *ABD* of Metz' (pp.311–12). Moshe, the son of Rabbi Shmuel Helman, was a leading member of the community in Glogau. (editor's note p.375)

3. Adolf Fränkl-Gruen, *Geschichte der Juden in Kremsier* (Breslau: S. Schottlaender, 1896), pp.84-85: 'he signed receipts for his salary Samuel Helman'. In the town record [Grundbuch] there is an entry 'son of Feivel of Krotoschin'. His cited approbations include publications at Jesnitz 1738, Berlin 1746, Fuerth 1762, Sulzbach, and Prague. There is a reference to Leopold Loewenstein's *History of the Jews in the Palatinate* (see below) and to Rabbi Ezekiel Landau's Memorial Address. Leopold Loewenstein, *Geschichte der Juden in der Kurpfalz* (Frankfurt: 1895), pp.198–202: a brief curriculum vitae tracing Helman from his birth in Krotoschin (no dates or name of father) through his student days under Abraham Broda in Prague, to the rabbinate in Kremsier, his call to Mannheim where he was responsible for actively furthering Torah studies and the publication of various literary works. He became involved in the long-standing

controversy with Jonathan Eibeschuetz who was suspected of being a supporter of *Shabbataianism* (see Glossary). This continued after Helman succeeded Eibeschuetz at Metz. Footnotes refer to Landau's Memorial Address and to Helman's family, including his son Uri Feivush, his daughter Jached, and her son Naftali Hirsch Katzenellenbogen. There are also brief references to Helman's son Moshe and daughter Beila. There is a note of Beila's daughter Eidel and her marriage. Reference is made to many of Helman's approbations: from his Mannheim period these were published at Fuerth 1728, Wandsbeck 1729 and Amsterdam 1730, while from his time in Metz they include Sulzbach 1762 and Fuerth 1765.

4. Abraham Cahen, 'Le Rabbinat de Metz pendant la periode francaise', *Revue des études juives*, xii (1886), pp.289–94. See also Nathan Netter, *Metz et son grand passé* (Paris: 1938), pp.113–14. Shmuel Helman's distinguished eighteenth-century predecessors at Metz, attracted by the importance and wealth of its community and royal patronage, were Gabriel Eskeles (1694–1703), Abraham Broda (1703–09), Jacob Reischer (1709–33), Jacob Joshua Falk (1733–40), and Jonathan Eibeschütz (1742–50).
5. R' Meir ben Isaac of Horochow, *Kosnoth Or* (Frankfurt-on/O. 1753). From the Introduction:

   > I am most grateful for the kindness of G-d in leading me to the house of the distinguished philanthropist Rabbi Shaul Parnes, the son-in-law of Reb Shlomo Charif. His sons and sons-in-law are all great Torah scholars and the most notable among them is the exceptional and sharp-minded scholar Rabbi Schraga Feivel, the son of the great Gaon Rabbi Shmuel Hillman, ABD and Head of the Yeshiva of Metz ... and his [Shaul Parnes'?] wife, the admirable lady Henelle, daughter of the late Gaon Rabbi Naftali Cohen who was ABD of Glogau.

6. Neil Rosenstein, *The Unbroken Chain* (New York, London, Jerusalem: CIS Publishers,1990), Vol.1, p.102.
7. See Note 2. Rabbi Eleazar Kallir, *Chavot Yair Hadas* (Prague: 1792):

   > These are the words of the son-in-law of the author, the great luminary Rabbi Moshe Halevi, ABD of Libna, son of the famous Gaon Rabbi Michel Halevi, ABD of Eisenstadt, son of the late great Gaon Rabbi Asher Lemel Halevi, ABD and Head of the Yeshiva of Eisenstadt and Head of the Beth Din of Glogau, son-in-law of the late great sharp minded scholar Rabbi Moshe of Glogau, son of the great Gaon, famous in his generation, Rabbi Hillman, ABD and Head of the Yeshiva of Metz.

8. Bernhard Wachstein, *Die Grabschriften des Alten Judenfriedhofes in Eisenstadt* (Vienna: R. Loewit, 1922). Tombstone inscriptions:
   No.412. Jached, d.1788, wife of Rabbi Asher Lemel Halevi (No.426) and daughter of Jechiel Michel of Glogau, author of *Neser HaKodesh*, d.Vienna 1730.
   No.426. Ascher Lemel Halevi, d.1789, whose ancestry goes back to Joel Sirkes.
   No.515. Chana, daughter of Moshe ben Samuel Helman, d.1805, wife of Chief Rabbi Michael ben Ascher Lemel Halevi of Glogau (No.594).
   No.802. Guetel Chaja, d.1843, wife of Jacob Gelles (No.933) d.1858.
   No.1039. Malka, d.1868, wife of Moses Elias Gelles (No.1013), son of Jacob Gelles.
   The tombstone inscription of Chana, daughter of Moshe of Glogau, praises her highly for her modesty, piety, kindness and loyal partnership to her husband in his work as rabbi. She appears to have died at a relatively young age, although she 'brought up fine children'. Her father is referred to as the great luminary Rabbi Moshe, son of the great Gaon Rabbi Shmuel Hillman ABD of Metz.
9. Shmuel Noach Gottlieb, *Ohalei Shem* (Pinsk: 1912), pp.261–2:
   Rabbi Nahum Uri Gelles, son of the Gaon Rabbi David Isaac Gelis. Born in 1855 [correct

date 1852], his father, the above-mentioned, was a brilliant and great Torah scholar, and was among the students of the Gaon Rabbi Meir, ABD of Glina, and then he set up a Yeshiva in Brody. Rabbi Nahum Uri was the descendant of Rabbi Moshe who was the Head of the Rabbinical Court of Glina, who was in turn the son of the Gaon Rabbi Shmuel Hillman, Head of the Rabbinical Court of Metz, the son of Israel Heilprin of blessed memory ... of Krotoschin, who was the son-in-law of the author of *Megaleh Amukot*, who in turn was the son of Rabbi Lipman of blessed memory, son of the Gaon who wrote *Ahavat Zion*, the *R"M* of Lvov of blessed memory.

10. See Note 8. Bernhard Wachstein, *Urkunden und Akten zur Geschichte der Juden in Eisenstadt* (Vienna and Leipzig: Wilhelm Braumuller, 1926): Page 214 gives the text of a ruling issued by the notables of the Eisenstadt community regarding the distribution of Synagogue honours for Simchat Torah (Rejoicing with the Torah: last day of the Festival of Succoth) dated 19th October 1859 signed by Ahron Ber Gelles and eight others. On p.706 the name of Ahron Ber Gelles appears on a list of representatives of the communities of Burgenland. He is referred to as Ahron Ber Gellis of Lorreto. The Jewish Museum in Vienna has a Torah Mantle presented by 'Rabbi Ahron Beer Gelles and his wife Feila on the occasion of their son Mordecai's Bar Mitzvah in 1858'. The museum catalogue suggests that it was given to the Stadt Tempel in Vienna, but an original dedication to the Eisenstadt synagogue is more likely.
11. Louis Lewin, *Die Geschichte der Juden in Lissa* (Pinne: N. Gundermann, 1904), pp.189–92. It is possible that Rabbi Uri Schraga Phoebus (Feivush), son of Samuel Helman of Krotoschin, the Rabbi in Mannheim and Metz, obtained his appointment at Lissa through the influence of his brother Moshe, who was prominent in nearby Glogau. Uri Feivush was at Lissa in the 1760s until about 1767, when he moved on to Bonn and Cologne after a brief sojourn in Berlin. He mentioned that his in-laws included the Berlin Rabbi David Fraenkel and the latter's son-in-law, the printer Isaac Speier. Uri Feivush went to Metz in 1770 to visit his father's grave and also to seek medical treatment for a condition of his foot. He died and was buried there beside his father. More is said about the Katzenellenbogen connection of his nephew Naphtali Hirsch and about Ezekiel Landau of Prague and the marriage of one of Uri Feivush's daughters, Hinde, to Ezekiel Landau's son Shmuel. On p.379 according to the Memorbook of Hanau, Uri Feivush took up his post there in 1758 following the death of his brother-in-law, the incumbent Isaac Rappaport. A. Jellinek, *Märtyrer und Memorbuch* (incl.) *Das alte Memorbuch der Deutzer Gemeinde von 1581 bis 1784]* (Vienna: Loewy & Alkalay, Pressburg, 1881). Referred to in short as the Deutzer Memorbuch and includes a glowing account of the life of 'our teacher and master Rabbi Uri Feivush, the Av Beth Din, son of the great gaon of blessed memory, Rabbi Shmuel Hillman'.
12. See Note 4. Jean-Claude Bouvat-Martin, *Memorbuch of Metz 1720–1849* (Paris: Cercle de Généalogie Juive, CGJ, 2001):
    No.2202. Samuel Helman, d.30 December 1764.
    No.2340. Sorle, his wife, d.27 July 1774.
    No..2282. Uri Schraga Feivush, d.20 October 1771.
13. Pierre-André Meyer, *Tables du registre d'état civil de la communauté juive de Metz (1717–1792)* (Paris: 1987): Births: children of Uri Feivush Helman: Hendlé 25 October 1752, Fratié 13 November 1753, Jutiel 3 June 1755, Salomon Léon 23 April 1757. Marriage: Chelle Helman, son of Salomon Léon, to Vogel Emerich 9 July 1780.
14. See Notes 3 and 11. Ezekiel Landau, *Ahavas Zion* – A Collection of Sermons delivered by Rabbi Yechezkiel Landau, ABD of Prague (Jerusalem: 1966):

    Sixth Sermon (pp.18–21) being a Memorial Address delivered on 10th February 1765 on the passing of the famous Gaon Rabbi Shmuel Hillman of blessed memory *ABD* Metz and of the pious Rabbi Anshel Ozer's o.b.m a member of the great Beth Din of Prague.

15. Jacob Jacobson, *Jüdische Trauungen in Berlin 1759-1813* (Berlin: Walter de Gruyter & Co., 1968), pp.296–7 and 445–6 refer to Beila, daughter of Samuel Hellman, wife of Jehuda Loeb, son of Oberlandesrabbiner David Hirsch Fraenkel, and the marriages in 1785 and 1802 of their son Michel Levi Fraenkel (1759–1840). Jacobson's earlier volume for the years 1723–1759 did not yield relevant information.
16. Rosenstein, *The Unbroken Chain*, Vol.2, p.723. Chaim Josef David Azulai, *Diaries (Ma'agal Tov)* Part I. Transl. Dr Benjamin Cymerman (Jerusalem: The Bnei Issakhar Institute, 1997), p.74 refers to meeting with Rabbi Isaac, son of Rabbi Israel of Hanau, the perfect son-in-law of Rabbi (Samuel) Hillman, the head of the Beth Din of the holy congregation of Metz, and also with the Rav's brother, Rabbi Wolff, head of the Beth Din of Kaluszyn (cf. previous ref). L. Loewenstein, *Das Rabbinat in Hanau* (Frankfurt a.M.: Jahrbuch der Juedisch Literarischen Gesellschaft, 1921),vol.14 provides further details on the family of Israel Ashkenazi who died in 1744, his wife Perl, daughter of Baruch Rappaport, the Rabbi of Fuerth, who predeceased her husband in 1737, and the families of their sons, Zeev Wolf who died in 1757, and Isaac Rappaport, who passed away in 1758 and was succeeded in the Hanau Rabbinate by his brother-in-law Uri Feivush Helman.
17. See Note 3. D. Feuchtwang, 'Epitaphien des Graeberfeldes zu Nikolsburg', in *Mitteilungen zur Juedischen Volkskunde* (1907), xxi, No.1. Deborah, d.1781, daughter of Rabbi Helman of Metz. For Deborah Helman see also Ref (4). She married (1) Rabbi Isaac Rappoport, grandson of Baruch son of Benjamin Wolf Rappoport of Fuerth, and (2) Rabbi Isaac Ducla of Pressburg.
18. http:/ / www. sdv.fr/judaisme/album/rabanim/nhirsch.htm /isidore.htm.
19. Manuscript Or. 12333 (part of the Gaster collection at the British Library), p.28 being a deed signed and witnessed at Ilbsheim near Mannheim on 15th April 1749 by Saralen and her husband Rabbi Shmuel Hillman making a financial settlement for the benefit of their daughter Yached, that she inherit 500 Reichsthaler from her mother and 1,000 Reichsthaler from her father 'one hour before their deaths' (so that these sums should not be deemed to be part of their estates and distributed amongst their sons only according to Jewish law).
20. Correspondence with Pierre-André Meyer, Pascal Faustini, Ira Albert, *et al.*
21. I.T. Eisenstadt (suppl. S. Wiener), *Da'at Kedoshim* (St Petersburg: J. Berman, 1897–98), pp.59–68.
22. Translation of an excerpt of the Zak Heilpren Ancestry from MS R. 761 at the Jewish Theological Seminary in New York:

> also on my mother Rebetzen Dinah's side, she was the daughter of the Gaon Rabbi Lipman ABD Chelm, who was the son of the Gaon Rabbi Israel who was known as Rabbi Israel Charnash who was the son-in-law of the Gaon Rabbi Natta Shapiro author of *Megaleh Amukot*. My ancestor Rabbi Israel Charnash had another son who is still alive now and he is the elderly Gaon Rabbi Helman ABD Metz. My ancestor, the above mentioned Gaon Rabbi Israel was ABD Krotoschin in Greater Poland and he had two brothers: one was the famous Gaon Rabbi Isaac ABD Tiktin and the third brother was the great and famous luminary Rabbi Zelki who was a preacher and Dayan in Posen, and to this day all the distinguished members of that community are descendants of his. The above-mentioned Rabbi Isaac had three sons: the Gaon Rabbi Yoel ABD Ostroh, the second was the Gaon Eliezer Lipman ABD Tarnograd and the name of the third is not known to me. They belonged to the Heilpern family.

23. Meir Wunder, *Elef Margoliot* (London & Jerusalem: Institute for the Preservation of the Galician Jewish Heritage and the Margulies family, 1993).
24. David Leib Zinz, *Gedullath Yehonathan* (Piotrkow: 1934), p.249 et seq.
25. Dov Weber, *Kol Todah* (New York: 1998), pp.40–2.

26. Leopold Loewenstein, *Index Approbationum* (Berlin: 1923), p.71. Samuel ben Israel Helmann: List of Approbations (Krotoschin 1, Mannheim 31, and Metz 24).
27. Yaakov ben Shmuel's Book of Responsa, *Beth Yaakov* (Duerenfuerth: 1696).
28. *Pinkas Vaad Arba Aratzoth*. Collected and edited with notes by Israel Halpern (Jerusalem: 1945), pp.xxxiii, 229, 230.
29. See Note 9. Stuart Steinberg, ''Shmuel Helman is the son of Israel Halpern', *Avotaynu,* xix, 4 (Winter 2003).
30. Gottlieb, *Ohalei Shem*, pp.352–3. Entry for Rabbi Eliyah Chaim ben Moshe Meisels (who became Chief Rabbi of Lodz in 1873). His ancestors include Rashi, Moses Isserles, and Nathan Nata Spiro. He was descended through his mother from a brother of Rabbi Shmuel Helman of Metz, stated to be the son of Rabbi Israel Charnash of Krotoschin.
31. See Note 4. Edouard Privat (ed.), *Histoire des Juifs de France* (Collection Franco-Judaica, 1972), pp.115, 319.
32. David Tebele Efrati, *Toldot Anshei Shem* (Warsaw: 1875).
33. See Note 11. E. Gelles, 'Finding Rabbi Moses Gelles', *Avotaynu,* xviii, 1 (Spring 2002).
34. R. Berndt, *Geschichte der Juden in Gross Glogau* (Glogau: 1873); M. Brann, *Geschichte der Juden in Schlesien* (Berlin: 1917). Franz D. Lucas and Margret Heitmann, *Stadt des Glaubens. Geschichte und Kultur der Juden in Glogau* (Hildesheim-Zurich-New York: G. Olms, 1991), pp.242–4 give additional information on the Rabbi Ascher Lemel ben Jehuda Selke Halevi, *Mechutan* of Ezekiel Landau, and also on his brother Joel's family.
35. Natan Zvi Friedmann, *Otzar Harabbanim* (Bnei Brak, Israel: 1973), No.14602.
36. H. Halpern (ed), *Memorial Book of Glina* (New York: Emergency Relief Committee for Glina, 1950), p.17.
37. Friedmann, *Otzar Harabbanim*.
38. Gelles, 'Finding Rabbi Moses Gelles'. Edward Gelles, My Father's People, *Sharsheret Hadorot,* 17, 1 (Feb. 2003). Stuart Steinberg, private correspondence.
39. Gottlieb, *Ohalei Shem*:

    Rabbi Moshe son of Rabbi Abraham Shmuel Helman. Born 1863. A descendant of Rabbi Yaakov Yosef of Ostroh and of the Gaon Rabbi Shmuel Hillman ABD of Metz. He was appointed Rabbi of Druia [in the Vilna region] in 1896. (p.342)

    Rabbi Dovber, son of the above Rabbi Moshe Helman ... He became Rabbi of Janowiczi [in the Witebsk region]. (p.352)

    Rabbi Shmuel Isaac Hillman of Glasgow is described as being a descendant of Rabbi Shmuel Hillman of Metz and as being 'a sixth generation descendant of Rabbi Yehezkel Katzenellenbogen ABD of Hamburg-Altona'. (p.450)

    Pages 37, 96 and 188–9 list rabbis by the name of Hilman-Helman-Gelman.
40. Sidney Hillman's entry in *Encyclopaedia Judaica,* 1971, vol.8, pp.493–4 and extensive coverage on the Internet. The subject of books by George Soule (1939), Jean Gould (1952), Matthew Josephson (1952), and Steven Fraser (1991).
41. familytreemaker.genealogy.com/users/r/h/o/Harold-Rhode-MD/.
42. Harold Rhode, 'Jewish Culture, History, and Religion', *Avotaynu,* xiv, 1 (Spring 1998).
43. Dr Jesse C. Hillman has prepared a paper on the geographical distribution and origins of the Hillman name.

סאלאטווינא הרב ר׳ **נחום אורי** בהרה״ג ר׳ דוד יצחק זצ״ל **געלים.**

(גאליציען)

נולד—תרט״ו, אביו הרה״ג הנ״ל זצ״ל הי׳ גדול בתורה וחריף עצום, מתלמידי הגאון ר׳ מאיר אבד״ק גלינא שקבע אח״כ ישיבתו בעיר בראדי. הרב ר׳ נחום אורי הנ״ל הוא נכד הגאון ר׳ משה אבד״ק גלינא בן הגאון ר׳ שמואל הילמאן אבד״ק מיץ, בן הגאון ר׳ ישראל היילפרין זצ״ל אבד״ק קראטשין [חתן הגאון בעל „מגלה עמוקות"] בן הגאון ר׳ ליפמאן זצ״ל בהגאון בעל „אהבת ציון" הר״מ דלבוב זצ״ל. הרב ר׳ נחום אורי הנ״ל נסמך להוראה מהגאון ר׳ צבי אורינשטיין זצ״ל, מהגאון ר׳ יצחק שמעלקיש מלבוב, מהגאון מהר״י ווידינפעלד אבד״ק הרומילוב, ומהגאון הר׳ יואל אשכנזי זצ״ל אבד״ק זלאטשוב. בשנת תרל״ז נתקבל לרב בעיר קידרניץ, ובשנת תרמ״ד בעיר סאלאטווינא הנ״ל. יש בידו בכתובים מסודר לדפוס ספר שו״ת, וגם דרושים והספדים.

Nuchim Jre Gellis Solotwina bei Stanislaw (Galizien.)

Figure 40
Pedigree of Rabbi Nahum Uri Gelles (1852–1934)
in *Ohalei Shem* (pp. 261–2) by Shmuel Noach Gottlieb, publ. Pinsk, 1912 [for translation see Ch. 33, note 9]

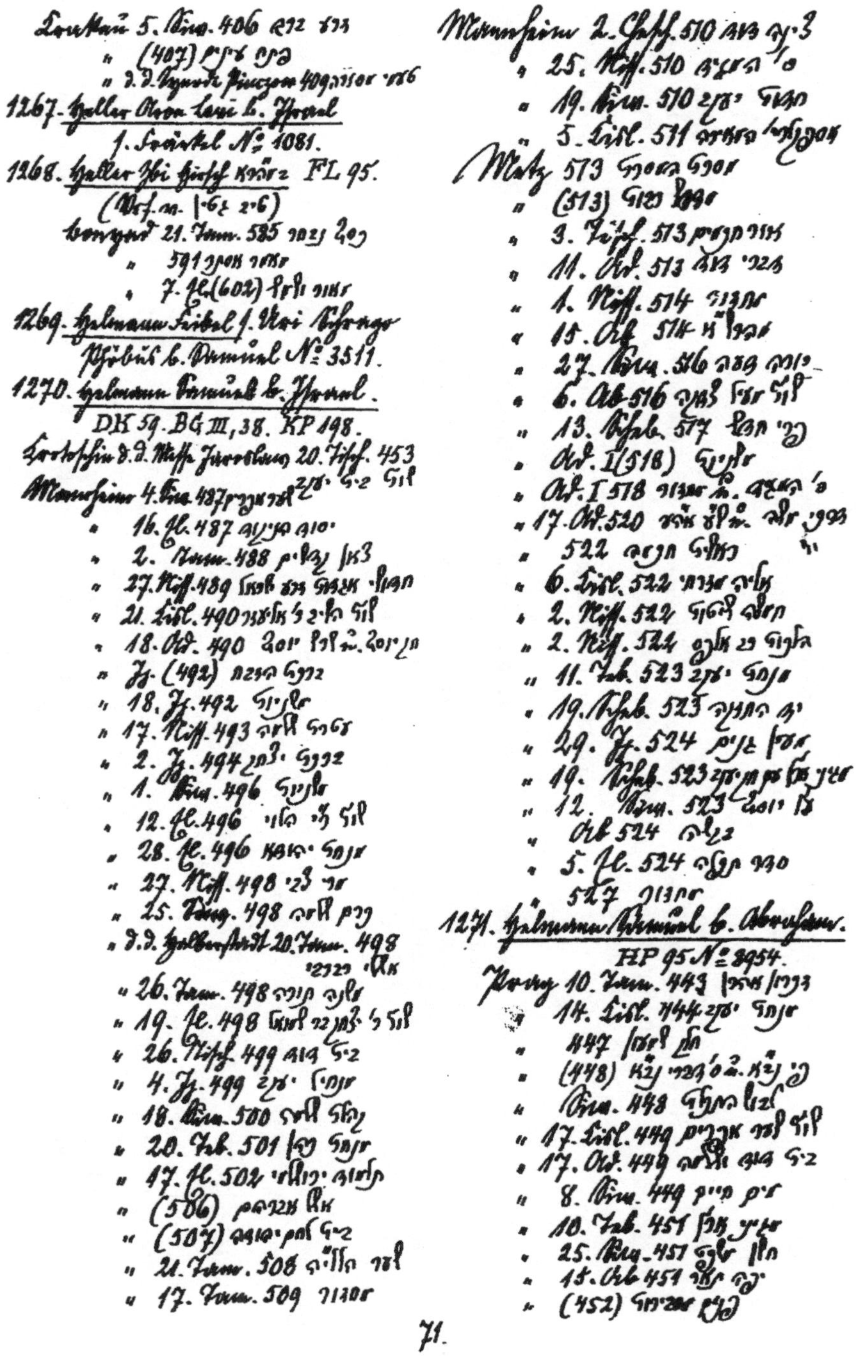

1267. Heller Aron Levi b. Israel

f. Fränkel № 1081.

1268. Heller Zbi Hirsch ... FL 95.

1269. Helmann Leibel f. Uri Schraga

Phöbus b. Samuel № 3511.

1270. Helmann Samuel b. Israel.

DK 59. BG III, 38. KP 498.

1271. Helmann Samuel b. Abraham.

HP 95 № 8954.

Figure 41

List of approbations by Rabbi Shmuel Helman of Metz

Table 28
FAMILY OF CHIEF RABBI SHMUEL HELMAN OF METZ

Shmuel Helman, born Krotoschin ca. 1670–d. Metz 1764
m. (1) ? from Glogau (2) (her sister ?) Sarah, d.Metz 1774

Moshe of Glogau[1]	Uri Feivush, d. 1771[2] ABD at Hanau, Lissa, Bonn, Cologne m. Chaja Ittel Parnes	Jached m. Eliezer Katzenellenbogen ABD of Bamberg & Hagenau ca. 1700–71 son of Moses of Schwabach	Beila, d. 1784 m. Juda Leib Fraenkel 1733–1806 son of David Fraenkel of Berlin[3]	Deborah, d. 1781 m. Isaac Rapaport[4] ca. 1706–58 son of Israel Ashkenazi ABD of Offenbach & Hanau
Chana, d. 1805 m. Yechiel Michal Segal[5] ABD of Eisenstadt ca. 1740–1819 son of Asher Lemel, 1705–89 ABD of Glogau & Eisenstadt	Hinde, 1752–1835, m. Shmuel Landau of Prague d. 1834 son of Ezekiel Landau ABD of Prague, 1713–93	Naftali Hirsch K., 1750–1823[6] of Frankfurt-on-O. & Alsace Head of Consistory of Upper Rhine m. Rachel, daughter of Feivel of Glogau	Michael Fraenkel 1759–1840 m. Riekel Riess	

Shmuel Helman had many other grandchildren whose progeny spread across Europe and is now worldwide. Helman was the teacher of his grandson Naftali Hirsch and of Benjamin Katzenellenbogen, later ABD of Krotoschin and Gelnhausen.

Notes:

1. Ancestor of a Gelles rabbinical line from Brody. Gelles were also found in Krotoschin, Eisenstadt, Vienna, and elsewhere. The name of Uri Feivush (or Feivel) recurs in the Gelles as well as the Helman family.
2. Uri Feivush's children whose births were recorded at Metz: Hinde (1752), Fratie (1753), Jutiel (1755) and Salomon Leon (1757).
3. David Fraenkel (1707–62) of Dessau. Chief Rabbi of Berlin. Author of *Korban HaEdah*, commentary on Jerusalem Talmud, and teacher of Moses Mendelssohn
4. Isaac followed his father as Rabbi of Hanau and was succeeded in 1758 by his brother-in-law Uri Feivush.
5. Taught at Vienna before becoming Chief Rabbi of Eisenstadt. He wrote *Sha'ar Hamaim.* He had two sons, Rafael of Glogau, RBD of Eisenstadt in 1810, and Moshe Halevi who was Rabbi at Tzelem (Deutschkreuz) and Libna, wrote *Sh'ar Hakatan,* and married the daughter of Eleazar Kallir, author of *Or Chadash* and other works. Moshe died in 1837. His son, Helman Halevi, was Rabbi at Scheinling around 1870.
6. Naftali Hirsch Katzenellenbogen (aka Hirsch Lazare) was summoned by Napoleon to attend his Great Sanhedrin in 1806. He was the author of *Sha'ar Naftali* etc. and nephew of Phineas Katzenellenbogen (ca. 1691–1765) who wrote *Yesh Manhilin.* Naftali Hirsch was the grandfather of Lazare Isidore 1813–88, Chief Rabbi of France.

CHAPTER THIRTY-FOUR

Patterns of Names

A line from Rabbi Uri Feivush of Vilna

Patterns of names are part of the warp and weft of Jewish genealogy. Such patterns can sometimes provide ancillary support for evidence from other sources and point towards further lines of enquiry. However, without primary source material the use of such patterns can at best be indicative.

In the Gelles family tree the first names of Moses, Isaac and David are found repeatedly in a pattern that includes the less common Uri or Uri Feivush. The Hebrew name Uri = light, and the Yiddish Feivush or Feivel = Phoebus, the Greek sun god. Another name that is sufficiently rare to suggest the possibility of a family connection is David Tebele. It is borne by some of our distant kinsmen. The Yiddish name Tebele or Teyvel = Theophilus, that is, beloved of God, as was King David.

Seven generations of Gelles rabbis can be traced back to Brody at the beginning of the eighteenth century.[1] This Galician line appears to overlap with an earlier Lithuanian line. David of Vilna, who was Chief Rabbi of that city at the beginning of the seventeenth century, was followed by his son Uri Feivush, and the latter's grandsons included Gershon Vilner of Shklov and Isaac of Siemiatycze. The matronymic second name of Gell(i)es appears in the latter's progeny. Taken together with the recurrence of first names and of certain towns there seemed to be a basis for further investigation of possible underlying genealogical connections.

Uri Feivush of Vilna went to Jerusalem in his old age around the year 1650 and became *Nasi* of the Ashkenazi community. This title was also held by R. Isaiah Halevi Horovitz (1568–1627), who ended his days in Safed and was widely known as the *Shelah* after the title of his book. Some writers have suggested that Uri Feivush was his son-in-law, confused perhaps with Chaim Feivush.[2, 3]

The name of Uri in the descendency of the Lithuanian line also turns up later in the connections of Shmuel Helman of Krotoschin. He was Rabbi of Kremsier and Mannheim and then became the distinguished Chief Rabbi of Metz, where he died at an advanced age in 1764. He married into a wealthy family of Glogau. One of his sons was called Uri Feivush and a grandson, Naftali Hirsch Katzenellenbogen, was the son-in-law of a Feivel (Feivush) of

Glogau. The records of Kremsier give their Rabbi's name as Shmuel Helman son of Uri Feivush of Krotoschin, but he was traditionally believed to have been a son of Israel Halpern, the son-in-law of Chief Rabbi Nathan Nata Shapiro of Cracow, and that belief was based on a persuasive contemporary family document. Be that as it may, it was not uncommon at the time to be sometimes referred to by one's father-in-law's name. Shmuel Helman might thus conceivably have been the son-in-law of an Uri Feivush.[4] My grandfather Rabbi Nahum Uri Gelles was certainly a direct descendant of Shmuel Helman (see Note 1). It is an interesting possibility that Shmuel Helman's family in Silesia had earlier connections to our Lithuanian Rabbis.

R' Isaac of Siemiatycze was the progenitor of a rabbinical line whose antecedents include R. Moses Lima (d.1658). The latter was Uri Feivush's successor as Chief Rabbi of Vilna.[5] It is not clear whether Isaac's son Shmuel Gelles, the ABD of Siemiatycze, is the Rabbi S. Gelles, whose daughter married Menachem Mendel Levush aka Moses Gelles of Brody (see Note 2). The identity of the R. Uri, whose son R. Isaac of Glina died in 1759, is intriguing. The latter was described on his tombstone in Brody as of distinguished lineage and a descendant of R. Moses Isserles. Furthermore, he is deemed to have a Rapaport connection.[6] He is a possible ancestor of the later Gelles line, as Table 29 indicates.

R'Gershon Vilner of Shklov was linked by marriage with the family of R'Yissachar Ber of Cracow and his wife Roza Yollis.[7] Yissachar Ber, who became President of the Council of the Four Lands, was a son of Chief Rabbi Abraham Joshua Heschel of Cracow (1596–1663). Roza's father, Mordecai Yollis was connected with the Chalfans of Venice, Prague and Vienna, and married a daughter of Moshe Halevi Yollis of Cracow.[8] Gershon Vilner was the brother-in-law of R' Zvi Hirsch Witeles Landau (1648–1714), the grandfather of Chief Rabbi Ezekiel Landau of Prague (1713–93).[9] From Gershon Vilner to his son-in-law, R' Nathan Nata of Brody (died 1764), and to the latter's son-in-law R' Nachman ben Chaim Rapaport of Glina, a connection goes back to R' Simcha ben Nachman Hakohen Rapaport (d.1717), and then to the latter's father-in-law, R' Israel Swincher.[10]

Israel of Swienush, called Swincher, a distinguished Rabbi of Dubno and Lutsk, was active in the Council of the Four Lands. He was the brother of Roza Yollis and a son of Mordecai Yollis of Cracow. There were marriages between descendants of Israel Swincher and of Abraham Joshua Heschel, as frequently happened in ancient families with established links.[11]

Simcha Hakohen Rapaport, the Chief Rabbi of Grodno and Lublin, had 15 children who all became rabbis or wives of rabbis. Simcha's sons included Chaim Rapaport (1700–71), the Chief Rabbi of Lvov, and Nachman Rapaport of Vaskiai. The latter's possible connection with the house of Moses Isserles of Cracow came through his marriage to a daughter of David Katvan, a wealthy rabbi and community leader in Zolkiew, whose family stemmed from Prague. Katvan married Toybe, the daughter of Rabbi Shabbatai Katz (known as the *Shach*) and Yente Leah Meisels, who was a direct descendant of the *Rema,* as Moses Isserles was called.[12] One authority has suggested that

David Katvan's daughters came from a first wife whose name is unknown.[13] Other genealogists thought that this hypothetical first wife was another daughter of the *Shach,* or indeed a daughter by the name of Esther.[14] The possibility of two marriages could obscure the picture as it emerges from a recently published book that marshals the available evidence.[15] However, it should be borne in mind that if Katvan did have another wife before he married Toybe, she might well have been her elder sister. This was quite common in an age when young first wives often died in childbirth.

From David Katvan and a daughter of Shabbatai Katz there could conceivably have been a line via their Rapaport son-in-law to R. Uri and then to R. Isaac of Glina. An analysis of the latter's identity and descent from Moses Isserles is the subject of a following chapter. Isaac's Rapaport marriage and sojourn in Glina suggests a link to R. Nachman ben Chaim Rapaport of Glina, who was the son-in-law of Chief Rabbi Nathan Nata of Brody and connects back to Gershon Vilner and the line from Uri Feivush of Vilna. These Rapaports link ancient family lines, as set out in Table 30.

Another son-in-law of David Katvan was Isaac Krakower (d.1704), who married his daughter Beile. Isaac Krakower was a son of Yissachar Ber and Rosa Yollis and hence a nephew of Israel Swincher. Isaac became Chief Rabbi of Brody. He was head of the Rabinowicz-Babad family, his issue being known by the acronym Babad (sons of the Av Beth Din).

Further ancestral links to be explored include that of Israel Swincher to his teacher and supposed cousin David Halevi Segal (1586–1667), Chief Rabbi of Lvov, known as the *Taz* from the title of his commentary the *Turei Zahav*.[16] The latter was the son-in-law of Joel Sirkes (1561–1640), the Chief Rabbi of Cracow, known as the *Bach* after his work the *Bayis Chadash*. Joel Sirkes was a Yaffe and cousin of Rabbi Mordecai Yaffe of Prague (1535–1612), called the *Levush* after his magnum opus.

David Tebele, son of Nathan Nata of Brody, became a notable Rabbi of Lissa in Silesia. He was connected by blood with many famous Rabbis of his time such as Chief Rabbis Ezekiel Landau of Prague and Zvi Hirsch Zamosz of Hamburg, and he wrote about his grandfather Gershon Vilner and their family connections. Israel Swincher is mentioned as belonging to his grandfather's family circle,[17] and it appears that Gershon Vilner and his brother-in-law Zvi Hirsch Witeles Landau were both connected by marriage to the Katzenellenbogen line of Abraham Joshua Heshel.[18] The links of David Tebele Lissa's namesakes, the writer and historian David Tebele Efrati, the Chief Rabbi of St Petersburg, David Tebele Katzenellenbogen, and the descendant of the distinguished Brody family, David Tebele Chayes, are set out in Table 31.[19]

NOTES

1. E. Gelles, 'Finding Rabbi Moses Gelles', *Avotaynu*, 18, 1 (Spring 2002). See Jewish community life in Brody (Chapter 30).

2. Hillel Noach Steinschneider, *Ir Vilna* (Vilna: 1900), pp.3–4, summarizes published data on Rabbi Uri Feivush Ashkenazi of Vilna and Jerusalem.
   [i] R' David Tebele of Lissa: 'I heard from my grandfather the famous Rabbi Gershon Vilner of Shklov, grandson of the Gaon Rabbi Feivush of Vilna, that he later left for the Holy Land where he was appointed Nasi, while he [Gershon] studied at the Yeshivah of the Gaon Yisrael Saba, the author of *Or Yisrael*'.
   [ii] the author of Kerem Shlomo [see following reference], who was a descendant of Uri Feivush, lists Rabbis Uri Feivush of Vilna, Isaac of Siemiatycze and David of Yanov and several sisters who were the children of the Gaon Rabbi M, the ABD of Horodicz.
   [iii] the author of Zir Yitzchak, Vilna 1876, writes that Rabbi Uri Feivush was Nasi in Jerusalem in 1650–53 and was twice mentioned in the Pinkas of the Sefardim of Jerusalem, where he signs as Feivush Ashkenazi, known as Uri Shraga, a disciple of the Maharam of Lublin'.
   [iv] an old rabbinical pedigree has the son-in-law of Reb Moshe Yurberger, son of Reb Leib Sheitels of Vilna, ABD Horodna (Grodno), son-in-law of Reb Dovid Chasid, son of Rabbi Feivush, son of Rabbi David of Vilna. It gives the pedigree of Rabbi David Tevele ABD Lissa, son of Rabbi Nathan Nata ABD Brody (son-in-law of the above-mentioned Rabbi Gershon of Vilna), son of Reb Leib Sheitels, son of Rabbi Nathan Nata ABD Belz, son of the Gaon Rabbi Zecharya Mendel author of Be'er Heitev, son of Rabbi Leib [Fischls] ABD of Cracow, son of Rabbi Zecharya Mendel ABD Lvov. This appears to be a very useful source. Steinschneider thinks there are serious errors in *Kerem Shlomo* and also in the pedigree of R' Rafael Nathan Nata Rabinowitz, given in his edition of the Responsa of Rabbi Meir of Rothenberg. Steinschneider also quotes *Shefa Tal* (Hanau: 1612). The introduction is by the 'young, scholarly, and pious Rabbi Feivel, son of the Gaon and Chassid Rabbi David Zacharya, known as Reb Mendelen, son-in-law of the great wonder of our generation, the holy flame, ABD and Rosh Yeshiva of Frankfurt, Rabbi Isaiah Segal Horovitz [the *Shelah*]'. Steinschneider suggest that this may possibly be the same Rabbi Feivel and that he inherited the title of *Nasi* in Jerusalem from his illustrious father-in-law (cf. Pinchas Pesses of Dubno, *Atereth Haleviyim* [Warsaw: 1902], p.63).
   [v] p.47 – footnote 4 identifies a son of Uri Feivush of Vilna as R' Meir of Horodycze.
   [vi] According to *Koreh Hadoroth* (Berlin: 1845) Rabbi Feivush Ashkenazi was considered a great halachic authority. He is also mentioned in *Sha'ar Efrayim* (Sulzbach: 1688), pp.63, 67, 68; *Torath Chessed* (Salonika: 1633), pp.32, 33; and *Perach Mate Ahron* (Amsterdam: 1703), Vol.1, p.44.

   See also the article on the Rabbis of Vilna in the *Jewish Encyclopaedia* and Berel Kagan's book on the History of Keidani, which mentions R' Avigdor as a grandson of R' Uri Feivush of Vilna and also the scholar and philanthropist R' Moshe ben R' Uri Rapaport, who died in Keidani around 1830.

   R' Shlomo Ahron Zelig son of Rabbi Yoel, *Kerem Shlomo* (Warsaw: 1841). The genealogical information on the Lithuanian Gelles connection overlaps with that of the previous reference. Disagreement on several points is due to failure to appreciate the recurrence of names, for example Uri Feivush as the grandson of Uri Feivush and so on. 'R' Mordecai was a son of the great and famous Rabbi Shmuel Gelles of Siemiatycze, son of the Gaon Rabbi Isaac ABD of Siemiatycze' … 'The wife of the famous Reb Shmuel Gellies and her brother the Gaon Rabbi Moshe ABD Przemysl were the children of the Gaon Rabbi Yosef of Novardok, Rosh Beth Din of Brisk. The above-mentioned R' Mordecai son of Rabbi Shmuel Gelles was the son-in-law of Rabbi Abele, son-in-law of Rabbi Yossel Yozel, son of the famous Rabbi Shmuel Ashkenazi, author of several works. Rabbi Yozel was the son-in-law of the Gaon Rabbi Lima ABD Kotzk, son of Rabbi Moshe Lima, author of Chelkath Mechokek.' … 'The above-mentioned Rabbi Mordecai, son of

Rabbi Shmuel Gelles, had another son, the Gaon Reb Yosef Yosel, the author of Minchas Oni and Sheyarei Mincha'.

3. David Tebele Efrati, *Toldot Anshei Shem* (Warsaw: 1875) On page 35 R' Ezekiel Landau of Prague (1713–93) addresses R' David Tebele ABD Lissa as a relative in the *Noda Be'yehuda*. R'Gershon Vilner, who was David Tebele's grandfather is stated to be a brother-in-law of R' Zvi Hirsch Witeles Landau (1648–1714), who was the grandfather of R' Ezekiel Landau. Pages 34–5: the Lithuanian Gelles connection outlined here can be summarized as follows: from R' Uri Feivush of Vilna through R' M. of Horodycze to several grand-children including R' Gershon Vilner of Shklov and R' Isaac of Siemiatycze. The daughter of the former Rabbi married R' Nathan Nata ABD Brody and their son was R' David Tebele ABD Lissa.

   R' Isaac of Siemiatycze had a son called R' Shmuel Gelles, his son R' Mordecai Gelles was a son-in-law of R' Abele, grandson of R' Yosef Yosel, son-in-law of R' Yehuda Leib, known as R' Leima of Wengrow (died 1707), who was the grandson R' Moses Lima (ca 1605–58), author of *Chelkas Mechokek* [The Staff of the Lawgiver].

   R' David Tebele was the father-in-law of R' Shlomo Zalman Lipschitz of Slutsk, the father of R' David Tebele Lipschitz of Slonim, father-in-law of R' Abraham Efrati of Meretz, father of the author R' David Tebele Efrati (1850–84).

4. E. Gelles, 'Rabbi Shmuel Helman of Metz and his Family Connections', *Sharsheret Hadorot*, 18, 2 (May 2004).
5. See Note 3.
6. N.M. Gelber made transcriptions of about 200 tombstones of the old cemetery in Brody. These are preserved in the Gelber Archives at the Central Archives of the History of the Jewish People, 46 Jabotinsky Street, Jerusalem. The tombstone of R'Isaac ben Uri reads, 'Here lies Rabbi Yitzchak Isaac, son of the great luminary Rabbi Uri, a descendant of the Gaon Rabbi Moshe Isserles, of distinguished lineage. Passed away 17th Shevat 5519 [1759].' A note by Gelber adds: 'R'Yitzchak, Rabbi of Glina, son-in-law of R' Nachman Barzap. [Abraham Jekutiel Zalman Pereles Rapaport known as Barzap died in 1799, so the father-in- law is most likely to have been a Rapaport of a previous generation].'
7. Louis Lewin, *Die Geschichte der Juden in Lissa* (Pinne: M. Gundermann, 1904), pp.192–204 for Rabbi David Tebele of Lissa and some family connections. He was the son of R' Nathan Nata ABD of Brody. His mother was the daughter of R' Gershon Vilner of Shklov. David Tebele became ABD of Lissa in 1774 and died there in 1792. His wife Feige died in 1797. On p.194, he refers to R' Gershon Vilner as of his family, and he wrote an approbation for a book by a Rabbi of his community, Rabbi Raphael ben Chaim Meisels to whom he was related by marriage (Meisels was a descendant of Joel Sirkes and Moses Lima). On p.199, he corresponds with his blood relative R' Ezekiel Landau, ABD of Prague. On p.200, R' Zvi Hirsch Zamosc, ABD of Hamburg is referred to as his blood relative. Page 204 refers to his son and daughter with their connections.
8. Yitzchak Shlomo Yudlov, *Sefer Yichus Belza* (the Lineage Book of the Grand Rabbis of Belz) (Jerusalem: Machon, 1984).
9. See Note 3.
10. Ahron Walden, *Shem Hagedolim Hachadash* (Jerusalem: 1965), p.52, a daughter of R' Nathan Nata of Brody married R' Nachman ben Chaim Hakohen Rapaport of Glina (cf. David Tebele Efrati, *Toldot Anshei Shem*, p.34, where Glina is rendered as Glogau). *Jewish Encyclopaedia*, 1904 edn. From the list of the Rabbis of Dubno:

    > Nachman ben Meir HaKohen Rapaport (also called Nachman Lifshes) died 1674 … Moses ben Joseph died at Lemberg … 1684, Israel ben Mordecai Yollis [also called Israel Swincher], Simcha ben Nachman HaKohen Rapaport died at Szeberszin … 1717, [he was the] son-in-law of Israel ben Mordecai, replaced the latter in the rabbinate of Dubno from 1682 to 1688, and became Rabbi of Grodno 1714, of Lublin 1717, called to the rabbinate of Lemberg in the same year and died on his way there.

> ... Eleazar ben Yissachar Ber of Cracow (Rabbi of Dubno1715–19), maternal grandfather of Ezekiel Landau.

Pinchas Pesses, *Ir Dubno Verabaneha* (Cracow: 1902), p. 17 refers to Israel Swincher:

> the Gaon famous in his generation Rabbi Israel, son of the Parnas R' Mordecai Yollis of Cracow, brother-in-law of the Parnas of his generation R' Yissachar Berish, son of the Gaon Reb Heschel of Cracow. Rabbi Israel was a mechutan of the Gaon Rabbi Nachman Katz Rapaport, his daughter married the Gaon Rabbi Simcha Rapaport. He was known as R' Israel Swincher ... and went on from Dubno to assume the position of ABD and Parnas of the Council of the Four Lands at Lutzk, where he is buried.

11. Neil Rosenstein, *The Unbroken Chain* (New York, London, Jerusalem: CIS Publishers, 1990), p.716: R. Chaim of Grodno, great-grandson of Abraham Joshua Heshel married a granddaughter of R. Israel Swincher of Slutsk
12. Shmuel Zanvel Cahana, *Anaf Etz Avoth* (Cracow: 1903), p.xii lists the four children of R. Nachman Hacohen Rapaport, the eldest being R. Simcha Rapaport, whose 15 listed offspring include R. Nachman of Viskiai (father of R. Joel of Bichow) and R. Chaim of Lvov.
13. Zvi Hirsch Horowitz, *Kitvei Hageonim* (Piotrkov: Chanoch Henoch Follman, 1928), p.35.
14. Salomon Buber, *Kiriya Nisgava* [Zolkiew] (Cracow: Josef Fischer, 1903), pp.55–6.
15. Neil Rosenstein, *The Lurie Legacy* (Bergenfield, NJ: Avotaynu, 2004), pp.280–2.
16. R' Zvi Hirsch Horovitz, *Letoldot Hakehiloth BePolin* (Jerusalem: Mossad HaRav Kook, 1978), p.377. Israel Swincher is described as a disciple and cousin of R' David Halevi (the *Taz*) and father-in-law of R' Simcha HaKohen Rapaport. The epithet of Israel ben Mordecai Yollis of Cracow appears to derive from the town name of Swienuch in Volhynia.
17. See Note 7.
18. See Notes 3 and 7.
19. Notes to Table 31:

For Nathan Nata's father, Aryeh Leib of Slutsk and Grodno, see Rosenstein, *The Unbroken Chain*, Vol.1, p.219. For Nathan Nata of Brody, see N.M. Gelber (ed.), *Arim VeImahot BeIsrael* (Brody) (Jerusalem: 1952), Vol.6, pp.56–7. For Nathan Nata's sons, David Tebele of Lissa and Aryeh Leib of Anikst, see Note 2, Walden, *Shem Hagedolim Hachadash* (The New Names of the Great Ones), Part 1, p.52, letter 'Teth' No.3, and p.43 letter 'Zayin' No.12. For further biographical details and family connections of David Tebele of Lissa see Note 7: Lewin, *Die Geschichte der Juden in Lissa*, pp.192–204.

For David Tebele Efrati, see Note 3, David Tebele Efrati, *Toldot Anshei Shem*.

For David Tebele Chayes, see entry in Rosenstein, *The Unbroken Chain*, Vol.2, p.806. See also Leo Lauterbach, *Chronicle of the Lauterbach family, 1800–1991* (El Paso, Texas: 1992, New Edition by Bernard S. Lauterbach), p.68.

For Isaac Chayes see Lewin, *Die Geschichte der Juden in Lissa*, p.204, also E. Gelles, 'Chief Rabbis in the Genes', *Manna*, No.69 (2000) and 'Chayes Family Connections', *Shemot*, 12, 2 (June 2004). David Tebele Chayes was most probably the son or nephew of Meir Chayes, son of Menachem Manish Chayes of Brody and Florence, son of the above-named Isaac Chayes.

For David Tebele Katzenellenbogen of St Petersburg, see Rosenstein, *The Unbroken Chain*, Vol.1, p.241; *Encyclopaedia Judaica* (1972), Vol.10, p.828, Shmuel Noach Gottlieb, *Ohalei Shem* (Pinsk: 1912), p.369, and Suwalki Yizkor Book (1961), pp.143–6. For his ancestry see his book, *Ma'ayan Mei Neftoach* (St Petersburg: 1923). Aryeh Leib of Anikst is taken as the son of Nathan Nata of Brody and brother of David Tebele of Lissa. I am following Neil Rosenstein and David Tebele of St Petersburg, though Louis Lewin states that Aryeh Leib was the third son of the Rabbi of Lissa (*loc cit.)*. Aryeh Leib of Anikst was the father of Saul of Vaslui, who married a daughter of Rabbi Meir Gunzburg. Their son was Aryeh Leib of Tauroggen, father of Naftali Hirsch, and grandfather of David Tebele, who was born in Tauroggen and became the Chief Rabbi of St Petersburg, assuming the name of Katzenellenbogen.

Table 29
NAME PATTERNS IN THE GELLES FAMILY

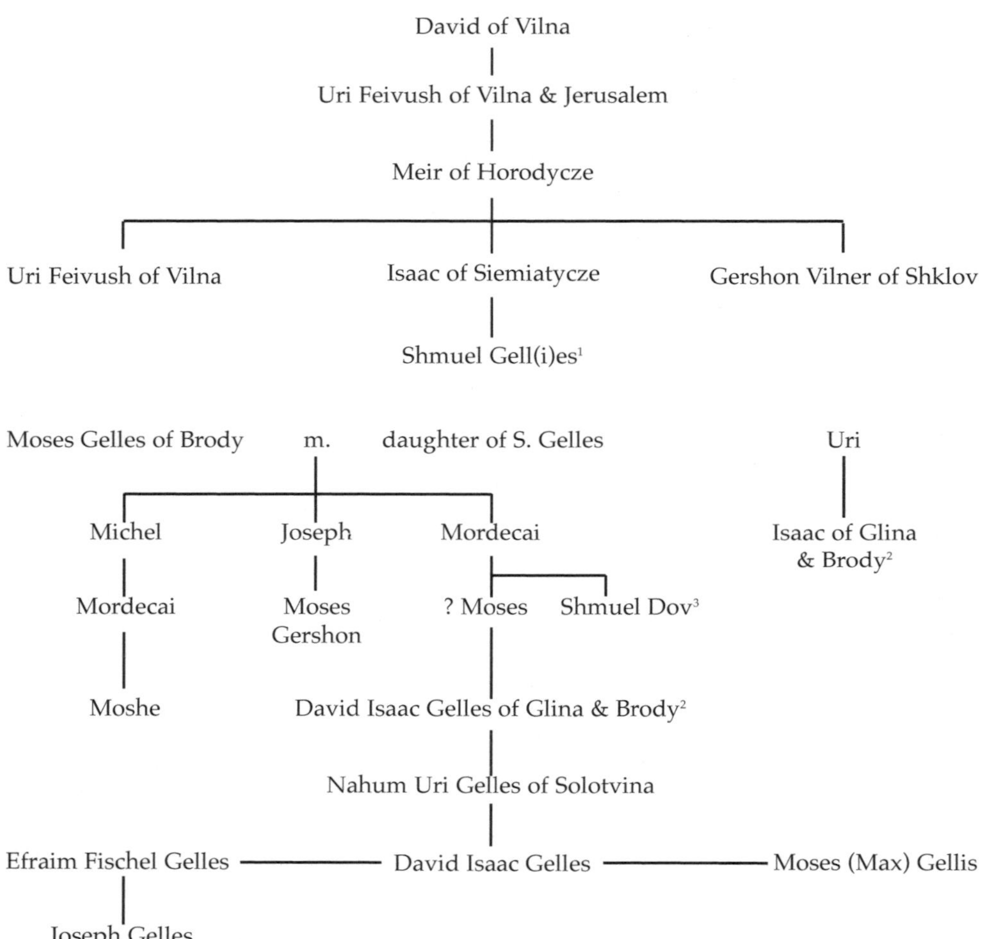

Notes:
1. R. Shmuel Gelles of Siemiatycze was the father of a R. Mordecai Gelles who was descended on his mother's side from R. Moses Lima (who succeeded Uri Feivush as Chief Rabbi of Vilna).
2. Rabbi Isaac ben Uri was Rabbi in Glina. His tombstone in Brody records his 'distinguished lineage' and his death in 1759. Rabbi David Isaac Gelles studied in Glina. He died around 1870 and his tombstone in Brody gives his father as R. Moshe Gelles.
3. R. Shmuel Dov, a son of Mordecai, son of Moses Gelles of Brody, married a daughter of R. Pinchas Shapiro of Koretz (1726–91). Shmuel Dov died in 1811.

Table 30
ANCIENT FAMILY CONNECTIONS

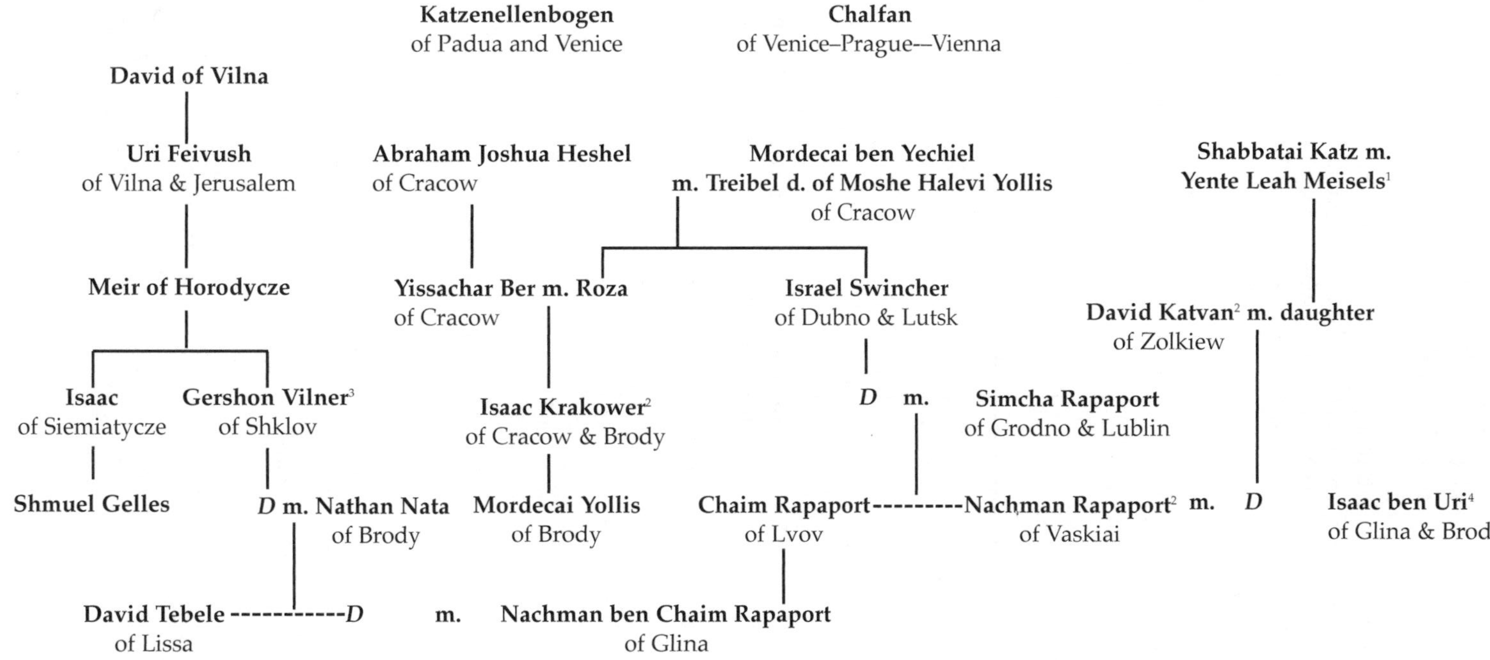

Notes:
1. Yente Leah Meisels was a direct descendant of Moses Isserles of Cracow.
2. Isaac Krakower and Nachman ben Simcha Rapaport were sons-in-law of David Katvan of Zolkiew.
3. Gershon Vilner and his brother-in-law Zvi Hirsch Witeles Landau were connected by marriage to the line from Abraham Joshua Heshel.
4. Rabbi Isaac ben Uri's descent from Moses Isserles is shown in Table 45. Isaac was Rabbi at Glina and married a Rapaport.

Table 31
WHAT'S IN A NAME?
DAVID TEBELE

Rabbi David Tebele of Brisk was a brother of the Chief Rabbi of Cracow known as the Hoicher Rebbe Leib or Leib Fischls. Two great-grandsons of Aryeh Leib Fischls were Nathan Nata, a Chief Rabbi of Brody, and Zvi Hirsch Berlin, who was known as Rabbi Hart Lyon while he was Chief Rabbi in London. The latter's grandson was David Tebele Berliner.

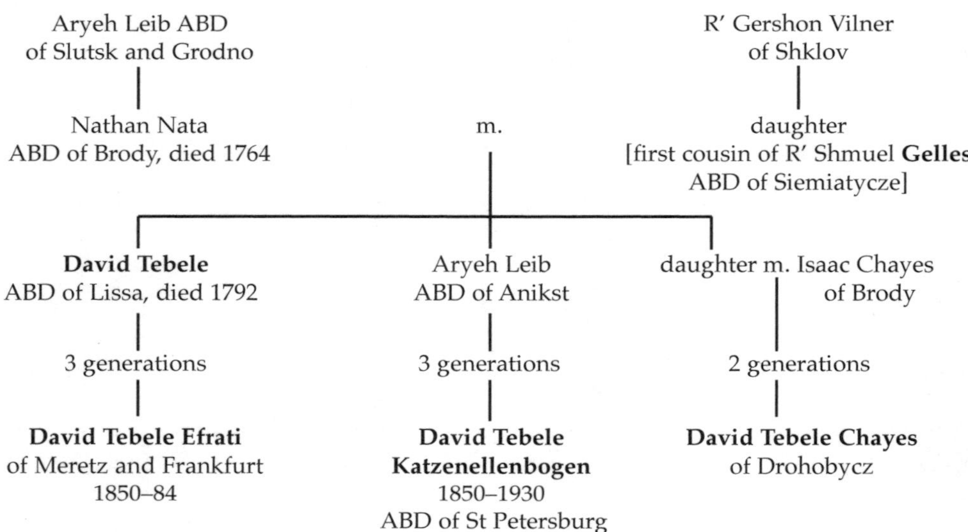

Chapter Thirty-Five

Enlightenment and Chasidism

Some genealogical background

INTRODUCTION

During the second half of the eighteenth century the ideas of the Enlightenment gradually spread from France to Germany and Eastern Europe. They were challenged by the Chasidic movement whose Polish origins date from the teachings of Israel ben Eliezer (1700–60), known as the *Baal Shem Tov*. His immediate follower was Dov Ber, the *Maggid* (preacher) of Meseritz, while a near contemporary was Pinchas Shapiro of Koretz. The ancestral background of these men is indicated in Table 32 that includes Menachem Nachum Twersky and the descendant Friedmans of Ruzhin, Sadagora, and Czortkow. These Chasidic sages came from a tightly knit group of rabbinical families.[1] The philosopher of the enlightenment, Moses Mendelssohn, sprang from a similar background.[2, 3]

Table 32 begins in the sixteenth century with Moses Isserles of Cracow, the Katzenellenbogens of Padua and Venice and the Shapiros who descended, via a nexus involving the Luria and Treves, from the great eleventh-century scholar and biblical commentator Rashi of Troyes. These families and others such as the family of Rabbi Judah Loew of Prague (c.1520–1609) belong to the millennial bedrock of European Jewry.

HISTORY OF IDEAS

The rationalist and mystical strands in Jewish thought since the middle ages can be traced from Moses Maimonides on the one hand, and from cabbalistic writings, particularly the influential *Zohar* on the other. In the sixteenth century, exponents of these two strands were Moses Isserles [the *Rema,* d.1572] and Isaac Luria [the holy *Ari,* d.1574]. Both strands were based on the Talmud and traditional Jewish learning, but the rationalists drew on Aristotle while the mystics had affinity with Neo-Platonic and Pythagorean ideas. These two strands were not mutually exclusive and many rabbis had greater or lesser sympathy with a study of the Cabbala.

Luria's teaching of the contraction of the Infinite before the creation of the world and of the creative power of numbers and letters was carried further by Nathan Nata Spiro of Cracow. Rabbi Loew of Prague showed sympathy with cabbalistic thought and Rabbi Isaiah Halevi Horovitz (1568–1627) wrote an ethical-mystical work that earned him the title of the *holy Sheloh* and aroused much interest in Eastern Europe. The pedigree of eighteenth-century Chasidism is thus a long one. It goes back to the mysticism of the Bible and Talmud and arrived in Poland via the medieval Cabbalists of Spain, Provence and Germany, and of the school of Safed, where Isaac Luria's teachings took root. This continuing tradition of Jewish mysticism is mirrored in the lineage of some of the afore-mentioned families.

SOCIO-ECONOMIC BACKGROUND

In the sixteenth century the Jewish communities in Poland enjoyed a high point of local autonomy and economic well-being. Many centres of learning attracted the leading rabbis of the day. Then the Polish-Lithuanian state went into gradual political decline and finally fell to Prussia, Austria and Russia in the three late-eighteenth-century partitions. The Jews had already suffered the catastrophe of the Chmielnicki massacres in the mid-seventeenth century and the following period brought further depredations. Rabbinical learning and leadership declined and the wretched state of the poor Jewish masses provided fertile ground for the new message of hope and joy brought by the Baal Shem Tov and his followers.

CHASIDIC TEACHING

The message was revealed to the masses in simple stories and parables and spoke of the sparks of God's holiness in all things. It encouraged the Chasidim to express their joy in his all-pervading presence through worship in which singing, dancing and story-telling played an important part. Ecstatic enthusiasm and constant devotion were emphasized in their prayers. The influence of the Cabbala was apparent in their liturgy, which drew particularly on the practice of Isaac Luria's school. Their beliefs included that of the transmigration of souls and the basis of their ethics was humility and love. The people flocked to the charismatic leader or *Zaddik*, who was held to have attained a degree of religious perfection. The founder's disciples and successors were men of great personal charisma whose emphasis on different aspects of religious piety gave their communities an individual character. Dov Ber of Meseritz took the lead in organizing the movement after the founder's death. Pinchas of Koretz was a towering figure of sublime ethical teaching who enjoined his following to love the evil-doer more, in order to compensate for the diminution in the power of love the sinner had caused in the world. Some masters like

Menachem Nahum Twersky believed that there is no place empty of the divine, everything that exists comes from God, and the power of the creator resides within each created thing. In such teaching Chasidism comes close to a pantheistic world view. Other leaders, not shown in Table 32, included Jacob Joseph of Polnoye, Schneur Zalman of Liadi who founded the *Chabad* school in Lithuania, and Nachman of Bratslav,

In the nineteenth century scores of Chasidic communities grew around their *Zaddikim,* who generally founded enduring dynasties. These rabbi-saints had a spiritual cohesion notwithstanding their differences and doctrinal squabbles. Among the most famous was the Rokeach dynasty of Belz. The Rokeachs were uncompromising in their rejection of any reformist and enlightenment ideas. Of equally ancient family were the Friedmans of Ruzhin, Sadagora and Czortkow. Their semi-regal style contrasted strangely with the saintly simplicity of the Court of Belz but their extraordinarily charismatic leadership drew followers from all over Galicia and beyond. Israel of Ruzhin was venerated in his time and even in 1933 his grandson Israel Friedman of Czortkow was mourned by thousands as they followed him to his grave in Vienna.

Moses Mendelssohn attempted to reconcile traditional Judaism with the Greek rationalist heritage. His ancestral roots and those of the Chasidic leaders were very similar but that could certainly not be said for the general state of education and the social conditions for Jews in Germany and Poland. Mendelssohn was a descendant of Moses Isserles and the Katzenellenbogens. Saul Wahl Katzenellenbogen was the progenitor of so many important lines. Some of these came together with other clans such as the Horovitz and Shapiro to bring forth leaders of the Chasidic movement. For example, the Wahl descendant Meir Horovitz of Tiktin was the forebear of Schmuel Schmelke Horovitz of Nikolsburg and of his younger brother Pinchas Horovitz of Frankfurt, who were both prominent disciples of Dov Ber of Meseritz. However, within these old rabbinical families there were often sharp divisions between adherents of Chasidism and opponents of the movement, particularly in the first two generations after its foundation.

CHASIDIC CONNECTIONS OF THE GELLES FAMILY

My ancestors were very much embedded in this great genealogical tapestry. Moses Gelles was a scholar of the prestigious Brody *Klaus* in the early part of the eighteenth century. He was also known as *Levush*, possibly after the epithet of Rabbi Mordecai Yaffe of Prague.[4] Moses Gelles was the great-grandfather of R. Moshe Gelles aka Levush, who was a grandson of a Rabbi Yehuda Zundel of Brody. The latter was probably the Rabbi Yehuda Leib Zundel *Ramraz* whose other grandsons included R. Shalom Rokeach (1779–1855), the first *Zaddik* of the great Belz dynasty. The older Moses Gelles was also the grandfather of Rabbi Shmuel Dov, who married

Sarah Rachel Scheindel, daughter of Rabbi Pinchas of Koretz. Various sources give Shmuel Dov as the son of Rabbi Mordecai, son of Moses Gelles of Brody, whose tombstone inscription refers to him as a 'servant of God'.[5] Shmuel Dov's letter of appointment in 1793 to the rabbinate of Kolibolet and the surrounding area describes him as the son of Rabbi Mordecai, and as the son-in-law of Pinchas 'the holy flame, the royal wonder of our generation ..., Rabbi of Shepetivka'. Shmuel's rabbinical post passed from father to son for five generations, as shown in Table 32.[6,7] His grandson, Rabbi Eliyahu Pinchas married Sima Wertheim, thus linking this Gelles-Shapiro line with Menachem Nahum Twersky's Shapiro-Katzenellenbogen ancestry.

My great-grandfather Rabbi David Isaac Gellis and his progeny were cousins of this line. His father Rabbi Moshe may well have been a brother or first cousin of Rabbi Shmuel Dov. David Isaac studied at Glina and was buried in Brody. His son, my grandfather Rabbi Nahum Uri Gelles (1852–1934), was descended from Rabbi Shmuel Hillman of Metz. The latter is generally taken as a grandson of Nathan Nata Spiro, the Chief Rabbi of Cracow and author of the important cabbalistic work *Megaleh Amukot* (Revealed Depths).[8] This rests largely on a persuasive contemporary family document, but other contradictory evidence on Helman's Shapiro connection remains to be resolved.[9] A direct line leads from Nathan Nata of Grodno in the sixteenth century to Nathan Nata of Cracow, to Pinchas of Koretz, and then to Yehuda Meir Shapiro (1887–1934), who was one of the most important Polish rabbis of the twentieth century. Meir Shapiro founded the Lublin Yeshiva where he taught my cousin Joseph Gelles, grandson of Nahum Uri and the last of our rabbinical line.[10] Joseph's brother Leo was a descendant of another Chasidic sage, Rabbi Meir of Przemyslany, the grandson of Meir ben Jacob.[11] The younger Meir was a close friend of Israel Friedman of Ruzhin. The latter's grandson and namesake Rabbi Israel Friedman of Czortkow had a large following which included my grandfather and Rabbi Meir Shapiro.

Rabbi Israel's great-grandson, Rabbi Israel Friedman of Manchester has written a book on the Czortkow dynasty.[12] It might be noted here that the proximity of the graves of my grandfather and Rabbi Israel Friedman in Vienna is in keeping with the close family connection mentioned in my father's obituary in the Viennese paper *Heruth* on 4 September 1964 (see Chapter 36).

The Czortkow connection has survived the holocaust as indeed have many other Chasidic families in their worldwide dispersion. The family links between several of the great Chasidic leaders encompass distinct lines of Gelles cousins. These sages made a unique contribution to the history of Jewish mysticism, which connected with other ancient philosophies and had a significant impact on Christian thought through the ages.

NOTES

1. Yehuda Klausner, 'The Hasidic Rabbinate', *Sharsheret Hadorot*, 16, 1 and 3 (Oct. 2001 and June 2002). Martin Buber, *Tales of the Chasidim* (London: Thames & Hudson 1956), *Die Erzählungen der Chasidim* (Zurich: Manesse Verlag, Conzett & Huber, 1949), footnote 1. Jiri Langer, *Nine Gates* (London: James Clarke & Co., 1961; Czech edition first published in 1937). Gabrielle Kohlbauer-Fritz, *Zwischen Ost und West. Galizische Juden in Wien* (Vienna: Jüdisches Museum Wien, 2001). Neil Rosenstein, *The Unbroken Chain* (New York, London, Jerusalem: CIS Publishers, 1990), pp.291, 1184–5.
2. Isidore Epstein, *Judaism* (Harmondsworth: Penguin Books, 1959).
3. Alexander Altmann, *Moses Mendelssohn. A Biographical Study* (Philadelphia: Jewish Publication Society, 1973).
4. E. Gelles, 'Finding Rabbi Moses Gelles', *Avotaynu*, 18, 1 (Spring 2002); E. Gelles, 'Jewish Community Life in Brody', *Sharsheret Hadorot*, 18, 4 (Nov. 2004).
5. Levi Grossman, *Shem U She'erit* (Tel Aviv: 1943), p.92. Shimson Aaron Polonsky, *Chidushei Horav MiTeplik* (Jerusalem: 1984).
6. Metityahu Yechezkel Guttman, *Rabbi Pinchas miKoretz* (Tel Aviv: 1950). Yaakov Y. Wahrman, *SeferYuchasin* (www.pikholz.org/Families/Wahrman).
7. A.J. Heshel, *Yivo Bletter*, vol.36, pp.124–5. Yechezkel Shraga Frankel (ed.), *Imrei Pinchas* (Bnei Brak, Israel: 5763 [2003]), vol.2, pp.486–8 (see footnote 2 and illustration).
8. Shmuel Noach Gottlieb, *Ohalei Shem* (Pinsk: 1912), pp.261–2.
9. E. Gelles, 'Rabbi Shmuel Helman of Metz and his Family Connections', *Sharsheret Hadorot*, 18, 2 (May 2004). Stuart Steinberg, 'Shmuel Helman of Metz is the son of Israel Heilprin', *Avotaynu*, 19, 4 (Winter 2003).
10. Yehuda Meir Shapira, *Imrei Da'as* (Bnei Brak, Israel: 1990). Josef Gelles, son of Rabbi Ephraim Fischl Gelles, is listed as a student at the Lublin Yeshiva.
11. Ahron Leib (Leo) Gelles, died New York 1973, son of Rabbi Ephraim Fischel Gelles, the eldest son of Rabbi Nahum Uri Gelles of Solotwina near Stanislau. Leo's mother was descended from R. Meir of Przemyslany through the Leifers of Nadworna (private communication from the Laufer family). Rosenstein, *The Unbroken Chain*, p.490. Meir Wunder, *Meorei Galicia* (Jerusalem: Institute for the Commemoration of Galician Jewry, 1978 *et seq*.), Vol.III, p.521.
12. Rabbi Israel Friedman, *The Rebbes of Czortkow* (New York: Artscroll Mesorah Publications, 2003).

Note on Pinchas of Koretz

Martin Buber wrote: 'In the period between the Baal Shem Tov and his great-grandson Nahman of Bratslav he has no equal in fresh and direct thinking, in daring and vivid expression. What he says often springs from a profound knowledge of the human soul and it is always spontaneous and great-hearted.' (*Tales of the Chasidim*, pp.19–20 of the English and pp.218–242 of the German Edition).

Pinchas Shapiro married Trani Weil, a descendant of Rabbi Moshe Meir Weil, known as the Maharam Ashkenazi Weil of Stühlingen.

Note on Shmuel Dov Gelles

The letters of appointment of Rabbi Shmuel Dov [Gelles] and of his grandson Rabbi Eliyahu Pinchas to the position of Av Beit Din (head of the rabbinical court) of Kolibolet and the surrounding area in 1793 and 1831 respectively, add much to the information provided in Notes 5–7. These two documents are shown in Figures 41 and 42. They set out the new rabbi's duties and his emoluments, specifying payments for sermons, contributions from inn-keepers, traders and tailors, and a variety of duties and privileges.

It appears that Shmuel Dov died in 1811 and that his son Ahron, who succeeded him as

Av Beit Din, passed away in 1830. The latter's son, Eliyahu Pinchas, then became the third Rabbi of the line. The letters of appointment refer to the exclusive right to the sale of candles. We found earlier that the heirs of Moses Gelles owned a wax chandlery in Brody and there were indications, as mentioned in Chapters 29 and 30, that the family enjoyed a monopoly for the sale of candles in that city.

Note on the Graves of Israel Friedman and Nahum Uri Gelles

Some details of the graves at the Zentral-friedhof in Vienna are available on the website of the Israelitische Kultusgemeinde Wien (IKG) and other details come from miscellaneous sources. Rabbi Israel Friedman, who followed his father David Moses Friedman as Admur of Czortkow, died in Vienna at the age of 79 years on 1.12.1933. He was married for 63 years to his first cousin Ruchama Batsheva Friedman, daughter of Abraham Jacob Friedman, Admur of Sadegora. She died on 1.11.1934 aged 78 years. Husband and wife are laid to rest in the family tomb covering the space of Nos.28–30 at Gate IV, Group 21, Row 16. Rabbi Nahum Uri Gelles, who died on 18.11.1934 aged 82 years, lies immediately next to this mausoleum in Row 16, Grave No.27. Another adherent of the Czortkower Rebbe and one of the latter's sons are buried in adjacent graves in Row 17, Nos.27 and 28.

תפו ——— אמרי פנחם — נספחים / תולדות רבינו

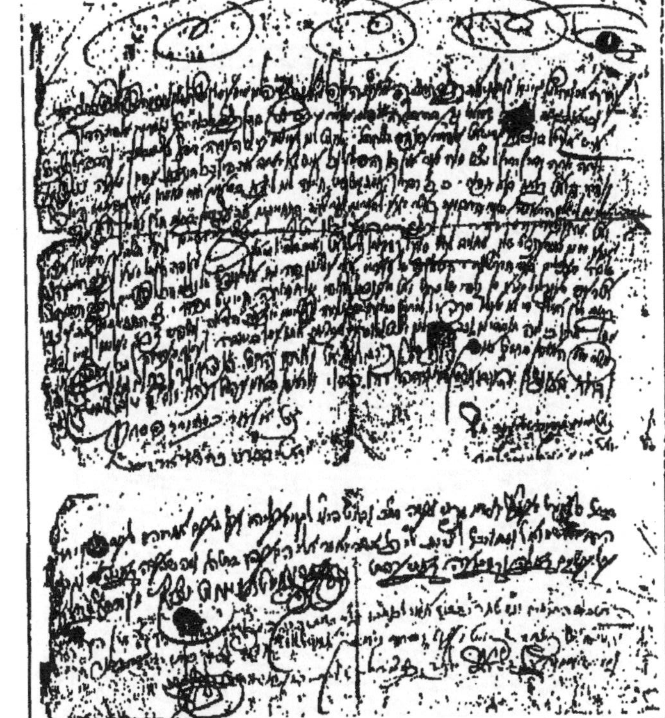

כתב הרבנות של הרה"ק רבי שמואל מקאלניבלאט

חתום בידי הרה"ק רבי יעקב שמשון משפיטיווקא, שכנראה כתב בעצמו את כתב הרבנות

(מתוך "ארץ ישראל על בעלזי" עמ' 94 ... יצחק שלום עליכם)

אמרי פנחם — נספחים / תולדות רבינו ——— תפז

כתב הרבנות של הרה"ק רבי שמואל מקאלניבלאט חתן רבינו

על האסף היום קיימו וקבלו את כבוד הרב המאה"ג המופלג... פלגי מים עמוקים והחיק ויוכם השלם. בתורה וביראה קשית מוהר"ר שמואל נ"י בהרבני המופלג מוהר"ר מרדכי ז"ל חתן כבוד מעלות הרב מובהק פאות הדור איש אלקים בוציגא קדישא מוהר"ר פנחס זללה"ה. להיות לנו לעינים עיני העדה דפ"ק קאלניבלאט והכפרים השייכים. יורה יורה ידין ידין מגח סלה ועד אין בו המסך, וכל איש לא יפתח את פיו ככל היוצא מפיו מעשה ומשמע וחרי הוא כלאו דלא תסור, כי כל דבריו אמת ומשפט, וחלילה לנו ליצא במקאון אחר מאמר מגסון מאמר מתנם המלך ועליו לשלם הראוי בעד הרבנות כאשר מגיע להאחוזה(!) ועוד זאת התחייבנו את עצמינו בחרב חזק ואמיץ ... דהיינו לפי חשבון הראוי אשר מגיע ממנו מאורענדי' שלו סחיב יחי' סלקו כסדורה ... אי קראב נובל מהאלף מקופת הקרל מגיע לכבוד הרב הנ"ל (!) שלשה רענדלין בעד הדרשות. הטאקסי של סוחרים אשר עשינו גם כם אורנדיי של נרות הכל שייך לכבוד הרב הנ"ל (!) אי רענדיל מגיע מן קלפי של קהל ואי רענדיל מקלפי של חברה הייטאם דפה.

כל זה התחייבנו את עצמנו בחרב חזק ואמיץ די לא מגזן (!) בכדי להחזיק בדקה של תורה שממנו יוצאה הוראה ומשפט צדק ועלינו לקיים גדלתו משל אתין כי זה חובתינו וכך יפה לנו מונה והרבה לעשות אתו עמי בטובה לעמוד בעזרה בכל... כאשר יהיית האופן נתון אופן וכל הנ"ל... כל אי מאתנו החיים בנדר גמור והחוב נמור צלול, וברור בענשין המבוארים בתורה גל יחל דבת ולראית באנו עתית וצתית יום ד' טוב שבט תקכ"ג.

נאי חיים במוהר"ר אליעזר ז"ל

נאי חיים

נאי אלעזר במוהר"ר פסח

נאי שבתי בהר"ר ארי'

——

[בצד שני של הדף:]

דברי התנאים מעליד ונעשו (!) בפני נעשת בתי"כ... לקיים עליהם ועל זרעם אחריהם לעד... הרב [מריחה] שמואל והחרובים מציין לוח כל אשר יאמר אליהם לפי דתיה והוה שמעת באנשי וקבלו על עצמם באלה ובשבועה באתי עתיה יעקב שמשון באמ"ץ המנוח מ' יצחק מעיר הק' טבריא

——

[בכ"י אחר:]

כתיבת התנאים וגם שאר המתגים אסור לכותבם בלי רשות הרב המפורסם כנוד... שמואל חתן המפורסם המנוח מרי פנחס שפירא... והסידור קידושין אסור לשום אדם לסדר בלתי ידיעת כבוד הרב ומי שיעבור על כל הנ"ל ילכד במצודת.

[יעקב שמשון באמ"ץ המנוח מ' יצחק מעיר הק' טבריא]

Figure 42
Letter of appointment of Rabbi Shmuel Dov Gelles

כתב הרבנות של הרה"ק רבי אליהו פנחס מקאלניבלאט
נכד הרה"ק רבי שמואל מקאלניבלאט
(ביטאון "יערי ישראל" של מעוזד עמ' 44 בנכד הרה"ג יצחק שליט"א)

כתב הרבנות של הרה"ק רבי אליהו פנחס מקאלניבלאט
נכד הרה"ק רבי שמואל מקאלניבלאט

אנחנו אלופי מנהיגי וראשי הקהילה וגם יחידי סגולה דפה ק"ק קאלניבלאט וגם הארנדארים מתושבי הכפרים השייכים לקהילתינו הסכמנו כולם כאחד בהסכמה אחת ובדעה אחת ובלב אחד ובפה אחד ברצונו הטוב ובנפשות חפצות בלי שום אונס כלל איך שהיה אצלינו פה בעירינו אב"ד ... הרב המאור הגאון הגדול המפורסם כש"ת מוהר"ר שמואל במוהר"ר מרדכי זללה"ה חתן הרב החסיד המפורסים בוצינא קדישא חסידא ופרישא כש"ת נודע בכל העולם מוהר"ר מנחם שפירא זצוקללה"ה והיה פה אצלינו לרב ושר"צ סך עשרים ושנים שנים שעשה אותו להיות רב אצלינו פה היה הרב המאור הגאון הגדול המפורסים בוצינא קדישא איש אלקי רבן של בני הגולה כש"ת מוהר"ר יעקב שמשון הרב דק"ק שעפעטיווקא ... וסמך ממנו.

ואחר זה בשנת תקע"ב לפ"ק ביום ד' בסקין נסתלק לעולמו ושבק לן חיים ומיד תיכף אחר פטירתו קיבלנו עלינו בהסכמת כל הקהל כאחד את בנו הרבני המופלג בתורה וביראה כש"ת מו"ה אהרן זללה"ה שהוא יהיה אצלינו פה לרב למלאות מקום אביו והיה אצלינו לרב פה סך תשעה עשר שנים וקצת ביום בי פ"ב אדר הלך לעולמו ושבק לן חיים ולכל ישראל.

בכן הסכמנו כל הקהל כאחד עם הארנדארים שסביבותינו בהסכמה אחת ובדעה אחת שבנו האברך המופלג בתורה וביראה כש"ת מוהר"ר אליהו פנחס בן הר"ב מו"ה אהרן זללה"ה נכד הרב הישיש הגאון הגדול מו"ה שמואל זללה"ה שהוא יהיה אצלינו פה בעירינו כרב אב"ד למלאות מקום אבותיו נ"ע וקבלנו עלינו בחיוב גמור לציית אותו בכל אשר יצא מפיו הן ע"פ ד"ת הסי הן ע"פ פשרה . וחולין וחלילה ואסור לשום אחד מאנשי קהילתינו וסביבותינו להמרות את פיו רק מוטל עלינו לאשר ולחזק ולקיים את הרבנות בכל תוקף חיוב כאשר היה בימי אבותיו נ"ע כן מחויב להיות בימיו וכל ההכנסות שהיו לאבותיו הן מהעיר והן מהכפרים שסביבותינו כפי אשר אישר וקיים הרב הגאון הגדול בוצינא קדישא נ"ע הרב דק"ק שעפיטווקא זצוקללה"ה והרע החזיקו הצדיקים הגדולים קדושי עליון יהינו הרב המאור הגאון הגדול המפורסים בכל קצוי ארץ רבן של בני הגולה כש"ת מוהר"ר אברהם יהושיע העשיל זצוקללה"ה מאפטא ויאסי ומעזבוז גם הרב החסיד בוצינא קדישא נ"ע כש"ת מוהר"ר בנימין זאב זצוקללה"ה מבאלטא וגם הרב הגאון הגדול נהורא דאורייתא ארי שבחבורה צנא מלא ספרא כש"ת מוה"ר ארי' יעקב זצוקללה"ה מק"ק סטילא וגם הצדיק שבדורינו שיחי' עד ביאת גואל המשיח הרב המפורסים בכל קצוי ארץ בוצינא קדישא רבא דעמא מופת דורינו רבן של בני הגולה כש"ת מו"ה משה צבי אב"ד דק"ק סאווראן

הכל קבלנו עלינו בחיוב גמור ליתן לו כל ההכנסות שהיו לאבותיו מאז ומקדם כולם נתונים נתונים המה לו להרב דקהילתינו המופלג בתורה וביראה מו"ה אליהו פנחס הנ"ל שיחי' דהיינו הטאקסע מן בהמות היינו מן גסה כשרה חמשה ל"ב (ז) . ומן גסה טריפה גימל נ"ג (ז) ... מן פלגא ובן שנה כשרה בי נ"ב (י) ... ומן פלגא ובן שנה טריפה א' נ"ב (ז) .. ומן דקה גסה כשרה ו' ק(אפיקעס); ומן דקה גסה טריפה ה' ק(אפיקעס); ומן דקה קטנה כשרה ה' ק(אפיקעס); ומן דקה קטנה טריפה גימל קאפיקעס; גם מן עופות ואווזים א' קאפיקע.

גם הארנדי מן הכרות דפה קהילתינו שייך נ"כ להרב הנ"ל ... ואסור לשום אדם דפה למכור נרות הן ליהודים הן לגויים, גם סדר קדושין וסדר גיטין וסדר חליצה הכל שייך לו וחלילה אסור לשום אדם לסדר גט או קדושין הן בקהילתינו הן בהכפרים שסביבותינו בלתי ידיעתו גם מחויבים אנחנו ליתן לו בכל ערב יום כפור מן תשעה ר"ת גם מכל סוכות סך שלושה ר"ת גם כל הכתבים (ז) מכל דבר שבעיר וגם קניינים הכל שייך לו גם הוספנו להרב הנ"ל סך חמשה ועשרים ר"ת לשנה זולת עתה גם הארנדארים מהכפרים שסביבותינו מחויבים ליתן לו מכל אלף והובים סך אר"ח כל זה עשינו וקבלנו עלינו בחיוב גמור בדעה אחת ובהסכמה אחת דלא השנאה ודלא ... בכל ימי חייו תיותו עד מאה ועשרים שנים ולהיות ביד הרב דקהילתינו הנ"ל לעדות ולראיה ולמזכרת באנו כולנו עה"ח בחי ממש.

היום גימל שנכפל בו כי טוב ב"ן אדר דהאי שתא תקצ"א לפ"ק פה ק"ק קאלניבלאט.

נאום... נאום... נאום...

Figure 43
Letter of appointment of his grandson Rabbi Eliyahu Pinchas

Table 32
AN ENLIGHTENMENT PHILOSOPHER AND SOME CHASIDIC SAGES

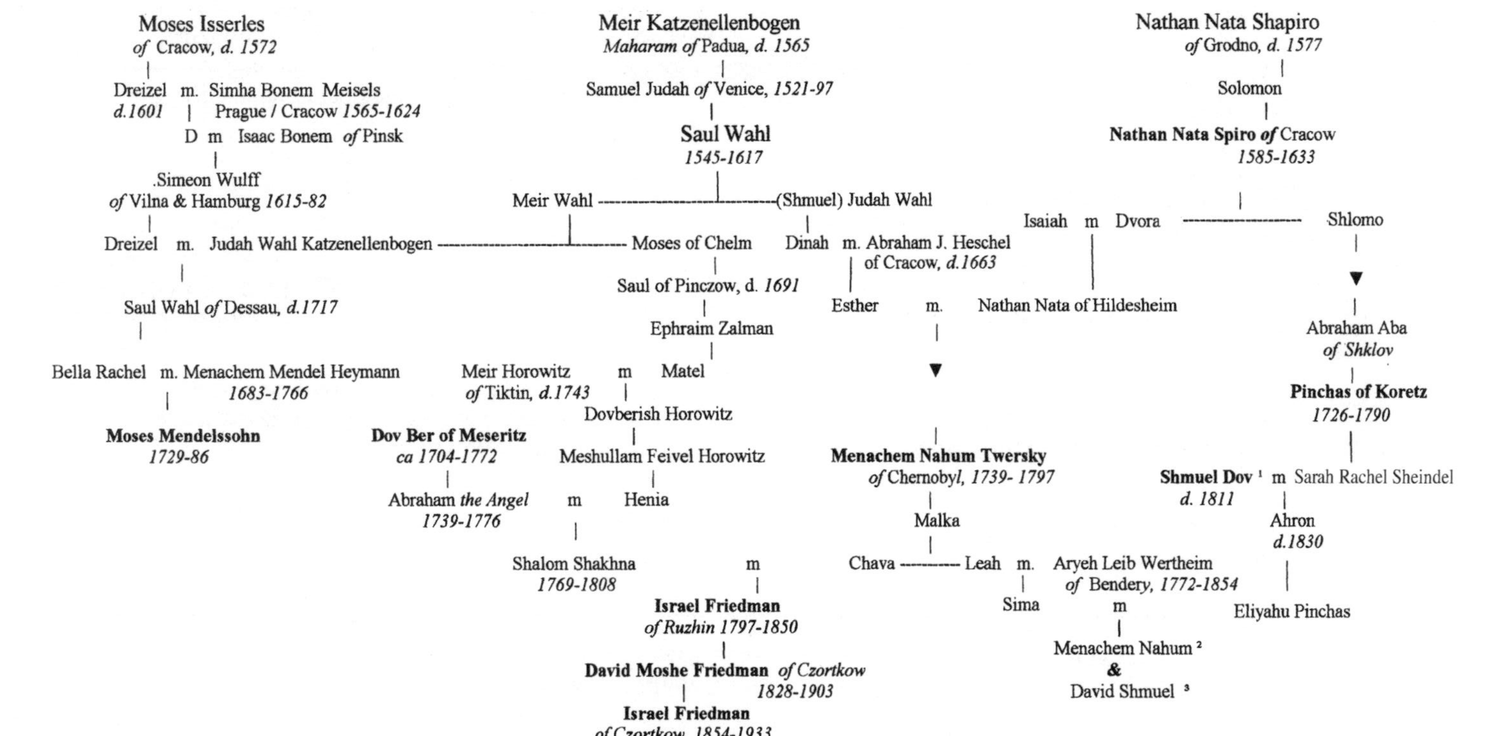

Notes

1. Son of R. Mordecai and grandson of Moses Gelles of Brody
2. Father of Abraham Isaac Polonsky, 1851–1900, fifth generation Rabbi of Kolibolet and surrounding area
3. Father of Levi Isaac of Nigrest whose branch was also linked by marriage to the lines from Levi Isaac of Berdichev, 1740–1810 and Meir of Przemyslany, 1780–1850. A line from Moses Gelles of Brody led to R. Nahum Uri Gelles, 1852–1934, who had a Czortkow connection. His grandson, Ahron Leib Gelles, was descended through his mother from Meir of Przemyslany.

Table 33
A GELLES–FRIEDMAN–SHAPIRO CONNECTION

Nathan Nata, *Av Beth Din* of Hildesheim, a grandson of Nathan Nata Spiro of Cracow married Esther, a daughter of Abraham Joshua Heschel of Cracow and a great-granddaughter of Saul Wahl. Their descendant was Menachem Nahum Twersky of Chernobyl (1739–97), whose wife's ancestor was Nathan Nata of Grodno, a grandfather of Nathan Nata Spiro.

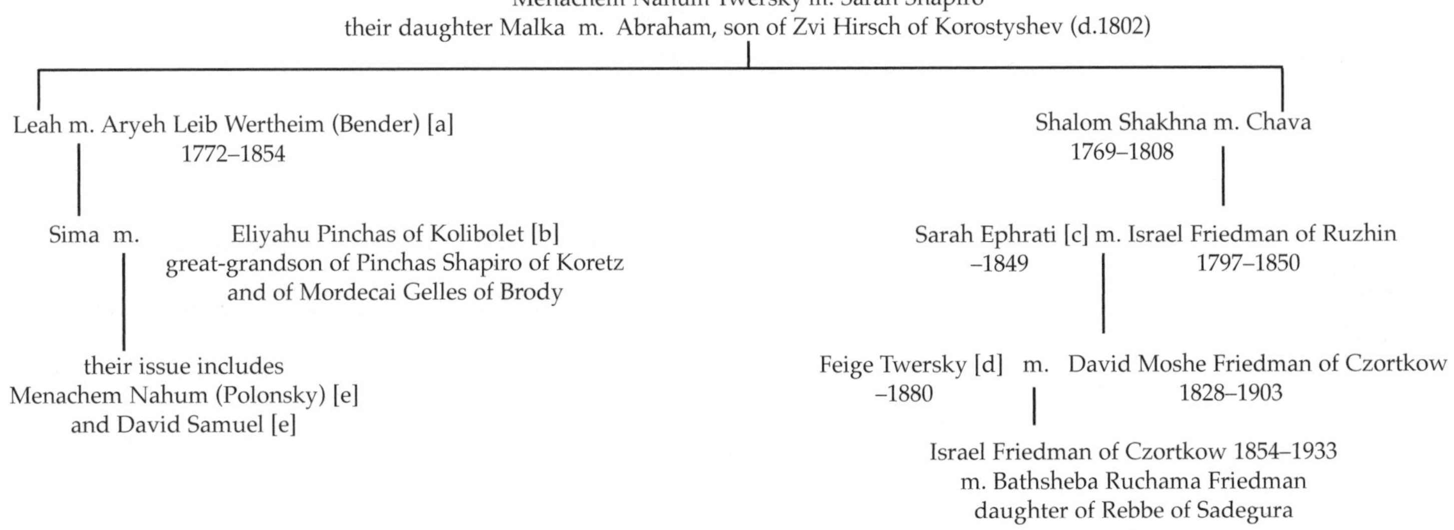

Notes

[a] Aryeh Leib Wertheim became Rabbi of Bendery in 1814
[b] son of Ahron, s, of Shmuel Dov, s. of Mordecai Gelles, s. of Moses Gelles of Brody
[c] daughter of Rabbi Moshe Ephrati, head of the Berdichev Yeshivah
[d] great grand-daughter of Menachem Nahum Twersky
[e] the lines from Eliyahu Pinchas through his sons Menachem Nahum Polonsky and David Samuel have marriage connections back to Levi Isaac of Berdichev (1740–1810)

Table 34
DESCENDANTS OF LEVI ISAAC OF BERDICHEV AND ELIYAHU PINCHAS (GELLES) OF KOLIBOLET

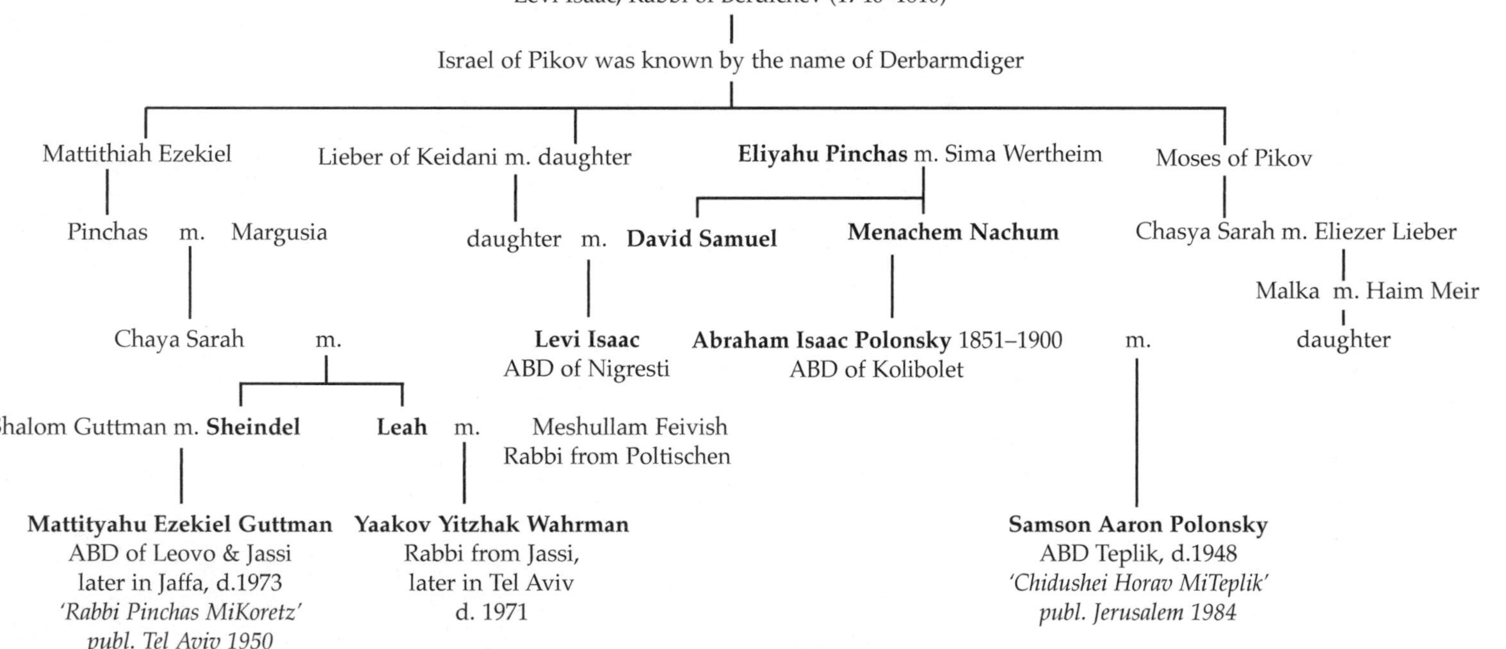

Eliyahu Pinchas, son of Ahron (d.1830), son of Shmuel Dov (d.1811), son of Mordecai, son of Moses Gelles of Brody.
Five generations from Shmuel Dov (Gelles) to Abraham Isaac (Polonsky) were ABD's of Kolibolet, Zvemgorod, Tolna, Shpola and Kalerka.
Shmuel Dov married Sarah Rachel Sheindel, daughter of Rabbi Pinchas of Koretz (1726–90) and there are several other Shapiro connections.
Eliyahu Pinchas married Sima, daughter of Aryeh Leib Wertheim, Admur of Bendery (1772–1854).
Sources include Neil Rosenstein, *The Unbroken Chain* (New York, London, Jerusalem: CIS Publishers, 1990), pp.291, 1184, 1185; Yaakov Yitzhak Wahrman, *Sefer Yuchasin* [www.pikholz.org/Families/Wahrman].

CHAPTER THIRTY-SIX

Gelles Rabbinical Ancestry

Links to ancient families and the great rabbis of the past

A JOURNEY OF DISCOVERY

The trail that is gradually revealing our ancient rabbinical ancestry began in Vienna. My father, Dr David Gelles (1883–1964), was an advocate in that city. He was the second son of R' Nahum Uri Gelles (1852–1934) of Solotvina near Stanislau. My grandfather's tombstone in Vienna and the Jewish community records pointed to a family connection with Brody in Austrian Galicia. The births and other details of my father and grandfather can also be found in Galician records.[1]

A hint of our ancestry came from the entries in the standard reference works on the Galician Rabbinate. It appeared that my great-grandfather R' David Isaac Gellis (ca.1790–1870) studied at Glina and that we were descended from R' Shmuel Helman of Metz via his son R' Moshe of Glogau.[2] There is documentary evidence to support the traditional view that Shmuel Helman's father was the Halpern son-in-law of Chief Rabbi Nathan Nata Spiro of Cracow. While this view is not uncontested, the evidence for a close Halpern connection is persuasive.[3] The Memorial Book of Glina gave some further details about my great-grandfather. It also contained other information about the town's rabbis, the significance of which emerged at a later stage.[4]

The discovery of David Isaac's tombstone in Brody revealed his father's name as R' Moses Gelles.[5] My researches continued to focus on Brody. In the middle of the eighteenth century this town had one of the largest Jewish communities in Europe. The old cemetery and many relevant documents have vanished. A fragment of the records of its Beth Din covering the years from 1808 to 1817 has survived.[6] So have the transcriptions of tombstones by Dr N.M. Gelber, which are preserved in the Jerusalem archives and were partially published in the Brody Memorial Book.[7] A project of cataloguing the extant tombstones in the 'new' cemetery is currently under way.[8]

A great amount of material pertaining to Brody is housed in the Lviv archives. This includes birth, marriage and death, as well as property records from the late-eighteenth century onwards. An analysis of the house numbers and the names of their occupants over several generations made it possible to construct a partial family tree. My great-great-grandfather R' Moshe was the grandson of Menachem Mendel Levush, known as Moses Gelles, who married a daughter of a Rabbi S. Gelles of Brody. Mordecai Gelles was a *mechutan* [in-law] of R' Pinchas Shapiro of Koretz (1726–91). The latter's daughter, Sarah Rachel Sheindel, is stated to have 'married Rabbi Shmuel, son of R' Mordecai, son of R' Moses Gelles, one of the scholars of the Brody Klaus, whose epitaph refers to him as *Moses the Servant of God*'.[9]

Mordecai's brothers included Joseph Gelles and Michel Levush. The issue of that generation were known variously by the names of Gelles and Levush. Details of these studies are to be found in preceding chapters and several published articles.[10] The Levush epithet very probably recalls descent from Mordecai Yaffe of Prague and the title of that Rabbi's magnum opus *The Levushim* or Rabbinical Robes of Learning. Within our line of pious and learned men, who were mostly rabbis in Brody, Glina and other small Galician towns, there were some hints of past glory. Tombstones referred to descent from Moses Gelles, scholar of the famous Brody *Klaus* or to a 'distinguished lineage', and there were references in the literature to others of our name as 'descended from great rabbis'.[11]

While it has been possible to trace the Gelles line in Brody to the beginning of the eighteenth century in spite of ambiguities of names, epithets and sobriquets, an extension to earlier times posed challenges that called for a different methodology. The rabbinic literature then became the main source for clues to ancestors who did not necessarily carry the matronymic by which the family was later known.

Gelles are recorded in Prague in the seventeenth and eighteenth centuries and there are hints that these may have originally come from Frankfurt. There was a well-marked migration from the Rhineland to Prague and then to Cracow and points further east, as for example in the family of R' David Gans of Prague (1541–1613). Gans was a first cousin of R' Nathan Nata Shapiro of Grodno.[12]

Eisenstadt in the Burgenland was the home of rabbis bearing the Gelles name in the nineteenth century. Some were most probably kinsfolk of the Brody line and are found side by side with the descendants of Moshe of Glogau, whose daughter Chana married Yechiel Michal Segal, son of Asher Lemel Halevi, ABD of Glogau and Eisenstadt.[13] There were Gelles in Vienna and elsewhere in the Austro-Hungarian Empire at that time. Rabbis of our name were in Krotoschin in German Poland at a later date, having moved there from Lithuania.[14]

URI FEIVUSH OF VILNA

A search for patterns in marriages and for patterns of personal and town names within ancestral lines proved particularly fruitful when applied to connections in Lithuania. Among the earliest Chief Rabbis of Vilna were R'

David and his son R' Uri Feivush. The latter went to Jerusalem in his old age around the year 1650 and became Nasi of the Ashkenazi community. The grandsons of Uri Feivush Ashkenazi, as he was known in the Holy Land, included Uri Feivush of Vilna, Isaac of Siemiatycze, and Gershon Vilner of Shklov. R' Isaac of Siemiatycze was the progenitor of a Lithuanian rabbinical line bearing the Gelles name. It is not clear whether Isaac's son Shmuel Gell(i)es, the ABD of Siemiatycze, is identical with the Rabbi S. Gelles whose daughter married Menachem Mendel of Brody.

R'Gershon Vilner had links with the family of R' Yissachar Ber of Cracow and his wife Roza Yollis. Yissachar Ber was President of the Council of the four Lands and a son of the Chief Rabbi Abraham Joshua Heschel of Cracow. There are complex links between the line of Uri Feivush of Vilna and the Heshel-Babad and Yollis lines. Yissachar Ber's brother-in-law Israel ben Mordecai Yollis, otherwise known as Israel Swincher, played a prominent role in the Council of the Four Lands. He was the father-in-law of Rabbi Simcha Hakohen Rapaport.[15]

SHMUEL HELMAN OF METZ

The name of Uri Feivush also occurs in later generations in the Silesian towns of Krotoschin and Glogau and hints at a connection with R' Shmuel Helman, the Chief Rabbi of Mannheim and Metz, who married into a wealthy family in Glogau. One of his sons was called Uri Feivush and a grandson, Naftali Hirsch Katzenellenbogen, was the son-in-law of a Feivel of Glogau.[16]

RAPAPORT CONNECTIONS

Simcha Rapaport's sons included Chaim Rapaport, who became Chief Rabbi of Lvov. His wife Miriam was a descendant of Mordecai Yaffe and Shlomo Luria. Chaim's brother Nachman Rapaport of Vaskiai married a daughter of David Katvan. She was probably a granddaughter of Shabbatai Katz and hence a descendant of Moses Isserles. Nachman ben Chaim Rapaport was a Rabbi of Glina. Isaac ben Uri, who died in 1759, had also been a Rabbi at Glina and was married to a Rapaport. According to his Brody tombstone he was a descendant of Moses Isserles.[17] These two Rabbis of Glina come into the tapestry of our family connections as outlined in Chapter 34.

MOSES ISSERLES

A link between Rabbi Isaac ben Uri of Glina and Brody and the later Gelles line does not have the backing of primary source material but a marriage of Isaac's daughter to Mordecai Gelles has a certain degree of plausibility. The marriages made by Mordecai's sons Shmuel Dov and Moses fit into the theory and so do the name and location of the latter's son, my great-grandfather Rabbi David Isaac Gellis, who studied at Glina and is buried in Brody. Isaac ben Uri's Rapaport connection at first suggested a descent from Moses Isserles via Rabbi Shabbatai Katz and Yente Leah Meisels, but the various dates did not fit.

A different Meisels connection came to light through the serendipitous discovery of an old text published in 1699 by Rabbi Shmuel Delugatch, who claimed Isserles descent through his father Rabbi Moshe of Grodno, the son of Uri Delugatch, the ABD of Satanov.[18] Shmuel Delugatch refers to his uncle Rabbi Aryeh Leib, known as Leib Chasid, the ABD of Lvov and Przemysl, and the latter's brother Rabbi Uri, ABD of Bodki. Rabbi Leib Chasid was born in Ludmir around 1640, became a member of the Four Lands Council, was appointed Rabbi of Przemysl in 1691 and died there in 1694. He was the son of R. Moshe Meisels of Ludmir and Lvov, who was a son of a son of R. Simcha Bonem Meisels, husband of Dreizel Isserles, daughter of the *Rema*.[19] Rabbi Uri of Bodki may well have been the father of the Rabbi Isaac of Glina who is claimed as a possible ancestor of the later Gelles line.

SHAPIRO AND FRIEDMAN

Moses Gelles of Brody was the progenitor of my immediate line and he was also the grandfather of Shmuel Dov, the son-in-law of R' Pinchas Shapiro of Koretz, a direct descendant of Nathan Nata Spiro of Cracow. A letter of appointment issued in 1793 speaks of Shmuel Dov as the son of R' Mordecai (son of Moses Gelles) and son-in-law of the 'royal wonder of our generation, the holy flame ... the Rabbi Pinchas of Shepetivka'. The great Rabbi Pinchas moved from Koretz to Shepetivka where he died in 1790 (see Chapter 35).

My father's obituary in a Viennese journal in 1964 asserted that we had a connection with the Friedmans of Czortkow.[20] I knew that my grandfather was a follower of R' Israel Friedman who died in Vienna in 1933. Our family and the Friedmans had some common ancestors and our cousins from the marriage between Shmuel Dov and Rachel Scheindel Shapiro shared with the Friedmans a connection from Menachem Nahum Twersky, who was also descended from Saul Wahl and Nathan Nata Spiro of Cracow.

R' Yehuda Meir Shapira (1887–1934), a descendant of Pinchas Shapiro in the direct male line through five generations, was a scholar, community leader, member of the Polish Parliament, educator and founder of the Lublin Sages Yeshivah.[21] His association with our family has emerged quite recently.

An entry in a Galician newspaper, *der Neuer Morgen Tagblatt* of 26 December 1934 read 'Solotwina has still not appointed a successor to the late R' Nachum Uri Gelles. Several factions have developed within the town ... One faction says that the old Rabbi's grandson should be appointed but there are very many who oppose this suggestion'.[22] According to the

Solotwina entry in *Pinkas Hakehilot,* my grandfather occupied the position of head of the rabbinical court until his death, and was succeeded in that post by R'Yoel Babad.[23] So who was this Yoel Babad and who was the 'grandson of the old Rabbi' mentioned in the newspaper?

The first question was not difficult to answer. The descendants of Isaac Krakower were generally known as Babad but some were also called by the name of their grandmother's family of Yollis, as for example Mordecai Yollis aka Mordecai Babad. His brother Jacob Babad who died in 1748 was the progenitor of several lines, including one at Mikulince and Podwoloczysca that included Yoel Babad, the last Rabbi of Solotwina.[24] Records of births, deaths and marriages and a nineteenth-century subscription list for a rabbinical work indicate the repeated occurrence of the Gelles name in these two towns.[25]

The answer to the second question came seemingly out of the blue. A list of students at Meir Shapira's Lublin Yeshiva appended to the Rabbi's book *Imrei Da'at* gave the name of Joseph Gelles, son of R' Efraim Fischel Gelles of Solotwina.[26] R' Ephraim Fischl (Philip) was the eldest son of my grandfather Nahum Uri. He was born in 1879 and died at a young age, perhaps during, or just after, the First World War. He and his siblings, including my father David, were fifth generation descendants of Moses Gelles.

Joseph Gelles was indeed the last of our rabbinical line. He may perhaps have been born to Efraim Fischel by a second wife some time after family contacts had been severed. Nahum Uri's wife Esther died in 1907, and some children emigrated to America or joined the process of assimilation in Vienna before the outbreak of the Great War. Joseph may have been too young for the vacant post in 1934 and probably perished in the holocaust. The mystery will not be solved until some further family records come to hand. R' Meir Shapira, who had taken Joseph Gelles under his wing, was not only a direct descendant of Pinchas Shapiro. The family connection goes further than that. He had been Rabbi of Glina where my great-grandfather David Isaac Gelles had studied at the beginning of the nineteenth century, and he was an ardent follower of the Rebbe of Czortkow like my grandfather.

Discovery of Joseph Gelles was followed by an equally remarkable rediscovery of his brother. A dinner was held in New York on 7 December 2003 to commemorate the seventieth anniversary of the death of Rabbi Israel Friedman of Czortkow and the centenary of the death of his father Rabbi David Moshe. The published programme carried a memorial for the soul of Ahron Leib Gelles of Lemberg and Vienna, of the old generation of Czortkow Chasidim, who died in New York in 1973. The programme led me finally to this missing cousin Leo and to his mother's family, the Leifers of Nadworna, who cared for Leo in his declining years. The Leifers are descendants of the saintly Rabbi Meir of Przemyslany (Chapter 35).

BABAD

The Babad family's genealogy is outlined in Dr Neil Rosenstein's *The Unbroken Chain*. Isaac Krakower's son, Mordecai Yollis Babad of Brody, was a prominent and wealthy Rabbi who acted as treasurer and secretary of the Council of the Four Lands. His sons included Israel Levitzer and Menachem Mendel of Brody. Rosenstein places Mordecai Yollis' death in 1743 and has his wife as a daughter of Jacob Shor, possibly relying on a letter from Josef Lewinstein of Serok. Other sources have Mordecai's wife as the daughter of R' Saul Katzenellenbogen of Pinczow [1617–93] and his second wife Yente Shor. According to Gelber's tombstone transcriptions Mordecai Yollis died in 1752. That is also the year given in David Wurm's book on the Babad genealogy that includes details of Mordecai's wife and children. Their son Menachem Mendel and his wife Frejda died in 1756 and 1757. Some of Mendel's approbations are mentioned in the literature. The identities of a possible first wife of Mordecai Yollis Babad and of Menachem Mendel's wife remain obscure.

Mordecai Babad's daughter Malka (died 1783) was the second wife of Yacov Charif ABD of Leshnov (whose first wife was a daughter of the Chacham Zvi Hirsch Ashkenazi). Yaacov was a son of Moses Phineas Charif (died 1702), the notable Chief Rabbi of Lvov, and his wife Gele Rapaport, who was a great-granddaughter of Saul Wahl. Moses Charif's father was Israel Charif. According to the published chart in David Wurm's work, Israel Charif was a son-in-law of Isaac Krakower. It thus appears that Mordecai Yollis Babad was the father-in-law and great-uncle of Yaacov Charif.[27]

HALPERN (HEILPRIN)

The identification of the father of Shmuel Helman of Metz was discussed in Chapter 33. Helman's son-in-law Eliezer Katzenellenbogen of Bamberg and Hagenau had a Halpern mother. Her father and Israel Halpern were blood cousins. It has recently been brought to my attention that an approbation of a book by R' Benjamin ben Saul Katzenellenbogen of Krotoschin written by R' Shmuel Helman refers to his erstwhile pupil Benjamin as belonging to his father's family.[28] The marriages of the Helman family with Katzenellenbogens support the Halpern connection of Shmuel Helman of Metz. Other Halpern connections include the in-laws of Shmuel Dov Gelles and his descendants, Rabbis Abraham Heilprin of Sudilkov and Israel Nachman Heilprin of Brzezany (see Table 36 and Notes 5–7 in Chapter 35).

Abraham Halpern of the Stanislau Halperns, who became a member of the *Reichstag*, the Austrian Parliament, married Nechama, a daughter of Rabbi Enzel Zausmer of Stryj, son of Menachem Nahum Zausmer. Enzel's sister was the mother of Efraim Fischel Horowitz, ABD of Munkacz (see under Horowitz and Note 45).

KLOISNER AND LOEW

R' David Tebele of Lissa, the son of Chief Rabbi Nathan Nata of Brody, wrote that he was a cousin of many notable eighteenth-century rabbis such as Ezekiel Landau of Prague and Zvi Hirsch Zamosc of Hamburg and that his grandfather R' Gershon Vilner of Shklov was a kinsman of Israel Swincher.[29] As for possible connections with the family of Judah Loew of Prague, a measure of uncertainty remains surrounding the family tree of one of the most famous rabbinical families. Genealogists such as Rabbi Englard have questioned the very existence of the elder Zacharya Mendel Kloisner and have cast doubt on a connection between Judah Loew of Prague, *der Hohe Rabbi Loew,* and Aryeh Leib Fischls of Cracow who was known as *der Hoicher Rebbe Leib*.[30]

The broader picture is indicated in Table 38. A grandson of Uri Feivush of Vilna was Gershon Vilner of Shklov. He was the father-in-law of Nathan Nata, the *ABD* of Brody. The latter's ancestry as given by at least three separate descendants as well as several other sources differs in several important details, but essentially the line goes back via Zacharya Mendel of Belz to Aryeh Leib Fischls of Cracow to Zacharyah Mendel 'the prophet' to Rabbi Benjamin of Posen known as Beinish Reb Mendels, and to Zacharya Mendel Kloisner Hazaken, believed to have been a brother-in-law of the Maharal.[31] From David Tebele Lissa and his siblings there are lines of descent to the nineteenth century writer David Tebele Efrati and the twentieth century Chief Rabbi of St Petersburg, David Tebele Katzenellenbogen. A connection with the Chayes family comes through the marriage of David Tebele's sister to R' Isaac Chayes of Brody (see Table 31).[32]

YOLLIS AND CHALFAN

The marriage of Roza Yollis and Yissachar Ber of Cracow gave rise to many children and some important links to various family lines. Roza Yollis was the daughter of Mordecai Yollis of Cracow and Teibel, daughter of Moshe Halevi Yollis. The latter was related by marriage to Isaiah Halevi Horowitz. Mordecai Yollis of Cracow was a son of Yechiel Chalfan, son of Yitzchak of Vienna, son of Yechiel, son of Eliyahu Menachem Chalfan of Venice, Rabbi and *Magister Artium et Medicinae,* who married Fioret, daughter of Kalonymos ben David. Kalonymos forebears had been in Italy, Provence and Germany since the tenth century or even earlier. Elias Menachem was a distinguished scholar and friend of Pietro Aretino. He was a member of the Rabbinical Court that was asked to give an opinion on the question of Henry VIII's divorce. His parents were the astronomer Abba Mari Delmedigo Chalfan and the daughter of Joseph Colon, who was known as the *Maharik of Mantua*. He was the most prominent Italian Rabbi of his time. His father was Shlomo Trabot, who came to Italy from France and whose ancient family often bore the name of Zarfati. The family history of the

Chalfans is bounded by the expulsions of Jews from Provence, to successive local difficulties in Venice, Prague and Vienna, and the general expulsion from that city in 1670. In the immediately preceding period there were marriage alliances between Chalfans and Heschels. Elias ben Abba Mari Chalfan (1561–1624) married Rebecca Heschel. The Chief Rabbi of Vienna, Chaim Menachem Man, was of the Chalfan family and an uncle of Mordecai Yollis of Cracow.[33]

LANDAU

Zvi Hirsch Witeles Landau and Eleazar of Dubno were the fathers of Judah and Chaya, the parents of Ezekiel Landau (1713–93). This Chief Rabbi of Prague was known as the *Noda B'yehuda* from the title of his book. Gershon Vilner was a brother-in-law of Hirsch Witeles and Gershon's grandson, Rabbi David Tebele of Lissa, was a cousin of Ezekiel Landau. Shmuel Helman of Metz appears to have been a blood relation of Ezekiel as well as his *mechutan*.[34] There may be a Landau connection to the marriage of R. Abraham Jonah (Gelles) of Brody and Chaya, daughter of R. Henoch Reich. R. Isaac Reich, son of Jonah Reich, married a daughter of Jacob Simcha Landau, ABD of Apt, and her sister Toybe was the wife of R. Naftali Herz Ettinge, ABD of Lvov.[35]

ALTSCHULER

A different perspective on our ancestral background emerges from a consideration of Shapiro descent through the female line. Rosa Eberles (Alvares) was the wife of Chief Rabbi Nathan Nata Spiro of Cracow. She came from a Provençal family of Sephardic origin. The family of R' Abraham Eberles, are believed to have brought stones of their destroyed synagogue with them to Bohemia and incorporated them in the construction of the Prague synagogue from which they took their new name of Altschuler. They were closely related to the Chayot or Chayes, who in the person of Rabbi Isaac Chayes, Chief Rabbi of Prague and brother-in-law of Rabbi Judah Loew, attained prominence during the sixteenth century. Moshe Altschuler, or Moshe ben Abraham Eberls Altschul, married Chana Treivish, daughter of the Alsatian Rabbi Eliezer Treves, thus joining two venerable lines going back to Rashi of Troyes in the eleventh century. The year 1542 saw one of the numerous periodical expulsions of the Jews from Prague. Altschuler foresaw the coming troubles and managed to escape with his possessions to Cracow, where he became one of the leading members of the community.[36]

Table 44 shows how Shmuel Helman's supposed Halpern-Shapiro descent through the female line could relate him to many important rabbis, but there are disagreements between recognized authorities concerning several links.

FISCHL AND MARGOSHES

In the later fifteenth century, Efraim Fischl Ashkenazi left Frankfurt and found his way to Cracow via Nuremberg and Prague. His descendants included bankers and physicians to Polish Kings and a Chief Rabbi of Cracow. Zvi Hirsch Fischl, who died in 1626, was the son of Efraim Fischl ABD of Brisk, whose wife was a daughter of the famous Rabbi Shlomo Luria of Lublin, known as the *Maharshal*. In the next generation, R' Efraim Fischl of Lvov became President of the Council of the Four Lands and Nasi in the Holy Land. He died in 1653. His daughter Jutta married Rabbi Aryeh Leib (Fischls) ABD Cracow known as *der Hoiche Rebbe Leib* (d. 1671). From R' Efraim Fischl of Lvov there is a line of descent to Rabbi Eliezer Margoshes (1730–1807), the last scribe and trustee of the Council of the Four Lands, his son Josef Margoshes (1770–1840) and then to Aryeh Shmuel Margoshes (1814–1880), who was the father of Joseph Eliezer Margoshes (1867–1955). According to this well-known journalist and author, the Margoshes came originally from Spain and were then in Opatow for a long time before going to Brody, Lemberg, Nadworna and Jassi. The Margoshes and Gelles were connected by marriage (see Chapters 29 and 30 for details from the Brody Beth Din Records) and their family lines touched in the distant past.[37]

HAKOHEN

Michel Levush (Gelles) married Feige, a daughter of Rabbi Joshua Heschel Hakohen of Brody, who was probably a member of the Heschel Hakohen family descended from a son-in-law of Rabbi Abraham Joshua Heschel of Cracow. There are links with the Fraenkels of Brody and Przeworsk (see below). The Heschel Hakohen genealogy is to be found in Moses Hakohen' *Assifat Hakohen* and elsewhere.[38] Some of its connections are shown in Table 45.

ZUNDEL RAMRAZ

Tables 26 and 27 show that Mordecai Levush married Sarah Bathya [Bassie], who was a daughter of Rabbi Yehuda Zundel of Brody. The city's vital records give her death in 1826 and that of her son R. Moshe Levush aka Gelles in 1851.[39]

Rabbi Yehuda Leib Zundel Ramraz (d.1804) was a scholar of the Brody Klaus, as indeed was his grandfather, R.Ahron Zelig ben Yehuda Zundel Segal (d.1731). The younger Zundel was called Ramraz after his father, Rabbi Moshe Reb Zelig's of Brody. The latter was the son of Rabbi Todros, a descendant of the famous Abulafia family of scholars, poets and courtiers that flourished in thirteenth- and fourteenth-century Spain. Rabbi

Zundel's wife is given by some sources as Malka, the daughter of R.Yehuda Leib Bick, and by others as (perhaps secondly) Frieda, daughter of R. Yitzchak of Sokol, a descendant of Judah Loew of Prague, Shlomo Luria, Yoel Sirkes and Moses Isserles. Rabbi Yehuda Zundel Ramraz was the grandfather of Moshe, a descendant of Moses Gelles of Brody, of Shalom Rokeach, the founder of this great Chasidic dynasty, and of the latter's wife Malka.[40] There are also connections between the Rokeach and the Brodsky family from Brody, who were of Shor descent. The descendants of Israel Brodsky were among the richest Jews in nineteenth-century Russia and largely instrumental in the development of the sugar industry in that country.[41]

FRAENKEL

Many Jews who came to Poland from Germany centuries ago adopted the name of Fraenkel to indicate their country of origin.[42] A family that settled in Przeworsk had kinsfolk in Grodno and spread to other towns such as Rzeszow in western and Brody in eastern Galicia. Later they were also found in Sanok and Linsk. One of the branches bore their old name of Engelhard. Some of them also carried epithets such as *Reisher* (coming from Rzeszow) or *Pashawer* (from Przeworsk). They produced a number of notable rabbis including Abraham Zeev Wolf Fraenkel (ca. 1780–1849), author of *Meshiv Kahalacha*, who was Dayan at Brody before becoming ABD of Przeworsk. His first wife was a descendant of Rabbi Shmuel Shmelke Horowitz of Nikolsburg and he married secondly a daughter of the Brody Rabbi David Nathanson. Abraham Zeev Wolf Fraenkel was a son of R' Benjamin of Linsk and Rzeszow, described as a wealthy man of good lineage. The latter's uncle Shmuel, ABD of Grodno, was the father of R' Dov Ber of Kolomea and R' Leib of Brody. Another R' Dov Ber, son of Benjamin's brother Moshe of Przeworsk, was the father of Rabbi Meir Shlomo Fraenkel of Brody who married a daughter of R' Josef, son of Moses Gelles. The Brody Beth Din Records for the period 1808–17 also refer to the wealthy Finkel, a sister of Meir Fraenkel and wife of Reb Wolf Bolechower, who sold one of her many synagogue seats to make a trust in memory of the late Feige, daughter of Rabbi Yoshua Heschel Hakohen and wife of R' Michel Levush, son of Moses Gelles (see Chapter 30). Evidently the branches using the names of Levush and/or Gelles formed a close-knit family in that period.[43] Meir Fraenkel's first cousins included Blume Engelhard-Fraenkel, daughter of Nathan Pashawer Fraenkel, who married Yakov Shaya Loew, the head of the Sedziszow family, who were later connected through a Wahl marriage to my mother's people (see Chapter 11 and Table 46).

HOROWITZ

This Fraenkel family had a number of connections with the Horowitz rabbis, including the Sedziszow and Bolechow lines. Rabbi Yehuda Aaron Fraenkel of Brody (see R' Leib of Brody above) was the father-in-law of Rabbi Jakob Jokel Horowitz, ABD of Bolechow and the grandfather of Rabbi Yehuda Aaron Horowitz. The latter's career led from Bolechow to Solotwina and ultimately to the Rabbinate of Saniawitz and Mihaileni in the Bukowina.[44] The post thus vacated by Yehuda Aaron Horowitz at Solotwina passed to Rabbi Zvi Aryeh Weinstein, who in turn was succeeded in 1884 by his son-in-law, my grandfather, Rabbi Nahum Uri Gelles (see Chapters 27 and 28 and Table 25).

Yehuda Aaron's half-brother Efraim Fischel Horowitz of Munkacz had connections with Rohatyn near Narayow where my grandfather was born. Nahum Uri named his eldest son Efraim Fischel and sent his second son to study at the Munkacz Yeshiva. From the late-eighteenth century the Horowitz family had such influence over rabbinical appointments in the area of Galicia immediately round Stanislau that rabbis not bearing their name would as likely as not be related to the family. It is thus quite possible that my paternal great-grandfathers, Rabbis David Isaac Gellis and Zvi Aryeh Weinstein had connections to these two Horowitz half brothers, as suggested in Tables 47 and 48.[45]

Efraim Fischel Horowitz of Munkacz was doubly descended from Judah Loew's daughter Vögele and Isaac Katz of Prague. The rabbinical Katz (Kohen-Zedek) family linked Judah Loew via Horowitz and Zausmer lines to the parents of Efraim Fischel Horowitz, as shown in Table 49.

CONCLUSION

Birth, marriage, death and property records, tombstone inscriptions, and a fragment of the Brody Beth Din records provide a basis for the construction of the Gelles rabbinical family tree from the beginning of the eighteenth century to the eve of the Second World War. The extension of the line from eighteenth-century Brody to earlier times relies on a variety of literary sources and on name patterns extending over a considerable period. Further evidence on a number of crucial links is needed before my Gelles line can be put firmly on the millennial map of European Jewry. There is no doubt however that a line of rabbis, who were well respected but little known outside their communities, had formed numerous distinguished connections over the centuries. The ghosts of many famous rabbis stand in the wings. Emerging from the mists of time is an outline of the thousand-year odyssey that has taken my family across the continent of Europe.

The Council of the Four Lands

Many of the rabbis mentioned in this chapter were associated with the Council of Four Lands. This was the name of the semi-autonomous governing body of Polish Jewry for about two hundred years until 1764. Its authority covered the lands of Great Poland (with its centre at Posen), Little Poland (Cracow), Polish or Red Russia including Galicia and Podolia (Lemberg), and Volhynia (Ostrog or Kremenetz). Lithuania had its separate Council from 1623. The Great Council comprised the leading Rabbis and Elders of the important kahals. The total membership varied from around 20 to 25. They would meet twice a year on fair days at Lublin and Yaroslav and sometimes elsewhere. In later days the meetings were once a year and became more irregular. The Council fulfilled judicial and tax-raising functions and represented the Jewish communities vis-à-vis the Polish Diet-the Sejm- and the King. In state documents the Council would be referred to as *Congressus Judaicus* and its members as *seniores* and *doctores judaeorum*. The Council officers included President, Treasurer and Secretary. The great rabbis exercised their functions as judges, teachers and community leaders. Through the Council they acquired a leading political role. After the partitions of Poland in the later-eighteenth century, political direction of Jewish affairs necessarily became fragmented. The records of the Council of the Four Lands (Pinkas Vaad Arba Aratzoth) from 1580 to 1764 have been collected and edited with notes by Israel Halpern (Jerusalem: 1945).

Titles for community heads in Ashkenaz included Manhig and Parnas. The title of Nasi or Prince was at different times bestowed on heads of certain substantial communities in the Holy Land and other countries in the East and also in Spain and Provence. Chief Rabbis appointed by communities were heads of the rabbinical court (Av Beth Din) to which the headship of the rabbinical school (Rosh Yeshiva) was usually subordinate but sometimes combined with the office of Av Beth Din in the person of the Chief Rabbi (see the Glossary for these and other community titles).

NOTES

1. Vienna, Israelitische Kultusgemeinde, Wien 1010, Seitenstettengasse 4. Dr David Isaac Gelles, born Kudrynce, Galicia 24 December 1883, died Vienna 20 August 1964, buried in the Jewish Section of the Vienna Central Cemetery [T4/0200/001/021]. Rabbi Nahum Uri Gelles, born Narayow, Galicia 18 February 1852 and died Vienna 18 November 1934. His tombstone in the Central Cemetery [T4/21/16/27] describes him as Rabbi of Solotwina near Stanislau of a family from Brody (see Register of Births 1823–95 at Melnitsa–Podolskaya and Register of Births 1839–69 at Narayow).

2. Natan Zvi Friedman, *Otzar Harabbanim* (Bnei Brak, Israel: 1973). R' Moshe Helman of Glogau is stated to have been in Glina ca. 1780, Shmuel Noach Gottlieb, *Ohalei Shem* (Pinsk: 1912), pp.261–2:

   > Rabbi Nahum Uri Gelles was the descendant of Rabbi Moshe, ABD of Glina, who was a son of the Gaon Rabbi Shmuel Hillman, ABD of Metz, who was in turn son of Yisrael Heilprin of blessed memory, the head of the rabbinical court of Krotoschin (the son-in-law of the author of *Megaleh Amukot*) who in turn was the son of Rabbi Lipman of blessed memory, son of the Gaon who wrote *Ahavat Zion*, the R"M of Lvov of blessed memory [Moses Ashkenazi Halpern].

   Cf. Meir Wunder, *Meorei Galicia* (Jerusalem: Institute for the Commemoration of Galician Jewry, 1978 *et seq.*), Vol.1, p.699.
3. E. Gelles, 'Rabbi Shmuel Helman of Metz and his Family Connections', *Sharsheret Hadorot*, 18, 2 (May 2004).
4. H. Halpern (ed.), *Memorial Book of Glina* (New York: Emergency Relief Committee for Glina, 1950), p.17. R' David Isaac Gellis studied in Glina under R' Meir Krasnipoller (died ca 1815) who later became ABD of Brody. Other Rabbis of Glina included R' Nachman ben Chaim Rapaport, who was succeeded by R' David ben R' Moses Menachem Mendel Cahane Bochner around 1805 (cf. Wunder, *Meorei Galicia*, vol.1, p.442). See R' Y. Hochberg, *Divrei Yechezkel*, published together with his responsa, *Mareh Yehchezkel* (Bilgoraj: 1938). Also see *Arim Veimahot BeIsrael*, vol.6, p.167.
5. Photograph of the Brody tombstone of R' David Isaac Gellis supplied by R' Dov Weber of New York (see Figure 5). The inscription refers to his father the late Rabbi Moshe Gelles of blessed memory. The grave lies between R' Moshe Nata Dayan Shamash who died in 1869 and R' Joseph, son of R' David Judah, author of Yad Yehuda and Rabbi of Radichow who died in 1873. The vital dates for R' David Isaac Gellis are circa 1790 to 1870.
6. Record of the Beth Din of Brody 1808–17, MS 4037, Jewish Theological Seminary, New York.
7. N.M. Gelber, *Arim Veimahot BeIsrael* (Jerusalem: 1955), Volume 6, on Brody, 'Here lies Rabbi Yitzchak Isaac, son of the great luminary Rabbi Uri, a descendant of the Gaon Moses Isserles, of distinguished lineage, passed away 17th Sehevat 5519 (1759).' Gelber's transcriptions of 200 tombstone inscriptions from the old cemetery at Brody (in the Gelber archive at the Central Archives of the History of the Jewish People, 46 Jabotinsky Street, Jerusalem) include this inscription with the note that Rabbi Yitzchak was a son-in-law of Rabbi Nachman Barzap (?).
8. Dr Neil Rosenstein and R. Dov Weber, Brody Cemetery Project started in 1996.
9. Levi Grossman, *Shem U'She'erit* (Tel Aviv: 1943), p.92.
10. E. Gelles, 'Finding Rabbi Moses Gelles', *Avotaynu*, xviii, 1 (Spring 2002). E. Gelles, 'My Father's People', *Sharsheret Hadorot*, 17, 1 (Feb. 2003). E. Gelles, 'Jewish Community Life in Brody', *Sharsheret Hadorot*, 18, 4 (Nov. 2004).
11. Brody tombstone of Leah (1838–94), daughter of R' Abraham Gelles, described as a descendant of Moshe Gelles of the Brody Klaus, and a Brody tombstone of Aryeh (Leibush) son of Rabbi Chayim Naftali Gelles, a young man who died in his father's lifetime 'from a distinguished family', died on 23 or 24 Nissan 5660 [1900]. Wunder, *Meorei Galicia*, Vol.3, pp.502–3, gives an anecdote involving a R' Yosef Charif Stern-Leichtug (1773–1857) and his wife, the daughter of the Parnas Reb Shmuel Gellis of Sanz, who was described as a descendant of the great Rabbis.
12. Alexander Dietz, *The Jewish Community of Frankfurt. A Genealogical Study 1349-1849* (Cornwall: Vanderher Publishing, 1988), pp.126,131–3, 446, 511, 551. Marcus Horovitz, *Die Inschriften des Alten Friedhofes der Israelitischen Gemeinde zu Frankfurt a.M. Kauffman* (Frankfurt: Kauffman, 1901), [No.626]. F.W. Ettlinger, *Ele Toldot* (Manuscript at the Leo

Baeck Institute, New York), see Ch. 32 on Rabbi David Gans: R' David of Frankfurt, the father of Geylin (d.1634), who lived at a house called the Schloss later joined to the Weisse Gans, may be identified with the Rabbi David Gans who took up residence in Prague in 1574.

Simon Hock, *Die Familien Prags nach Epitaphien des Alten Jüdischen Friedhofes* (Pressburg: Adolf Alkalay, 1892). Gelles tombstones include 5392 [1632] Tziperl, daughter of R' Yakov Zalman, 5411 [1651] the honourable Rabbi Mendel son of Zalman Gelles, 'emissary of the Beth Din', 5423 [1663] R' Chaim son of R' Yerucham, 5487 [1727] Freidel wife of R'Benjamin Gellis Katz, 5505 [1745] Rafael son of Jacob Gelles.

David Gans, *Zemach David* (Prague: 1592), Paragraph 5367 [1507], 'Rabbi Nathan of Horodna, son of my uncle Rabbi Shimshon Shapira ... left two learned sons, R' Yitzchok, Rosh Yeshiva of Kovlo and R' Yissachar, Rosh Yeshiva of Pinsk and now Rosh Yeshiva and ABD of Worms.

13. Eleazar Kallir, *Chavot Yair Chadash* (Prague: 1792), p.114a: 'the son-in-law of the author, the great luminary Rabbi Moshe Halevi ABD Libna, son of the famous Gaon Rabbi Michel Halevi ABD Eisenstadt, son of the late great Gaon Rabbi Asher Lemel Halevi ABD and Head of the Yeshiva of Eisenstadt and Head of the Beth Din of Glogau, son-in-law of the late sharp minded scholar Rabbi Moshe of Glogau, son of the great Gaon, famous in his generation, Rabbi Hillman ABD and head of the Yeshiva of Metz'.

    B. Wachstein, *Die Grabschriften des Alten Judenfriedhofes in Eisenstadt* (Vienna: R. Loewit, 1922). See tombstone inscriptions Nos. 412, 426, 515, 594, 802, 933, 1013 and 1039. B. Wachstein, *Urkunden und Akten zur Geschichte der Juden in Eisenstadt* (Wien und Leipzig: Wilhelm Braumüller Universitäts-Verlagsbuchhandlung, 1926): p.214 – document of the Eisenstadt community dated 19 October 1859, signed by Ahron Ber Gellis and eight others; p.706 – a list of representatives of the Burgenland includes Ahron Ber Gellis of Lorreto.

    The Jewish Museum in Vienna has a Torah mantle presented by 'Rabbi Ahron Beer Gelles and his wife Feila on the occasion of their son's Bar Mitzvah in 1858'.

14. *Biographisches Handbuch der Deutschsprachigen Emigration nach 1933* (München: V.G. Saur, 1980), p.217 contains brief biographical entries for Rabbi Dr Siegfried Gelles (Krotoschin 1884–London 1947) and his son Rabbi Dr Benjamin Gelles (Lissa 1916–Jerusalem 2000) who were scholars of a rabbinical family that came from Lithuania to Krotoschin in the eighteenth century and have issue in England. Johanna, the daughter of their forebear Rabbi Benjamin Gelles of Krotoschin, married Julius Kyanski, and their issue included Judge Bernard Gillis, QC (1905–96). There may have been a distant connection with my Gelles family. See also *Biographisch-Bibliographisches Kirchenlexicon*, Vol.xxi (2003) and Gillian Shaw's website (the Dear Benny letters), www.users.globalnet.co.uk/~dlshaw/kyanski.htm.
15. Hillel Noach Steinschneider, *Ir Vilna* (Vilna: 1900), pp.3–4, summarizes published data on Rabbi Uri Feivush Ashkenazi of Vilna and Jerusalem (see Chapter 34). David Tebele Efrati, *Toldot Anshei Shem* (Warsaw: 1875). Louis Lewin, *Die Geschichte der Juden in Lissa* (Pinne: Verlag M. Gundermann, 1904).
16. Gelles, 'Rabbi Shmuel Helman of Metz and his Family Connections'.
17. See Note 7.
18. R. Shmuel Delugatch, *Agudas Shmuel* (Amsterdam: 1699). Rabbi Gabriel Eskeles of Metz refers to the author as a relative who describes himself as 'Shmuel, son of the great gaon the pious Rabbi Moshe Delugatch of Grodno ... son of the great gaon Rabbi Uri of Satanow, descendant of the great gaon Rabbi Moshe Isserles' and goes on 'my late uncle the pious gaon Rabbi Leib ABD Lvov and Przemysl and his brother the gaon Rabbi Uri ABD Bodki'. The name D(e)lugatch meaning 'the long fellow' in Polish is Langer in German. Cf. Rabbi Uri Langer and possible Gelles connections (see Note 45).
19. Zvi Hirsch Horowitz, *Letoldoth Hakehilot BePolin* (Jerusalem: Mosad Horav Kook, 1978),

pp.472–3, 'Rabbi (Moshe) Aryeh Yehuda Leib known as Reb Leib Chasid, son of R. Moshe Meisels, descendant of the *REMA*, a son of a son of R. Simcha Bonem Meisels, son-in-law of the *REMA*'.

Solomon Buber, *Anshei Shem* (Cracow: 1895), pp.36–7, refers to Rabbi Aryeh Yehuda Leib as ABD and Rosh Yeshiva of Przemysl and Lvov, known as Leib Chasid, descendant of the *REMA*, to his tombstone and memorial address where the date of his death is given (1694), and to his signatures in the communal *Pinkas* and in an approbation to a Bible printed in Amsterdam – 'Aryeh Yehuda Leib of Ludmir' and 'Aryeh Yehuda son of R. Moshe of Ludmir residing in Lvov'.

Chaim Lieberman, *Ohel Rachel* (New York: ca 1980), pp.310–29: a discussion of the book written by Rabbi Shmuel Delugatch mentions in a footnote (9) that the latter's grandfather, Rabbi Uri of Satanov, was the subject of a memorial address delivered in 1636 by Rabbi Abraham Shrentzel Rapaport (1586–1651) ABD of Lvov.

Abraham Shrentzel Hakohen Rapaport, *Eisan Ha'ezrachi* (Ostrog: 1796), refers to the memorial address to Rabbi Uri, ABD Satanow, the date of his death in 1636, and Uri's manuscript commentary to *Shulchan Aruch Even Ha'ezer* which is to be found in Oxford.

Joseph Heimann Michael, *Ohr Hachayim* (Frankfurt: 1891; New York: 1965), p.152, refers to Rabbi Uri 'Delugatsch', a disciple of Rabbi Yehoshua Falk, whose writings are in his possession (which later passed to the Bodleian Library).

20. Dr David Gelles, obituary notice in *Heruth,* Vienna, 4 September 1964.
21. Biography of Rabbi Yehuda Meir Shapira, Memorial [Yizkor] Book of Piotrkow Trybunalski, Poland (New York: 1991; see translation on the jewishgen.org web site).
22. *Der Najer Morgen*, Lwow, Stanislawa Nr.297 of 26 December 1934, p.4.
23. Solotwina – *Encyclopaedia of Jewish Communities in Poland,* Vol.2, p.350, Translation from *Pinkas Hakehillot Polin* (Jerusalem: Yad Vashem, 1980).
24. R' A.M. Babad (Sunderland), *Imrei Tava* (Bnei Brak: 1983), p.192 gives R' Yoel Babad as ABD Solotvina, describing him as a grandson of R' Isaac ben Chaim Babad ABD Sassow (cf. Wunder, *Meorei Galicia*, vol.1, p.399).
25. The Jewish.gen *JRI-Poland* databases include for Mikulince a Moses Gelles (1839–84) and Osias Nathan Gelles (1854–91), as well as the infant Isaak, whose death in 1895, at the age of 5, is recorded with the names of his parents as Osias Nathan Gelles and Hinde Friedman. In Podwoloczyska another Osias Gelles married Mirl Gruenberg and there is a record of a Chaim Srul Gelles and his wife Chaya Dechtar with numerous issue.

    R' Israel Rapaport, *Tifereth Israel* (Husiatin: 1905) (collection of Chasidic teachings by Rabbi Israel Friedman of Czortkow). Its list of subscribers included Yehuda Leib Gelles of Podwoloczyska. Mikulince and Podwoloczyska are quite close to Narayow where my grandfather was born. He and his father-in-law lived and officiated for a time in Kudrynce, which is only a few miles from the larger towns of Mielnica and Skala and also not all that far from Czortkow. Gelles were also recorded in nearby Brzezany and Zbaraz, and also in Tarnopol, Lemberg and Cracow. Other books with interesting subscription lists include *Nezir Hashem* and *Semichas Moshe* by R' Shmuel Schmelke Horovitz of Nikolsburg and his son R Zvi Yehoshua of Trebicz published in Lemberg in 1869. Subscribers included Reb Yehuda Meir Gelles and Reb (Uri) Shraga Feivel Gelles of Dobromil. The names and known connections between Dobromil and Siemiatycze suggest that the latter were probably our kinsmen.
26. Yehuda Meir Shapira, *Imrei Da'as* (Bnei Brak, Israel: 1990). The list of students at the Lublin Sages Yeshivah appended to this book includes the name of Josef Gelles, son of R' Ephraim Fischel Gelles of Solotwina. The entrance requirements included a thorough knowledge of 200 folios of the Talmud with the commentaries of the Tosefoth.
27. Neil Rosenstein, *The Unbroken Chain* (New York, London, Jerusalem: CIS Publishers, 1990), Vol.2, p.759 et seq., 'David Katvan was according to the Zolkiew Pinkas ... the exalted official, head and captain, leader (Manhig) of the district of Lvov and warden

(Parnas) of the Council of the Land of Poland'. David Katvan was born in Prague and died in Zolkiew in 1698.

Ner Tamid: Yizkor LeBrody (An Eternal Light: Brody in Memoriam) (published by the Organisation of Former Brody Residents in Israel, 1994): 'Mordecai Aba'D of Brody fulfils an important role in the Council of the Four Lands as a Trustee in 1724. Among other responsibilities it falls upon him to distribute the quotas of the head tax to the Jewish communities in all Poland' (p.22). 'Rabbi Isaac ben Issachar-Berish, who was known as Cracower after his birthplace, a leader of the Council of the Four Lands and the grandson of Rabbi Heschel of Cracow. Rabbi Isaac headed the Brody community in the years 1690–1704. As a mark of respect and esteem his children were known as the children of the Aba'D, the Av Beit Din (head of the Rabbinical Court) or B'Aba'D (B'nai Av Beit Din) and in Polish documentation as Rabinowitz, that is the son of the Rabbi. The Babad family attained great importance in the life of the Brody community and achieved similar standing in autonomous Jewish institutions throughout Poland.' (p.23)

Zvi Hirsch Horovitz, *Kitvei HaGeonim* (Piotrkow: Chanoch Henoch Follman, 1928; New York: 1959), pp.35 et seq. Details of the family of Isaac Krakower and Beila Katvan. Their son R' Mordecai Yollis Babad of Brody had numerous children including Menachem Mendel of Brody and Israel Levitzer of Rovno.

Chaim Zvi Teomim, *Zikaron Larishonim* (Kolomea: 1914), p.48. Aryeh Yehuda Leib Lipschitz, *Avoth Atara Lebanim* (Rabbi Shaul Wahl-King of Poland) (Warsaw: 1927), *Shalshelet Hayuchsin*, pp.4–5 gives the children of Saul Katzenellenbogen of Pinczow and Yente Shor, including the wife of Mordecai Babad, and there is a full list of the latter's issue including R' Menachem Mendel of Brody, R' Israel of Rovno known as Israel Levitzer, and Malka, the wife of R' Yaacov Charif ABD of Leshnov. There are a number of patent errors in this text but it does agree by and large with the following details:

David Wurm, *Z dziejow zydostwa brodzkiego za czasow dawnej rzeczpospolitej* (Brody: 1935). Wurm's Babad family chart gives Yaacov Charif of Leshnov (died 1765) as the husband of Malka, daughter of Mordecai Babad, and also shows Yaacov as the son of Moses Charif of Lvov, son of Israel Charif, son-in-law of Isaac Krakower. Mordecai Babad is not only Yaacov's father-in-law but also his blood relative of the Babad lineage.

R' Menachem Mendel of Brody wrote an approbation to Migdal David, Prague. *Sha'arei Benyamin* by R' Benyamin Zev, son of R' David Ashkenazi of Zamosc (published in Zolkiew: 1752) carries an 'approbation' by the 'Holy Committee of the Lvov area', signed by numerous rabbis including R' Menachem Mendel, son of the wealthy Rabbi Mordecai Babad of Brody.

Samuel Z. Kahana, *Anaf Etz Avoth* (Cracow: 1903), lists the issue of Moses Charif, including R' Yaakov Charif ABD Leshnov, son-in-law of the Chacham Zvi and of R' Mordecai Babad.

Pinchas Pesses, *Ir Dubno Verabaneha* (Cracow: 1902), p.31, writes that a learned philanthropist of Dubno called R' David Parnas (died 1821) was the son-in-law of Reb Tzadok *der Reicher*, who was a son of Rabbi Moses Pinchas Charif of Lvov. This family was later known as Marshalkowitz.

28. David Leib Zintz, *Gedullath Yehonathan* (Pietrokov: 1934), p.242, reference to an approbation by Shmuel Helman of a book by his pupil and relative, Benjamin ben Saul Katzenellenbogen, *Or Chachamim* (Frankfurt-on-Oder: 1752).

    Shmuel Helman describes the author as a member of his father's family (see Leopold Löwenstein, *Index Approbationum* [Berlin: 1923] for a record of this approbation).
29. Lewin, *Die Geschichte der Juden in Lissa*.
30. Rabbi Shlomo Englard, 'Common Errors in Genealogical Charts', *Tzefunoth*, 11 (Nissan 5751) [April 1991]. He disputes the generally accepted link from Judah Loew of Prague (der Hohe Rabbi Loew of Prague) to Rabbi Aryeh Leib (Fischls) ABD Cracow (Hoicher Rebbe Leib). The tradition of R' David Tebele and the family of Chief Rabbi Nathan Nata

of Brody is that the line of ascent goes from them to Aryeh Leib of Cracow and then through the Kloisners to the family of the Maharal, but various published family trees differ in several respects.

31. Englard quotes R' Joseph Judah 'from the writings of his ancestor Rabbi David Tebele Brisker [from whom many David Tebeles of later generations appear to take their name!] who was a brother of the famous Gaon Rabbi Aryeh Loeb ABD Cracow' – *Asifath Yehuda* (Frankfurt-on-Oder: 1763). David Tebele Katzenellenbogen, *Ma'ayan Mei Neftoach* (St. Petersburg: 1923). R'Nathan Nata Rabinowitz, his lineage is given at the end of his edition of the Responsa of Rabbi Meir of Rothenburg (Lemberg: 1860). David Tebele, *Nefesh David* and *Michtov Le'David* (Przemysl: Alexander Sender Chaim Amkraut, 1878) with a pedigree affirming the descent of R' David Tebele ABD Lissa from R' Judah Loew of Prague.
32. David Tebele Efrati, *Toldot Anshei Shem.*
33. J. Aronus, *Regesten zur Geschichte der Juden im Französischen und Deutschen Reiche bis 1273* (Berlin 1887–1902), No.136, p.58. M. Steinschneider, *Catalogus Librorum Hebraeorum in Bibliotheca Bodleiana* (Berlin: 1931), No.6067 Kalonymus ben David, ex familia Kalonymorum. Alfred Julius Bruck, *The Bruck Family* (New York: 1946, Historia Judaica), vol.viii, p.159 et seq., 'Chalfan ... a renowned Sephardic family of Vienna that originated in Provence, settled in Italy after the expulsion of 1394 and was prominent in Venice and later in Prague. The oldest recorded date concerning the family goes back to the middle of the 15th century'.

    B. Wachstein, *Inschriften des Alten Judenfriedhofes in Wien* (Vienna: 1912), for translation of tombstone of Isaac Chalfan see L.A. Fraenkel, *Zur Geschichte der Juden in Wien* (Vienna: 1853), No.20. For Elias Menachem Chalfan and the divorce of Henry VIII see Paul Rieger, *Geschichte der Juden in Rom, II* (Berlin: 1895), pp.51–4, 95.
34. R' Chaim Nathan Dembitzer, *Kelilas Yoffi* (Cracow: 1888), Part 2, p.70 footnote 13, quotes from a printed work by R' Ezekiel Landau in which he writes: 'I heard from my grandfather the Gaon Rabbi Elazar in the name of his ancestor Rebbe Reb Heschel'. Shimon Shlesser, *Otzar Ha'Rebbe Reb Heshel* (Jerusalem: 1989), quotes R'Yakovka Landau that his father Ezekiel was descended from Rabbi Heschel on his father's and his mother's side, The Gelber archives, loc.cit give Rabbi Elazar of Dubno, ABD and Rosh Yeshiva of Razinai in Lithuania, son of the renowned Rabbi Yissachar Berish, son of the master of the entire exile R' Heschel, ABD Cracow, died 16th Sevat 5501 [February 1741] ... buried next to his wife Chana, died 15th Ellul 5496 [September 1736]. David Wurm, loc.cit gives Chana as the daughter of the Chacham Zvi Ashkenazi. Rabbi Elazar was the father of Ezekiel Landau's mother Chaya who died in 1740.
35. Rosenstein, *The Unbroken Chain*, pp.755–7.
36. Yitzchak Shlomo Yudlov, *Sefer Yichus Belza*, the Lineage Book of the Grand Rabbis of Belz (Jerusalem: Machon, 1984). Yisrael Asper kindly drew my attention to passages in *SeferYichus Belza*, in particular pp.188–9: 'Rosa Eberls was the daughter of Rabbi Moshe Eberls of Cracow, also called Rabbi Moshe Reb Yeklish. He was the brother of Rabbi Isaac Reb Yeklish and they were the sons of Rabbi Yaacov Eberls of Cracow, son of Rabbi Moshe Altschuler of Prague and husband of Gittel, daughter of Rabbi Moshe benYekutiel Landau Halevi.' Josef Kohen Zedek, *Dor Yesharim*, pp.20–1, is quoted in *Sefer Yichus Belza* p.189 on the origin of the Altschuler family. Michael Honey, Historical Clock, *the Megaleh Amukot Chart* gives the Avarles descent but does not have the Landau connection
37. Josef Margoshes, *Ereinerungen fun mein Leben* [Yiddish] (New York: Max N. Maisel Verlag, 1936; for an English version, see Select Bibliography). Wunder, *Meorei Galicia*, vol.3, pp.900–3.
38. Rosenstein, *The Unbroken Chain*, p.725. A. Schischa, *The Author of Assifat Hakohen and his Pedigree* (Jerusalem-London: Keren Yisrael, 2000), pp.123–35.

39. Gelles, 'Finding Rabbi Moses Gelles'. Gelles, 'Jewish Community Life in Brody'.
40. Yudlov, *Sefer Yichus Belza*. N.M. Gelber, *Arim Veimahot BeIsrael*, vol.6 (Brody), pp.54, 56, 69–70. Wunder, *Meorei Galicia*, vol.4, pp.844–907 and 967–9.
41. Rosenstein, *The Unbroken Chain*, pp.806–7 and 1103–4.
42. Olivier Giroud-Fliegner, 'Histoire des Fraenkel & Apparentés', http://www.osiek.org/ogf/fraenkel2.html.
43. Gelber (ed.), *Arim Veimahot BeIsrael*, vol.6 (Brody), pp.70–1, 167, 223. Wunder, *Meorei Galicia*, vol.4, pp.274–8 has much detail on the Fraenkel Rabbis of Brody and Przeworsk.
44. Wunder, *Meorei Galicia*, vol.2, pp.220, 236, 295 has information on Rabbi Yehuda Aaron Horowitz. Horowitz, *Letoldot Hakehilot BePolin*, p.110, supplementing and confirming these details. Rosenstein, *The Unbroken Chain*, does not have Rabbi Yehuda Aaron Horowitz. Cognizance is not taken of his father's third marriage, but issue by an earlier marriage is listed on p.983. Rosenstein has some information on the Fraenkels and much more on the numerous Horowitz branches descending from Isaac 'Hamburger' Horowitz, often complementing and sometimes disagreeing with Meir Wunder. See p.307 *et seq.* on a Fraenkel-Thumim line, p.1006 *et seq.* on the Horowitz of Stanislau, p.1016 *et seq.* on the Ropshitz dynasty, p.1029 *et seq.* on the Horowitz Sedziszow line, and so on. Chaim Horowitz, 'The Horowitz Families in Romania', www.jewishgen.org/yizkor/Bukowinabook/buk1_001 and related articles on other web sites. Chaim Horowitz refers to Mihaileni as a centre of Jewish culture and to its Rabbi Yehuda Aharon Horowitz, who was followed by his son, the outstanding Rabbi Naftali. He also mentions Horowitz rabbis who were descended from this family. The memoir by Dr Zisu Lebel entitled *My Dear Shtetl Mihaileni* (Haifa: 1998), (ed. Hecht) describes Jewish life in pre-war Mihaileni. There is a brief article on this town in the *Jewish Encyclopaedia*. An old map in Wunder's *Meorei Galicia* shows the two adjacent towns of Sinouc de Sus (Saniawitz) and Mihaileni on the borders between the Bukowina and Bessarabia and about 25 miles to the south-east of the city of Czernowitz. Kudrynce at the eastern most tip of Galicia is at a similar distance to the north-east of Czernowitz. Map 3 indicates the routes linking the towns of south-eastern Galicia to Czernowitz and other towns in the Bukowina.
45. The relationship between the two half brothers, Rabbis Yehuda Aaron Horowitz and Efraim Fischel Horowitz, is set out in Table 25. Wunder, *Meorei Galicia*, vol.2, pp.171, 176–7 gives some details on Efraim Fischel Horowitz (1790–1860) and his family, including his eldest son Joshua who became ABD of Rohatyn and a daughter, Esther Rivka, who married Eleazar Horowitz (1826–1912), ABD of Mariampol and Rohatyn. This couple's daughter Beila married Joshua Heschel Fraenkel-Teomim (d.1894), ABD of Narayow and Lubatchow. My grandfather's place and date of birth suggests a connection with the family nexus in Rohatyn-Narayow. Incidentally, Rabbi Uri Langer of Rohatyn and my grandfather Nahum Uri Gelles were both followers of the Chasidic Rabbis of Czortkow. The names of Efraim and Fischl are found in the Gelles family at an earlier date. Efraim (1816–37), a son of Moses Gershon Gelles, and Fischel Leib (1818–29), son of Abraham Gelles, are in the Brody Registers of Births 1815–40 and Deaths 1829–48. The names of Efraim and Fischel appear to have come at that time from the marriages with the Margoshes family (see records of the Brody Beth Din discussed in Chapters 29 and 30). My grandfather's eldest son, Efraim Fischel, born in 1879 might have been named after Rabbi Efraim Fischel Horowitz, whose father-in-law was Nahum Zausmer. Neil Rosenstein records Zausmer–Landau–Horowitz family links in *The Unbroken Chain* (pp.449, 458, 755, 757, 983, etc.). Eleazar and Esther Rivka Horowitz had a son David Halevi Horowitz who became a distinguished Chief Rabbi of Stanislau and married a daughter of Haim Babad, the ABD of Mikulince. The latter was a great-grandfather of Yoel Babad, the last Rabbi of Solotwina. Babad descent from Isaac Krakower, grandson of Chief Rabbi Abraham Joshua Heschel of Cracow is set out in

Neil Rosenstein's book, where numerous marriages between Horowitz and Babads are recorded (pp.709–803, 1013). Table 47 on the Rabbis of Solotwina suggests some possible connections.

Table 48 of Babad descent from Jacob Babad, son of Isaac Krakower, including the connection with Isaac Hamburger Horowitz, is based on Wunder's *Meorei Galicia* (vol.2, pp.122–5) and a collection of responsa by Isaac Horowitz which has a biography by the publisher R' Eliezer Schonfeld of Lodz (*Matamei Yitzchak* Pt. 1 [Piotrkov: 1904]).

Other in-laws in this Horowitz–Babad nexus were the Kliger Rabbis of Graiding and the Avigdor line from Brody whose Jacob Avigdor (d.1967) became Chief Rabbi of Mexico (see Neil Rosenstein, The Unbroken Chain, loc. Cit., pp.1014, 1036–7).

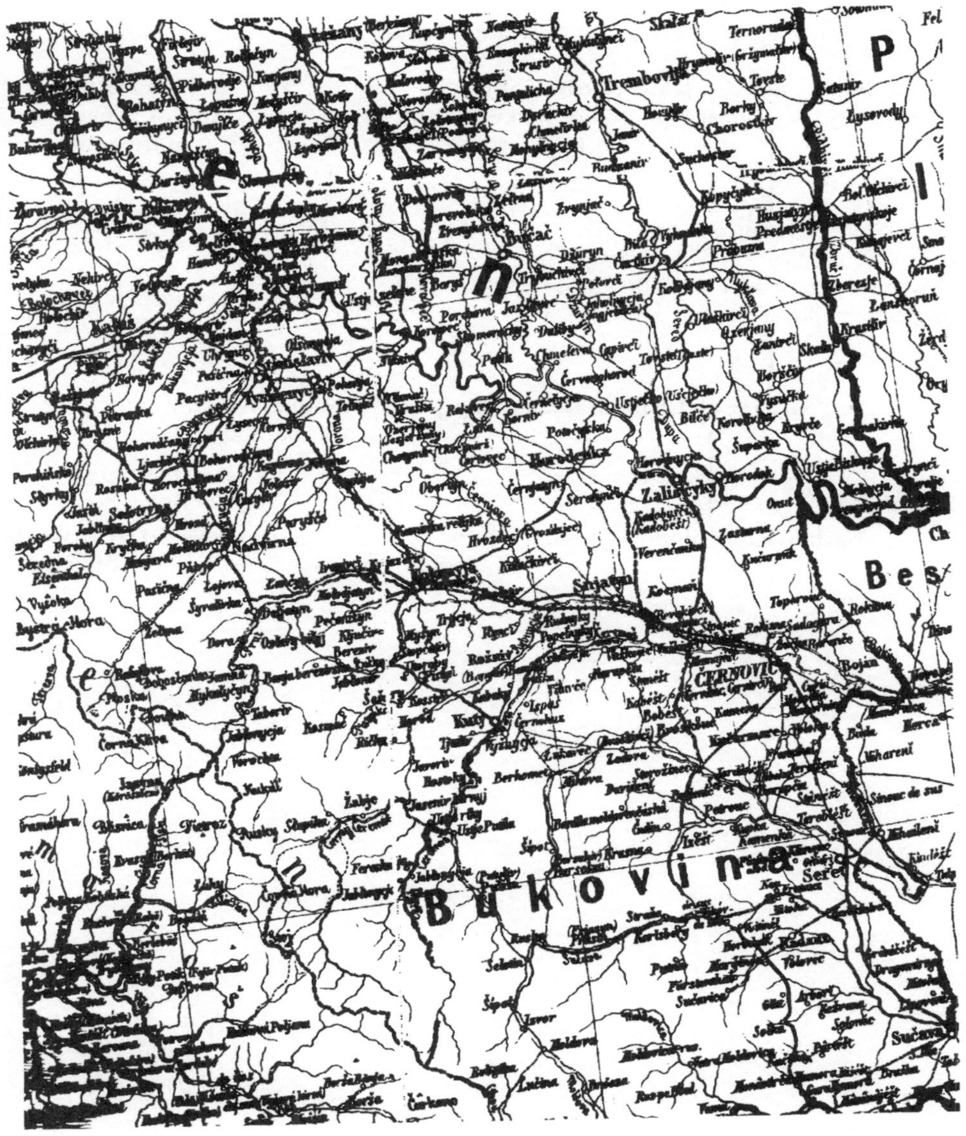

Map 3
Borderland between Galicia and Bukowina

Table 35
YAFFE–RAPAPORT CONNECTION

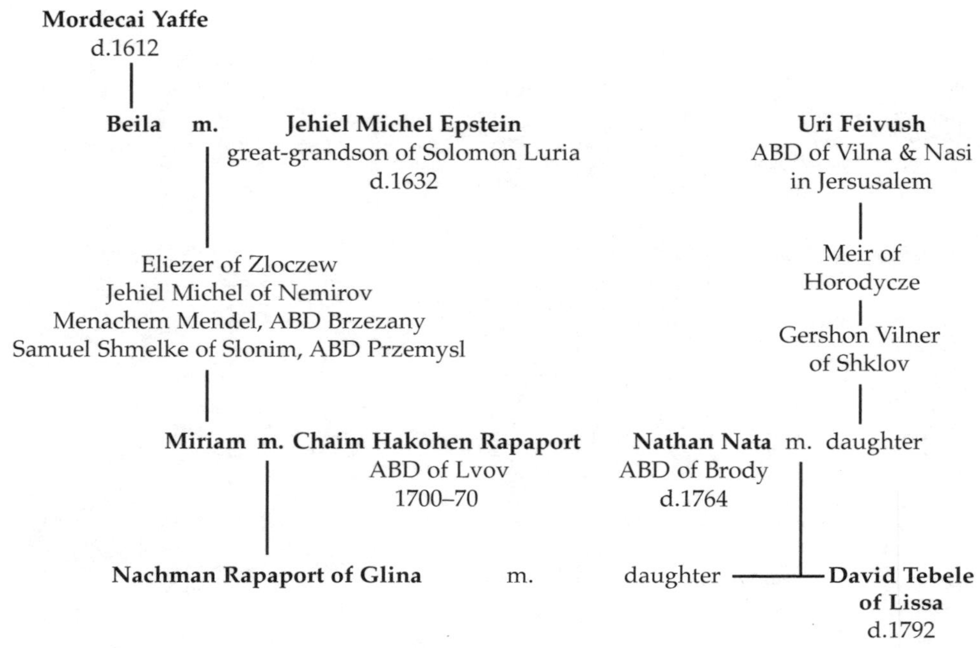

Table 36
HEILPRIN CONNECTIONS

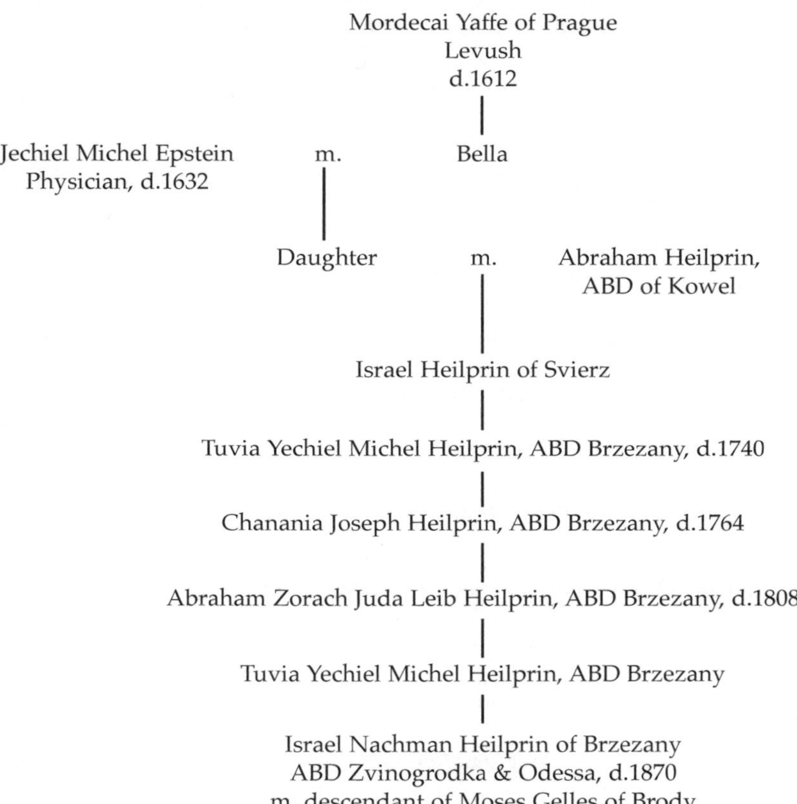

Notes:

A daughter of Shmuel Dov, grandson of Moses Gelles of Brody and son-in-law of Pinchas Shapiro of Koretz, married Rabbi Abraham Heilprin of Sudilkov.

For the Heilprins of Brzezany, see Dr Neil Rosenstein, *The Lurie Lagacy*, Avotaynu 2004, pp.356–7; and Rabbi Meir Wunder, *Meorei Galizia*, Vol.2, pp.563–6.

Table 37
THE SHAPIRO LINE

Nathan Nata of Grodno is descended from Rashi [Salomon ben Isaac of Troyes] through the medieval Rabbis of France of the Treves family

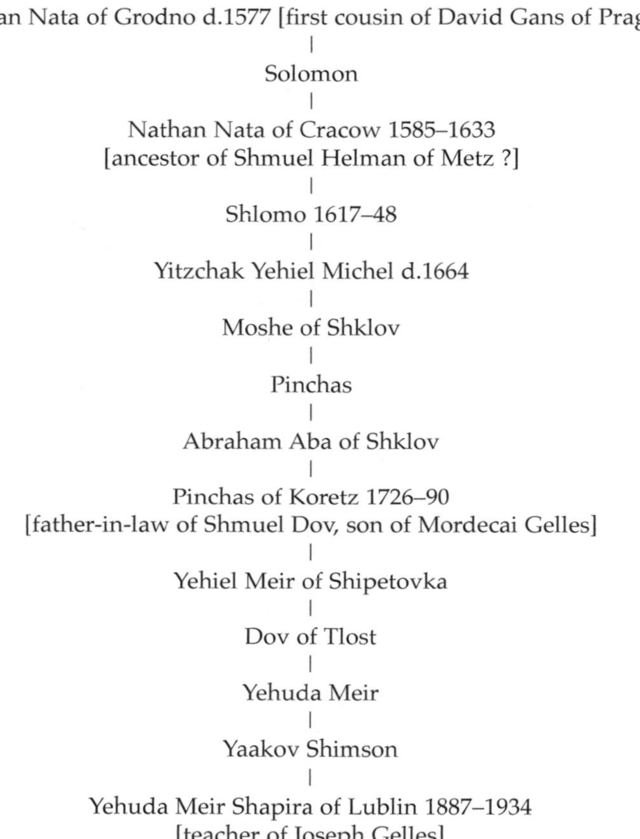

Nathan Nata of Grodno d.1577 [first cousin of David Gans of Prague]

Solomon

Nathan Nata of Cracow 1585–1633
[ancestor of Shmuel Helman of Metz ?]

Shlomo 1617–48

Yitzchak Yehiel Michel d.1664

Moshe of Shklov

Pinchas

Abraham Aba of Shklov

Pinchas of Koretz 1726–90
[father-in-law of Shmuel Dov, son of Mordecai Gelles]

Yehiel Meir of Shipetovka

Dov of Tlost

Yehuda Meir

Yaakov Shimson

Yehuda Meir Shapira of Lublin 1887–1934
[teacher of Joseph Gelles]

The Gelles family had ties of long standing with the millennial Shapiro line.

Table 38
KLOISNER

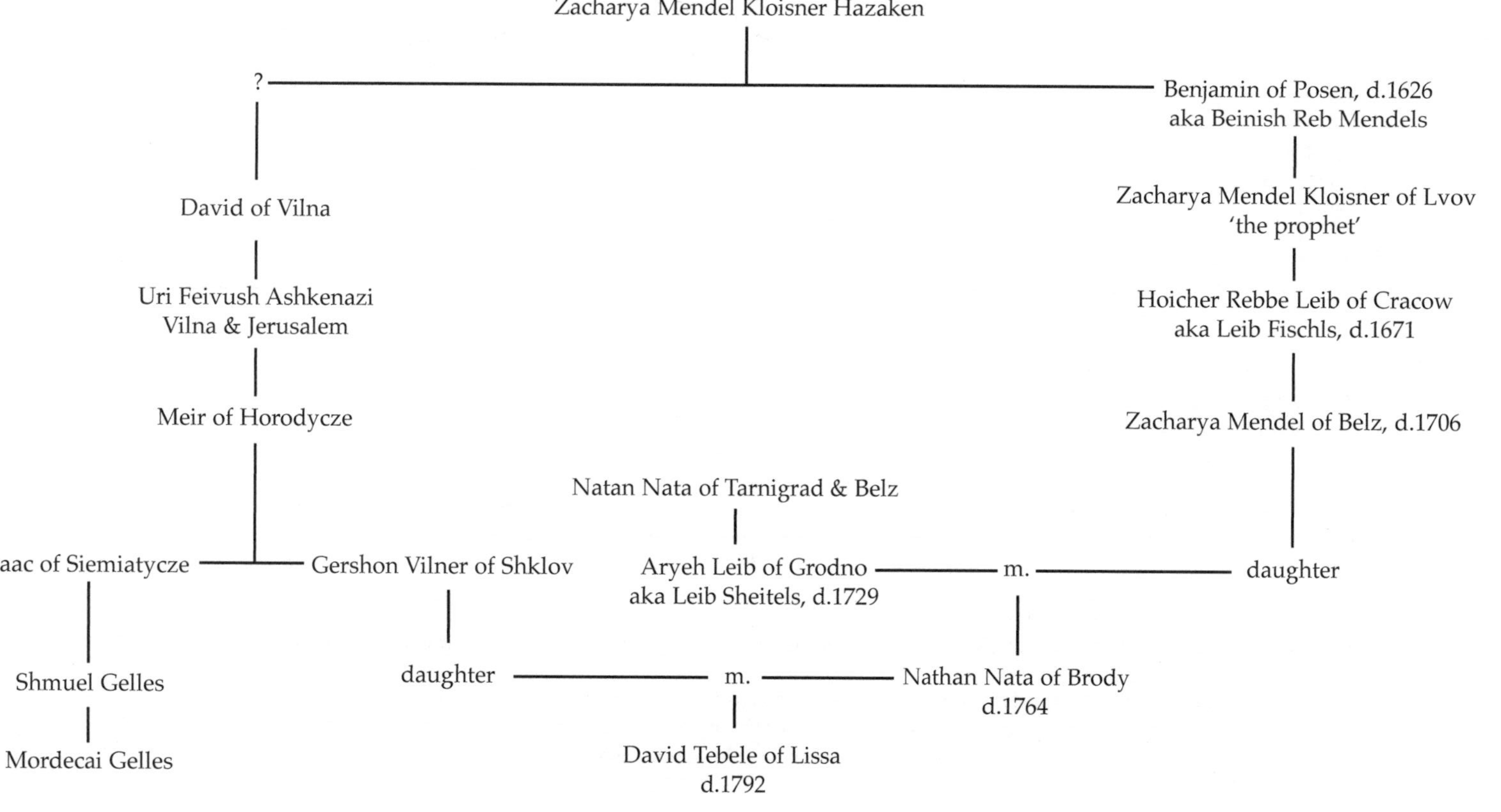

Table 39
CHALFAN FAMILY TREE

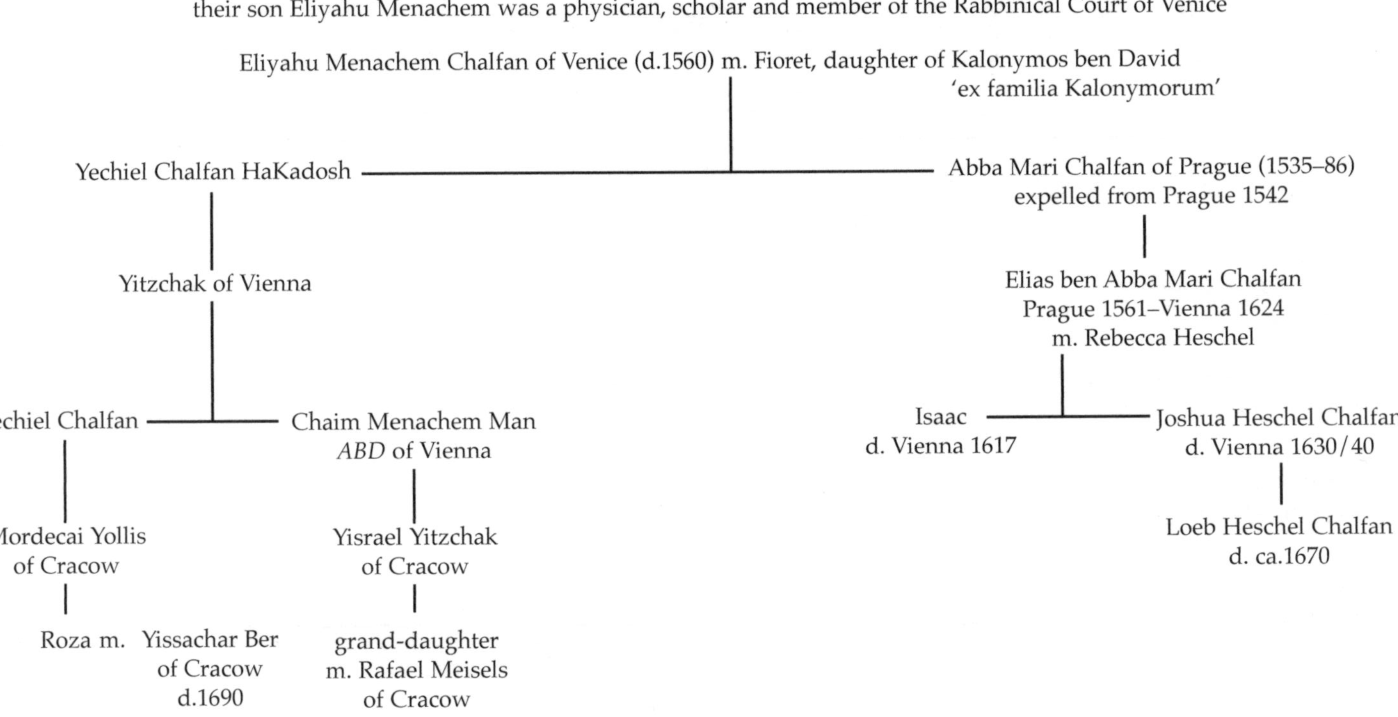

Table 40
FISCHL AND MARGOSHES

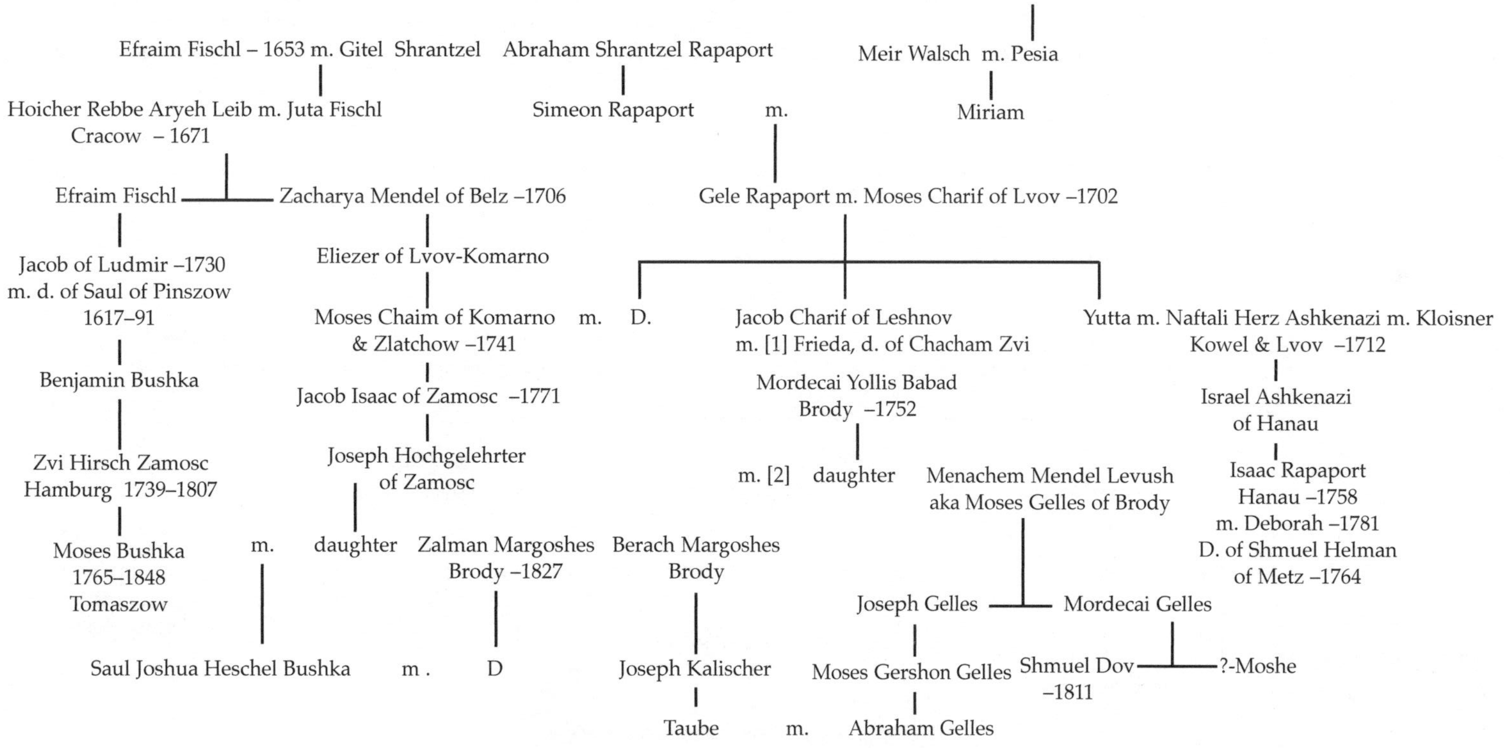

Efraim Fischl, president of the Four Lands Council, who died in Lvov in 1653 was the grandson of Efraim Fischl, ABD of Brisk, who married Valentina, daughter of Rabbi Solomon Luria of Lublin. The Margoshes descent from Efraim Fischl is recorded by Joseph Margoshes (1866–1955).

Table 41
ASHKENAZI–RAPAPORT

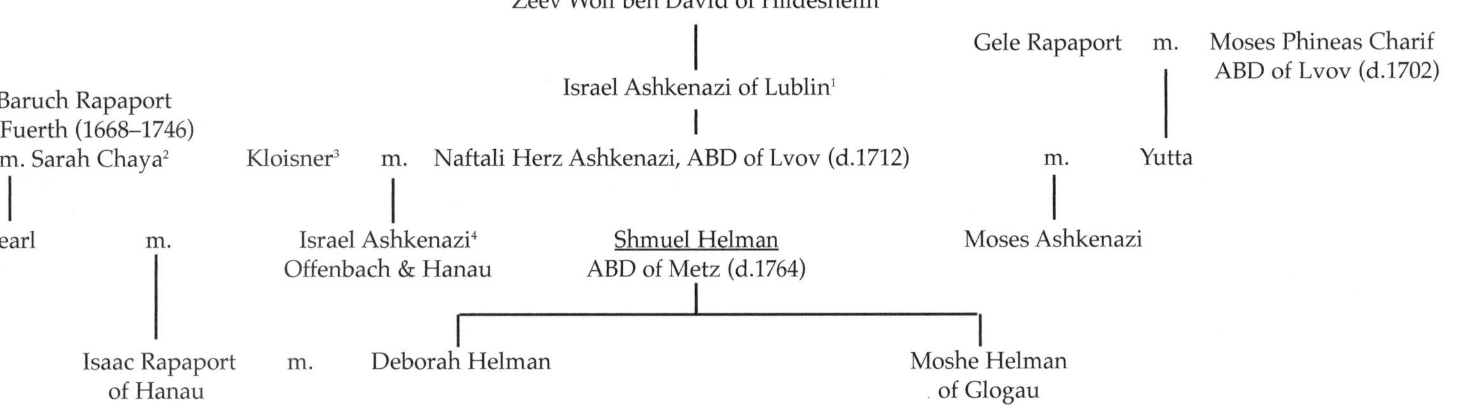

Notes:

1 The sons of Israel of Lublin included Yaacov of Jaroslaw, whose daughter married Zvi Hirsch of Drohobycz and that couple's daughter was the wife of David Wahl, ancestor of the Wahls of Nadworna (see Chapter 5).

2 Sarah Chaya, wife of Baruch Rapaport, was a granddaughter of Abraham Joshua Heschel of Cracow.

3 The first wife of Naftali Herz Ashkenazi was a daughter of Zeev Wolf, son of Zvi Hirsch ABD of Lvov, son of Zacharya Mendel Kloisner.

4 Israel Ashkenazi of Hanau's brother Zvi Hirsch, the first of the Halberstadt line, married Yente, a daughter of Simcha Rapaport, and his sons included Solomon DovBerish Halberstadt ABD of Glogau, Simcha Halberstadt ABD of Sokol and Dessau who married his first cousin, daughter of Moses Ashkenazi, and Naftali Herz Halberstadt, ABD of Kowel and Dubno, whose wife was Frodel, daughter of Jacob Babad.

Table 42
LANDAU CONNECTION

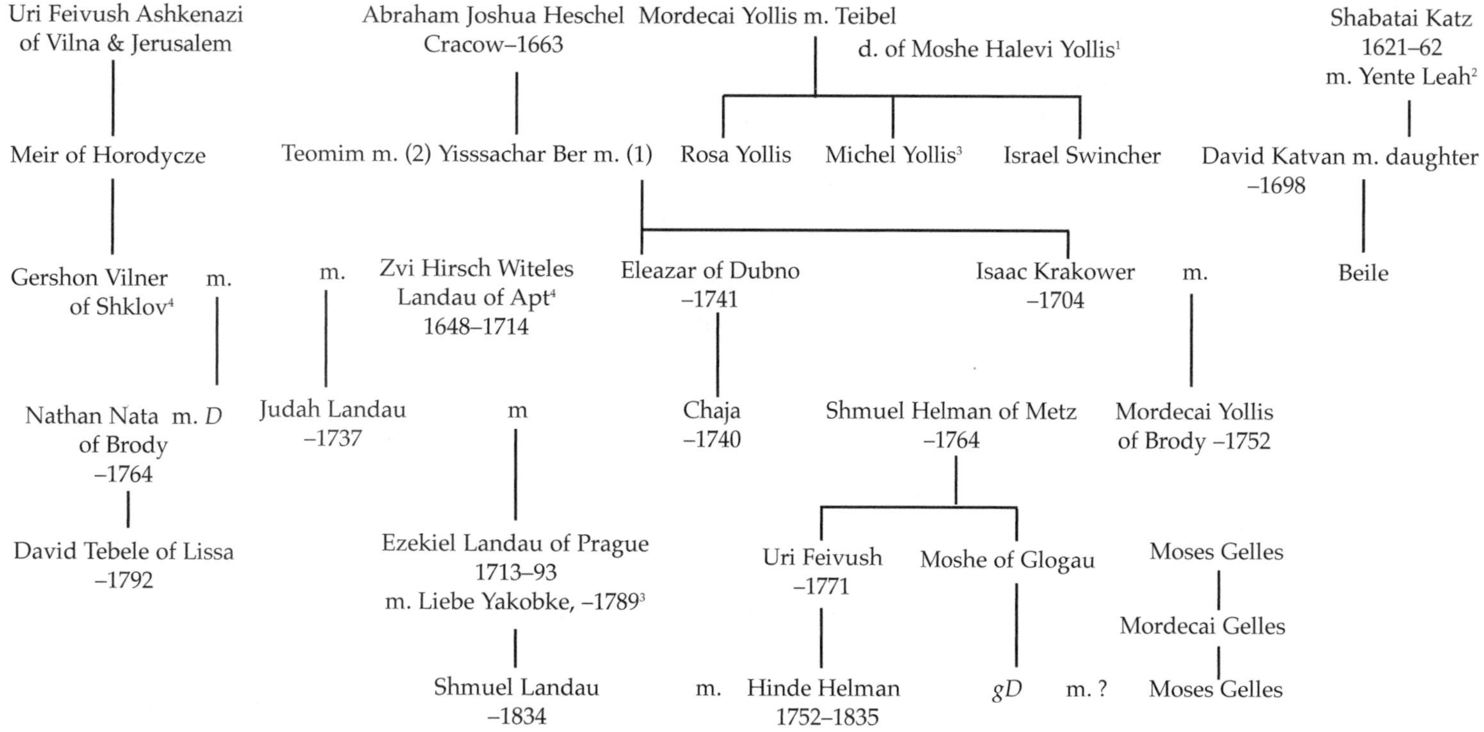

Uri Feivush Ashkenazi of Vilna & Jerusalem | Abraham Joshua Heschel Cracow–1663 | Mordecai Yollis m. Teibel d. of Moshe Halevi Yollis[1] | Shabatai Katz 1621–62 m. Yente Leah[2]

Meir of Horodycze | Teomim m. (2) Yisssachar Ber m. (1) | Rosa Yollis | Michel Yollis[3] | Israel Swincher | David Katvan m. daughter –1698

Gershon Vilner of Shklov[4] m. | m. Zvi Hirsch Witeles Landau of Apt[4] 1648–1714 | Eleazar of Dubno –1741 | Isaac Krakower –1704 m. | Beile

Nathan Nata m. *D* of Brody –1764 | Judah Landau –1737 | m | Chaja –1740 | Shmuel Helman of Metz –1764 | Mordecai Yollis of Brody –1752

David Tebele of Lissa –1792 | Ezekiel Landau of Prague 1713–93 m. Liebe Yakobke, –1789[3] | Uri Feivush –1771 | Moshe of Glogau | Moses Gelles

Mordecai Gelles

Shmuel Landau –1834 m. Hinde Helman 1752–1835 | *gD* m. ? Moses Gelles

Notes:
1. Related by marriage to Isaiah Horowitz (1568–1627).
2. Yente Leah Meisels, descendant of the Rema, Moses Isserles (1525–72).
3. Yakubka rabbinical line connects Yollis and Landau.
4. The brothers-in-law Gershon Vilner and Zvi Hirsch Witeles Landau are closely related to the Heschel and Yollis families.

Table 43
SOME LINES OF DESCENT FROM SAUL WAHL

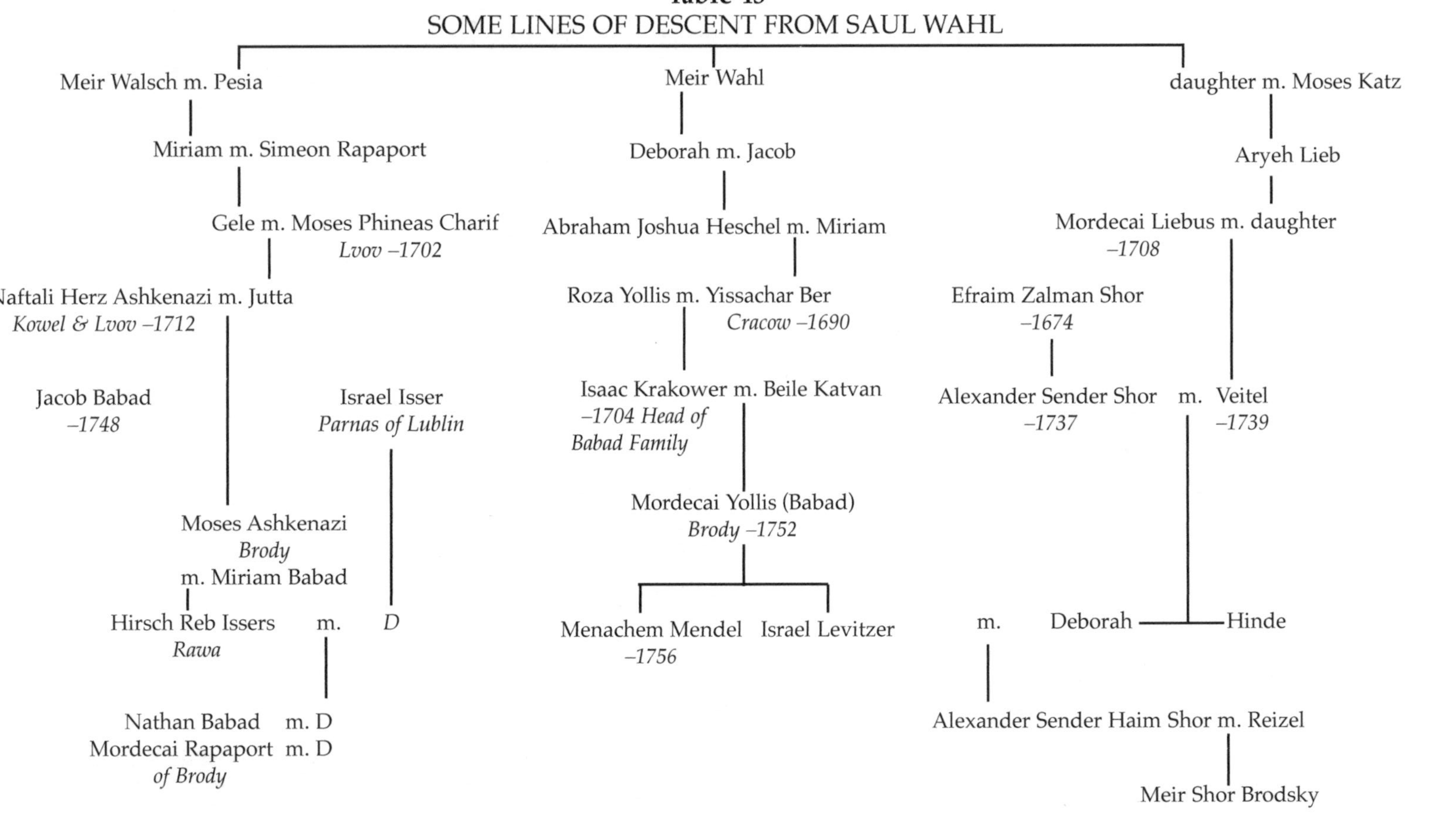

Notes:
Abraham Joshua Heschel, the Chief Rabbi of Cracow, died in 1663.
Efraim Zalman Shor was the son-in-law of Alexander Sender Shapira.
Mordecai Liebus was the father of Veitel Shor and of Israel Isser.
Hinde Shor married Menachem Meinish Margolioth. Their daughter was the wife of Abraham Jekutiel Pereles Rapaport of Brody, who died in 1798, and was the father of Mordecai Rapaport.

Mordecai Yollis Babad and Jacob Babad were sons of Isaac Krakower.
Mordecai Yollis married a daughter of Saul Katzenellenbogen of Pinczow and Yente Shor (a daughter of Jacob Shor).
Israel Babad of Rovno, known as Israel Levitzer, was the brother of Menachem Mendel whose wife Frieda died in 1757.
Israel Levitzer's grandson was Meir Shor Brodsky. He was the progenitor of the Brodsky family who became one of the richest Jewish families in nineteenth-century Russia.
Moses Ashkenazi of Brody married Miriam, the daughter of Jacob Babad.

For the Babad family tree see David Wurm, *Z dziejow zydostwa brodzkiego za czasow dawnej rzeczpospolitej* (Brody: 1935) (Note 27 in Chapter 36, discussing this and other sources)
For the Shor–Rokeach connections see Neil Rosenstein, *The Unbroken Chain* (New York, London, Jerusalem: CIS Publishers, 1990) and *The Lurie Legacy* (Bergenfield, NJ: Avotaynu, 2004).

Table 44

SOME DESCENDANTS OF MOSHE ALTSCHULER AND CHANA TREIVISH

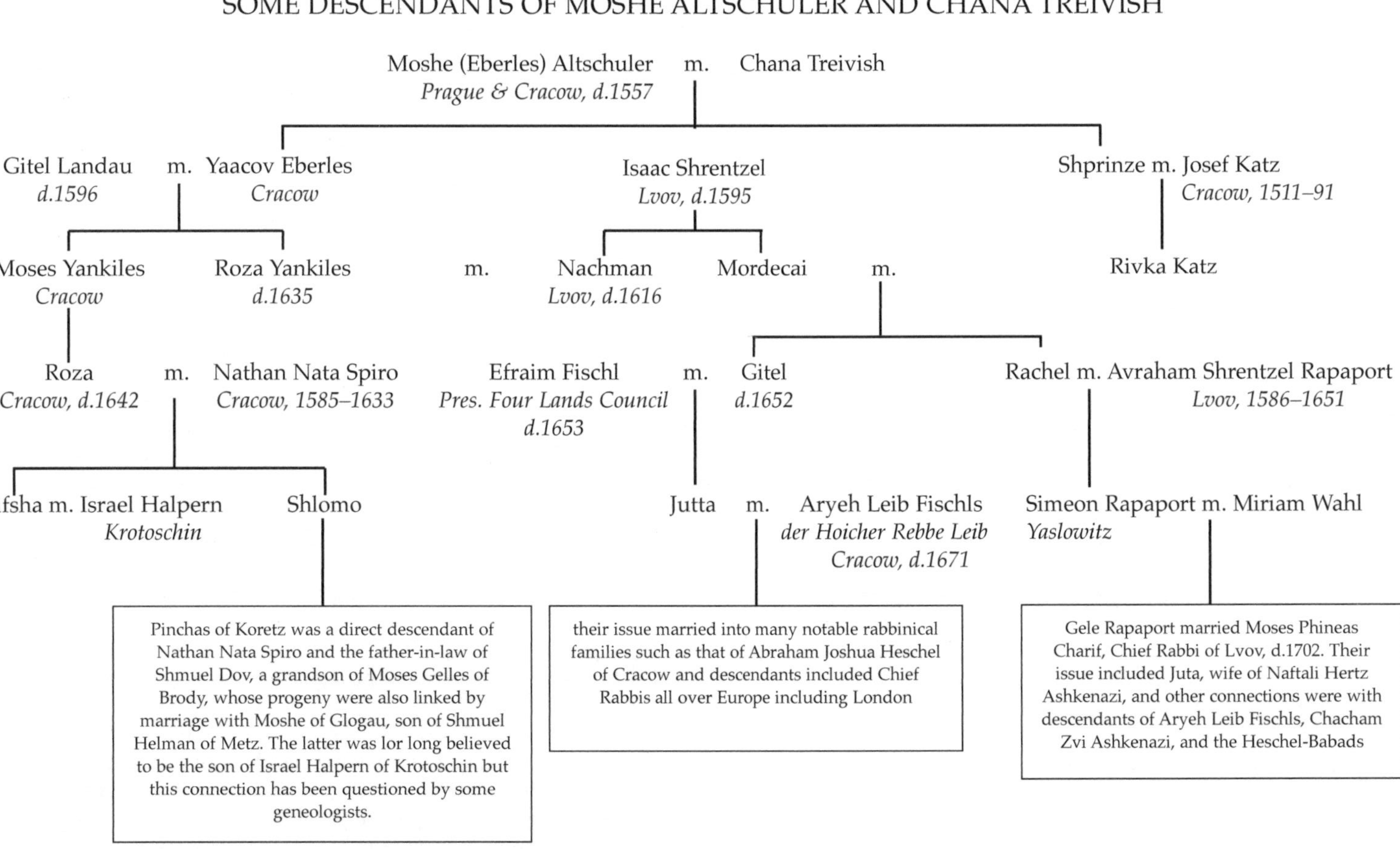

Notes:

Yaacov Eberls appears to have been married twice – to Gitel Landau and to a daughter of R. Aryeh Leib Katz Rapa, ABD of Prague (Yodlov, Cahana). Gitel Landau was a daughter of Moshe ben Yekutiel Landau Halevi, whose descendant Chief Rabbi Ezekiel Landau of Prague was believed to be a blood relation as well as in-law of Shmuel Helman of Metz. The traditional belief that the Rabbi of Metz was the son of Israel Halpern of Krotoschin has been challenged, but Shmuel Helman certainly belonged to the Halpern-Katzenellenbogen family nexus. Josef Katz, the son of Mordecai Gershon HaKohen and brother in-law of Chief Rabbi Moses Isserles, was Head of the Yeshivah of Cracow. Efraim Fischl of Lvov, a descendant of Solomon Luria of Lublin, married Gitel, a daughter of Mordecai ben Isaac or of Mordecai ben Nachman Shrentzel. She was therefore a sister or cousin of Rachel Rapaport. Abraham Shrenzel Rapaport belonged to the family of Aryeh Leib Katz Rapa of Prague.

Roza Yankiles (Eberls), who married Nachman Shrentzel, was known as *die goldene Roiz* (Cahana, Josef Kohen-Zedek). Gele Rapaport, the daughter of Simeon Rapaport and Miriam Wahl, was a great-granddaughter of Saul Wahl.

Aryeh Leib and Jutta Fischl were parents of Zecharya Mendel of Belz and of Efraim Fischl of Ludmir. A line from Zacharyah Mendel goes to Chief Rabbi Nathan Nata of Brody, who is connected by marriage to the descendants of Chief Rabbi Uri Feivush of Vilna. Efraim Fischl of Ludmir was the father of Jacob of Ludmir who married Hinde Katzenellenbogen. They are ancestors of the later Chajes line. The descendants of Efraim Fischl of Lvov include the Margoshes of Brody, in-laws of the later Gelles line. Aryeh Leib and Jutta Fischl were parents-in-law of Samuel ben Uri Feivush of Shidlow and Fuerth, whose son-in-law, Uri ben Naftali Hertz Breslauer aka Aaron Hart (1670–1756) became the first Chief Rabbi of the Ashkenazi Jews in England. Another daughter of Aryeh Leib and Jutta Fischl, named Esther, married Saul Loewenstam, the son of Chief Rabbi Abraham Joshua Heschel of Cracow. Esther and Saul were the grandparents of Zvi Hirsch Berlin (1720–1800) who became Chief Rabbi in London, where he was known as Rabbi Hart Lion. His son Solomon Hirschel or Hershell (1762–1842) was the first Chief Rabbi in London to be also recognized by the provincial and colonial communities (Rosenstein, Cecil Roth).

Various sources including Yitzchak Shlomo Yudlov, *Sefer Yichus Belza* (Jerusalem: Machon, 1984), pp.33, 188, 343; Shmuel Zanvel Cahana, *Anaf Etz Avoth* (Cracow: 1903), p.143, 158, 216, 222; Salomon Buber, *Anshei Shem* (Cracow: 1895), p.379; Josef Kohen-Zedek, *Dor Yesharim* (Berdichev: Chaim Jacob Sheftel, 1898); Neil Rosenstein, *The Unbroken Chain* (New York, London, Jerusalem: CIS Publishers, 1990), pp.553 et seq; Cecil Roth, *The Great Synagogue of London 1690–1940*,Chs.5, 9 and 13.

Table 45
MORE LINES FROM SAUL WAHL AND MOSES ISSERLES

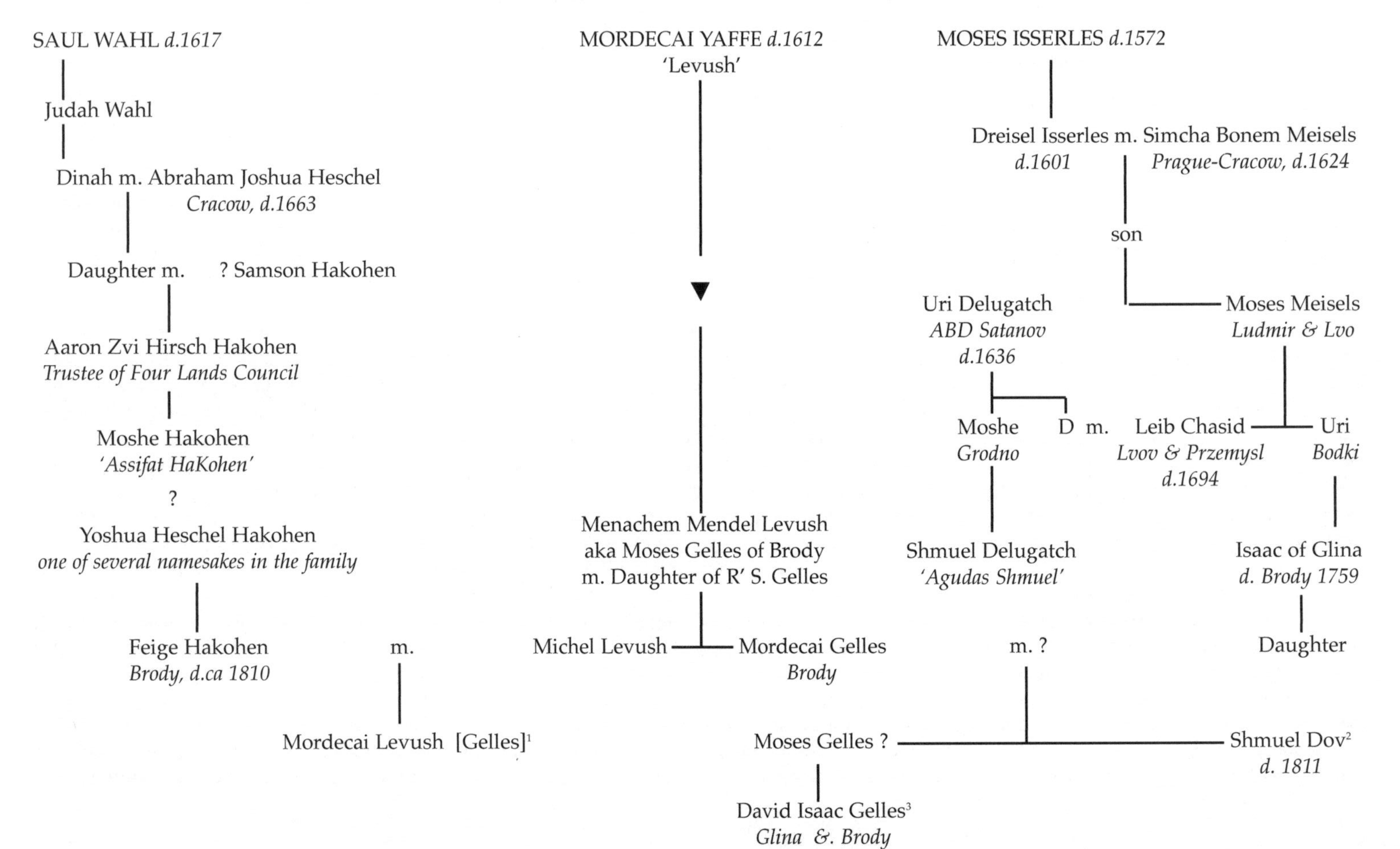

Notes:
1. Son-in-law of Yehudah Leib Zundel of Brody, d. 1804.
2. Son-in-law of Pinchas Shapiro of Koretz, d. 1791.
3. Father of Nahum Uri Gelles, d. 1934, the father of David Isaac Gelles, d.1964.

Michel Levush, a son of Moses Gelles of Brody, married Feige Hakohen, daughter of Rabbi Yehoshua Heschel Hakohen, who may be amongst the descendants of Abraham Joshua Heschel of Cracow, scion of the Katzenellenbogens , going back to Saul Wahl and the Rabbis of Padua and Venice. Moshe Hakohen records his wife's family connection with Yomtov Lipmann Heller, the great Rabbi of Vienna, Prague and Cracow, and also that there were several Yoshua Heschels in the Hakohen family tree named in memory of their distinguished ancestor. Through the alliance with the Zundel Ramraz family, Michel Levush's grandson Moshe Levush aka Gelles was a cousin of Shalom Rokeach, the first Rebbe of the Belz Chasidic dynasty.

Table 46 shows a Samuel Hakohen as the son-in-law of Abraham Zeev Wolf Fraenkel, ABD of Przeworsk. The Fraenkels of Przworsk and Brody were linked by marriage to the descendants of Michael Levush's brother, Josef Gelles.

My great-great-grandfather Moses Gelles was the father of Rabbi David Isaac Gellis of Glina and Brody, the father of Rabbi Nahum Uri Gelles, who was the father of Dr David Isaac Gelles of Vienna. The pattern of first names, the coincidence that my ancestor David Isaac Gelles studied in Glina and was buried in Brody around 1870, that Isaac ben Uri was a Rabbi of Glina, died in Brody in 1759, and was a descendant of Moses Isserles, as stated on his tombstone and numerous references to such descent in the rabbinical literature, combine to indicate that Moses Isserles might perhaps be among our forebears. The line from Moses Isserles goes via his daughter Dreizel who married Simcha Bonem Meisels, to their grandson Moses Meisels of Ludmir and Lvov, who was the father of Uri, ABD of Bodki. A book by R' Shmuel Delugatch, the grandson of Uri Delugatch, ABD of Satanov, and nephew of R' Aryeh Leib aka Leib Chasid, ABD of Lvov and Przemysl, throws light on the Meisels-Isserles descent, and there are several other supporting texts.

Sources:
E. Gelles, 'Finding Rabbi Moses Gelles', *Avotaynu*, xviii, 1 (Spring 2002).
E. Gelles, 'Jewish Community Life in Brody', *Sharsheret Hadorot*, 18, 4 (Nov. 2004).
E. Gelles, 'Rabbi Shmuel Hillman of Metz and his Family Connections', *Sharsheret Hadorot*, 18, 2 (May 2004).
Neil Rosenstein, *The Unbroken Chain* (New York, London, Jerusalem: CIS Publishers, 1990), p.725 but this is somewhat at variance with A. Schischa, *The Author of Assifat Hakohen and his Pedigree* (Jerusalem-London: Keren Yisrael, 2000), pp.125–35.
Dr N.M. Gelber's tombstone transcriptions at the Central Archives of the History of the Jewish People, Jerusalem.
Shmuel Delugatch, *Agudas Shmuel* (Amsterdam: 1699).
Z.H. Horowitz, *Letoldot Hakehilot BePolin* (Jerusalem: Mosad Horav Kook, 1978), pp.472–3.
Salomon Buber, *Anshei Shem* (Cracow: 1895), pp.36–7.
Chaim Lieberman, *Ohel Rachel* (NewYork: 1980).
Abraham Hakohen Shrentzel Rapaport, *Eisan Ha'Ezrachi* (Ostrog: 1796).
Joseph Heimann Michael, *Ohr Hachayim* (Frankfurt: 1891; New York: 1965).

Table 46
HOROWITZ–FRAENKEL–GELLES

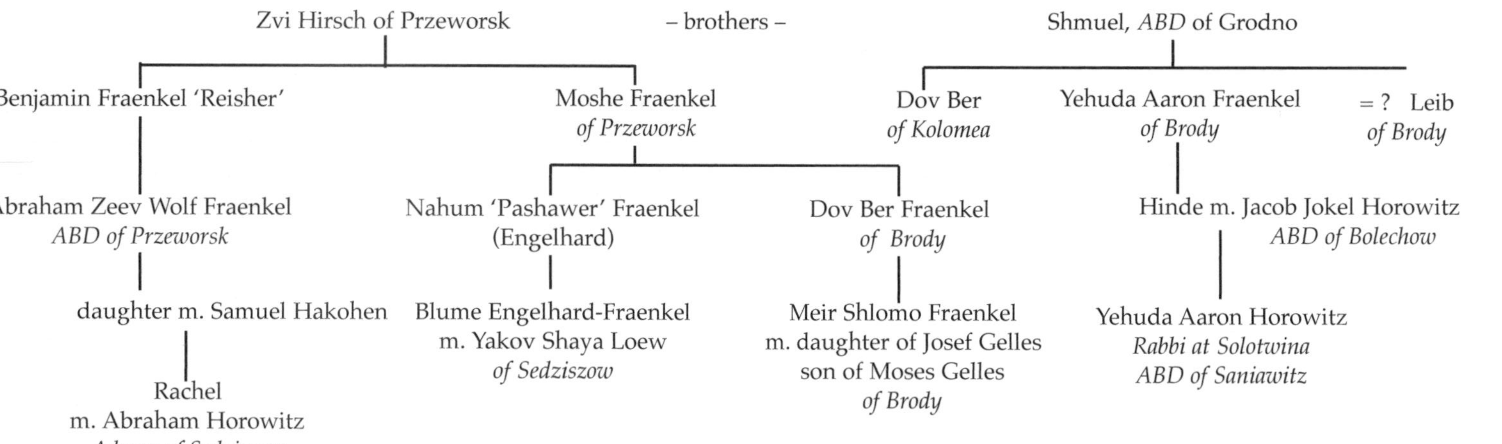

Notes:
Arim Veimahoth BeIsrael (Vol. 6, Brody) mentions R' Aaron Fraenkel, a friend of Rabbi Efrayim Zalman Margolioth (p.70), R' Yosef Fraenkel, one of the Gabbaim of the new Brody synagogue built in 1801 (p.167), and Nachman Fraenkel who was born in Brody in 1833 (p.223).
Abraham Horowitz of Sedziszow was a grandson of Naftali Zvi, the founder of the Ropshitz dynasty, a son of Menachem Mendel Rubin, ABD of Lesniow and Lesko, by his wife Beila Horowitz. She was a daughter of Isaac Horowitz, the Chief Rabbi of Hamburg, a grandson of Meir Horowitz, known as the *Maharam* of Tiktin. Abraham Zeev Wolf Fraenkel of Przeworsk, the author of Meshiv Kahalacha, married firstly a granddaughter of Rabbi Shmuel Shmelke Horowitz of Nikolsburg and secondly a daughter of Rabbi David Nathanson of Brody (see *Arim Veimahoth BeIsrael*, Vol.6 Brody, p.71; Meir Wunder, *Meorei Galicia* [Jerusalem: Institute for the Commemoration of Galician Jewry, 1978 *et seq*.], vol.2, p.357 and vol.4, pp.274–7; Neil Rosenstein, *The Unbroken Chain* [New York, London, Jerusalem: CIS Publishers, 1990], pp.970, 991,1029). Nahum Pashawer Fraenkel married a Fraenkel cousin.

Rabbi Meir Horowitz, a great-grandson of Abraham Horowitz of Sedziszow and descendant of Abraham Zeev Wolf Fraenkel of Przeworsk, set out the Horowitz–Fraenkel–Loew connections in a letter addressed to Max Low dated 6 September 1966. For the Gelles–Fraenkel connections in Brody, see Edward Gelles, 'Finding Rabbi Moses Gelles', *Avotaynu*, xviii, 1 (Spring 2002), and 'Jewish Community Life in Brody', *Sharsheret Hadorot*, 18, 4 (Nov. 2004). For Yehuda Aaron Fraenkel, see Wunder, *Meorei Galicia*, vol.2, pp.220, 236. Yehuda Aaron Horowitz was the son (by his third marriage) of Jakob Jokel Horowitz of Bolechow, who was a brother of Naftali Zvi of Ropshitz. (See also Rosenstein, *The Unbroken Chain*, pp.1016, 1039; Wunder, *Meorei Galicia*, vol.2, pp.176–7, 295; Zvi Hirsch Horowitz, *Letoldoth Hakehilot BePolin* [Jerusalem: Mosad Horav Kook, 1978], p.110.]

Table 47
THE RABBIS OF SOLOTWINA NEAR STANISLAU

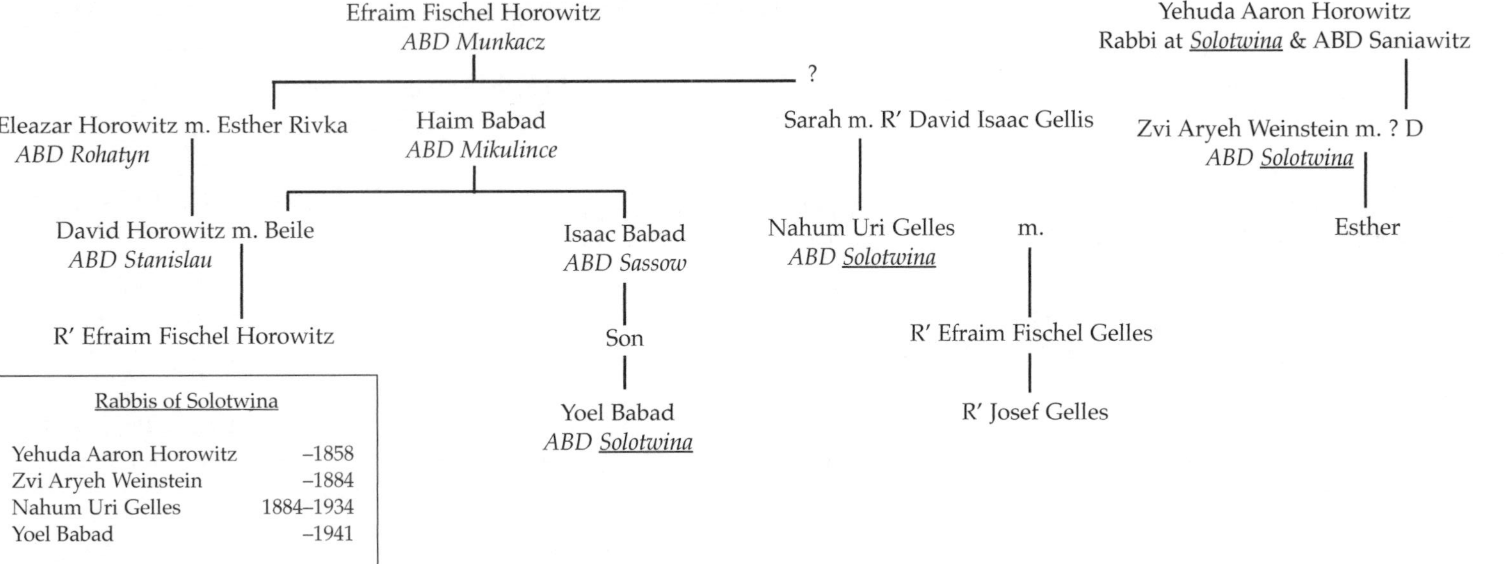

Rabbis of Solotwina

Yehuda Aaron Horowitz	–1858
Zvi Aryeh Weinstein	–1884
Nahum Uri Gelles	1884–1934
Yoel Babad	–1941

Notes

Efraim Fischel Horowitz (1790–1860) and Yehuda Aaron Horowitz were sons of Jacob Jokel Horowitz (1773–1832), ABD of Bolechow, by his first and third wives, who were daughters of Menachem Nahum Zausmer of Stryj and of Yehuda Aaron Fraenkel of Brody. Menachem Nahum Zausmer's son, Rabbi Enzel Zausmer of Stryj, was the father- in-law of Abraham Halpern of the Stanislau Halperns.

Eleazar Horowitz (1826–1912) was a son of Meshullam Issachar Horowitz (1808–88), the ABD of Stanislau. Eleazar's son David Halevi Horowitz (1862–1934) and his first wife Beile (1857–94) had offspring including a son called Efraim Fischel. Beile's father, Haim Babad (1811–89), ABD of Mikulince, was a descendant of Isaac Krakower (died 1704), the ABD of Brody, and head of the Babad line belonging to the wider Katzenellenbogen family (going back to the Rabbis of Padua and Venice).

Nahum Uri Gelles (1852–1934) was a descendant of Moses Gelles, an eighteenth-century scholar of the Brody *Klaus*. Nahum Uri's eldest son Efraim Fischel was born in 1879 and his second son David Isaac (1883–1964) was sent to study at the Munkacz yeshiva (see Table 46).

Table 48

SOME LINES OF DESCENT FROM ISAAC KRAKOWER, HEAD OF THE BABAD FAMILY

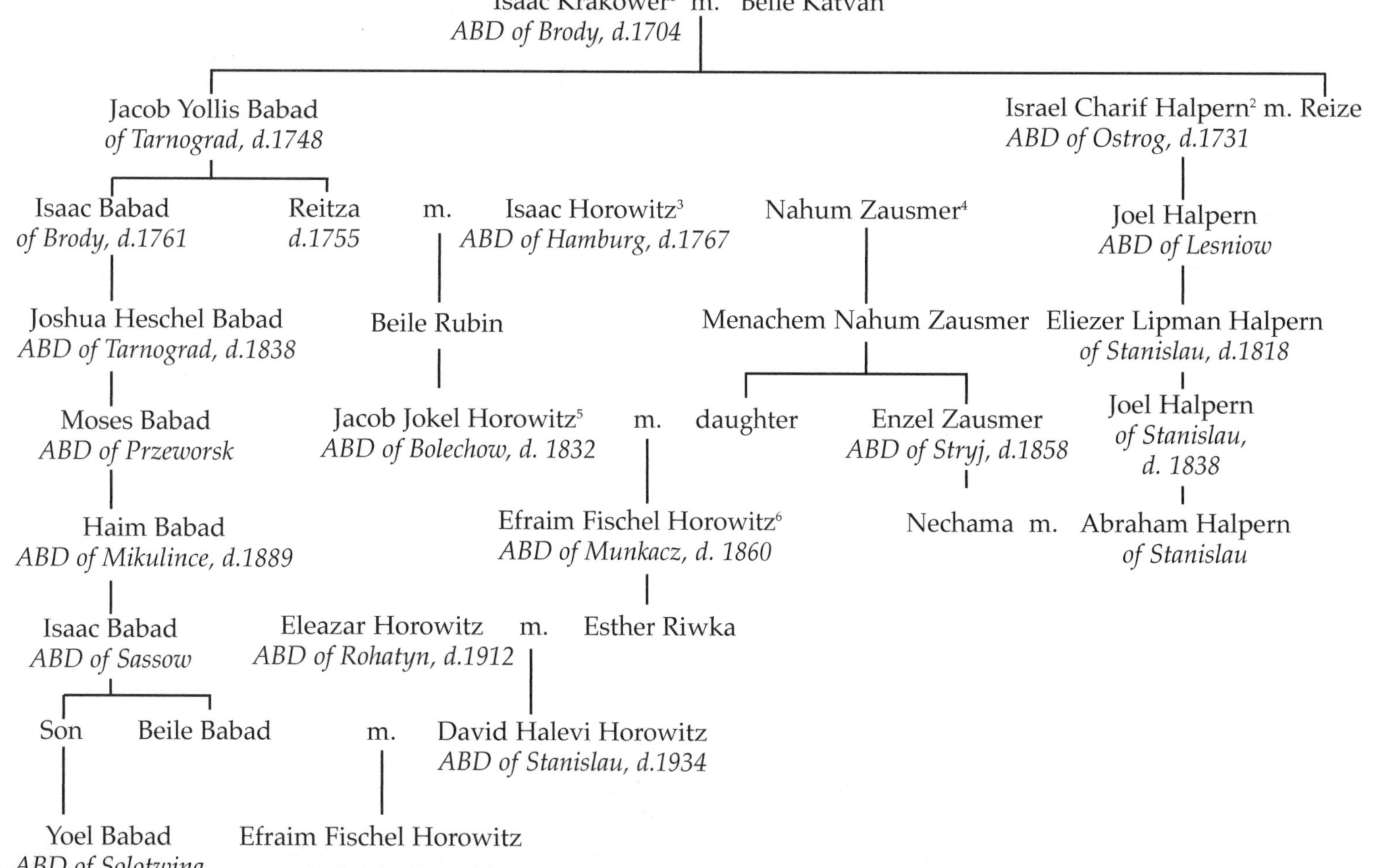

Notes:

1. Son of Yissachar Ber, President of the Council of the Four Lands, who was a son of Abraham Joshua Heschel, the Chief Rabbi of Cracow.
2. Son of Eliezer Lipman Halpern of Tarnograd, a son-in-law of Jacob Shor, who was a grandson of Saul Wahl.
3. Grandson of Meir Horowitz, the Maharam of Tiktin.
4. Married daughter of Isaac Katz, descendant of Saul Wahl and Judah Loew of Prague.
5. By a later marriage, father of Yehuda Aaron Horowitz, Rabbi at Solotwina, etc.
6. Possibly grandfather of Nahum Uri Gelles (1852–1934), ABD of Solotwina, whose eldest son was Rabbi Efraim Fischel Gelles and whose second son studied at the Munkacz yeshivah. Nahum Uri was succeeded at Solotwina by Yoel Babad.

Table 49

DESCENT FROM JUDAH LOEW OF PRAGUE VIA THE KATZ FAMILY

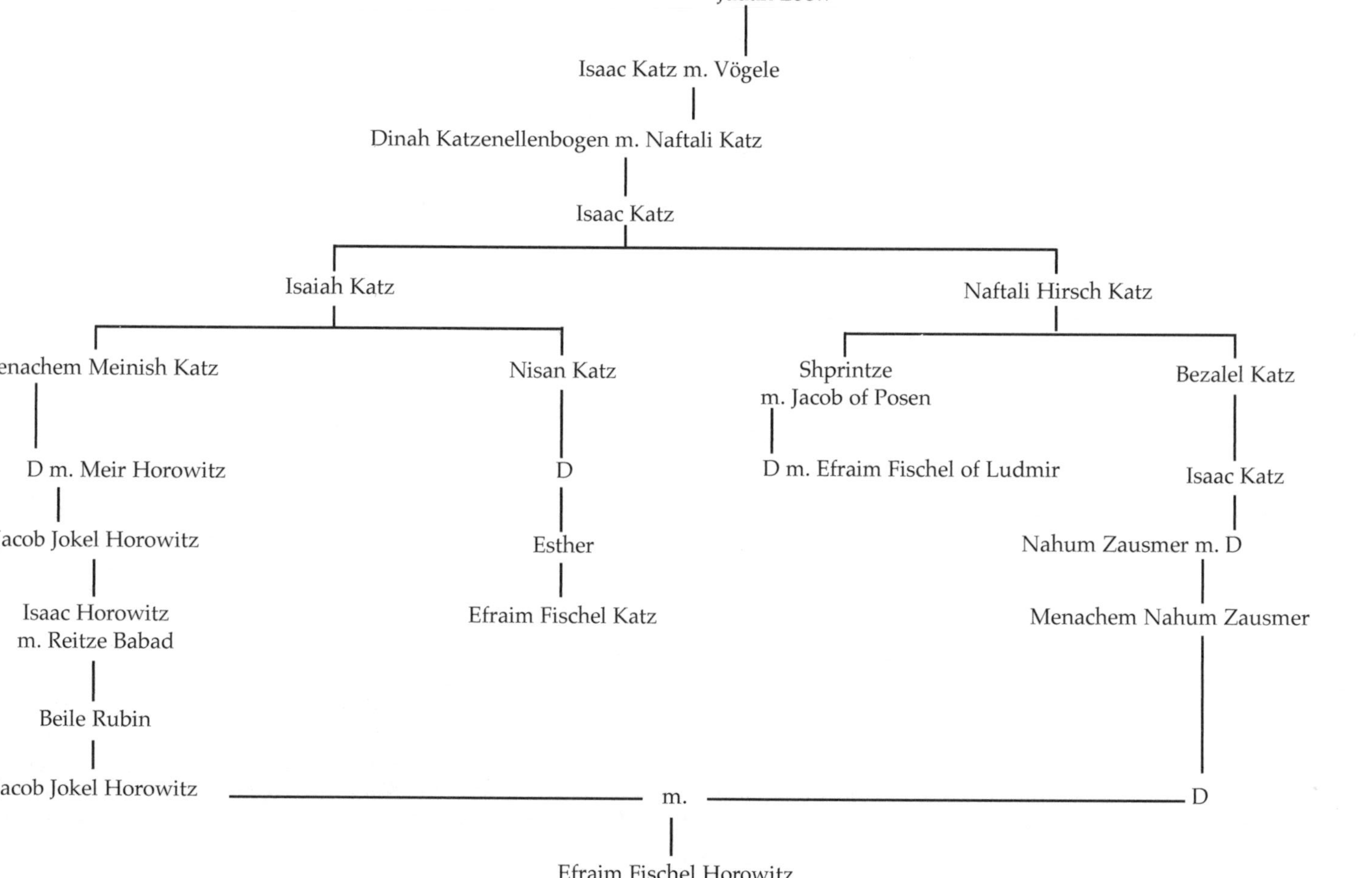

Notes:
Judah Loew of Prague (ca. 1525–1609) – the *Maharal* – married (1) a sister of Rabbi Isaac ben Abraham Chayes of Prague, and (2) Perel, daughter of Schmelke Reich. Efraim Fischel of Ludmir, scion of the Kloisner line, was a son of Aryeh Leib Fischls (d.1671), known as the Hoicher Rebbe Leib, who became Chief Rabbi of Cracow in succession to Abraham Joshua Heschel. Aryeh Leib married Jutta, the daughter of Efraim Fischel of Lvov (d.1653), President of the Council of the Four Lands. The line also goes back to the family of Judah Löw of Prague via Aryeh Leib's father, Zacharya Mendel the Prophet, son of Benjamin of Posen (d.1626), son of Zacharya Mendel Kloisner Hazaken of Posen, who married a sister of Judah Loew. Isaac Katz of Prague (d.1624) married Vögele (d.1629), a daughter of the *Maharal*. Naftali Katz, ABD of Lublin (d.1649), married Dinah Katzenellenbogen, who after his death became the second wife of Abraham Joshua Heschel of Cracow (d.1663). Naftali's son, Isaac Katz, was ABD of Stepan in Volhynia. His sons included Naftali Hirsch Katz of Frankfurt and Isaiah Katz, who was a *dayan* in Brody.

Descent from Naftali Hirsch Katz:
Naftali Hirsch Katz had a daughter Shprintze who married Jacob (Ashkenazi-Katzenellenbogen) of Posen. Their daughter was the wife of Efraim Fischel Kloisner of Ludmir. Shprintze's brother Bezalel Katz (d.1717) was ABD of Ostrog, and his son Isaac Katz (d.1734) followed him to become ABD of the Ostrog *Klaus*. One of the latter's daughters married Nahum ABD of Zausmer (Sandomierz). Their son born after his father's death was Menachem Nahum Zausmer. His children included Rabbi Enzel Zausmer of Stryj and a daughter who married Jacob Jokel Horowitz (1773–1832), ABD of Bolechow. The latter couple were the parents of Efraim Fischel Horowitz (ca. 1790–1861), ABD of Munkacz. Efraim Fischel Horowitz of Munkacz was the grandfather of David Horowitz (1862–1934), ABD of Stanislau, and perhaps of Nahum Uri Gelles (1852–1934), ABD of Solotwina near Stanislau. These two rabbis were respectively the fathers of Efraim Fischel Horowitz and Efraim Fischel Gelles.

Descent from Isaiah Katz:
His son Menachem Meinish Katz had a daughter who married Meir Horowitz (d.1746), called the *Maharam of Tiktin*. This line goes via Isaac Hamburger Horowitz (1715–67) and his wife Reitze Babad (d.1755) to Jacob Jokel Horowitz of Bolechow and Efraim Fischel Horowitz. A brother of Menachem Meinish Katz, Nisan Katz, was the ancestor of the scholar Efraim Fischel Katz.

IX.

PAST, PRESENT AND FUTURE

For a thousand years in thy sight
are but as yesterday when it is past
and as a watch in the night

Psalm 90: 4

Chapter Thirty-Seven

Davidic Descent

Historical impact of ancient myth

There is a grey area between legend and documented fact which should be of concern, not only to antiquarians, but also to serious genealogists and historians, at least in so far as ancient legends have sometimes cast a long shadow over subsequent periods of history.

For a long time most Jews believed that God had assigned rule over their people to King David and that the Messiah would be his descendant. Early Christians were at pains to advance a convincing Davidic pedigree for Jesus. The Jewish idea of a divinely appointed and consecrated kingship, hereditary to the seed of David, provided an inspiring model for the Christian rulers of Europe and had far-reaching political consequences, involving questions such as the divine right of kings and the limitation of their royal power. The legacy of the first great king of Judah and Israel was of significance in the medieval power game. It led to arguments between rival religious factions. It has also had a deep and lasting impact on Western literature and art.

Britain has given hospitality to a complex of legends and romances about the lost ten tribes of Israel, Joseph of Arimathea and the Holy Grail, the origin of the stone of destiny, and so on. They are all part of the religious culture of this country. Claims of Davidic descent for Britain's Royal House go back to ancient Irish chronicles and were elaborated by genealogists in the nineteenth century.

When Jerusalem was overwhelmed by the Babylonian king Nebuchadnezzar in 586 BC, most of the Jews were carried off into captivity. The story goes that two daughters of Zedekiah, the last Jewish king, managed to escape to Egypt with the prophet Jeremiah. After many wanderings they reached Spain. Thence the princess Tamar or Tea Tephi, with the prophet and a small entourage, finally came to Ireland. They were said to have brought with them Hebrew heirlooms including the breast plate of the high priest and the stone known as Jacob's pillow, the stone of destiny which was later called the stone of Scone after the coronation site of Scottish kings. Tea Tephi married Eochaide the Heremon, who became High King of Ireland. From this royal pair the line of kings of Ireland and then of Scotland continued to Kenneth MacAlpine, followed by a long line of succession to the House of Windsor.

More than half a millennium before the great dispersion of the Jews following the destruction of the second temple, the Babylonian conquest gave rise to an outflow of refugees. Their settlements in Europe at such an early date are unsubstantiated, but these are not isolated legends. For example, a Jewish presence in Worms is mentioned by Benjamin of Tudela (died ca. 1173). The tale has often been recounted that these Jews brought with them earth from the Holy Land and claimed that Worms and their synagogue had become their new Jerusalem and temple.

Echoes of the distant past are heard at our sovereign's coronation, when Handel's Messiah recalls Zadok, the priest of David, who anointed his son, Solomon.

Zadok and the following high priests of ancient Israel were descendants of Aaron, the brother of Moses. The anointment of kings at their enthronement was only a part of the complex ritual, which evolved in ancient times, and which has been discussed at length by scholars such as Raphael Patai. Conferment of divine authority by the hands of the consecrating priest became a millennial practice at coronations in Europe. The power thus supposedly conferred was demonstrated by English and French monarchs in the practice of 'touching for the king's evil' in order to heal scrofula, a tubercular condition of the neck. In England this royal ceremony persisted from the beginning of the second millennium into the eighteenth century. The Fitzwilliam Museum in Cambridge has a pierced gold 'angel' from the time of Charles I, a coin which was presented to sufferers by the king, to be hung round their neck as an amulet. Dr Samuel Johnson refers to one of the last of these occasions in the reign of Queen Anne.

It is no coincidence that the case for the divine right of kings came to the forefront of political discourse during the seventeenth century, which brought challenges to the absolutist pretensions of numerous rulers. King James I was an ardent supporter of the theory of divine right and wrote a book about it, while Charles I lost his head in its defence. In the hands of Bossuet and Louis XIV theory and practice did better in France, at least for a while. The traditions of Davidic descent were an important part of such monarchical pretensions.

In earlier times, the Merovingian kings of France laid claim not just to Davidic descent, but harboured the idea of descent from Jesus himself or at least from one of his brothers, who was supposed to have reached France and married into a local ruling family. Several noble houses subsequently attempted to trace their lineage from this progeny. These assertions and rumours stirred up much religious antagonism and political rivalry during the early medieval period and are supposed to have contributed to the eventual downfall of the Merovingians and the rise of Charlemagne's house.

The Carolingians enjoyed the backing of the Roman Church, which was of course implacably opposed to the heretical views of those who propagated the Merovingian claims. These continued to strike a chord in later times within societies such as the Rosicrucians and Templars. The beliefs of these groups were heavily influenced by mystical ideas of gnostic origins and were expressed with the frequent employment of cabbalistic symbolism. A sceptical view of these fanciful tales does not conflict with recognition of their historical influence.

Assertions made for a number of European royal houses include, for example, that of the descendants of William, Count of Toulouse, whose mother was a sister of Charlemagne's father, Pepin. She is supposed to have married an eighth-century descendant of Babylonian Exilarchs, who were indubitably of the House of David.

Amongst many Jewish families the subject of lineage continues to fascinate. During the millennia of their dispersion and its countless persecutions vital documentary material has been lost. While there are many claimants to a Davidic connection, there are almost always gaps in the chain of descent. From the time of the Babylonian captivity Jews survived there, and the descendants of the exilarchs who led them can be traced for the best part of two thousand years until the trail is lost in medieval Spain. Undoubtedly, some Sephardic families had respectable claims. But ancient tradition and partial pedigrees do not amount to proof.

Among the good cases that have been made, a noteworthy recent publication by Moshe Shaltiel-Gracian sets out to trace his family from Princes of the Babylonian Exile to Spain and later to the Ottoman Empire, North Africa, Italy and England. His studies combine ancient and medieval documentation, artefacts such as tombstones, seals and escutcheons, and a programme of DNA testing. The Charlaps, who were settled in Poland for hundreds of years, had early connections with the Shealtiels, and trace their clan via rabbis of Portugal and Spain to the Exilarchs and to earliest times.

This is a subject that has naturally interested family historians and has attracted some of the leading genealogists, who have investigated the Davidic claims of Ashkenazi families.

One linchpin to the ancient past is the fifteenth-century Rabbi Jechiel Luria of Alsace. From him many old rabbinical families are descended, including the Katzenellenbogen of Padua. A long lost pedigree scroll of the Luria family is supposed to have confirmed their descent from Salomon ben Isaac of Troyes, the great scholar and Bible commentator, who lived in the eleventh century and was known as Rashi. This pedigree includes members of other ancient rabbinical clans. From Rashi the ascent is deemed to go back to Johanan Ha-Sandelar, who lived in the second century of our era and came from the circle of Rabbi Akiba.

Johanan Ha-Sandelar was a fourth generation descendant of the Babylonian Talmudic sage Hillel. The belief that Hillel was of Davidic lineage was expressed by Moses Maimonides in the twelfth century, relying primarily on passages in the Babylonian Talmud. There are other sources supporting the pedigree of Hillel and the connection of the latter to Rashi.

Second only to Rashi as a key figure in the genealogical links with the ancient past is Judah Loew the Elder, the great-great-grandfather of the sixteenth-century Rabbi Judah Loew of Prague. Rashi and Judah Loew have been venerated for their wisdom and scholarship, and both have become figures surrounded with potent legends, as indeed were Hillel, Rabbi Akiba and the sages of their day.

Numerous miracles are associated with the story of Rashi's life. Among the legends about his prophetic gifts, the best known is that of his meeting with Godfrey of Bouillon before the latter set out on the first Crusade. Rashi is supposed to have foretold him the failure of his mission in circumstantial detail.

Rabbi Judah Loew was known as the *Hohe Rabbi Loew* of Prague or the *Maharal*. He was a renowned scholar and a master of the cabbala, alchemy, and all other branches of arcane knowledge. He impressed not only the common people, who were prepared to credit him with supernatural powers such as the creation of the 'Golem', his servant, reportedly fashioned out of clay and brought to life through magical invocation. This was a time when both Jewish secret lore and alchemy were at the height of their influence and captivated the highest in the land, including the Emperor Rudolf II. Three generations later, the great Sir Isaac Newton was still interested in alchemy. The beginnings of modern chemical science were nearly two centuries in the future.

From ancient times, the potency of many kings, princes, prophets and sages has been connected with the royal line of David. Legends that have had such an impact from the days of the Bible and the Talmud through millennia of European history surely belong to more than the outer periphery of our cultural inheritance.

NOTES

Rashi of Troyes was of Kalonymos descent. The Kalonymos, whose Greek name means literally 'Good name' from the Hebrew 'Shem Tov', were pre-eminent among medieval families held to be of Davidic descent. Benjamin of Tudela, who records his visit to Narbonne in 1166, refers thus to the Kalonymos, the princely leaders of that community. Related ancient Sephardic families are Shem Tov and Shaltiel. The Dayan family is in the forefront of Davidic claimants. The Charlaps who lived in Poland for centuries derive their name from the Hebrew acronym for *Chief Sage of the Exile in Poland* and claim descent from the Ibn Yahya rabbis of Spain and Portugal. Arthur F. Menton, the author of *The Book of Destiny: Toledot Charlap* and of *Ancilla to Toledot Charlap*, King David Press, also edits the Charlap-Yahya Newsletter.

Among the ancient families that span *Sefarad* and *Ashkenaz* are the Horowitz family, who are believed to go back to the Shem Tov Halevi of Spain and took their present name from *Horovice* near Prague in the late-fifteenth century (see below for web site).

Genealogical reference works on Ashkenazi roots include Dr Neil Rosenstein's well-known compendium of the Katzenellenbogen descendancy, *The Unbroken Chain* (New York, London, Jerusalem: CIS Publishers, 1990), and his new book, *The Lurie Legacy. The House of Davidic Royal Descent* (Bergenfield, New Jersey: Avotaynu, 2004).

DISCUSSION OF DAVIDIC DESCENT IN JEWISH GENEALOGICAL JOURNALS

Avotaynu:
Neil Rosenstein, 'A Response to Jacobi's Rashi Article', vi, 2 (Summer 1990).
Neil Rosenstein, 'A Seventeenth Century Luria Manuscript', vii, 2 (Summer 1991).
Neil Rosenstein, 'Rashi's Descent From King David', viii, 3 (Fall 1992)
David Einsiedler, 'Can We Prove Descent From King David?', viii, 3 (Fall 1992).
Laurence S. Tauber, 'From the Seed of Rashi', viii, 3 (Fall 1992).
Laurence S. Tauber, 'The (Maternal) Descent of Rashi', ix, 2 (Summer 1993).
David Einsiedler, 'Descent From King David – Part II', ix, 2 (Summer 1993).
Mitchell Dayan, 'Dayan Family of Aleppo: Direct Descendants of King David', xx, 2 (Summer 2004).

Sharsheret Hadorot:
Yehuda Klausner, 'Torah and Jewish Genealogy', 15, 1 (Nov. 2000).
Moshe Shaltiel-Gracian, 'Tracing a Davidic Line from Babylon to the Modern World', 16, 2 (Feb. 2002).
Andrés J. Bonet, 'The Bonet-Kalonymos-ShemTovs', 17, 2 (Feb. 2003).

WEBSITES

The Shealtiel family websfor.me.uk/shealtiel/
The Charlap–Yahya family charlap.org/
Shem Tov Halevi – Horowitz Rav-Sig Links
www.jewishgen.org/Rabbinic/links/bio.htm

MISCELLANEOUS INFORMATION ON THE INTERNET

Merovingian claims – Who Was Dagobert II? http://www.dagobertsrevenge.com/articles/dag.html
The Holy Grail – http://www.thedyinggod.com/holygrail.htm
The King's Evil – http://www.bbc.co.uk/education/medicine/nonint/renaiss/am/reamgs.shtm
http://www-cm.fitzmuseum.cam.ac.uk/coins/CoinOfTheMoment/angel/angel.html
Queen Elizabeth II's Descent from King David and the legend of Tamar, daughter of Zedekiah, King of Judah – http://www.bibleprobe.com/lineage.html
http://www.potts.net.au/tree/misc/adam.html

CHAPTER THIRTY-EIGHT

From Europe to America and Israel

1492 and all that

OUR EUROPEAN ODYSSEY

Jews left their mark all over the Mediterranean littoral before the fall of Jerusalem to the Babylonians. There are legends of Jewish refugees who settled in Worms after the destruction of the first temple and of a Jewish princess who made her way to Spain and then to Ireland at that time. Many more came to Europe before and after the destruction of the second temple.

From this date to the late middle ages a large Jewish community in exile flourished in Baghdad. The Caliph Haroun al–Rashid sent an embassy to the court of the Emperor Charlemagne. The Jewish envoy's descendants are believed to have intermarried with the ancient Kalonymos family. This was the period during which many Jews were transplanted from their Babylonian exile to Byzantium and to Spain, where they enjoyed a brilliant cultural life and contributed much to the transmission of the Greek heritage to western Europe. Centuries later, many Jews fleeing from Spain and Portugal sought new homes in Constantinople, Salonika and other parts of the Ottoman Empire, and in due course the indigenous Romaniot Jews merged with these incoming Sephardim. From Constantinople some travelled to Italy and beyond, while others reached Poland by the eastern route up the Pruth valley, to be joined eventually by Ashkenazi Jews fleeing from oppression in their German and Austrian homelands. Refugees from the Iberian peninsula at the end of the fifteenth century also went to Holland. Some of these Jews later settled in England while others ventured to start a new life in North and South America.

The odyssey of migrations from France and Germany to Italy, from these countries to Bohemia and Poland, Lithuania and Russia, and back again, is now ended. The holocaust and the Second World War effectively destroyed the Jewish communities in central and eastern Europe. How we came to be there, what we achieved, and how it all nearly ended a little while ago, is a story that will be written and rewritten for a long time to come.

RETURN TO THE HOLY LAND

While the Jews were driven from one country to another they gradually became part of a pan-European culture. But contact with the Holy Land was never broken. During the centuries of Ottoman rule in Palestine pious Jews continued to dream of Jerusalem and some did embark on the arduous pilgrimage. Many more came after disaster overtook the communities in Portugal and Spain. The town of Safed became famous in that period as a centre of Jewish mysticism and the study of the cabbala, whose foremost exponent, Rabbi Isaac Luria, lived and died there in 1572. A number of other notable scholars were attracted to Safed.

Among those who returned to their ancient homeland was Isaiah Halevi Horovitz, whose family was associated with the city of Prague. He was Chief Rabbi of Frankfurt, which he left soon after the anti-Jewish riots of 1612. The holy *Shelah,* as he was called after the title of his principal work, died in 1627 and was buried in Tiberias.

In the next generation, Uri Feivush, the elderly Chief Rabbi of Vilna, travelled to Jerusalem. Around 1654 he became head of the Ashkenazi community there and was also honoured with the title of *Nasi*. He is recorded as Uri Feivush Ashkenazi, pupil of the Maharam of Lublin. His great-grandson was Rabbi Shmuel Gellies of Siemiatycze. The latter's descendants retained the Gelles name. My family, who were Rabbis in Galicia, appear to have a connection with this line (Chapter 34).

A century after Uri Feivush went to the Holy Land a family from Grodno in Lithuania undertook the long and hazardous journey. They believe their name comes from an ancestress called Gele. Rabbi Israel Gellis of Jerusalem is her tenth or eleventh generation descendant (see Notes)

Centuries separate these early links with the Holy Land from the Jewish immigrants of recent times. These were spurred on by an increasing anti-Semitism in much of Europe, of which the Russian pogroms were a particularly virulent form, and by the idealism of the modern Zionist movement, that arose as a direct reaction to the extreme nationalism then sweeping the European continent. The pressures of two world wars and the holocaust finally led to the gathering of survivors and the creation of the modern State of Israel.

THE DISCOVERY OF AMERICA

The connection of European Jews with America is necessarily not so ancient. Columbus, or at least a number of his intrepid mariners, are deemed to have been *conversos* of Jewish descent. The name of Louis de Torres is most often mentioned. The physician Maestre Bernal, the inspector Roderigo Sanchez de Segovia, and the sailor who supposedly first sighted land, Roderigo de Triana, were of the company. The oldest Jewish congregation in North America was that of Newport, Rhode Island. The origin of this community lay in the seventeenth century, when Portuguese Jews who had taken refuge in Holland and then in Brazil were joined by others from Curaçao. Later arrivals from Portugal included Aaron Lopez, who was born in Lisbon in 1731 and settled in Newport in 1752. He was involved in the construction of the Touro synagogue, which was inaugurated in 1763. It is the oldest extant synagogue in the United States.

However, it is the Bohemian mining engineer Chaim Gans, aka Joachim Gaunse, who was probably the first professing Jew to set foot on the North American mainland. A kinsman of the famous Rabbi David Gans of Prague (1541–1613), he came to England in 1581, made significant contributions to the copper industry here, and was sent to America by Sir Walter Raleigh in 1584. The purpose of this expedition to Virginia was to explore and evaluate mineral prospects. The path of some of the Gans family from Germany to Bohemia and then to Poland and their family connections are close to those of my forebears (Chapter 32).

Jews have played an increasing role in the history of the United States since its inception. George Washington expressed his hopes for religious harmony in addresses to several Jewish congregations, including the abovementioned Touro synagogue.

A trickle of immigrants became a flood in the closing years of the nineteenth century. Those who escaped from want and oppression in the Russian Empire were later joined by refugees from Nazi persecution in central Europe.

OUR CULTURAL HERITAGE

The rabbinical tradition in my family was concentrated in the ancient Wahl-Katzenellenbogen and Chayes families with whom my mother's people, the Griffels, were connected by marriage. It was particularly strong in my paternal Gelles line. The Griffels, and their cousins also had some rabbinical connections.

Our cultural and intellectual heritage comes from countless generations who studied the Talmud and the commentaries. Some rabbis at least had a broader knowledge, particularly of languages and of medicine. Popes, emperors, kings, sultans and nobles had their Jewish physicians through the ages. From the times of the early Renaissance a small number of Jews were allowed to study medicine at Universities such as Montpellier and Padua. A few of these doctors rose to positions of influence with their powerful patrons through the exercise of their gift for international diplomacy. Many rabbis through the centuries carried out one or more of the functions of teacher, judge and community leader. With the enlightenment and emancipation more and more descendants of the old rabbinical families received secular educations and began to enter the liberal professions and the public service. They took to the law and medicine, to philosophy, science and literature with an ease coming from centuries of intellectual inbreeding.

Even in the oldest rabbinical families not all were cut out to be scholars, and the majority had to make a living in the few areas open to Jews at the time. Thus some became moneylenders. The stigma widely attached to that occupation tended to fade when the Jew became a rich merchant banker or even a *Court Jew*.

My maternal ancestors included successful entrepreneurs, who flourished in the old Austro-Hungarian Empire. Their wealth was often based on natural resources and on the management and development of landed estates and property (Chapters 20 and 21).

OLD AND NEW HOMES

My family has ceased to exist in central and eastern Europe. My maternal grandparents disappeared in the holocaust as did scores of other relatives of the Griffel, Taube, Loew and Safier families. All other survivors of our immediate family left Europe long ago. The majority are in the United States and Israel, but there are also a few in Australia and elsewhere.

My immediate Gelles line came from Austrian Galicia and they also had close connections to the neighbouring province of Bukowina and its capital, Czernowitz. My father settled in Vienna and from there we finally came to England. My aunt Lotte Gelles was a Zionist like my father but, unlike him, she emigrated to Palestine in the 1930s. She was married twice, firstly to a lawyer in Vienna and then in Tel Aviv to a doctor who hailed from Berlin. My father's eldest sister Bertha went to America in 1910. Her grandsons Stuart and Robert Rothenberg are both doctors. Stuart is an expert in Ayurvedic medicine. One wonders whether the doctors and mystics among his Gelles forebears predisposed him towards his life's work. Uncle Max had a daughter Elsa who lives in New York, and her son Peter specializes in rehabilitation medicine (Chapter 27). My paternal grandmother Esther died in 1907. Her father was a Rabbi Weinstein, hailing from the Bukowina. At least two Weinstein descendants in America were lawyers (Chapter 28)

My maternal uncles Zygmunt and Edward Griffel went to America in 1939. Zygmunt's son Eric held a senior position in the US Foreign Service and Edward's son David built up a successful computer software company. Dr Jacob Griffel was my mother's first cousin. He was a trained lawyer who had studied at Cracow and Vienna before going into the family oil business. He became famous for rescuing thousands of Jews during the Second World War. He and his many siblings have left scores of descendants divided between America and Israel. Jacob Griffel's brothers included the lawyer Shmuel and Rabbi Henry Griffel. Yehuda Nir, Stephen Lamm and Max Griffel are among the doctors of this family (Chapters 15 and 16).

Some Wohls of Cracow, who were related to the Griffels by marriage, lived in Switzerland and their descendants are in England, America and Brazil (Chapter 18). Wahls hailing from my grandmother's birthplace Tarnobrzeg are flourishing in France and may well be distantly related (Chapter 14). The

Wahls of Zurich and their relatives in America are among the descendants of the nineteenth century Chief Rabbi of Nadworna (Chapter 5).

The Loews are another large tribe. Some cousins have been in America for nigh on a hundred years. One of the most distinguished was my mother's first cousin Dr Abraham Loew, who emigrated in 1921 and attained a degree of eminence as a psychiatrist in Chicago. He was a pioneer of community self-help mental health care. One of his daughters, Marilyn Low, a retired professor of art history, worked for the Getty museum in Los Angeles. Dr Willy Low is a distinguished physicist in Israel (Chapter 11).

My mother's first cousin Ziga Taube settled in Los Angeles. His son Tad has become a major philanthropist whose good works transcend his home base of California, taking in Israel and his native Poland, where he is supporting foundations devoted to Jewish history and culture (Chapters 22 and 23).

The Safiers of Tarnobrzeg were the family of my great-grandmother Sarah. They were linked by marriage to our Wahl and Taube lines. The Safiers sustained grievous losses in the holocaust. Many members of the succeeding generation are now dispersed to America and Israel, and there is also a strong contingent in Australia, where the versatile Marcel Safier maintains a website devoted to the family records. The Australian Safiers include quite a number in the medical profession. In America, Henry L. Safier is a consultant gastroenterologist. Emil Safier is another American cousin. He is a scientist who developed a specialist computer firm connected with the film industry in Los Angeles (Chapter 19).

Barbara Taube Safier, who married the late civil engineer Nick Welner, is the daughter of Isaac Safier and Sarah Taube. Sarah's father was Feivel Taube of Lemberg and Przemysl. The Welners thus stem from a union of the Safier and Taube families. Dr Michael Welner is a prominent forensic scientist, who has held professorships in law and psychiatry. His brother Alan is a doctor, and his sister, the late Dr Sarah Welner, achieved much for the medical care of disabled people and has been posthumously honoured in 2004 by the National Hall of Fame for Persons with Disabilities.

The family of my great-grandmother Sarah Chajes were from Kolomea (Chapter 8). From their ancestral base at Brody in Galicia the Chajes family spread far afield. From the late-eighteenth to the early-twentieth centuries a branch flourished as merchant bankers in Livorno and Florence (Chapter 7). The grandchildren of the notable nineteenth-century Rabbi Zvi Hirsch Chayes of Zolkiew included not only the Chief Rabbi of Vienna but the lawyer and scholar Adolf Chayes, the doctor Herman Chayes, Sophie, the wife of the Viennese philologist Professor Solomon Frankfurter (uncle of US Supreme Court Justice Felix Frankfurter), Benno Chayes, Professor of Medicine in Berlin, and the bibliographer Saul Chayes (Chapter 6). New shoots have taken root in America and Israel.

CONCLUSION

My family in its diverse branches has been on a long journey. This journey from country to country and from continent to continent has been one of discovery – of new vistas, new ideas and new insights. Reflecting on our history, one cannot fail to be struck that through the enormous changes in our material and social environment over the centuries the essence of our great spiritual and cultural heritage has survived and proved its lasting worth.

NOTES ON SOME GELLES AND GELLIS FAMILIES

Grodno was a historic Lithuanian city, lying between Vilna and Brest. It had a large Jewish community, which in its time attracted great Rabbis such as Nathan Nata Shapiro, who was a first cousin of David Gans of Prague, and Mordecai Yaffe of Prague whose progeny was to be found in many Lithuanian towns including Gorzd, Kretinga, Plungian and Keidani. Kretinga (Krottingen) and Gorzd (Garsden) were important trading centres in the early eighteenth century. They were near the border of Prussia and Lithuania and not many miles from the German port of Memel. A town like Gorzd performed an entrepot function not dissimilar to that of Brody in Galicia on the border between the Austrian and Russian Empires. Gelles or Gellis lived in these towns side by side with Yaffes and others with whom marriages are on record (Chapter 32).

GELLIS OF GRODNO

Rabbi Israel Gellis of Jerusalem refers to his late father, the author and historian Rabbi Yaacov Gellis. Their family came to Palestine from Grodno in the eighteenth century, and they believe that their family name was derived from a lady called Gele whose four sons, Abraham Israel, Moshe, Efraim and Gershon adopted the matronymic. One wonders whether they had any links with Prague. Families of that name found in other Lithuanian towns might have come from the Grodno stock.

GELLIS OF GORZD AND KRETINGA

The two neighbouring towns in the Gubernya of Kovno harboured Gellis families. It is quite likely that some made their way to German Poland (Silesia) and elsewhere. Many emigrated to England and America in the nineteenth century, and descendants are also to be found in South Africa and Israel. Professor Harold Gellis of New York and some of his relatives have studied the genealogy of these lines.

GELLES OF KROTOSCHIN AND LISSA

From rabbis settled in these Silesian towns in the nineteenth century came Rabbi Siegfried Gelles and his son Rabbi Benjamin Gelles, who ultimately found a new home in England. Rabbi Benjamin Gelles was Rabbi of Finchley and ended his days in Jerusalem. The family included Judge Bernard Gillis (see Chapter 36). One of Rabbi Benjamin's sons, Dr Jonathan Gelles, lives in England and another is in Israel. They may have come to Krotoschin from Lithuania. Indeed my Gelles of Brody appear to have had early Lithuanian connections and Krotoschin comes into our family story (Chapter 33), but possible links with these Silesian Gelles Rabbis remain obscure.

ISAAC GELLIS 'DELI KING OF NEW YORK'

Isaac, the son of Shalom Gellis and Elke Abrams, was born in 1850 and came to America at the age of 19. He married Sarah Schmulewitz and raised a large family. He was a pioneer in the manufacture of Kosher provisions and became President of the Eldridge Street synagogue, which was built by and for nineteenth-century east-European immigrants (Eldridge Street Synagogue, National Historic Landmark Nomination). He died in 1906 leaving a widow, seven children, and a substantial fortune. His obituaries in the *New York Times* and in the *Hebrew Standard* (30 March 1906) extol his many charitable works, and the latter journal records that his funeral service was attended by 3,000 mourners, who crowded into the synagogue, and a further 10,000 who stood bare-headed outside under the protection of 500 mounted policemen.

It is not too far fetched to wonder whether this Isaac was of the same stock as his namesakes who moved to Hungary and Austria in the eighteenth century. From these came Aaron Gellis, recorded in the 1780s as a *traiteur* in Baden near Vienna, who received a grant of permanent residence in 1805.

Isaac's obituary gives his origin as Mennel [?] in Russia. I believe this should read Memel (Klaipeda) not far from towns such as Kretinga and Gorzd in Russian Lithuania where Gellis and allied families such as the Lapin and Dreben lived. Other towns in this area were Taurage (Tauroggen) and Plungian. This family nexus had many relatives in Grodno and there are also recorded family movements to the Ukraine. The death certificate of Sarah Gellis (1845–1926) gives her parents as Abraham Schmulewitz and Annie Dreben. An account of the Drebens by Louise Lapin Haines in the Newsletter of the Worldwide Congregation Charlap/Yahya (vol.12, 4) records that Sarah Gellis was the aunt of Charles Dreben who married Rosa Lapin. The 'fighting Drebens' included an American hero, 1st Sergeant Sam Dreben (1878–1925). The Lapins belonged to the great and ancient Charlap clan (see Charlap Newsletter, vol.6, 3, p.4 and also Chapter 37).

GELLES OF KISHINEV

From the Moldavian city of Kishinev came some families bearing the names of Gelles and Chalfon (Halfin). The New York cardiologist, Dr Jeremiah M. Gelles, and the Israeli computer specialist Guy Bashkansky have recounted the intricate family connections that took some of them to Czernowitz, the capital of Austrian Bukowina, to Belgium, and later to

America and Israel. The Gelles–Halfin links make Jerry Gelles a cousin of Diane Halfin, who married Prince Egon von Fürstenberg. Diane Fürstenberg became a leading designer of clothes and jewellery in America. Her story of triumph over great adversity was published by Simon & Schuster in New York in 1998.

There is no immediate link to the members of my family who lived in Czernowitz during the nineteenth and early-twentieth centuries (Gelles, Weinstein, Brenner). However, there was a constant flow from the towns of eastern Galicia such as Kolomea and Stanislau to Czernowitz, as described in Hugo Gold's *History of the Jews in the Bukowina* (*Geschichte der Juden in der Bukowina* [Tel Aviv: Olamenu, 1958/62]). Kishinev too, though within the Russian Empire until the First World War, had received many Galician Jews, who in later days fled westward from Tsarist persecution. It was strategically placed between Czernowitz and Odessa on the Black sea. The route from Brody to Odessa was of considerable importance in a bygone age and has become so again today.

The movements of Rabbi Yehuda Aaron Horowitz and his family between Solotwina in Galicia and Mihaileni/Saniawitz on the Moldavian/Bessarabian borders (cf. Chapters 28 and 36) are relevant to the discussion of family links across the borders of these lands in the nineteenth and early-twentieth centuries.

GELLES IN HUNGARY

Our links to Eisenstadt and Munkacz have been discussed. The printer Moshe Eliyahu Gellis of Ungvar is a possible connection (see Menashe Simcha Davidowitz, *Toldot Afsei Aretz* [Ramat Hasharon: 1996]).

GELLES OF GALICIA

The story of my immediate Gelles family with their ancient base in Brody and their dispersion to other Galician towns is recounted in earlier chapters. The Gelles name was particularly strong in eastern Galicia. Lemberg, Tarnopol, Kolomea, Stanislau, Berezhany, Mikulince, Podwoloczyska and Dobromil were mentioned in this connection. In Przemysl too, and in Novy Sacz and Krakow in western Galicia, Gelles could be found at a relatively early date. Migrations to Brody from Bohemia, Lithuania and Silesia, and from Galicia to Bukowina, Moldavia, Hungary and Austria are indicated on Map 4.

There are a number of prominent academics in America bearing the Gelles name. Among those who are descended from Galician families, mention might be made of Richard James Gelles, who is Dean and Professor of Child Welfare and Family Violence at the University of Pennsylvania, and whose grandfather came from Przemysl.

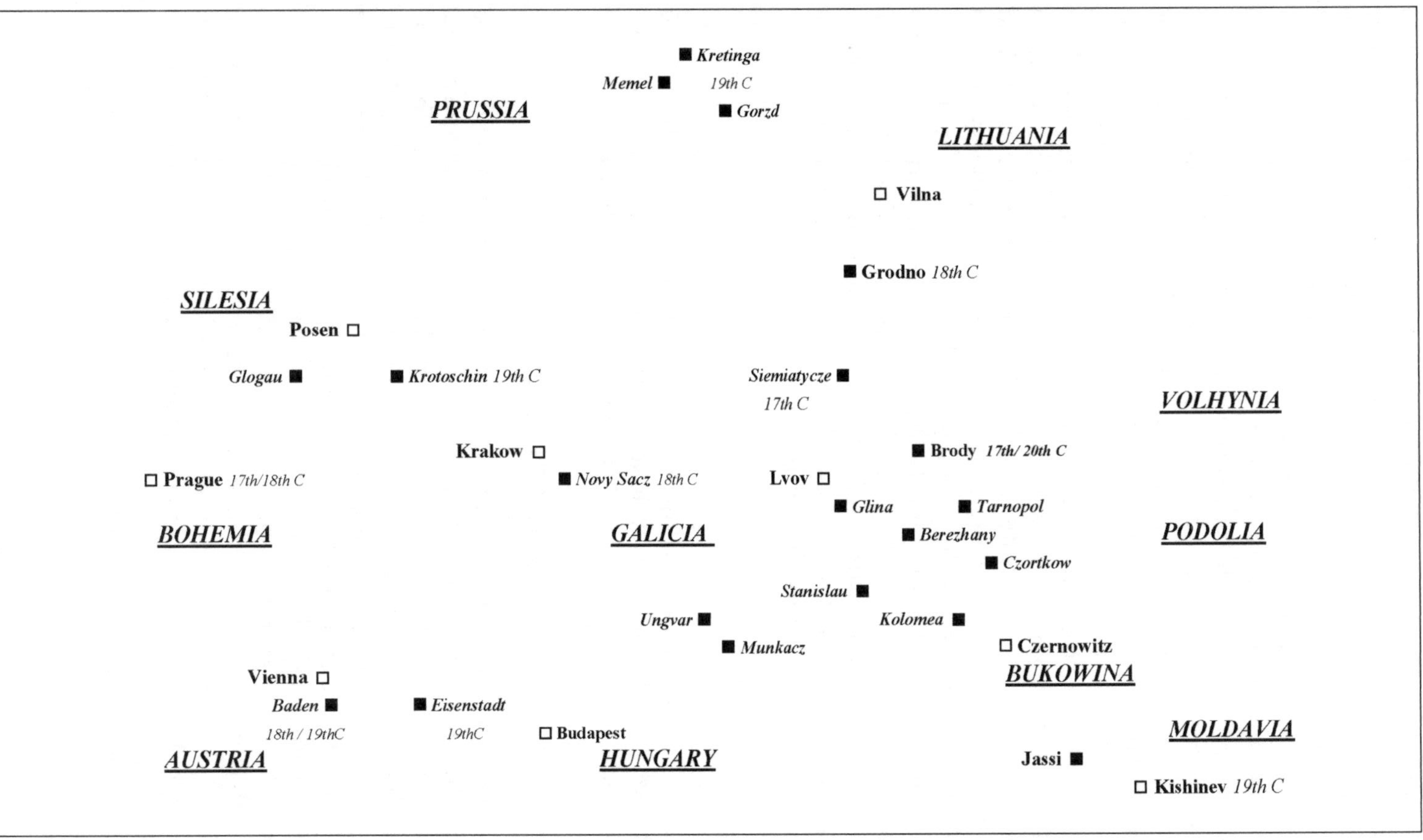

Map 4
Incidence of the Gelles name with some approximate dates

NOTES ON SOME CHAYES COUSINS

Different branches of the Chayes family have variously written their name with a 'y ' or a 'j'.

Oscar Chajes was born in Brody in 1873 and died in New York in 1928. He became one of the most successful chess players in the opening decades of the twentieth century. He won the US Western Open championship in 1909, and beat the world champion Jose Capablanca in 1916. Oscar Chajes was No. 10 in the world chess rankings in 1918–20.

Abraham Chayes was born in Chicago in 1922 and died in Boston in 2000. He was the Felix Frankfurter Professor of Law at Harvard University, adviser to John F. Kennedy, sometime legal adviser to the Department of State, influential teacher and author of books on international law. The five children of his marriage to Professor Antonia Handler Chayes include Professor Lincoln Chayes of UCLA and the reporter and journalist Sarah Chayes who lives in Paris. Abraham's father, Edward Chayes was born in Chicago in 1895. Professor Lewis Glinert, who is a distant Chajes cousin, traces the family back via Abraham Chayes (born ca. 1870 in Russia) to Yehuda Leib Chajes, who was perhaps a sibling of Rabbi Zvi Hirsch Chajes of Zolkiew. They came to the United Sates via Brazil and Argentina. The family count themselves as of the Chayes clan although the precise connection to the Brody family remains to be clarified.

Julius Chajes was born in Lemberg in 1910 and died in Detroit in 1985. He gave public performances as a pianist at the age of 9 and composed a string quartet when he was 13. At the age of 15 Chajes performed his Romantic Fantasy with the Vienna Symphony Orchestra. In 1933 he won the prize for pianoforte in the International Music Competition held at Vienna and a year later he became head of the piano department at the School of Music in Tel Aviv. During his stay in Israel Chajes conducted extensive research on ancient Hebrew music. In the wake of these studies and local influences Chajes transformed his style of composition and became known as one of the foremost composers of modern Israeli music. After coming to the United Sates in 1937 he gave several recitals in New York Town Hall. In 1940 he accepted positions in Detroit including a teaching post at Wayne State University. Julius Chajes was survived by a widow Annette and one son, Yossi Hillel Chajes (born 1965), who is Professor of History at Haifa. Julius Chajes' archives are to be housed and studied at the Jewish Music Archive of Hebrew Union College, Cincinnati. Aron Marko Rothmüller wrote, 'Chajes is particularly successful in employing and arranging Palestinian folk-songs and religious melodies. In this connection we must mention his Palestinian Dance and Palestinian Melodies for piano, and several psalms for soli and chorus'. Henryk Szering often played Chajes' violin sonata in recitals and wrote (in a letter dated 3 August 1978) 'his music is to Israel, what Chopin's was to Poland, de Falla's to Spain, and Bartok's to Hungary'.

Julius Chajes was the elder son of the gynaecologist Dr Joseph Chajes (Lemberg 1875–Tel Aviv 1944) and of his wife Valerie Roth (1893–Detroit 1970). Joseph Chajes was the son of Marcus Chajes who, according to Dr Neil Rosenstein, was a nephew of Rabbi Zvi Hirsch Chajes of Zolkiew.

Figure 44 shows Julius Chajes taking a class, assisted by his little son Yossi, who has now grown into a distinguished professor of Jewish history. Joseph, Julius and Yossi, and his progeny are an enduring paradigm for our wider family's journey from Europe, to America, and Israel.

Figure 44
Julius Chajes and his son Yossi

Chapter Thirty-Nine

My European Heritage

Cultural roots

INTRODUCTION

So many strands are woven into the tapestry of our ancient descent. Some of these strands go back to medieval Portugal, Spain and Provence. Others appeared in Italy, the Rhineland and northern France. Some of my forebears dwelt in these countries at least since the days of Charlemagne. The Sephardic roots have the glamour of a golden period of Jewish culture. Many Ashkenazi families laid claim to, or cherished memories of, such origins as they moved on from Germany and Austria to Bohemia and then to Poland, Lithuania and Russia. Our sojourn in eastern Europe may in some ways have had less cultural impact, in spite of its more recent past, than our history in western and central Europe. We were in the lands of the erstwhile Holy Roman Empire for over a thousand years.

SEPHARDIC ROOTS

In the late-fourteenth century many Jews fled from persecution in Spain. The final catastrophe in the Iberian peninsula followed a hundred years later. At the same time there was a general expulsion from Provence, where Jewish communities had flourished for centuries.

Sephardic origins in medieval Barcelona have been claimed for the Horovitz family who are better known for their association with the city of Prague and their later achievements in Poland and elsewhere. Pinchas Horovitz, the President of the Council of the Four Lands, the semi-autonomous governing body of Polish Jewry, was a *mechutan* (in-law) of our ancestor Saul Wahl.

My father's people in eighteenth-century Brody had marriage links to families with Sephardic roots such as Margoshes and Zundel Ramraz, who looked back to ancient times in Toledo and other cities of Spain.

The Chalfans of Provence distinguished themselves as scholars and physicians in Venice, Prague and Vienna where they flourished for several centuries. The progenitor of the Chayes family, Isaac ben Abraham 'of the wise men of Provence', became Chief Rabbi of Prague in the sixteenth century. From this Provençal family came the Altschulers, named after their association with the Prague synagogue which they helped to build. They were allied with the Treves who furnished Chief Rabbis in medieval France and were descended from Rashi.

RASHI AND THE MEDIEVAL RABBIS OF FRANCE

The ancient Kalonymos rose to prominence in the ninth and tenth centuries in northern Italy, in the Rhineland cities of Speyer and Mainz, in Provence at Nimes and Arles, and in Narbonne.

Rashi (Salomon ben Isaac) was born in 1040 at Troyes in Champagne, which already had a considerable Jewish community by the tenth century. His father was Isaac Zarfati (that is, from France) and his mother was of Kalonymos descent. Rashi studied at Worms and founded a school around 1070. He is famed for definitive commentaries on the Bible and Talmud, and he thus influenced generations of Jews and Christians. The first printed Hebrew book was his commentary on the Pentateuch. His glossaries describing common tasks of daily life used French words spelt in Hebrew characters. Quite apart from their religious importance these texts have been useful in the reconstruction of the old French *langue d'oïl*. Rashi has been the subject of much study and many old families with rabbinical connections claim descent from him. It is thought that his cousin, Aaron the physician, was sent to Rome by the Byzantine Emperor Constantine X to treat Pope Urban II. The millennial Jewish contribution to the study and practice of medicine is well documented. Aaron's people were doctors and rabbis in Italy and France. A descendant, Moses Aaron was a thirteenth-century Chief Rabbi of Orleans and Cracow. Five generations down his line, around 1360, there flourished Samson Luria, a physician of Orleans, who found refuge at Erfurt during one of the not-infrequent temporary expulsions of the Jews from France. The Luria family, with Italian and French origins, developed branches in a number of countries. Samson Luria was a contemporary of Matithia Treves of Provence, who became Chief Rabbi of Paris in 1364 and whose father was Johanan ben Matithia Treves, Chief Rabbi of France.

Marriages between these Treves, Spiro and Luria families formed a nexus between the earlier times and the late medieval period when other families became prominent. The Katzenellenbogens are among the descendants of Yehiel Luria of Alsace (d. ca.1470/90) and can therefore trace their lineage back to Rashi and hence to biblical times. From their base in Germany, they moved to Prague, Padua and Venice, and then to Poland.

GERMAN ROOTS

The rabbinical clans of the middle ages often took their names from their geographical origin. The Treves family may have derived their name from Trier, an Imperial city of Roman times. The descendants of Samuel of Speyer adopted the name of Shapiro (Spiro). The Halperns were from Heilbronn. There are the eponymous Katzenellenbogen, Oppenheim, Landau and other families.

Ancient towns with famous Jewish communities include Mainz (Kalonymos, Minz) and Worms (Loew). Gelles or Gellis is accepted to be a matronymic derived from the medieval German girl's name Gele (the yellow or fair-haired). Gelnhausen was an important city in the middle ages, when it was known as *Geilinhus* (Geile's houses). The city lies quite close to Frankfurt and numerous Gelhausers lived in Frankfurt during the fifteenth to seventeenth centuries. According to the tradition in my father's family some of our forebears were in Frankfurt at one time. Rabbi David Gans of Prague studied in Frankfurt and his daughter Geyle died there. There were numerous descendants of Gans and of Gelles in Prague in the immediately succeeding period.

REFUGE IN ITALY

In the middle ages there were some Jews in the little German town of Katzenellenbogen. Persecution in their homeland set some on a journey that ended in Padua. Meir Katzenellenbogen was head of a famous Jewish academy there. His son, Samuel Judah, in turn, became Chief Rabbi of Padua and Venice. He was the father of Saul Wahl.

Saul went to Poland as a young man to continue his studies. He rose to eminence in the late-sixteenth century through the patronage of the princely Radziwills, at a time when the state of Poland-Lithuania reached the zenith of its political power. The Poles possibly called him Wahl because in medieval usage the name suggested his Italian origin. Karl Marx, Moses and Felix Mendelssohn, and the Rothchilds are the best known of innumerable descendants who have attained prominence in many countries to the present day.

Saul Wahl's mother was a Yaffe. There were numerous marriages between the Wahl and Yaffe families. An appended chart shows a line of descent from Moses Yaffe of Bologna who took his family to Prague in the late-fifteenth century. Generations of this family prospered in Italy, Bohemia and Poland under the patronage of a King of Hungary and of successive Jagiellon and Habsburg rulers. The family's movements across central and eastern Europe reflected to a large extent the fortunes of their patrons.

Rabbi Mordecai Yaffe was a scion of this ancient family. He took refuge in Venice for ten years when the Jews were expelled from Prague in 1561. He was in touch with some of the leading scholars of his day, and wrote on many subjects including astronomy and political science. He is best remembered as the author of the major commentary *The Robes of Learning* and he was also a community leader who was largely responsible for the foundation of the Council of the Four Lands in Poland-Lithuania.

The flow of Jewish refugees from the Iberian peninsula and Provence brought many to Italy. The afore-mentioned Chayots moved on from Prague to Poland where the family, henceforward known as Chayes, established themselves in the little Galician town of Brody. The family included Zvi Hirsch Chayes, the nineteenth-century Rabbi of Zolkiew and his grandson Zvi Perez Chayes, who became professor at the University of Florence, Chief Rabbi of Trieste, and ultimately Chief Rabbi of Vienna in the period between the two world wars.

Another branch of the Chajes family settled in Livorno and Florence in the eighteenth century, where they enjoyed an enlightened economic regime and liberal approach to Jewish communal autonomy. Menachem Manish Chajes of Brody had come here after marrying the daughter of Wolf Berenstein, son of the first Chief Rabbi of Galicia. He and his family prospered in the coral trade, which laid the basis for the commercial bank, Berenstein, Chajes & Co. of Florence.

The Wahl-Katzenellenbogen family tree sprouted innumerable branches. In the nineteenth century many were still based in Poland. It was a long way from sixteenth-century Padua and Venice to nineteenth-century Galicia and to the Europe riven by the two great world wars. A long cry from 'living happily in Padua, living wealthily in Padua' of Shakespeare's day!

However, Italy once again gave refuge to one of their number in the century that has just ended. Lucia Ohrenstein was, like my mother, a granddaughter of Shulim Wahl of Tarnobrzeg. She married Livio Tripcovich who came from a Dalmatian shipping family based in Trieste. His family was ennobled in 1936 and the name is presently borne by a nephew, the composer Baron Raffaello de Banfield Tripcovich.

Scholars, civic leaders and entrepreneurs, and also a charming butterfly have woven their strands into the tapestry of our Italian experience. Our journey has taken us from Portugal, France and Germany, to Bohemia and Austria. Our long sojourn in Poland, where at first we were welcome and honoured guests came to an end in the horror of world war. But it is the ancient Italian and German dimensions that are central to our cultural background.

PRAGUE AT THE CROSSROADS

The Jewish community of Prague had a glorious history. Its heyday was in the sixteenth century when the city stood at the crossroads of Europe and of Jewish migrations from Germany and Austria to Poland and the east. The great Rabbis of Prague in this period included Judah Loew whose family hailed from Worms in Germany, his brother-in-law Isaac ben Abraham

Chayes from Provence, Mordecai Yaffe whose family had come to Prague from Italy and who were to shine later in Poland and elsewhere, and Judah Loew's pupil, the historian and astronomer David Gans, who had studied in Frankfurt before settling in Bohemia

The times were far from tranquil. Many times the Jews were expelled from Prague. But they were needed for their contribution to commerce and finance. Thus, their great community leader Mordecai Marcus ben Samuel Meisel left with the others in 1542 and again in 1561, only to return and to become in the words of a leading historian 'the first Jewish capitalist in Germany'. He obtained the novel privilege of being able to lend money on property mortgages and promissory notes and he went on to finance the Turkish wars of the Emperor Rudolf II. With his immense fortune he became the outstanding philanthropist of his age. Members of his family duly participated in the general drift to Poland and Lithuania. Simcha Bonem Meisels married a daughter of Moses Isserles, the famous Rabbi of Cracow.

SOJOURN IN POLAND

My ancestors were in Germany long enough to form ties that for good or ill have persisted to this day. The so-called Ashkenazi Jews were subjected to periodical persecutions and expulsions for hundreds of years, but they both absorbed and contributed to German culture while they were there. The names of the great rabbinical families remind one of their medieval German origins.

Polish kings had encouraged Jewish immigration for sound economic reasons since the days of Casimir the Great in the fourteenth century. In the sixteenth century the influences of renaissance and reformation and the increased wealth of the landed nobility combined to produce for a time a state of comparative religious tolerance and economic opportunity, which attracted many Jews who were under pressure elsewhere. Jewish communities grew rapidly in Poland and Lithuania. They contributed greatly to the economic life of the country, in provision and management of credit, and in diverse trades and enterprises. For two centuries until 1764 the Council of the Four Lands was the semi-autonomous governing body of Polish Jewry with internal taxation and judicial powers and spoke for its community in matters of State. As the community flourished a number of towns became centres for religious learning and attracted some of the leading rabbis of the age.

The Katzenellenbogens became eminent rabbis in Italy, but they had come from Germany via Prague, and with Saul ben Judah Katzenellenbogen, known as Saul Wahl, they entered Polish history. His family and also that of other forebears such as the Chayes produced many rabbis throughout the seventeenth to nineteenth centuries. But the decline of the Polish state and that of Jewish communal life set in with the Cossack rising of Bogdan Chmielnicki in the mid-seventeenth century. By the eighteenth century when Poland succumbed to a series of partitions, a long period of depression, not to say of degeneration, had set in for the Jews of that country. In reaction, there arose the Chasidic movement, which in the following century competed with the gathering enlightenment and beginnings of emancipation. The latter movements gradually affected the whole of Europe, and led to a reversal of the age-old eastern migration, with many Jews yearning to gain entry into the full cultural life of the continent denied to them for so many centuries.

The general pattern was migration from Germany and Italy, to Prague and Vienna, and to Poland and Lithuania, following waves of persecution and periodical expulsion. In line with the growth and decline of Jewish communities my ancestors might have travelled this road to Cracow, Breslau or Posen, and then spread further afield. In the early eighteenth century the Galician border town of Brody became an important Jewish centre for a relatively short while. The city of Glogau in German Silesia as well as the nearby towns of Lissa and Krotoschin also come into our family history at that time.

One of our forebears was Samuel Helman, who was born in Krotoschin, studied in Prague, and then became in turn Rabbi of Kremsier in Moravia, Chief Rabbi of Mannheim in Germany, and finally Chief Rabbi of Metz in Lorraine, where he died in 1764. His wife came from Glogau in German Poland. His daughters married into some leading rabbinical families of their day, Katzenellenbogen, Rapaport and Fraenkel. One was the daughter-in-law of David Mirels Frankel, the Chief Rabbi of Berlin, a granddaughter married the son of Ezekiel Landau, the Chief Rabbi of Prague, a grandson, Naftali Hirsch Katzenellenbogen was Chief Rabbi of the Palatinate, and the latter's grandson became Chief Rabbi of France.

From Krotoschin and from a similar background of the Halpern–Katzenellenbogen nexus came eighteenth-century immigrants to England such as the Samuel family, who rose to importance and affluence in their new home.

The nearby Silesian town of Lissa had a notable Rabbi in David Tebele, the son of Chief Rabbi Nathan Nata of Brody. They were descendants of Aryeh Leib Fischls, known as der Hoicher Rebbe Leib, who succeeded Abraham Joshua Heschel of the Katzenellenbogen family in the Chief Rabbinate of Cracow in the seventeenth century.

Movements from east to west in the next century are exemplified by the descendants of these Rabbis. Zvi Hirsch Berlin, known in England as Rabbi Hart Lion (1721–1800), and his son Solomon Herschel Berliner (1762–1842), both occupied the post of Chief Rabbi of the Ashkenazi community in London, the latter becoming the first Chief Rabbi of the British Empire.

Other important communities in western Europe attracted Polish scholars from this wider ancestral circle. Thus, Hamburg in this period had Ezekiel Katzenellenbogen, Isaac Horowitz and Zvi Hirsch Zamosc among its Chief Rabbis.

AT HOME IN THE AUSTRO-HUNGARIAN EMPIRE

In the eighteenth century many Moravian and Galician Jews migrated to Hungary. The town of Eisenstadt, which had already provided a shelter from persecution in the seventeenth century, then became an important centre of Jewish learning. There was a family connection between German Poland, Austrian Galicia and the Burgenland.

On my mother's side, branches of our family flourished in Austrian Galicia until the eve of the First World War. They were generally among the leaders of their communities in a number of small towns. Later in the nineteenth century they gradually left their provincial centres for Lemberg, Cracow and Vienna. Between the two world wars Galicia became again a part of Poland. When that country was overrun in 1939, many had already gone to England and the Americas, to Italy, and elsewhere. Survivors whose families are now flourishing, say in France, are descendants of Jews who were driven to migrate eastwards from these lands in the middle ages.

In the period from Charles V to Maria Theresa, Austrian Jews went through many of the trials and tribulations that was their lot elsewhere. Residence, occupation and dress, access to educational facilities and much else were matters subject to restrictions amounting to onerous civil disabilities. The principal grounds for anti-Jewish feeling were religious and economic. These led to periodical expulsions, but as in some German states and in Poland, the rulers were unwilling or unable to manage their economic affairs without Jewish bankers. So the mass expulsion from Vienna in 1670 was relaxed within a generation.

The so-called Court Jews provisioned armies, financed military campaigns, and raised state loans. One of the first was Mordecai Meisel in Rudolf II's Prague, but they are generally thought of as a seventeenth to eighteenth century phenomenon. However, their sixteenth-century precursor, Saul Wahl, was rather more than a royal agent in Poland. He played a role in the affairs of state on the political level as well as in economics. Like the Austrian Court Jew, Samson Wertheimer, who became Imperial *Hof-Faktor* and *Landes-Rabbiner* of Hungary a hundred years later, this was not just an outstanding entrepreneur but a cultured man steeped in Jewish learning. Wahl moreover had received the best classical education that Renaissance Padua had to offer.

Jewish financiers could and did rise to great wealth and influence. Jews had also been prominent in the service of princes in other ways. Rabbis studied medicine and there were many prominent Jewish Court physicians. Their international connections qualified some to engage successfully in diplomacy. Incumbents of the great rabbinical posts included some with family connections, but there were of course many more rabbinical ancestors who were unknown worthies in small provincial towns.

Enlightenment and gradual emancipation from the reign of Joseph II more or less coincided with the Polish partitions and the acquisition of Galicia. The Jews of the Empire were concentrated there and in other outlying provinces such as Bukowina. In the course of the later nineteenth century more and more newly emancipated Jews sought higher education, and entry into the professions. There were massive inflows to Vienna and Budapest. Arts, journalism and the liberal professions began to be dominated by them. The great Jewish bankers were still indispensable to the Government finances through most of the nineteenth century. In the era of assertive nationalism all this gave rise to increasing resentment.

However, there is no doubt that the period up to the outbreak of the First World War was a golden age for Austrian Jewry. The later Habsburg Empire was quite liberal and philosemitic. After all, the Kaiser ruled over and balanced so many ethnic minorities. The Jews of Galicia like others in the Empire sent their members to the Imperial Parliament, they were loyal subjects of the crown and distinguished themselves in its civil and military service. This period saw Vienna attain a level of cultural distinction which becomes more impressive with the passage of time, and in which the specifically Jewish contribution is increasingly recognized.

In the year the old Emperor Franz Joseph died my father was admitted to the roll of advocates in Vienna. David Gelles and his brother Max as well as his sister Lotte were doctors of law of Vienna University. Their father was almost the last of a long line of rabbis who had traversed the continent over the centuries to take up posts in many lands. Descendants of Moses Gelles of Brody had connections with Chasidic sages such as Pinchas Shapiro of Koretz and the Friedmans of Czortkow. The Chasidic movement, which found fertile ground in eighteenth-century Galicia, had its roots in age-old Jewish mysticism, in the medieval study of the Cabbala, and in the school of Isaac Luria at Safed in the sixteenth century. Chasidism combined Talmudic Judaism with ideas close to those found in Plato and in Neo-Platonic and Pythagorean philosophy.

SUMMARY

From ancient roots we eventually found our way to Padua and Venice, Vienna and Prague, Cracow and Vilna, and beyond. In the sixteenth century Prague was the outstanding crucible for some of our forebears, and seventeenth-century Cracow became another great centre of Jewish culture. By the end of the eighteenth century the descendants of Meir Katzenellenbogen of Padua, of the above-mentioned great men of Prague, and of the later Rabbis of Cracow, such as Nathan Nata Shapiro, Abraham Joshua Heschel, and Aryeh Leib Fischls, were prominent on a pan-European stage. Many instances of the multiple connections between these and other ancient families have been given in the preceding pages. One might mention again that the mother of Saul Wahl Katzenellenbogen was a Yaffe. Chief Rabbi Joel Sirkes of Cracow was of Yaffe descent and David Halevi Segal, the Chief Rabbi of Lvov, was his son-in-law. The latter was a kinsman of the Yollis family who were connected by marriage with the Katzenellenbogen clan. There were Yollis connections back to the Chalfans and with Horovitz and Rapaport. The Kloisner line of Aryeh Leib Fischls went back to the family of Judah Loew, Abraham Joshua Heschel was a scion of the Katzenellenbogen, and Nathan Nata Shapiro of Grodno, the grandfather of the famous Cracow Rabbi of that name, was a first cousin of David Gans. This is the genealogical framework, extending over hundreds of years and across the entire continent, into which my forebears on both my father's and my mother's side are deeply embedded.

My rabbinical ancestors were guardians of Jewish law and teachers of the ethical code to which the civilization of Christian Europe is heavily indebted. Law and medicine, logic and the study of languages had been the concern of rabbis through the centuries. The process of assimilation into the mainstream of European culture therefore came easily to their emancipated progeny. It is gratifying that the present generation is increasingly interested in the Jewish heritage and in the Jewish involvement with the history of our continent.

Table 50

CONNECTIONS BETWEEN ANCIENT CLANS

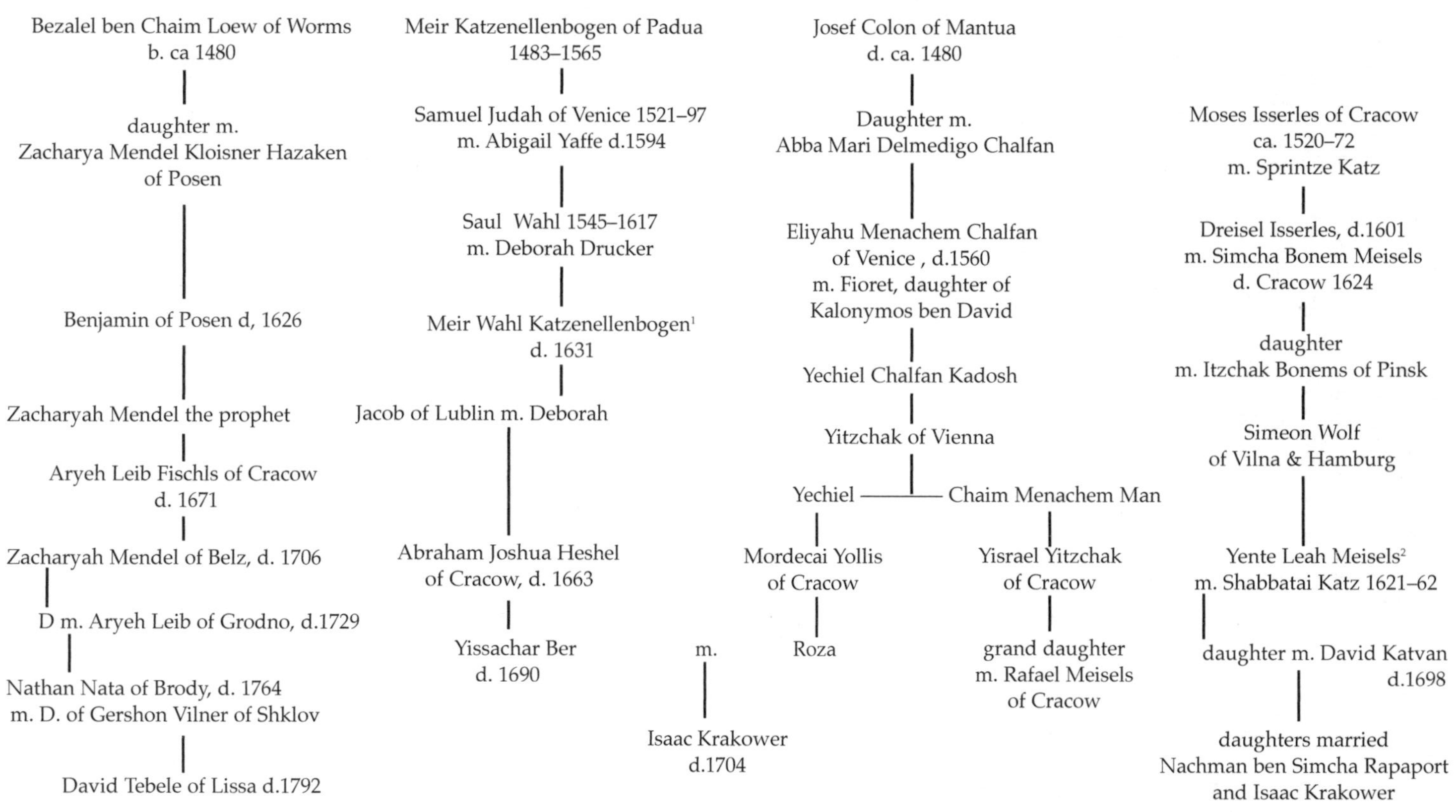

Notes:

1. Loew-Katzenellenbogen connection through the marriage of Sara, daughter of Benjamin of Posen [Beinish Reb Mendels] to Moses of Chelm, the son of Meir Wahl Katzenellenbogen. Their son Saul Katzenellenbogen of Pinczow (1617–91) and Yente, daughter of Jacob Shor, had a daughter who married Jacob of Ludmir (d.1730), the grandson of Aryeh Leib Fischls (der Hoicher Rebbe Leib of Cracow).
2. Yente's sister Dreizel and Judah Wahl Katzenellenbogen were the forebears of Moses Mendelssohn.

Table 51
KALONYMOS–CHALFAN

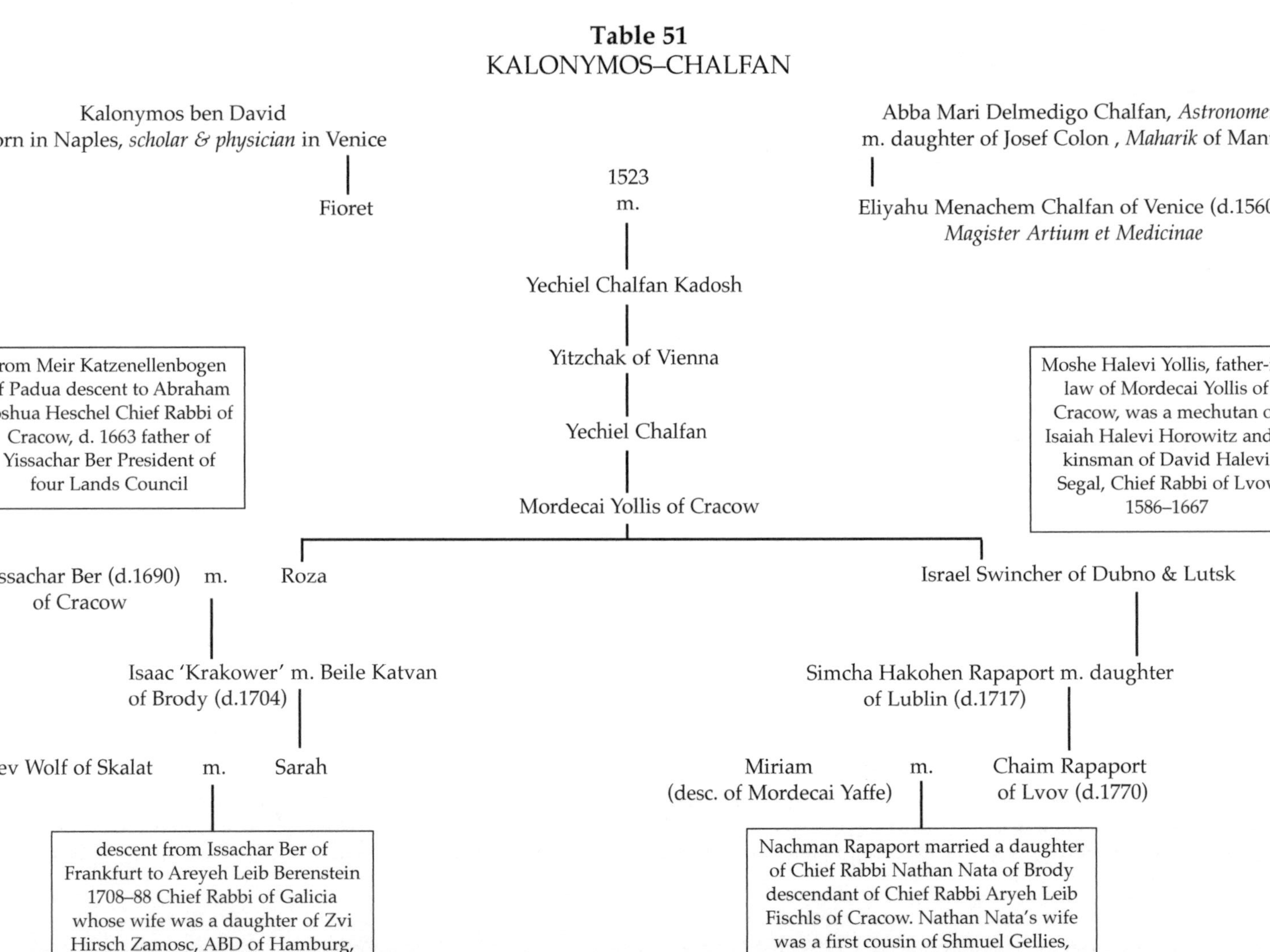

Notes:
Various sources including A.J. Bruck, *The Bruck Family* (New York: 1946, Historia Judaica No.8); Yitzchak Shlomo Yudlov, *Sefer Yichus Belza* (Jerusalem: Machon, 1984) (but cf. Englard, *Tzefunot* 4:3, pp.87–8); Hillel Noach Steinschneider, *Ir Vilna* (Vilna: 1900); David Tebele Ephrati, *Toldot Anshei Shem* (Warsaw: 1875); Louis Lewin, *Die Geschichte der Juden in Lissa* (Pinne: N. Rudermann, 1904); Neil Rosenstein, *The Unbroken Chain* (New York, London, Jerusalem: CIS Publishers, 1990); *Jewish Encyclopedia* 1904 edn; etc.

Table 52
A FRAGMENT OF CHAYES FAMILY HISTORY

AD	Chayes Line
	Isaac ben Abraham, ca. 1538–1610, Chief Rabbi of Prague
1600	Menachem Manish, 1560–1636, Rabbi of Vilna
	Jacob
	Isaac ben Jacob, ca 1660–1726, Rabbi of Skole
1700	Eliezer, ABD of Nemirow and Psheworsk, d.1767
	Isaac, member of Four Lands Council, d. in the Holy Land
	Meyer, ABD of Tysmienica
	Isaac of Brody, d.1807 m. daughter of Nathan Nata, ABD of Brody, d.1764
	Menachem Manish of Brody, Livorno & Florence, d.1832 m. grand-daughter of Aryeh Leib Berenstein, d. 1788 Chief Rabbi of Galicia
1800	Meir, banker of Florence and Brody, d.1854 m. Esther, desc of Issachar Ber of Frankfurt *Leone of Brody, b. 1794, settled in Livorno* Zvi Hirsch of Brody, 1805–55, Rabbi of Zolkiew *Giacomo, son of Leone, d. 1869* Salomon of Brody, 1835–96 m. Rebecca Shapiro *Adolfo of Livorno, d.1889*
1900	Zvi Hirsch Perez of Brody, 1876–1927 Chief Rabbi of Vienna *Count Guido de Chayes of Livorno, d.1906* *Count Giorgio de Chayes, d.1913*

Background

The Chayes family had ancient Sephardic origins in Portugal and Provence. They came to Bohemia in the fifteenth century, like others such as the related Altschulers. Isaac ben Abraham was a brother-in-law of Judah Loew of Prague, whose family hailed from Worms in Germany. Isaac Chayot, Judah Loew, and Mordecai Yaffe alternated in the post of Chief Rabbi of Prague. At this time Prague had a large Jewish community and was at the crossroads of migration from Germany and Italy to Poland and Lithuania. The resurgent Habsburg power was represented by Emperor Rudolf II who made his Court in Prague. In the sixteenth century Poland had flourished under the Jagiellonian kings. In 1569 the Union of Lublin joined the kingdom with the Grand Duchy of Lithuania and shortly afterwards the state became an elective monarchy. Under the Swedish king Zygmunt III (Vasa) the Jews continued to flourish with a substantial measure of self-government (this was the period when Saul Wahl rose to importance in the Polish Commonwealth). Isaac Chayot's son went to Vilna, and his descendants established themselves at Brody in Galicia, which prospered for a century as 'a free city' and entrepot between the Austrian and Russian Empires. The Chayes, as they were now called, produced many scholars and rabbis. A marriage with the Berensteins, who were of the Katzenellenbogen clan, brought a branch of the family to Tuscany in the eighteenth century. They were successful merchants and bankers in a traditionally liberal atmosphere, which was maintained by the Habsburg successors to the Medici rulers and continued into the days of the Risorgimento and the Kingdom of a united Italy. Livorno like Brody was for long a 'free city' and an important entrepot. In the nineteenth century the family produced great Rabbis in Zvi Hirsch Chajes of Zolkiew and his grandson Hirsch Perez Chajes, who was Professor at Florence, Chief Rabbi of Trieste, and an outstanding Chief Rabbi and community leader in Vienna in the inter-war years.

Table 53
A FRAGMENT OF YAFFE FAMILY HISTORY

AD	Yaffe Line	
1400		
	Moses of Bologna	– *financed wars against the Ottoman Turks, moved to Prague*
1500		
	Abraham of Bohemia	– *Appointed in 1512 Prefect of the Jews of Poland*
	Eliezer	– *remained in Poland*
	Joseph of Prague	
	Abraham of Prague	– *his brothers were Isaac and Eliezer of Mantua*
	Mordecai of Prague	– *ca. 1530–1612 The LEVUSH Scholar & Community Leader*
1600		
	Perez	
	Abraham Aberle of Nikolsburg	– *financial services in Moravia*
	Joseph of Posen	
1700		
	Mordecai of Plungian, Lithuania	– *born 1721 Rabbi of Keidani 1756*
	Joseph of Keidani	– *President of the Council of Lithuania*

Political Background

John Hunyadi defeated the Turks at Belgrade in 1456 His son Matthias Corvinus became King of Hungary in 1458. This Renaissance Prince was politically involved in Italy and a great patron of literature and the arts. His second wife was Princess Beatrice of Naples. Following Bohemian entanglements, he occupied Vienna in 1485, but after his death in 1490 Hungary passed to the Jagiellonian rulers of Poland and Bohemia. Abraham Yaffe was recommended by Vladislaw Jagiellon of Bohemia to his brother Zygmunt I of Poland (1506–48) who was married to Bona Sforza, daughter of the Duke of Milan. The rivalries of Habsburg, Jagiellon and the Hungarian nobility, and the religious struggles in Bohemia opened the way to Ottoman Turkish incursions. Louis Jagiellon, King of Hungary and Bohemia, fell at the battle of Mohacs in 1526. Most of Hungary remained under Ottoman rule until the late seventeenth century. After Mohacs, the Habsburgs continued to expand their Austrian power base as the last bulwark against further Turkish advance. Joseph Yaffe appears to have returned from Poland to Prague at the behest of the Habsburg ruler of Bohemia. The peregrinations of Mordecai Yaffe from Prague to Italy, Lithuania and Poland, back to Prague, and finally to Posen are well known. He was the prime mover in the creation of the Jewish Council of the Four Lands. His grandson Abraham Aberle of Nikolsburg and the latter's son Joseph appear to have enjoyed the patronage of succeeding Habsburg rulers. Joseph Yaffe travelled from Moravia to Posen and was killed on a journey from Posen to Plungian during the War of the Polish Succession.

Table 54
A FRAGMENT OF GELLES FAMILY HISTORY

AD	Gelles Line
1600	
	Rabbi S(hmuel) Gelles
1700	
	Menachem Mendel Levush aka Moses Gelles of Brody *Scholar of the Brody Klaus*
	Mordecai Gelles
	Moses Gelles
1800	
	Rabbi David Isaac Gellis
	Rabbi Nahum Uri Gelles
1900	
	Dr David Isaac Gelles *Advocate in Vienna*
	Edward Gelles *in England since 1938*

Background

Our ancestors were among the rabbinical families emanating from the Rhineland and northern Italy who congregated in sixteenth-century Prague and then proliferated in Lithuania, Silesia, and Galicia. The most prominent of these families included those of Judah Loew, David Gans and Mordecai Yaffe. Primary sources such as tombstone inscriptions and vital data from Jewish community and civil records as well as evidence from the rabbinical literature reveal a direct Gelles line going back to the Galician city of Brody and to a scholar of the Brody Klaus, whose epithet of *Levush* –passed down by some in his family for several generations – can be shown as indicative of descent from Rabbi Mordecai Yaffe of Prague (1530–1612).

The Jewish community of Brody grew rapidly at the beginning of the eighteenth century with an influx of Rabbis from Lithuania and these included some of our forebears. Brody became part of the Austro-Hungarian Empire at the first of the three Polish partitions in 1772 and remained so until the end of the First World War. In the later eighteenth century many Jews moved from Galicia and Bukowina to Hungary (Eisenstadt) and to Austria, including Vienna, whose old community had been expelled in 1670 but was reinvigorated in the following generations. The descendants of Moses Gelles of Brody had links by marriage with many Rabbis including Samuel Helman of Metz (died 1764) and Pinchas Shapiro of Koretz (died 1791).

CHAPTER FORTY

Conclusion

Genealogy and history

I have approached the history of European Jewry through a genealogical study of my own family. Vast impersonal forces undoubtedly underlie great historical movements, but I believe that individuals are endowed with a measure of free will and have the capacity to alter the course of human history.

Individuals are the quintessential raw material of genealogy. The questions a genealogist seeks to answer concern the names of individuals, where they came from, who their parents, siblings, spouses and children were, how they lived, and what characteristics distinguished their ancestors or progeny. These questions take one into the fields of onomastics, geography and demography, history, genetics, philosophy and religion.

Individuals belong to families. A network of links with other families can produce groups that develop economic ties and a common culture. Generally such groups tend to settle in one region or country, but the Jews have been uprooted time and again by religious persecutions or economic pressures and were forced to move across the European continent. The historical events that gave the impetus to these migrations are well known and have left their mark in the records of many families. There were of course individual transplantations for a variety of reasons. Rabbis, in particular, were notably peripatetic as they followed the fall and rise of Jewish communities. I have found much that is relevant to Jewish as well as a wider European history from my study of a limited number of families.

The information that is encapsulated in ancient Jewish names can throw invaluable light on in-laws and their social standing, geographical origin, occupations, the titles of scholarly books, and even physical or mental attributes. All this was before family names became general at the end of the eighteenth and the beginning of the nineteenth centuries. The deciphering of the messages within names is one of the primary tasks of genealogical methodology.

For a few ancient families it is possible to trace their progress across Europe, gaining insights into the rise and fall of Jewish communities over the centuries. The vital data on these families show how they fit into the great tapestry of the Ashkenazi rabbinate.

Without going too far into the debate on nature versus nurture, one cannot help wondering whether ten or twenty generations of rabbis and scholars in such lineages as the Katzenellenbogen, Shapiro or Chajes are evidence of genetic inheritance in an intensively inbred elite and to what extent early childhood environment has contributed to their continuing intellectual vigour. Stories are told about sermons being given by a three year old, and a child of five years absorbing the contents of a French dictionary in a week, but these boys were no doubt exceptionally precocious. The rabbinical families tended to marry into others of similar standing, and a place within one ancient rabbinic clan made it likely that there would be more connections to other clans as one goes back in time. It is thus not extraordinary to find family connections to most of the great Ashkenazi Rabbis of the past 500 years. These inevitably take one back to Rashi of Troyes and the Kalonymos family. Claims linking Rashi, the Lurias, Judah Loew's ancestors, and others to biblical times and to the family of King David have respectable foundations but are not pursued in a book that is primarily concerned with Europe in the second millennium of our era.

Some of the Chasidic leaders who briefly make an appearance in these pages were credited with extraordinary psychic powers. A common belief in reincarnation and the transmigration of souls was part of a religious way of life that lifted them and some of their followers to another plane of existence. These saintly Rabbis gave the impression of being able to pass freely to and fro from the mundane world of our everyday experience, which is governed by historical time, to a timeless spiritual world which most of us glimpse only at rare moments during our earthly sojourn. They believed that God dwells in all things and their message was that we should allow him fully into our lives to re-establish the unity between the two worlds. A philosophy that takes the purpose of history to be the education of human souls is enriched by this great Jewish heritage.

Glossary

Admur:	Chasidic Rabbi / leader of community group
Agudas:	Society or Party, e.g. Agudas Israel
Amoraim:	Talmudic sages
Arendar:	purchaser of a licence to run an estate with the benefit of specified monopoly rights for a fixed period
Ashkenazi:	pertaining to central and east European Jewry / speaking *Yiddish* (Judeo–German)
Av Beth Din:	Rabbinical head of the religious court of a community – abbreviated ABD
Avot:	Forefathers
Beit Hamidrash:	House of study
bat:	daughter of
ben:	son of
Besht:	Israel Baal Shem Tov, founder of Chasidism
Cabbala:	Tradition/an ancient corpus of Jewish mysticism and esoteric knowledge
Chabad:	Lubavich branch of Chasidic movement
Chacham:	title of Sephardic Rabbi/a wise man
Charif:	sharp-witted/cf. Witteles, Spitzkopf, Chacham
Chasidim:	members of the Chasidic movement established during the eighteenth century
Chazan:	Synagogue overseer/Cantor
Chevra Kadisha:	burial society
Chidushei:	Novellae
Dayan:	judge, a member of the Rabbinical court
Diaspora:	Greek word for dispersion – the world wide dispersion of the Jews
Emunah:	belief

Gabbai: elected synagogue official/attendant to a rabbi
Gaon: ancient title given to heads of academies/rabbinical eminence
Gedulat: greatness of
Gemarrah: the collected commentaries of the *Amoraim* of Babylon and the Holy Land on the Mishna and other related traditions
Ghetto: quarter of a city to which Jews were restricted
Golah: exile/emigration

Haggada: legend, anecdote, or parable of rabbinic literature
Halacha: Jewish religious law
Haskalah: Jewish enlightenment in eighteenth- and nineteenth-century Europe
Herem: excommunication

Kahal/Kehillot: Jewish community/communities
Keneset: gatherings
Kohen/Kohanim: of the priestly caste – descendants of Aaron, the High Priest
Khazaria: tribal kingdom north of the Black Sea that flourished in the seventh to tenth century; some of its Turkic ruling class converted to Judaism in the ninth century
Klaus: collegiate house of study
Kinnui: nickname or secular given name

Levi: of the priestly tribe of Levi

Maggid: preacher
Manhig: community leader, see *Parnas*
Marranos: Iberian converts to Christianity who remained hidden Jews
Maskilim: members of the *Haskalah* movement
Mechutan: relationship of the parents of a married couple (as well as the respective siblings of the parents)
Megilla: scroll
Melamed: teacher
Meorei: luminaries
Mitnagim: Jewish opponents of Chasidism
Mishna: the earliest recorded rabbinic work of Jewish Law
Mishpachot: families
Moreh: religious teacher

Nasi: prince or president/also a rabbinical title more honorific than ABD
Ne'eman: treasurer/secretary of community

Nefesh: soul

Parnas: warden of community
Parochet: curtain covering the Holy Ark in synagogue
Pilpul: dialectic used in the exposition of the Talmud
Pinkas: community record
Pogrom: Russian word for destruction or devastation used with particular reference to late nineteenth- and early twentieth-century anti-Jewish attacks in Russia and Ukraine
Rabbi: religious scholar and/or teacher/also title for religious leader of community
Reb: courtesy title of a gentleman
Rebbe: title of Chasidic Rabbi
Rebetzin: title of Rabbi's wife
Romaniot: Jew of Byzantine extraction
Rosh: head, e.g. Rosh Yeshivah – Head of the Yeshiva

Sanhedrin: Jewish High Court of 71 elders in ancient times
Schul: Yiddish colloquial for Synagogue
Sephardi: Jew of Iberian extraction/speaking *Ladino*
Sefer: book
Sefiroth: ten emanations or divine attributes of the *Cabbala*
Sha'ar: gate
Shabbataianism: beliefs associated with the followers of the false Messiah Shabbatai Zvi (1626–1716)
Shamash: Synagogue beadle
Shechinah: the Divine presence
She'er: remnant
Shem: name
Shtadlan: negotiator with authorities on behalf of a Jewish community
Shtetl: little town

Talmud: body of Jewish oral law comprising the Mishna and Gemarrah
Tannaim: Sages of the Mishna
Targum: Aramaic translation/exposition of the Bible
Tikkun: restoration of harmony in the universe – a cabbalistic concept
Torah: instruction or Divine Law/the Pentateuch

Vaad arba arazot: Council of the Four Lands – Governing Body of Eastern European Jewry

Yahrzeit: anniversary of death

Yeshiva: Talmudic academy of higher learning
Yichus: pedigree or lineage
Yizkor: memorial prayer
Yochasin: genealogical tree

Zaddik: saint/title of Chasidic master
Zikaron: memorial
Zimzum: contraction of the Infinite (En Sof) – a cabbalistic concept

ENGLISH TITLES OF A FEW SELECTED HEBREW RABBINICAL WORKS

Ahavat Zion: Love of Zion (Moses Ashkeanzi Halpern)
Bayis Chadash: New house (Joel Sirkes)
Chelkas Mekokek: Staff of the Lawgiver (Moses Lima)
Da'at Kedoshim: Knowledge of the Holy Ones (I.T.Eisenstadt)
Aseret Levushim: Garments or Robes {of Learning] (Mordechai Yaffe)
Ma'a lot Hayochasin: Steps of Pedigree (Ephraim Zalman Margulis)
Megale Amukot: Revealed Depths (Nathan Nata Spiro)
Meginei Shlomo: Protectors of Solomon (Yehoshua Heshel of Cracow)
Ohalei Shem: Tents of Names i.e. notables or men of learning (Shmuel Nach Gottlieb)
Otzar Harabbanim: Treasury of Rabbis (Nathan Zvi Friedman)
Pnei Yehoshua: Face of Yoshua (Jacob Joshua of Frankfort)
Seder Hadoroth: Order of Generations (Jechiel Heilprin)
Shem Hagedolim: Names of the Great Ones (Chayim Josef David Azulai)
Siftei Kohen: The Lips of a Priest (Shabatai Katz)
Toldot Anshei Shem: Generations of Men of Note (David Tebele Efrati)
Letoldot Hakehilot Bepolin: Generations of Polish communities (Zvi Hirsch Horowitz)
Tevuot Shor: The Produce of the Ox (Alexander Sender Shor)
Tosafot Yomtov: Additions of Yomtov (Yomtov Lipmann Heller)
Turei Zahav: Rows of Gold (David Halevi Segal)
Yesh Manhilin: Some Bequeath (Phineas Katzenellenbogen)
Zemach David: Sprig of David (David Gans)
Zohar: The Book of Splendour – early work of Jewish mysticism attributed to the *Tannai* Rabbi Shimon ben Yochai and circulated by Moses de Leon of Granada (died c.1305)

Figure 45

The Seal of Kalonymos ben Todros of Narbonne, circa 1300, showing lion rampant within shield, with inscriptions in Hebrew (obverse) and Langue d'oc (reverse). See Daniel M. Friedenberg, *Medieval Jewish Seals from Europe* (Wayne State University Press, 1987), pp.71–6.

SOME OF THE SYMBOLS ON JEWISH TOMBSTONES, FAMILY CRESTS, ETC.

The Star of David (Magen David), now the most common Jewish symbol, was adopted by the Zionist movement, and is incorporated in the flag of Israel. An older, specifically Jewish, symbol is the seven-branched candelabrum or the nine-branched Menorah associated with the festival of Chanukah. The crown, the Torah scroll, and two tablets representing the Ten Commandments are frequently seen on tombstones and crests. The ancient tribes of Israel each had their separate standard, that of the lion being associated with the tribe of Judah and particularly with King David and his royal line. The Kalonymos of Narbonne displayed a lion rampant. The seal of Saul Wahl reportedly had a lion rampant holding the two tablets of the Decalogue (see Chapter 4). This family is believed to be of Davidic descent as is that of Judah Loew of Prague (see Chapter 37). The descendants of Aaron, the high priest and brother of Moses, were of the tribe of Levi. The symbol of the priests is the two hands raised in benediction with the four fingers of each hand divided into two sets of two fingers. These families were called Hakohen or Katz (a Hebrew acronym of righteous priest). Some families who were of priestly descent combined this symbol with a family emblem. For example, some Rapaports had a crest of the Kohanic blessing with the bird of the Rapa (rabe = raven). The Levites, who in ancient times were in charge of the Ark of the Covenant and its household and ministered to the Kohanim, displayed as their emblem the pitcher, symbolic of their privileges that included the washing of the priest's hands. Levite families called Halevi (and sometimes Halevi Segal) include some Yollis, Landau and Horowitz. David Halevi Segal, the seventeenth-century Chief Rabbi of Lvov, belonged to this family nexus.

Select Bibliography

References to material from archives, periodicals, journals and web sites are to be found in the notes appended to individual chapters. The bibliography includes a section on relevant Yizkor books.

Adler, Avraham, *The Righteous Man and the Holy City* (Jerusalem: Jerusalem Library)

Adler, Marcus Nathan, *The Itinerary of Benjamin of Tudela* (Oxford: Oxford University Press, 1907)

Adlersberg, Alexander Yoel Hakohen, *Magen Avoth* (Stanislau: ed. and published by B. Schmerler, 1936)

Altman, Alexander, *Moses Mendelssohn. A Biographical Study* (Philadelphia: Jewish Publication Society of America, 1973)

Apih, Elio, *Trieste. Storia della citta Italiana* (ed. Laterza, 1988)

Arim Veimahot BeIsrael (ed. Y.L Maimon) (Jerusalem, 1952 and later)

Arim Veimahot BeIsrael volume 5 (Stanislau, ed. Dov Sadan and Menachem Gelernter)

Arim Veimahot BeIsrael volume 6 (Brody, ed. N.M. Gelber)

Assouline, Hadassah and others, Polish Sources at the Central Archives of the History of the Jewish People (Jerusalem: Avotaynu, 2004)

Avigdor, Isaac C., *Faith after the Flames* (New Haven: Rodgiva Publishing, 2005)

Azulai, C.Y.D., *Shem Hagedolim Hashalam* (with notes by Menachem Mendel Krengel of Krakow, published by Rabbi Joel Teitelbaum, Jerusalem: 1979)

Azulai, Chaim Josef David, *Diaries (Ma'agal Tov)* Part I. Transl. Dr Benjamin Cymerman (Jerusalem: Bnei Issakhar Institute, 1997)

Babad, A.M., *Imrei Tava* (Bnei Brak, Israel: 1983)

Beider, Alexander, *A Dictionary of Jewish Surnames from the Russian Empire* (NJ: Avotaynu, 1993)

Beider, Alexander, *Ancient Ashkenazi Jewish Surnames from Prague, 15th–18th Centuries* (NJ: Avotaynu, 1995)

Beider, Alexander, *A Dictionary of Jewish Surnames from the Kingdom of Poland* (NJ: Avotaynu, 1996)

Beider, Alexander, *A Dictionary of Ashkenazi Given Names: Their Origins, Structure, Pronounciation and Migrations* (NJ: Avotaynu, 2001)
Beider, Alexander, *A Dictionary of Jewish Surnames from Galicia* (NJ: Avotaynu, 2004)
Beller, Steven, *Vienna and the Jews 1867–1938. A Cultural History* (Cambridge: Cambridge University Press, 1989)
Berkley, George E., *Vienna and its Jews* (Madison Books, 1988)
Berndt, R., *Geschichte der Juden in Gross Glogau* (Glogau, 1873)
Bevan, Edwyn R. and Charles Singer (eds), *The Legacy of Israel* (Oxford: Clarendon Press, 1927)
Biographisches Handbuch der Deutschsprachigen Emigration nach 1933 (München: V.G. Saur, 1980)
Bonar, A.A. and R.M. McCheyne, *Narrative of a Mission of Inquiry to the Jews from the Church of Scotland in 1839* (Edinburgh: William Whyte, 1842)
Bonfil, Robert, *Rabbis and Jewish Communities in Renaissance Italy* (Oxford University Press/Littman Library, 1990)
Bouvat-Martin, Jean-Claude, *Memorbuch of Metz 1720–1849* (Paris: Cercle de Généalogie Juive, CGJ, 2001)
Brann, M., *Geschichte der Juden in Schlesien* (Berlin: 1917)
Brody, 'Records of the Beth Din 1808–1817' (New York: Jewish Theological Seminary, Manuscript MS 4037)
Brook, Kevin Alan, *The Jews of Khazaria* (Jason Aronson, 1999)
Bruck, Julius, *The Bruck Family* (New York: 1946, Historia Judaica No.8)
Bryce, Lord, *The Holy Roman Empire* (Macmillan, 1961)
Buber, Martin, *Die Erzählungen der Chasidim* (Zürich: Manesse Verlag, Conzett & Huber, 1949)
Buber, Solomon, *Kiriya Nisgava* (Cracow: Josef Fischer, 1903)
Buber, Solomon, *Anshei Shem* (Cracow: 1895)

Caro, Yehezkiel, *Geschichte der Juden in Lemberg* (Krakau: Josef Fischer, 1894)
Cohen, Yitzchak Yosef, *Chachmei Transylvania* (Jerusalem: Machon, 1989)

David Tebele, *Nefesh David* and *Michtov Le'David* (Przemysl: Alexander Sender Chaim Umkraut, 1878)
Davidowitz, Menashe Simcha, *Toldot Afsei Aretz* (Ramat Hasharon: 1996)
Davies, Norman, *God's Playground. A History of Poland* (London: Clarendon Press, 1981)
Davies, Norman, *Europe. A History* (Oxford: Oxford University Press, 1996)
Delugatch, Shmuel, *Agudas Shmuel* (Amsterdam: 1699)
Dembitzer, Chaim Nathan, *Kelilas Yoffi* (Cracow: 1888)
Dietz, Alexander, *The Jewish Community of Frankfurt. A Genealogical Study 1349–1849* ed. Isobel Mordy (Cornwall: Vanderher Publishing, 1988)
Dubnow, Simon, *Weltgeschichte des Jüdischen Volkes* (Jerusalem: 1937)

Edelmann, Hirsch, *Gedullath Shaul* (London: 1854)
Efrati, David Tebele, *Toldot Anshei Shem* (Warsaw: 1875)

Eisenstadt, I.T., *Da'at Kedoshim* (St Petersburg: J. Berman, 1897–98)
Encyclopedia Judaica (Jerusalem: Keter Publ., 1972)
Epstein, Isidore, *Judaism* (Harmondsworth: Penguin, 1959)
Ettlinger, F.W., *Ele Toldot* (Manuscript at the Leo Baeck Institute, New York)

Falk, Yosef, *Mivchar Kethavim* (ed. and introduced by Dov Sadan) (Tel Aviv: Yosef Shimoni-Mefitz Hasefer, 1974)
Feuchtwang, D., 'Epitaphien des Gräberfeldes zu Nikolsburg', in *Mitteilungen zur Juedischen Volkskunde* (1907)
Feuer, Lewis S., *Francis Bacon and the Jews. Who was the Jew in the New Atlantis?* (reprinted from the Transactions of the Jewish Historical Society)
Feuer, Lewis S., *The Life and Work of Joachim Gaunse, mining technologist and first recorded Jew in English-speaking North America* (Cincinnati: American Jewish Archives, 1987)
Fisher, H.A.L., *A History of Europe* (Fintana Library, 1960)
Fischler, Yehiel Michel, *Chasdei Avoth* (Lemberg: 1880)
Fraenkel, Louis and Henry, *Forgotten Fragments of the History of the Fraenkel Family* (K.G. Saur Verlag, 1999)
Fränkel-Grün, Adolf, *Die Geschichte der Juden in Kremsier* (Breslau: S. Schottländer, 1896–1901)
Fraenkel, L.A., *Zur Geschichte der Juden in Wien* (Vienna: 1853)
Freidenreich, H.P., *Jewish Politics in Vienna 1918–38* (Indiana University Press, 1991)
Friedenberg, Daniel M., *Medieval Jewish Seals from Europe* (Wayne State University Press, 1987)
Friedenson, Joseph, *Dateline Istanbul* (New York: Mesorah Publications Ltd, 1993)
Friedman, Israel, *The Rebbes of Czortkow* (New York: Artscroll Mesorah Publications, 2003)
Friedman, Nathan Zvi, *Otzar Harabbanim* (Bnei Brak, Israel: 1973)
Fuchs, Abraham, *The Unheeded Cry* (New York and Jerusalem: Artscroll Mesorah Publications, History Series, 1984)
Fuenn, S.J., *Kiryah Ne'emanah* (Vilna: 1860)

Gans, David, *Zemach David* (Prague: 1592)
Gellis, Max, *Kommentar zum GMBH-Gesetz* (Vienna: Linde Verlag, 2004 5th edn)
Gellis, Yaakov, *Encyclopedia LeChachmei Eretz Israel* (Jerusalem: 1975 et seq.)
Gilbert, Martin, *Atlas of Jewish History* (London: Routledge, 1993)
Gold, Hugo, *Die Juden und Judengemeinden Mährens in Vergangenheit und Gegenwart* (Brünn: Jüdischer Buch und Kunstverlag, 1929)
Gold, Hugo, *Geschichte der Juden in der Bukowina* (Tel Aviv: Olamenu, 1958/62)
Gold, Hugo, *Die Geschichte der Juden in Wien. Ein Gedenkbuch* (Tel Aviv: Olamenu, 1966)

Gold, Hugo, *Zvi Perez Chajes* (Tel Aviv: Olamenu, 1971)
Gottlieb, Shmuel Noach, *Ohalei Shem* (Pinsk: 1912)
Graetz, Heinrich, *Volkstümliche Geschichte der Juden* (Berlin and Wien: B. Harz, 1923)
Grossman, Levi, *Shem U'She'erit* (Tel Aviv: 1943)
Guggenheimer, Heinrich W. and Eva H., *Jewish Family Names and their Origin; An Etymological Dictionary* (US: KTAV Publishing House, 1992)
Guttman, Matityahu Yechezkiel, *Rabbi Pinchas MiKoretz* (Tel Aviv: 1950)

Hanks, Patrick and Flavia Hodges, *A Dictionary of Surnames* (Oxford: Oxford University Press, 1988)
Herz, Ludwig, *Die Sechshundertjährige Geschichte der Familie Gans 1330–1930* (Wiener Library, London: microfiche WLMF 89151)
Hock, Simon, *Die Familien Prags nach Epitaphien des alten Jüdischen Friedhofes* (Pressburg: Adolf Alkalay, 1892)
Horowitz, Marcus, *Die Inschriften des alten Friedhofes der Israelitischen Gemeinde zu Frankfurt a.M.* (Frankfurt: Kauffman, 1901)
Horowitz, Zvi Hirsch, *Kitvei Hageonim* (Piotrkov: Chanoch Henoch Follman, 1928)
Horowitz, Zvi Hirsch, *Letoldoth Hakehilot BePolin* (Jerusalem: Mosad Horav Kook, 1978)

Israel, Jonathan I., *European Jewry in the Age of Mercantilism 1550–1750* (Oxford: Clarendon Press, 1985)

Jacobson, Jacob, *Jüdische Trauungen in Berlin 1759-1813* (Berlin: Walter de Gruyter & Co., 1968)
Jäger-Sunstenau, *Geadelte jüdische Familien* (Salzburg: Verlag des Kyffhäuser, 1891 3rd edn)
Jellinek, A., *Märtyrer und Memorbuch,* (including) *Das Memorbuch der Deutzer Gemeinde 1581-1784* (Vienna: Loewy & Alkalay, 1881)
Jewish Encyclopaedia (New York and London: 1904)

Kahane, Samuel Z., *Anaf Etz Avoth* (Cracow: 1903)
Kallir, Eleazar, *Chavot Yair Chadash* (Prague: 1792)
Katzenellenbogen, David Tebele, *Ma'ayan Mei Neftoach* (St Petersburg: 1923)
Katzenellenbogen, Phineas, *Yesh Manhilin* (Jerusalem: Machon Chatham Sofer, 1984)
Kleiman, Yaakov Hakohen, *DNA and Tradition – The Genetic Link to the Ancient Hebrews* (Devorah Publishers, 2004)
Kochan, Lionel, *Jews, Idols and Messiahs* (Oxford: Blackwell, 1990)
Kochan, Lionel, *The Making of Western Jewry 1600–1819* (Basingstoke: Palgrave Macmillan, 2004)
Kohen-Zedek, Josef, *Dor Yesharim* (Berdichev: Chaim Jacob Sheftel, 1898)
Kohlbauer-Fritz, Gabrielle (ed.), *Zwischen Ost und West. Galizische Juden und Wien* (Vienna: Jüdisches Museum der Stadt Wien, 2000)

Kranzler, David, *Thy Brother's Blood* (New York: Mesorah Publications, 1987)
Kranzler, David and Eliezer Gevirtz, *To Save a World* (New York, London, Jerusalem: CIS Publishers, 1991)

Landau, Ezekiel, *Ahavas Zion* (including) 'Memorial Address delivered 10 February 1765 on the passing of the famous Gaon Rabbi Shmuel Hillman, ABD of Metz'(Jerusalem: 1966)
Landshuth, Leiser, *Sammlungen der Grabinschriften vom alten jüdischen Friedhof in Berlin* (Berlin: 1884)
Langer, Jiri, *Nine Gates* (English translation, London: James Clarke & Co. Ltd, 1961, published in Czech 1937)
Lauterbach, Bernard S., *Chronicle of the Lauterbach Family* (El Paso, TX: revised edition 1992)
Lewin, Louis, *Die Geschichte der Juden in Lissa* (Pinne: N. Gundermann, 1904)
Lieberman, Chaim, *Ohel Rachel* (NewYork: 1980)
Lipschitz, Aryeh Yehuda Leib, *Avoth Atara Lebanim* (Warsaw: 1927)
Lipschitz, C.U. and Neil Rosenstein, *The Feast and the Fast* – edited translation of *Megilas Eivah* (New York and Jerusalem: Maznaim, 1984)
Low, Abraham A., *Mental Health through Will-Training* (Glencoe, IL: Willett Publ, 1950)
Löwenstein, Leopold, *Geschichte der Juden in der Kurpfalz* (Frankfurt: 1895)
Löwenstein, Leopold, *Das Rabbinat in Hanau* (Frankfurt: Jahrbuch der Jüdisch Literarischen Gesellschaft, 1921)
Löwenstein, Leopold, *Index Approbationum* (Berlin: 1923)
Lucas, Franz D. and Margret Heitmann, *Stadt des Glaubens. Geschichte und Kultur der Juden in Glogau* (Hildesheim-Zürich-New York: Georg Olms Verlag, 1991)

Macartney, C.A., *The Habsburg Empire 1770–1918* (London: Weidenfeld & Nicholson, 1968)
Margolis, Ephraim Zalman, *Ma'alot Hayochasin*, ed. A.S. Ettinge (Lemberg: 1900)
Margoshes, Joseph, *Memoirs of my Life* (New York: Posy-Shoulson Press, 1936)
Mayer, Sigmund, *Die Wiener Juden* (Wien and Berlin: R. Loewit, 1917)
Meir ben Isaac of Horochow, *Kosnoth Or* (Frankfurt-on-Oder: 1753)
Mendelsohn, John, *The Holocaust: Relief and Rescue of Jews from Nazi Oppression, 1943–45* (New York: Garland, 1982)
Menton, Arthur F., *The Book of Destiny: Toledot Charlap* (King David Press)
Menton, Arthur F., *Ancilla to Toledot Charlap*
Meyer, Pierre-André, *Tables du registre d'état de la communauté juive de Metz 1717–1792* (Paris: 1987)
Michael, Joseph Heimann, *Or Hachayim* (Frankfurt: 1891; New York: 1965)

Netter, Nathan, *Metz et son grand passé* (Paris: 1938)
Nir, Yehuda, *The Lost Childhood* (New York: Harcourt, Brace, Jovanovich, 1989)

Patai, Raphael, *The Messiah Texts* (New York: Avon Books, 1979)
Patai, Raphael, *Robert Graves and the Hebrew Myths* (Detroit: Wayne State University Press, 1992)
Pennell, Joseph, *The Jew at Home. Impressions of a summer and autumn spent with him in Russia and Austria* (London: Heinemann, 1892)
Perels, Meir, *Megillath Yuchasin Mehral miPrag* (Warsaw: 1864)
Pesses, Pinchas, *Ir Dubno Verabaneha* (Cracow: 1902)
Pickholz, Judah Gershon, *Chidushei Hagershuni* (Kolomea: 1890)
Pinkas Hakehilot Polin (Jerusalem: Yad Vashem, 1980) (See Vol.II for chapters on Stanislau and Solotwina)
Pinkas Vaad Arba Aratzoth (ed. Israel Halpern) (Jerusalem: 1945)
Polonsky, Shimson Aaron, *Chidushei Horav MiTeplik* (Jerusalem: 1984)
Privat, Edouard, *Histoire des Juifs en France* (Collection Franco-Judaica, 1972)
Proszyk, Jacek, *The Jewish Cemetary in Bielsko-Biala* (Bielsko: 2002)

Rapaport, Abraham Shrentzel Hakohen, *Eisan Ha'ezrachi* (Ostrog: 1796)
Rapaport, Israel, *Tifereth Israel* (Husiatin: 1905)
Rau, N. and M., *My Dear Ones* (Chicago: Recovery Inc., 1986)
Rieger, Paul, *Geschichte der Juden in Rom* (Berlin: 1895)
Rosenfeld, Moritz, *Oberrabbiner Hirsch Perez Chajes, Sein Leben und Werk* (Vienna: 1933)
Rosenstein, Neil, *The Unbroken Chain* (New York, London, Jerusalem: CIS Publishers, 1990)
Rosenstein, Neil, *The Lurie Legacy* (Bergenfield, NJ: Avotaynu, 2004)
Rosman, M. J., The Lord's Jews (Boston, MA: Harvard University Press, 1990)
Roth, Cecil, *Venice* (Philadelphia: Jewish Publication Society of America, 1930)
Roth, Cecil, *The History of the Jews in Italy* (Philadelphia: Jewish Publication Society of America, 1946)
Roth, Cecil, *History of the Great Synagogue* (London: Edward Goldston & Son Ltd, 1950)
Roth, Cecil, *A History of the Jews in England* (Oxford: 1964)
Roth, Joseph, *The Wandering Jews* (London: Granta Books, 2001)
Rozenblatt, Marsha L., *The Jews of Vienna 1867–1914* (Albany: State University of New York, 1983)
Ruderman, David, *Preachers of the Ghetto, Essential Papers on Jewish Culture in Renaissance and Baroque Italy* (Berkeley: University of California Press, 1992)

Sachs, Viola, *Idee przewodnie literatury amerykanskiey* (Warsaw, 1966 [revised 1992])
Sachs, Viola, *The Game of Creation* (Paris: Editions de la Maison des Sciences de l'Homme, 1982)
Samuel, J. Burnford, *The History of the Samuels* (Philadelphia: Lippincott, 1912)

Schischa, A., *The Author of Assifat Hakohen and his Pedigree* (Jerusalem-London: Keren Israel, 2000

Schwerdscharf, Moses Yaakov, *Hadras Zvi* (Sziget: 1909).

Selig, Shlomo Aaron, *Kerem Shlomo* (Warsaw: 1841)

Shaltiel-Gracian, Moshe, *Shaltiel* (Chicago: Academy Chicago Publishers, 2005)

Shapira, Yehuda Meir, *Imrei Da'as* (Bnei Brak, Israel: 1990)

Shlesser, Shimon, *Otzar Ha'Rebbe Reb Heshel* (Jerusalem: 1989)

Shpiro, Yakov Leib, *Mishpachot Atikot BeIsrael* (Ancient Families of Israel) (Jerusalem: Chulyot, 1981)

Slomka, Jan, *From Serfdom to Self-government. Memoirs of a Polish Village Mayor 1842–1917* (London: Minerva, 1941)

Steinschneider, Hillel Noach, *Ir Vilna* (Vilna: 1900)

Steinschneider, M., *Catalogus Librorum Hebraeorum in Bibliotheca Bodleiana* (Berlin: 1931)

Sternhel,Yitzchak, *Kochvei Yitzchok* (New York: 1979)

Teomim, Chaim Zvi, *Zikaron Larishonim* (Kolomea: 1914)

Vital, David, *A People Apart: The Jews of Europe 1789–1939* (Oxford: Oxford University Press, 1999)

Wachstein, Bernard, *Die Grabschriften des alten Judenfriedhofes in Eisenstadt* (Vienna: R. Loewit, 1922)

Wachstein, Bernard, *Inschriften des alten Judenfriedhofes in Wien* (Vienna: 1912)

Wachstein, Bernard, *Urkunden und Akten zur Geschichte der Juden in Eisenstadt* (Vienna: Wilhelm Braumüller, 1926)

Walden, Aaron, *Shem Hagedolim Hachadash* (Warsaw: 1864)

Weber, Dov, *Kol Todah* (New York: 1998)

Weimarer Historisch-Genealogisches Taschenbuch des gesamten Adels jehudäischen Ursprungs (Weimar: Kyffhäuser, 1912)

Wistrich, Robert S., *The Jews of Vienna in the Age of Franz Joseph* (Littman/Oxford University Press, 1990)

Wunder, Meir, *Meorei Galicia* five volumes (Jerusalem: Institute for the Commemoration of Galician Jewry, 1978 *et seq.*)

Wunder, Meir, *Elef Margoliot* (London & Jerusalem: Institute for the Preservation of the Galician Jewish Heritage and the Margulies family, 1993)

Wurm, David, *Z dziejow zydostwa brodzkiego za czasow dawnej rzeczpospolitej* (Brody: 1935)

Yaffe, Israel, *Or Israel* (Frankfurt-on-Oder: 1703)

Yudlov, Yitzchak Shlomo, *Sefer Yichus Belza* (Jerusalem: Machon, 1984)

Zintz, David Leib, *Gedullath Yehonathan* (Piotrkow: 1934)

Zipperstein, Steven, *The Jews of Odessa 1794–1881* (Stanford: Stanford University Press, 1986)

YIZKOR (MEMORIAL) BOOKS:

Belz (*Sefer Zikaron* published by Belz Societies in Israel and America, Tel Aviv 1974)

Berezhany-Narayow (ed. Menachem Katz, Memorial Book published by Berezhany-Narayow Societies in Israel and the United States, Haifa, 1978)

Bielsko-Biala (History of the Jews from Bielsko-Biala, published by Irgun Yotsei Bielsko-Biala, Tel Aviv, 1987)

Brody (*An Eternal Light: Brody in Memoriam* [Israel: Organisation of former Brody residents, 1994])

Glina (Asher Korech, *The Community of Glina 1473–1943; its History and Destruction*, Jerusalem, 1950)

Gorzd (ed.Y.Alperowitz, Tel Aviv, 1980).

Kolomea (ed. D. Noy and M. Schutzman, *Sefer Zikaron le'Kehilat Ve'hasevivah* [published by former residents of Kolomey and surroundings in Israel: Tel Aviv, 1972])

Nadworna (ed. Israel Carmi, Memorial Book and Records, Landmannschaft of Nadworna in Israel and America, 1975)

Piotrkow Trybunalski (ed. Y. Melz and N. Lau, published by former residents of Piotrkow Trybunalski in Israel, 1965) and (ed. Ben Giladi, *A Tale of One City*, Shengold, New York in cooperation with the Piotrkow Trybunasky Relief Association in New York, 1991)

Przemysl (ed. Arie Menczer, published by Irgun Yotsei Przemysl, Israel, 1964)

Tarnobrzeg-Dzikow (ed. Yakov Yehoshua Fleisher [Tel Aviv: Tarnobrzeg-Dzikow Society, 1973])

PUBLISHED ARTICLES BY EDWARD GELLES

'Saul Wahl. A Jewish Legend', *Judaism Today,* 14 (Winter 1999–2000).

'In Search of My Pedigree', *Shemot,* 8, 2 (June 2000).

'The Wahls of Nadworna', *Shemot,* 8, 3 (Sept. 2000).

'Chief Rabbis in the Genes', *Manna,* 69 (Autumn 2000).

'All Quiet on the Eastern Front', *Avotaynu,* xvi, 4 (Winter 2000).

'Searching for Eve: A Methodological Lesson', *Avotaynu,* xvii, 2 (Summer 2001).

'Galician Roots', *The Galitzianer,* 9, 1 (Nov. 2001).

'Capitalists and Rabbis', *The Galitzianer,* 9, 2 (Feb. 2002).

'Economic Background to some Family Links', *The Galitzianer,* 9, 3 (May 2002).

'Finding Rabbi Moses Gelles', *Avotaynu,* xviii, 1 (Spring 2002).

'Abraham Low's Ship's Manifest', *Shemot,* 10, 2 (June 2002).

'Genealogy for Moral Support', *The Galitzianer,* 9, 4 (Aug. 2002).

'The Safiers of Tarnobrzeg', *Shemot,* 10, 3 (Sept. 2002).

'My Mother's People', *Sharsheret Hadorot,* 16, 4 (Oct. 2002).

'A Tale of Two Cities', *The Galitzianer,* 10, 1 (Nov. 2002).

'My Father's People', *Sharsheret Hadorot,* 17, 1 (Feb. 2003).

'The Wohls of Cracow', *The Galitzianer,* 10, 2 (Feb. 2003).

'Davidic Descent', *Sharsheret Hadorot,* 17, 2 (June 2003).

'A Nineteenth Century Pictorial Record of Brody', *The Galitzianer,* 10, 4 (Aug. 2003).

'David and Chaim Gans of Prague', *Shemot,* 12, 1 (March 2004).

'Rabbi Shmuel Hillman of Metz and his Family Connections', *Sharsheret Hadorot,* 18, 2 (May 2004).

'Chayes Family Connections', *Shemot,* 12, 2 (June 2004).

'Jewish Community Life in Brody', *Sharsheret Hadorot,* 18, 4 (Nov. 2004).

'Genealogical Background of some Hasidic Sages', *Sharsheret Hadorot,* 19, 1 (Feb. 2005).

'Rabbis of Solotwina near Stanislau', *Sharsheret Hadorot,* 19, 4 (Nov. 2005).

'Gelles of Brody and some Fraenkel-Horowitz Connections', *Sharsheret Hadorot,* 20, 1 (Feb. 2006).

Index of Family Names

* Note:
Katz is from an acronym of Kohen Zedek = righteous priest
Segal is a surname of Levites as in Halevi Segal (perhaps from the acronym of Se Gan Leviyyah = assistant to a priest)

FAMILY NAMES OF A FEW RULING HOUSES

Habsburg:	Great European family providing ruling dynasties in Austria and Spain over many centuries. Holy Roman Emperors, Dukes and later Emperors of Austria, Apostolic Kings of Hungary, Kings of Bohemia (e.g. Maximilian II, 1564–76 and Rudolf II 1576–1612) and many other lands, including the Kingdom of Galicia and Ladomeria (1772–1918).
Hohenzollern:	Prussian dynasty 1688–1918 (Frederick the Great 1740–86).
Jagiellon:	Kings of Poland (e.g. Sigismund I, 1506–48 and Sigismund Augustus II, 1548–72) and sometime Kings of Hungary and Bohemia (Vladislav 1490–1516 and Louis, killed at Mohacz, 1526).
Medici:	Banking family who were rulers of Florence and produced four Popes and two Queens of France. Cosimo I de Medici became the first Grand Duke of Tuscany in 1569. His ducal line survived until 1737 and was succeeded by the House of Habsburg-Lorraine.
Romanov:	Russian dynasty 1613–1917 (Peter the Great 1689–1725, Catherine the Great 1762–96).
Sforza:	Francesco Sforza, Duke of Milan 1450–66 (successors to the Visconti)
Vasa:	Swedish dynasty and sometime Kings of Poland (Sigismund III, 1587–1632 and his two successors).
Wettin:	Kings of Saxony and sometime Kings of Poland (August II, 1697–1704 and 1710–33, August III, 1733–63).

Index of Place Names

Katzenellenbogen
Keidani
Kishinev
Klausenburg (Koloszvar)
Kolerka
Kolibolet
Kolomea (Kolomya, etc)
Koretz
Kovno
Krakow (Krakau)
Kretinga (Krottingen)
Kremsier
Krotoschin (Krotoszyn, Krotchin, etc)
Krystynopol
Kudrynce
Leipen
Leipnik
Lippstadt
Lisbon
Lissa
Livorno (Leghorn)
London
Los Angeles
Lublin
Lutsk
Lvov (Lemberg)
Mainz
Mannheim
Mantua
Marseilles
Melbourne
Memel (Klaipeda)
Meretz
Meseritz
Metz
Mexico City
Mielnica
Mihaileni
Mikulince (Mikulintsy)
Minsk
Monte Carlo
Montpellier
Munkacz (Mukachevo)
Nadworna
Naples
Narayow
Narbonne
New York
Nigresti
Nikolsburg (Mikulov)
Nimes
Novogroduk (Navahradek, Nowogrodek, etc)
Novy Sacz (Zanz)
Odessa
Ofen (Budapest)
Orleans
Padua
Paris
Pinczow
Pinsk
Plungian
Podwolocziska
Posen (Poznan)
Prague
Przemysl
Przemyslany
Przeworsk
Rio de Janeiro
Rome
Ruzhin
Sadegora
Safed
Salonika (Thessaloniki)
Sandomierz
Sao Paulo
Satanow
Sedziszow (Shendishov)
Siemiatycze
Sinouc de Sus (Saniawitz)
Shepetivka
Shklov
Shpola
Skala
Slutsk
Solotwina (Solotvina)
Speyer
Stanislau (Stanislawow, etc)
Stanford
St Petersburg (Petrograd, Leningrad)